W9-BAI-451

GULLIBLE
SUPERPOWER

U.S. SUPPORT
FOR BOGUS
FOREIGN DEMOCRATIC
MOVEMENTS

GULLIBLE
SUPERPOWER

TED GALEN CARPENTER

CATO
INSTITUTE
WASHINGTON, D.C.

ISBN: 978-1-944424-92-3
eISBN: 978-1-944424-93-0

Jacket design: Jon Meyers.
Printed in the United States of America.

Library of Congress Cataloging-in-Publication Data

Carpenter, Ted Galen, author.
Gullible superpower : U.S. support for bogus democratic movements / Ted Galen Carpenter.

page cm

Washington, D.C. : Cato Institute, 2019.

Includes bibliographical references.

ISBN 9781944424930 (ebook) | ISBN 9781944424923 (hardback)
1. Democratization--Government policy--United States. 2. Democracy--Government policy--
United States. 3. United States--Foreign relations--1989–. 3. United States--Foreign relations--1981–1989.
4. United States--Foreign relations--1977–1981.

JZ1480

327.73--dc23   2018041025

To my wife Barbara, my lifelong loving companion, my biggest fan, and my most persistent, constructive critic.

CONTENTS

ACKNOWLEDGMENTS

I owe a debt of gratitude to many people for making this book possible. A special thank you goes out to Christopher A. Preble, vice president for defense and foreign policy studies at the Cato Institute. Chris is my successor in that post, and in addition to becoming a distinguished foreign policy scholar in his own right, he has helped build the Institute's defense and foreign policy program into a major factor in the ongoing debate about America's role in the world. I am especially grateful to him regarding this book project. Not only did he offer insightful critiques and suggestions about the manuscript, but he exercised extraordinary patience even when the target date slipped because of serious health problems that I had to battle.

Other scholars also were kind enough to review the initial draft of the book and provide important observations and insights. Helpful Cato colleagues included John Glaser, director of foreign policy studies, senior fellow Doug Bandow, and research fellow Emma Ashford. Other constructive manuscript critics included Independent Institute scholar Ivan Eland, and Charles Koch Foundation executive Will Ruger. Travis Evans and James Knupp both provided invaluable assistance in researching this topic.

My thanks also go out to the book production and marketing staff at Cato, especially to Jason Kuznicki, Eleanor O'Connor, and Robert Garber.

They managed to keep the book on schedule, despite an assortment of obstacles and difficulties. Jon Meyers designed a bold and impressive cover.

Finally, I want to express my appreciation to Cato's ever-supportive management team. Chairman Robert A. Levy and the board of directors, President and CEO Peter Goettler, Executive Vice President David Boaz, and Vice President Gene Healy all have encouraged the principled, iconoclastic work of Cato's foreign policy scholars. They have remained steadfast in their support even when that work sometimes has come under intense fire for daring to challenge a stale and dangerous policy status quo. *Gullible Superpower* is written in that tradition of speaking truth to power.

INTRODUCTION

A TRADITION OF CAUTION BETRAYED

Foreign insurgent groups have a distressing record of manipulating U.S. political figures, policymakers, and opinion leaders into supporting their causes. Frequently, those groups have engendered support that has gone far beyond just rhetorical endorsements. On several occasions during the late 20th and early 21st centuries, foreign lobbying efforts have led the United States to give financial and even military assistance to highly questionable organizations and movements. Examples include the Nicaraguan Contras, Angola's National Union for the Total Independence of Angola (UNITA), the Kosovo Liberation Army (KLA), and the Iraqi National Congress (INC). At times, those efforts even have entangled the U.S. military in bloody, unnecessary, and morally dubious wars, such as in Kosovo, Iraq, Libya, and, most recently, Syria.

U.S. officials often have aligned themselves with murky factions, painting them as freedom fighters who are dedicated to overthrowing oppressive regimes and installing democratic governments. In retrospect, those officials often failed to define clearly what they meant by "freedom fighters"; indeed, they swept highly diverse movements into that category. Especially during the latter stages of the Cold War, American policymakers and opinion leaders tended to equate resistance to Soviet-sponsored regimes with a commitment to Western democratic political values. Most of the time, conflating those goals proved to be erroneous.

Since the post–Cold War era began in 1991, such policy confusion has continued unabated. Because rebel movements such as the KLA and the Iraqi National Congress sought to unseat or gain independence from tyrannical governments, American supporters contended that those insurgencies were seeking to bring freedom and democracy to their countries. Again, those portrayals were exaggerated at best and spectacularly inaccurate at worst. What is less certain is whether U.S. policymakers sincerely believed the democratic credentials of their foreign clients, or whether they merely portrayed them as freedom fighters to win support from an otherwise skeptical American public. Even if America's democracy exporters were sincere in their beliefs, they should have been more diligent and skeptical about the factions they were supporting. Such activists obviously sought U.S. assistance to overthrow the regimes they opposed, and they were prepared to tell potential American supporters whatever they wanted to hear in order to get it.

Washington's support for indigenous regime-change forces also has been characterized by U.S. leaders' tendency to misconstrue or inflate the American interests at stake. Officials and their media and think tank allies typically have acted as though the existence of an unpleasant, repressive regime in a far-away country axiomatically impinges upon vital American strategic interests and moral values. In reality, few of the situations arguably did so. Moreover, on several occasions, the changes that U.S. policy brought about in support of the insurgencies produced chaos and undermined the modest strategic interests that were involved. That was especially true in Afghanistan, Iraq, Libya, and Syria.

American supporters of so-called freedom fighters have tended to be overly optimistic about prospects for democracy in most of the countries in which Washington has embraced insurgents. Countries such as Afghanistan, Angola, Iraq, Libya, and Syria have had little or no experience with democratic governance, and the foundations for installing such a governmental system in those places often have been inadequate. In most of those countries, allegiances primarily are tribal, ethnic, or religious; allegiance to the nation state (or to abstract political values) is secondary, if present at all. Private sector institutions typically are weak and underdeveloped, with few capable nongovernmental organizations committed to democratic values or individual rights. To expect democracy to flourish under such unfavorable conditions shows insufficient awareness of the daunting obstacles at hand.

Even in countries where the economic and social conditions for democracy are more favorable and which have had greater exposure to Western values, establishing honest, capable democratic systems is not easy. That point became evident during the 2013–2014 turmoil in Ukraine, when supposedly pro-freedom demonstrators sought to unseat autocratic (but democratically elected) President Viktor Yanukovych. Prominent Americans portrayed the episode as a Manichean struggle between good and evil. Yanukovych was designated as the villain, while ostensibly pro-Western demonstrators in Kiev and other cities were considered heroic members of a democratic resistance.

The U.S. government clearly supported the latter faction. Sen. John McCain (R–AZ) showed up in Kiev to lend his vocal support to the demonstrators, as did other U.S. political and diplomatic figures. Assistant Secretary of State for European and Eurasian Affairs Victoria Nuland was caught on tape expressing Washington's choices for personnel in a post-Yanukovych government, even while the beleaguered Ukrainian president still held office.[1]

Such interference in another country's internal affairs is inappropriate in any case, but it was especially so in Ukraine's. The opposition contained many genuine democrats, but some authoritarian and ultra-nationalist elements also were involved; the anti-Yanukovych coalition even included outright anti-Semitic, neo-Nazi factions. They weren't just minor players, either—some of them were appointed to significant posts in the new government. Yet U.S. supporters of Yanukovych's ouster either ignored or downplayed the role of such undesirable figures. Moreover, even though Ukraine is nominally democratic, autocratic policies and pervasive corruption have manifested themselves in numerous ways: today's Ukraine is little more than a quasi-democratic kleptocracy.

Washington's policy toward the Syrian insurgency attempting to overthrow dictator Bashar al-Assad was perhaps even more myopic. The Obama administration conducted a dogged search for secular moderates among the armed insurgents—and in the process provided aid to some

highly dubious factions. The administration did so despite evidence
that the Syrian insurgent movement contained a large and increasingly
powerful contingent of Islamist fighters, including members of Jabhat
al-Nusra, which at one time was al Qaeda's Syrian affiliate. Even after
that revelation, the administration did not stop providing financial and
military aid to "selected" rebel groups—those supposedly composed of
moderates. As critics of that policy point out, however, the term "moderates" in the Syrian power struggle hardly means the same as it does in
a Western political context. Most supposedly moderate factions still are
strongly Islamist rather than secular.[2]

The goal of this book is to shine a spotlight on the faulty reasoning
underlying continued U.S. support for so-called democratic activists.
The forcible democracy-promotion and regime-change strategies Washington has pursued are not warranted either on geopolitical or moral
grounds. U.S. leaders need to learn from their failures and return to an
earlier, more prudent, realistic, and sensible policy tradition.

CARELESS SUPPORT REPLACES A TRADITION OF CAUTION

The first few generations of American leaders made a sharp distinction
between the republic's legitimate interests on one hand and foreign causes
that purportedly sought to overthrow tyrants and enshrine democratic
polities based on respect for fundamental rights on the other. No one
made that distinction more emphatically than President James Monroe's
secretary of state, John Quincy Adams.

In a celebrated Fourth of July address in 1821, Adams implicitly
rebuked growing calls for Washington to support republican independence movements in places ranging from Greece to Latin America. The
United States, Adams noted, "has abstained from interference in the
concerns of others, even when conflict has been for principles to which
she clings." He added: "Wherever the standard of freedom and independence has been or shall be unfurled, there will her heart, her benedic-
tions and her prayers be. But she goes not abroad, in search of monsters
to destroy. She is the well-wisher to the freedom and independence of
all. She is the champion and vindicator only of her own." He stressed

the imperative reasons for such a stance: "She well knows that by once enlisting under other banners than her own, were they even the banners of foreign independence, she would involve herself beyond the power of extrication, in all the wars of interest and intrigue, of individual avarice, envy, and ambition, which assume the colors and usurp the standard of freedom."[3]

That is an essential lesson that recent generations of policymakers have forgotten, at great cost to the nation. The United States going abroad "in search of monsters" is a problem that has been building for decades, but it has grown worse since the early 1980s. Ronald Reagan's administration took an especially fateful step in that direction by adopting the so-called Reagan Doctrine of providing aid to anti-Soviet insurgents in a variety of geopolitical settings. Although most applications of that strategy would take place in the Third World, the first prominent example occurred in Eastern Europe, specifically in Poland.

THE RISE OF THE REAGAN DOCTRINE

Conservative activists had urged the United States to go on the offensive and support anti-communist insurgents in Eastern Europe and elsewhere long before the Reagan presidency. During the early years of the Cold War, the Central Intelligence Agency (CIA) assisted a number of anti-Soviet groups operating behind the Iron Curtain, especially in Ukraine.[4] But that strategy of trying to "roll back" Soviet power never gained much traction, especially after communist authorities repeatedly managed to infiltrate and destroy would-be insurgent groups. Eventually, though, during Reagan's administration the roll-back strategy received not only a new lease on life but also a dramatic boost. Even before any administration official articulated the strategic rationale or used the term "Reagan Doctrine," some substantive elements of the strategy were in place (most notably, financial aid to Poland's Solidarity labor movement; financial and military aid to resistance fighters in Afghanistan; and similar aid to rebels in Nicaragua).

Washington's support for Solidarity was especially significant and passionate. Richard Pipes, director of Soviet and East European Affairs for the National Security Council, circulated a memo in the summer of 1981 arguing that Moscow feared widespread adverse consequences to its interests if Solidarity survived and flourished. That virus of freedom, Pipes contended, already was spreading to the Baltics and other portions of the Soviet empire. According to writer and conservative activist Peter Schweizer, who examined the Reagan administration's foreign policy in depth and had exceptional access to former senior officials, the Pipes memo was circulated to the president and all other senior members of the National Security Council; says Schweizer, "It had a galvanizing effect."[5]

The Polish regime's declaration of martial law in December 1981 led to a dramatic increase in U.S. support. According to Schweizer, "The declaration of martial law in Poland was a turning point for the administration. It solidified support behind an offensive strategy to roll back Soviet power. Within months, secret directives would be signed making it explicit U.S. policy to undermine Soviet power." Specifically, "Opportunities would be sought for sowing dissent in Eastern Europe."[6]

Despite some opposition from both Vice President George H. W. Bush and Secretary of State Alexander Haig, who worried that such a strategy would unduly provoke Moscow, the administration adopted a policy of extensive covert aid to Solidarity.[7] By mid-February 1982, CIA Director William Casey had developed a comprehensive plan for such assistance, and the aid began to flow (including not only U.S. intelligence assistance but also financial subsidies).[8] By 1985, the cash flow alone had reached $8 million a year.[9] Washington also looked elsewhere in Eastern Europe to find opportunities for democratic subversion similar to the Solidarity model.[10]

The Reagan administration's support for Solidarity became an important building block for a wider policy of assisting anti-communist elements in places where Soviet power was entrenched or seemed to be increasingly prominent, especially Afghanistan, Nicaragua, and Angola. But U.S. officials misconstrued the Solidarity precedent. A sizable number (probably a solid majority) of Poles in the Solidarity movement were Western-style democrats, but that was not true of the other movements. Thus, the Reagan Doctrine was built upon a conceptual fallacy from the outset.

The most detailed exposition of the policy that eventually became known as the Reagan Doctrine came from Reagan's second secretary of state, George Shultz, during a crucial speech to the Commonwealth Club in San Francisco on February 22, 1985. The title of his talk was "America and the Struggle for Freedom."[11]

"A revolution is sweeping the world today," Shultz proclaimed, "a democratic revolution."[12] He emphasized that in the West's global ideological struggle with the Soviet Union, the United States was determined to wrest the initiative from Moscow. "For many years we saw our adversaries act without restraint to back insurgencies around the world to spread communist dictatorships." Moreover, "Any victory of communism was held to be irreversible" (the infamous Brezhnev Doctrine). But those days were over, Shultz emphasized. "In recent years, Soviet activities and pretensions have run head-on into the democratic revolution. People are insisting on their right to independence, on their right to choose their government free of outside control."[13]

He specifically cited Poland's Solidarity movement and the armed resistance forces in Afghanistan, Cambodia, Nicaragua, Ethiopia, and Angola. He also included dissident activities in the Soviet Union and throughout Eastern Europe in the democratic revolution category. Shultz even gave a perfunctory nod to advocates of peaceful change in autocratic states such as South Africa, South Korea, the Philippines, and Chile. All of those people, he stressed, sought independence, freedom, and human rights.

Therein lay the core problem with the Reagan Doctrine: Shultz conflated very different movements in an incredibly diverse range of societies as manifestations of a global democratic revolution—a shockingly naive interpretation. Many of the countries he mentioned had no experience with democracy, and they lacked even the basic building blocks of such a system. Arguing that some Eastern European nations might hope to establish democratic governance was one thing (especially a country like Czechoslovakia, which had been democratic between the two world wars). But arguing that a consensus in favor of democratic governance existed in a place like South Korea, where democratic traditions were both weak and sporadic, was quite another. And assuming that people who had never experienced even a semblance of democracy nevertheless were committed to it, people in countries such as Afghanistan, Angola, Cambodia, and Nicaragua, was a colossal stretch of logic. No evidence existed that they sought to achieve "independence, freedom, and human rights." They likely wanted independence, but many of the "democratic" movements most definitely were not working toward any concept of freedom or human rights.

Nevertheless, Shultz and other administration officials casually identified America's interests and values with those of foreign insurgent groups. The new revolutionary trend "we are witnessing around the world—popular insurgencies against communist domination—is not an American creation," Shultz stated. He did give the administration a little policy wiggle room: "The nature and extent of our support—whether moral support or something more—necessarily varies from case to case." Nevertheless, "There should be no doubt where our sympathies lie."[14]

And he was not above tugging on emotional heart strings. "How can we as a country say to a young Afghan, Nicaraguan, or Cambodian: 'Learn to live with oppression; only those of us who already have freedom deserve to pass it on to our children.'"[15] Shultz added that "the forces of democracy around the world merit our standing with them; to abandon them would be a shameful betrayal—a betrayal not only of brave men and women but of our highest ideals." Once again, he assumed that such insurgents were seeking Western-style freedom and democracy in spite of the dearth of evidence to support his assumption.[16]

Reagan administration officials invoked the term "freedom fighters" in a disturbingly promiscuous manner. Shultz and other administration leaders even applied that label to the Afghan mujahideen, although the word "mujahideen" translates as "holy warriors," not "freedom fighters."[17] Indeed, a disproportionate percentage of insurgents in Afghanistan were Islamic extremists. Many of them, especially the Arab "foreign volunteers," later migrated to terrorist movements around the world (including al Qaeda) after they helped expel the Soviets from Afghanistan. Washington's imprimatur for the Afghan insurgents proved not only embarrassing but also tragic.

President Ronald Reagan himself was laudatory regarding various anti-Soviet movements; his lack of skepticism reached telling levels in his assessment of the Contras, who were trying to overthrow the pro-Soviet Sandinista regime in Nicaragua. On one occasion, he even stated that the Contras were the "moral equal of our founding fathers," and that, "We owe them our help."[18] In his first summit meeting with Mikhail Gorbachev in 1985, the president severely chastised the Soviet leader for his country's determination to suppress national resistance groups in Afghanistan, Poland, Nicaragua, Angola, and elsewhere that "simply wanted their freedom."[19] Reagan implicitly (and naively) equated the nationalistic desire to resist Soviet hegemony (which was very real in all of those locales) with a desire for "freedom."

The central problem with the Reagan Doctrine was that most of the so-called freedom fighters were not advocates of freedom and democracy, even given very generous definitions of those concepts. Anti-Soviet and anti-communist insurgent groups were a diverse collection of secular authoritarians, religious zealots, and genocidal psychopaths, with a sprinkling of genuine, pluralistic democrats thrown in. Even in a country such as Nicaragua (which had some aspects of Western heritage and culture), bona fide democrats constituted a minority of the fighters. In such places as Afghanistan and Angola, they were almost entirely absent.

Despite his overall enthusiasm for the Reagan Doctrine, George Shultz drew the line at supporting some supposed freedom fighters. He was especially skeptical of the anti-communist insurgency in Mozambique led by the Resistência Nacional Moçambicana (RENAMO). When implementing the Reagan Doctrine in specific countries, he recalled, "I took care to know who and what the United States was funding." And he was frustrated with fellow conservatives who seemed to exhibit no such caution. "Despite heated demands from the right-wing fringes of the administration and Congress, I steadfastly insisted that we refuse to give backing to the atrocity-prone RENAMO."[20] Not only did some conservatives misrepresent the behavior and ideological nature of RENAMO, they wildly exaggerated the success of the insurgency and the extent of the support it enjoyed from the people of Mozambique. Shultz noted that in late 1985, briefers from the CIA (apparently acting on instructions from Director William Casey) "were

showing their audiences in the administration and Congress a map of
Mozambique to indicate—falsely—that RENAMO controlled virtually
the entire country."[21]

Unfortunately, the appropriate skepticism that Shultz exhibited regarding RENAMO was not shown in other theaters where
the administration invoked the Reagan Doctrine. Indeed, too often
Shultz himself behaved in the same manner for which he criticized
other conservatives regarding their enthusiasm toward the unsavory
Mozambique rebels.

Angola was an especially odious case. There, the United States
embraced an insurgent leader even though the U.S. security rationale
was weak and the client was a psychopathic charlatan. Leading conservatives hailed Jonas Savimbi, the leader of UNITA, as a charismatic,
pro-Western political figure and a genuine freedom fighter. Jeane Kirkpatrick, U.S. ambassador to the United Nations, went so far as to call
him a "true hero for our time."[22]

As noted in Chapter 3, Savimbi's checkered past and disturbing
(sometimes even horrifying) behavior did not warrant such enthusiasm. Critics noted that even UNITA's official seal proclaimed it to be
a socialist organization and that Savimbi started out as a loyal client
of communist China.[23] Even worse, by the late 1970s and early 1980s,
evidence clearly indicated that Savimbi encouraged a cult of personality
typically found in countries run by megalomaniacal dictators. Additionally, allegations arose (since confirmed) that Savimbi had ordered the
assassination of UNITA rivals to preserve his own dominant position.
U.S. officials and conservative proponents of the Reagan Doctrine had
more than enough evidence proving that the individual they portrayed
as a democratic freedom fighter was nothing of the sort.

When U.S. officials tried to justify the Reagan Doctrine on moral
grounds, especially in regions where the United States had few strategic or economic interests, their arguments came across as either naive
self-deception or cynical propaganda designed to mislead the American people. If a legitimate case could be made for U.S. involvement, it
needed to be on the basis of a country's supposed relevance to important,
tangible American interests, especially security interests.

From a purely strategic standpoint, one can understand why the Reagan administration opted to aid some of the anti-communist insurgencies. Given the global interventionist orientation of U.S. foreign policy, Washington believed that it had significant, even vital, interests at stake in several regions. Keeping the Soviets away from the Persian Gulf's oil riches became a key rationale for backing the Afghan mujahideen. Preventing Moscow and its Cuban surrogates from gaining a foothold in southern Africa was a major motive for Washington's support of UNITA insurgents in Angola, and it drove some particularly vocal conservatives to embrace even the highly suspect RENAMO rebels in Mozambique. And strategic motives, as well as ideological considerations, generated support for backing the Nicaraguan Contras, who were trying to unseat the radical leftist government. While the credibility of the strategic rationales varied, the ideological and moral cases fell short (often far short) of the mark.

Misplaced U.S. Enthusiasm for Phony Foreign Democrats Persists

Washington's habit of engaging in wishful thinking about so-called freedom fighters did not disappear at the end of the Cold War. The Clinton administration's de facto alliance with the KLA (an insurgent force seeking to gain independence for Serbia's restless, predominantly Albanian, province of Kosovo) is a case in point. Significantly, U.S. backing for the KLA took place even though the Cold War was over, and even though no credible strategic motive existed for Washington to meddle in a civil war in the Balkans. The rationale for adopting such a course was based almost entirely on supposed moral imperatives. Proponents of U.S. intervention hyped the evil nature of Serbia's regime—even warning of a repeat of the Holocaust if Washington did not take action to support the Kosovars.

Along with magnifying Serbian President Slobodan Milošević's evil deeds, American admirers of the KLA exhibited a massive blind spot about that organization's beliefs and conduct. Perhaps the most absurdly romanticized view of the insurgents was Sen. Joseph Lieberman's (D–CT) assertion that America and the KLA stood for the same political and moral principles. Lieberman even insisted that "fighting for the KLA is fighting for human rights and American values."[24]

Washington's bias had important policy implications. The United States led a 78-day North Atlantic Treaty Organization (NATO) air war against Serbia that killed hundreds of Serb civilians. Those air strikes compelled Belgrade to relinquish control of Kosovo to an international peacekeeping mission under the nominal auspices of the United Nations (UN) Security Council. A new government (dominated by KLA leaders) took power in Pristina; in February 2008, the United States and its allies bypassed the UN Security Council and recognized Kosovo's unilateral declaration of independence.

The aftermath has been far different from Washington's pie-in-the-sky expectations that post-war Kosovo would be a model of multiethnic comity. After NATO's 1999 war, more than 240,000 Serbs and other ethnic minorities fled or were driven from Kosovo. Since that ethnic cleansing campaign, Muslim Kosovars systematically desecrated numerous Christian churches and other religious sites, some hundreds of years old. An investigation by a European Union commission also found that the KLA committed an array of war crimes, including murdering Serb civilians and prisoners of war and selling their organs on a gruesome international black market.[25]

Yet another insurgent group that beguiled U.S. officials, members of Congress, and journalists was the INC. Neoconservatives and other advocates of a U.S. campaign to overthrow Saddam Hussein touted the alleged virtues of the INC and its leader, Ahmed Chalabi. The underlying logic of the Iraq Liberation Act, which Congress passed in 1998, was that modest U.S. financial aid and political support would enable the INC to spark an insurgency that would topple Saddam and establish democratic rule. Washington's alliance with Chalabi and his associates grew even stronger during George W. Bush's presidency. Indeed, the INC was the most important intelligence source for the allegations that Iraq possessed weapons of mass destruction.

The fear that Saddam had such weapons was the principal reason the United States launched the invasion and occupation of Iraq in 2003. The KLA had lured Washington into a small war to secure Kosovo's secession from Serbia, but Chalabi and the INC lured Washington into a far larger, more destructive war in Iraq. When the U.S. occupation failed to find any weapons of mass destruction, thereby debunking the INC's "evidence," Chalabi nonchalantly responded that he and his colleagues had been "heroes in error."[26] Long-standing U.S. expectations that Chalabi would become Iraq's first freely elected leader proved as erroneous as the INC's intelligence. When parliamentary elections were held in 2005, Chalabi's party received barely 0.5 percent of the vote and failed to win a single seat. To add insult to injury, evidence emerged that a key INC member may have been an Iranian agent, and Chalabi himself soon adopted a stance that was noticeably friendly to Tehran.

Unfortunately, U.S. policy in such places as Libya and Syria indicates that few members of the American foreign policy community have learned from the previous ill-starred ventures in Afghanistan, Angola, Kosovo, and Iraq. The Obama administration's decision to lead a NATO campaign of aircraft and cruise missile attacks to help insurgents overthrow Libyan dictator Muammar Qaddafi reflected the assumptions of Secretary of State Hillary Clinton and other officials that a post–Qaddafi government would be stable and democratic. Instead, Libya has fragmented into a chaotic arena of violence, with multiple armed factions vying for power. Today, the country more closely resembles anarchic Somalia, Yemen, or South Sudan than it does a stable polity—much less a stable and democratic one.

The situation is at least as bad in Syria, where the Assad government, with assistance from Russia, continues to battle an array of insurgents that includes the Islamic State of Iraq and Syria (ISIS), rival Islamist factions such as the Nusra Front (now Jabhat Fateh al Sham), Kurdish separatists, and a meager contingent of supposed democrats in the Free Syrian Army and the Syrian Democratic Forces.[27] Most of those factions have spent as much time battling each other as they have waging war against Assad's Syrian national army. The result is an ongoing bloodbath that by mid-2017 had claimed more than 400,000 lives. Yet both the Obama and Trump administrations persisted in efforts to identify and strengthen alleged moderates who supposedly would represent a viable alternative to both Assad and the prospect of a hard-core Islamist regime. Although President Donald Trump's administration muted the verbal support for supposed moderate Syrian rebels, the substance of U.S. policy has remained largely the same.

The lengthy—and lengthening—roster of failed U.S. regime-change crusades for democracy should thoroughly discredit advocates of that approach. Most supposedly democratic rebels receiving Washington's backing have turned out to be corrupt, often vicious, authoritarians. Whether American cheerleaders for such movements are useful pawns that foreign activists manipulate for their unsavory purposes, or whether the cheerleaders themselves disingenuously use the lure of expanding democratic values to new regions in order to gain support for military interventions from an otherwise reluctant American public matters little. The various examples in this book provide support for both scenarios, although the bulk of the evidence points to the former.

The depressing reality is that the negative impact of the resulting policies on American values and interests is essentially the same in either case. U.S. leaders and the American people must absorb those painful lessons and revive the vital distinctions that Adams articulated so well. Otherwise, the policy tragedies of recent decades will persist and multiply.

CHAPTER ONE

THE NICARAGUAN CONTRAS: THE "MORAL EQUAL OF AMERICA'S FOUNDERS"?

President Ronald Reagan often was effusive in his praise of anti-communist insurgents who challenged Soviet-backed governments. That was especially true regarding the Nicaraguan Contras, who were seeking to unseat the leftist Sandinista regime. Reagan and members of his foreign policy team went far beyond strategic considerations in justifying support for such insurgent forces.

A reasonable security rationale existed—one that was significantly stronger than in other arenas where the administration endeavored to apply the Reagan Doctrine of providing aid to anti-Soviet insurgents. U.S. officials understandably were worried about deeper communist penetration into the Western Hemisphere. Indeed, even President Jimmy Carter's administration had grown increasingly uneasy as the Sandinista revolution seemed to turn more radical and as evidence of growing Soviet backing for Daniel Ortega's regime mounted. Once Reagan became president, Washington's alarm grew even stronger. Cuba had been a loyal Soviet client and a geopolitical headache for the United States for more than two decades, and the Sandinista revolution in Nicaragua appeared to be producing a second Cuba. U.S. leaders also worried that the communist contagion might infect the other countries in Central America and the Caribbean—and perhaps beyond.[1]

Evidence already indicated that Nicaraguan authorities were providing funds and weapons to leftist rebels in El Salvador, and American officials were especially focused on the danger to that country. Even before the Reagan administration took office, Washington was sending financial and military aid to El Salvador's government to help it fend off the growing insurgency.[2]

In its attempts to justify assistance to the anti-Sandinista faction solely on pragmatic, strategic grounds, though, Reagan administration officials sensed a problem. Both the public and Congress—severely scarred by the divisive, disastrous war in Vietnam—were wary of arguments that yet another small nation was now crucial to America's security and therefore warranted significant intervention. Reagan's second secretary of state, George Shultz, and other administration policymakers were exasperated that members of Congress did not seem to appreciate the fact that Nicaragua and other Central American countries were close U.S. neighbors, not unfamiliar lands 5,000 miles away. Administration officials were certain that events in that part of the Western Hemisphere automatically affected America's safety and other important interests.

Portraying the Sandinistas as odious Soviet puppets and their opponents as freedom fighters became an important way to broaden the appeal of U.S. aid to the Contras, especially among people who might not respond well to arguments based on cold calculations of realpolitik. Accurately assessing the Contras—defects and all—risked undermining the administration's moral argument, thereby reducing prospects for congressional and public support for efforts to counter the Sandinistas and their Soviet and Cuban sponsors.

Conflating Strategic and Moral Assumptions

But many Reagan administration officials and their domestic political allies seemed sincere in their arguments that the Contras were genuine freedom fighters worthy of American assistance and that the United States had a moral imperative to support them. As they had in so many other Cold War theaters, administration policymakers conflated very different ideological concepts and motives on the part of the

Nicaraguan rebels. Because the insurgents were hostile to communist ideology and the specter of Soviet imperialism, Reagan and his advisers blithely concluded that they also were committed to democracy, capitalism, and civil liberties. Blurring such diverse lines, U.S. leaders used the term "freedom fighters" in an extremely vague, promiscuous fashion. That tendency was evident in other Cold War arenas, such as Afghanistan (Chapter 2) and Angola (Chapter 3), but it was especially strong regarding the situation in Nicaragua.

Reagan heaped praise on anti-Sandinista fighters, asserting that they were nothing less than the "moral equal of our founding fathers," and that "we owe them our help" in their efforts to topple the Sandinistas.[3] Nearly a decade later, the former president still was describing the anti-Sandinista forces as "freedom fighters" in his memoirs.[4] He also railed against most American journalists, contending that they were too favorable to Ortega's government and far too negative toward the Contras. "Perhaps after Vietnam when many reporters had cast Uncle Sam in the role of the villain," Reagan speculated, "they didn't want to put white hats on the Contra freedom fighters because the U.S. government was supporting them."[5] He implicitly rejected the possibility that critical journalists had reason to conclude that many of the Contras weren't wearing metaphorical white hats.

Reagan clearly was frustrated that Congress and the public also weren't eager for the United States to assist the Contras. In a March 15, 1985, diary entry dealing with recent polling data, the president wrote, "Our communications on Nicaragua have been a failure. 90% of the people know that it is a communist country, but almost as many don't want us to give the Contras $14 mil. for weapons. I have to believe it is the old Vietnam syndrome."[6] But that was not the only reason for the country's recalcitrance, in his view. On another occasion, he asserted that "the Sandinistas have a disinformation program that has fooled a lot of people." Some of those people, he concluded sarcastically, "want to be fooled."[7]

The president was not the only member of the administration to exhibit such a blind spot regarding the Contras. Years later, Reagan's White House Chief of Staff James A. Baker III asserted that

"President Reagan correctly called the contras 'freedom fighters,'" and Baker lamented that "maintain[ing] public support for a rebel army's effort to overthrow a government, even one as anathema as the Sandinistas," had proved so difficult.[8] A training manual that the CIA prepared for Contra forces in 1984 contained the following preface: "This book is a guerilla training manual for Psychological Operations, and it is applied to the specific case of the Christian and democratic crusade being conducted in Nicaragua by the Freedom Commandos."[9] Even allowing for hyperbole in both internal documents and propaganda tracts, that kind of gushing description seems a bit over the top if the authors were not true believers.

CIA Director William J. Casey was an avid supporter of the Contras, and even though he was a crusty veteran of the intelligence wars with the Soviet Union and its allies, his support for the Nicaraguan rebels seemed motivated by more than realpolitik calculations. When he died in May 1987, his will established the William J. Casey Fund for Nicaraguan Freedom Fighters, and his widow donated $140,000 to the Contras the very day her husband died.[10] Using his personal wealth in that fashion suggests Casey's sincere belief in their cause.

WASHINGTON BEGINS ACTIVELY BACKING THE CONTRAS

Moral considerations and national security concerns aside, U.S. leaders were tempted to play offense for once—not merely attempt to contain an embryonic Soviet client but actually help anti-communist Nicaraguans harass and perhaps oust the offending government. Indeed, the Reagan administration already had opted for that strategy in late 1981, more than three years before the proclamation of the Reagan Doctrine. The new administration had broken off talks with the Sandinistas in late October, apparently abandoning any hope of enticing Ortega's government out of the Soviet orbit. CIA planning for an alternative strategy proceeded rapidly, and in November the agency presented a two-part scheme to the National Security Planning Group. One part called for building popular support for an opposition front throughout Central America that would be "nationalistic, anti-Cuban and anti-Somoza."[11]

The last reference was to Nicaragua's anti-communist—but thoroughly corrupt—former dictator, Anastasio Somoza Debayle. That was a sensitive point with administration officials, because Washington had backed the Somoza family for decades.[12] Administration policymakers wished to distance their Central American policy from that legacy—one that was extremely unpopular in Nicaragua and the rest of the region.

The first component of the Reagan administration's approach was only slightly more ambitious than the Carter administration's; however, the second component was much more hardline and confrontational. It called for funding an armed force of 500 soldiers on the Honduran border consisting of Nicaraguans and some Cuban exiles not associated with Somoza. That unit was formed not only to collect intelligence but also to "engage in paramilitary and political operations" inside Nicaragua. Such "Contras" were now under the umbrella of a CIA covert operation.

Reagan signed National Security Decision Directive 17 on November 23, 1981, approving assistance to the new armed insurgents and to Nicaragua's peaceful internal political opposition factions. From the outset, the aid program's orientation was utterly inconsistent with any realistic notion of promoting freedom and democracy. The decision directive specified that the composition and control of the insurgent groups would depend on discussions with Argentina and U.S. partners in Central America.[13] At the time, Argentina was ruled by a ruthless military junta amassing a dreadful record of human rights abuses, yet the regime was a favorite of Secretary of State Alexander Haig (Shultz's predecessor) and other officials.

Indeed, in his first meeting with Argentine diplomats, Haig told them that they had heard their last public lecture from the United States on human rights.[14] His assurance was a direct repudiation of the Carter administration's emphasis on human rights. That administration had maintained a rather frosty relationship with Buenos Aires because of the latter's notorious conduct—including imprisoning and murdering political dissidents and putting their children up for adoption to regime loyalists. Giving the Argentine junta an important voice in policy toward the Contras guaranteed a bias against democrats in favor of authoritarian elements.

Significant aid began to reach the Contras by the spring of 1982, and by 1986 the United States was funding the insurgency to the tune of $100 million a year. One underlying motive for the support was clear: according to Haig, both he and the president "knew that Moscow and Havana were behind the troubles in Central America."[15]

Haig's analysis oversimplified matters. True, the USSR and Cuba were avidly fishing in Central America's troubled political waters and providing material support to extreme socialist or pro-communist forces, but long-standing internal social, political, and economic tensions created conducive conditions for left-wing movements in Central America.[16] Washington's hostility to left-of-center reformist political forces and support for friendly, but often unpopular, dictators[17] in places like Nicaragua, Honduras, and Guatemala throughout the 20th century had exacerbated such problems and increased popular support for radical left-wing movements.[18]

Unfortunately for the Reagan administration, suspicions about the Contras abounded in Congress and among influential American groups. Harvard University Professor Gregory F. Treverton noted the Contras' acute image problems:

> Initially the Contras did not enjoy a good press in the United States. They usually were represented in Congress, and on American TV, by hefty men in dark sunglasses, looking uncomfortable in suits and uttering monosyllabic assents to arguments made on their behalf by their American supporters. Their shortcomings were apparent to all. They seemed both savage and feckless on the battlefield, more adept at excess or sabotage than combat.[19]

The CIA desperately sought to counteract its client's negative image. When allegations of human rights abuses and outright atrocities began to plague the Contras, the CIA took the lead in producing a new operations manual, "Psychological Operations in Guerrilla Warfare," mentioned previously. Unfortunately, many of the actions suggested in that manual—such as assassinating local leaders to intimidate villagers—were as offensive to human rights proponents as the Contras' original conduct had been. Moreover, having a foreign government write an operations manual did not help the Contras' claim to being an indigenous national liberation movement.

Agency leaders were especially determined to change the widespread impression that the Contras were dominated by military commanders— many of whom had been officers in Somoza's infamous National Guard. That was not an easy task, because the impression largely was true, especially with regard to the largest Contra faction, the Nicaraguan Democratic Force (FDN), which was the recipient of most of the U.S. aid. The head of the Contras' military arm, Enrique Bermúdez, had been a colonel in Somoza's Guard. His background was far from unique— a 1985 study by the Congressional Arms Control and Foreign Policy Caucus found that 46 of the top 48 commanders were Guard veterans.[20]

A State Department analysis the following year tried to rebut that conclusion, contending that only 30 percent of Contra commanders had been Somoza Guard members. But as Illinois State University Professor James M. Scott pointed out, the State Department arrived at that fig- ure only by adding lower-level officers, thereby diluting the Somocista presence in the total. The truly top-level commanders, in fact, had been members of the military hierarchy in the old regime.[21]

American diplomats and CIA handlers pressed the various Con- tra factions to mute their differences and unite under the supposedly civilian-controlled FDN. The FDN's legitimacy as a genuine, indigenous, democratic revolutionary movement was not enhanced, though, when the organization's principal offices were located in Miami. Moreover, Washington bullied perhaps the most genuine nationalistic, democratic faction, which was headed by Sandinista defector Edén Pastora—the CIA reportedly terminated aid to Pastora in April 1984 because he refused to join the U.S.-sponsored FDN common front.[22]

Trying to prevent factionalism among the Nicaraguan rebels was not the only headache for U.S. officials. As Treverton points out, his- torically, when Washington has sponsored a foreign government or political movement, "The United States becomes associated with 'their' purposes. Like it or not, American covert support for foreign groups inevitably identifies the United States with those groups."[23] Even when administration officials are appalled at a client's conduct and may try to make a distinction between U.S. goals and the client's, outside observers are likely to be unimpressed. Moreover, such distinctions "cannot be sustained inside a messy foreign reality, when U.S.-supported groups [pursue] ambitions of their own and where connections among groups and causes [are] fleeting, often ambiguous."[24] Those problems accurately describe Washington's effort to back the Contras.

THE FIGHT OVER CONTRA AID

Many members of Congress simply did not believe the assertion of U.S. officials and their think tank and media allies that the Contras were genuine freedom fighters. Moreover, the Reagan administration's conduct did little to inspire congressional trust. A November 8, 1982, issue of *Newsweek* broke the story that the U.S. ambassador to Honduras, John Negroponte, was involved in a covert mission to train and equip Contra fighters. The State Department's response was part grudging acknowledgment that the *Newsweek* article was accurate and part disingenuous regurgitation of previous assertions about supposedly restrained U.S. policy objectives. The administration conceded that the United States was supporting small-scale military operations against the Nicaraguan government, but the supposed purpose of that effort was merely to put pressure on the regime, not oust it. Thomas O. Enders, assistant secretary of state for Inter-American Affairs, argued that aiding the guerrillas might prod the Sandinista government toward democratic reforms. It was, he claimed, a "lowball option, a small operation not designed to overthrow."[25] Beyond the goal of getting the Sandinista government to negotiate with its domestic opponents, administration officials insisted that funding an insurgent force inside Nicaragua was the most effective way to choke off the flow of arms from Nicaragua to leftist forces in El Salvador.[26]

The reaction in Congress and the media was a mixture of incredulity, apprehension, and anger. At a minimum, the administration's response, even if sincere, seemed to ignore the difficulty of calibrating assistance to rebel forces so precisely that they could "pressure" the Sandinista regime without ousting it. Yet as *New York Times* correspondent

Tim Weiner noted, "President Reagan stuck with the cover story maintaining the fiction that the United States was not seeking to topple the Sandinista regime";[27] the president even gave that assurance publicly to a joint session of Congress. But to outside observers, the Contras' interest in merely applying pressure seemed improbable; their agenda was to overthrow their enemies and take power. The CIA-directed aid program also effectively circumvented Congress, which was a very sensitive matter, especially in light of revelations during the mid-1970s of the executive branch's abuses in the conduct of U.S. foreign policy during previous decades; the Senate committee headed by Sen. Frank Church (D-ID) had uncovered information that was especially damning.[28]

Most critics of the Reagan administration weren't buying the assurances of a limited goal. Congress, particularly wary after the debacle in Vietnam, was alarmed that the United States seemed to be drifting into another murky conflict, this time in Central America. Treverton notes correctly that the Contras "did not have limited purposes, much less ones that suited American convenience." What was not clear, he contends, "is whether the administration misled itself *and* Congress or just Congress" regarding the Contras' objectives.[29]

The negative congressional response was swift and decisive. On December 8, 1982, the House of Representatives passed the Boland Amendment, named for its chief sponsor, Rep. Edward Boland (D-MA), which prohibited the Defense Department and the CIA from providing military equipment, training, or advice for the purpose of overthrowing the Nicaraguan government.

Of course, if the Reagan administration was sincere in its claims that the objective of sending assistance to the Contras was not to overthrow the Ortega regime but merely to create greater pressure for political reform and negotiations with opposition forces, the Boland Amendment should have been irrelevant. After all, the limited, supposedly nonlethal aid to opposition factions that Congress had approved was not automatically terminated. Yet the fact that the president and his advisers—along with their conservative supporters in the media and the policy community—asserted that the Boland Amendment crippled U.S. efforts to prevent Sandinista and Cuban subversion in Central America was a tacit admission that forcible regime change was the real goal of U.S. policy.

American admirers of the Contras did not disguise their irritation with the Boland Amendment, and they diligently worked to repeal the measure. Sen. Barry Goldwater (R-AZ) asserted flatly, "The Boland Amendment is unconstitutional. It's another example of Congress trying to take away the constitutional power of the President to be Commander in Chief and to formulate foreign policy."[30] Syndicated columnist George Will observed: "The Brezhnev doctrine asserts that the process of becoming a Soviet satellite is irreversible. The Boland Amendment forbids support to freedom fighters attempting to liberate Nicaragua from a satellite regime. Republican Representative Don Ritter of Pennsylvania rightly says that the amendment makes the United States the enforcer of the Brezhnev doctrine."[31]

Rep. Tom Loeffler (R-TX) argued that failing to provide aid to the Contras would "crown the Sandinistas as the permanent rulers of a Communist Nicaragua."[32] A young Republican congressman from Georgia, Newt Gingrich, was even more caustic. "A vote for the Boland Amendment," he charged, "is in fact a vote for the unilateral disarmament of the side that favors freedom in Central America."[33]

Although the GOP-controlled Senate was willing to continue funding the operation to assist the Contras, the Democrat-controlled House balked following passage of the Boland Amendment. The two chambers eventually compromised in conference in the autumn of 1983, agreeing to continue aid but limiting the amount to $24 million a year. Congressional sentiment turned even more negative in the spring of 1984, and in October of that year, Congress voted to cut off any additional money until February 1985. Even then, funds could flow only if the administration certified compliance with several conditions, including taking steps to ensure that the Contras were not committing human rights violations.

The erosion of congressional support infuriated American backers of the Contras. Veteran CIA official David Phillips fumed, "Whatever the merits of the various 'freedom fighters,' we should recognize that once our country makes a commitment to them, it is unfair, and perhaps immoral, to turn our backs."[34] Administration officials also increasingly

argued that the alternatives to supporting the Contras were utterly unpal-
atable. Elliott Abrams, assistant secretary of state for Inter-American
Affairs, asserted that without generous aid to the Contras, the choice
would be either U.S. troops in direct combat roles "or surrender."[35]

The president and his advisers stepped up their efforts to get Congress to restore aid, arguing that the stakes were nothing less than preventing a communist takeover of all Central America. That propaganda
effort paid off to some extent in 1986, when first the House and then
the Senate reversed course and approved the administration's proposal to
spend $100 million in aid to the Contras. By the summer of 1986, the
CIA had dropped 90 tons of guns and ammunition to Contra forces in
southern Nicaragua.[36]

Even though legitimate American interests were imperiled by the
emergence of another Soviet ally in the Western Hemisphere, U.S. officials tended to overstate the stakes involved, as well as the magnitude
of the danger. Shultz, for example, asserted that "if the U.S. backed off
from the situation and Nicaragua became the dominant power in the
region, the U.S. would eventually not be able to tolerate it." He added
that "to back off now would eventually mean a war"; conversely, he
said that at the moment, "we have friends in the area who are ready
to resist."[37] Such comments reflected an excessive fear of Nicaragua's
potential clout. The country was, after all, a small, poor, third-tier or
fourth-tier power.

The apocalyptic warnings also ignored the rather obvious flaws
of many of America's "friends." The governments of Honduras and
Panama were thoroughly corrupt and authoritarian, and the car-
ousel of military regimes in Guatemala was even worse. More than
100,000 civilians already had perished in that nation's seemingly inter-
minable counter-insurgency war, and the situation would get worse
throughout the 1980s. Human rights groups excoriated the Guatemalan
government and military for its horrific record of atrocities.[38] As noted
previously, the Contras' behavior with respect to human rights also left
much to be desired.

But questions about the Contras' conduct did not inhibit their
American supporters, who deflected criticism by stressing the perils

to the United States of *not* supporting the insurgents. Shultz's warning about the dangers of that course was restrained compared to the hysteria of U.S. ambassador to the United Nations Jeane Kirkpatrick. She argued that if U.S. support for the Contras faltered, the damage would "not be controllable." Kirkpatrick believed that "Nicaragua would consolidate itself as the new Cuba, and the others in the region would 'Finlandize,'— accommodate to this new Communist power. Panama would go with Cuba, and 'we will confront MiGs before November.'"[39]

Reagan himself posited an even more expansive domino theory. "Although El Salvador was the immediate target," he conceded, "the evidence showed that the Soviets and Fidel Castro were targeting all of Central America for a Communist takeover. El Salvador and Nicaragua were only a down payment. Honduras, Guatemala, and Costa Rica were next, and then would come Mexico."[40]

That view magnified the Sandinista regime—which was at most an annoying, upstart challenger—into an existential threat to the security of the United States. The notion of a communist menace to Mexico was so far-fetched that it verged on being a paranoid fantasy. No credible evidence of a serious domestic communist movement in that country existed. Indeed, communist forces in Mexico always had been weaker than in virtually any other country in Latin America. And to suppose that even the most committed revolutionaries in tiny Central American nations could destabilize a much larger and more powerful Mexico—a country whose citizens tended to view their southern neighbors with a mixture of patronizing indulgence and contempt—strained credulity.

Yet the fear among U.S. policymakers that a communist tide might sweep not only through Central America but beyond apparently was quite real. That fear helps explain why the Reagan administration made such a high priority of undermining Moscow's latest client in the region by backing the Contras.

THE IRAN-CONTRA AFFAIR AND ITS IMPLICATIONS

Administration officials were so frustrated with the Boland Amendment's strictures that they ultimately sought to bypass the congressional appropriations process entirely and generate funds for the Contras another way. CIA Director Casey, National Security Adviser John Poindexter, and National Security Council staff member Oliver North were the principal parties to that effort. (Reagan denied knowledge of the scheme, and Poindexter later insisted that the president's denial was true.) The effort to send "off budget" covert assistance to the Contras culminated in the bizarre Iran-Contra affair, in which Washington sought to raise funds for the Contras by selling arms to Iran and then sending the proceeds to the Nicaraguan rebels.[41]

The Iran-Contra scandal highlighted the perils posed to America's democratic, constitutional system by Washington's regime-change policies and support of supposedly democratic insurgents. Administration officials were so determined to execute their foreign-policy priority of aiding people whom they regarded as freedom fighters that they were willing to adopt wholly unconstitutional measures to do so. Congressional control of appropriations is absolutely vital to preventing chief executives from amassing dangerously expansive powers and jeopardizing the system of checks and balances.

Congress's growing willingness to abdicate its power to declare war (the authority to determine when—or if—the republic goes to war) had already led to an extremely unhealthy development: the imperial presidency. But even the most ambitious and pro-war president was dependent on de facto congressional approval of U.S. involvement in a conflict, because the legislative branch controlled whether to authorize continued funding. Had the Iran-Contra scheme succeeded, it would have set a crucial precedent for the executive branch's being able to secure war funding without any congressional approval (or even input).

Bitter Divisions in U.S. Public Opinion about the Contras

Even before the Iran-Contra scandal erupted, domestic opposition to aiding the Contras was ferocious. Most liberals and many moderates viewed the rebels as little more than thuggish, diehard remnants of the former Somoza dictatorship. Liberal critics noted in particular that Contra leader Bermúdez had been a high-ranking officer in Somoza's infamous

National Guard, which had committed many human rights violations during the dictator's long rule.[42] Rep. Thomas Downey (D-NY) was especially caustic, and he summarized the prevailing attitude of liberals in the United States when he labeled the Contras "thieves, brigands, and butchers."[43]

Although Downey's blistering verdict accurately described a significant portion of the insurgent forces, his assessment was not entirely fair. The Contras included some moderate elements—even some committed democratic ones—as well as Somocistas. One problem in the domestic debate over U.S. policy in Nicaragua is that both sides caricatured the Nicaraguan faction they didn't like. Reagan and his allies portrayed the Sandinistas as a monolithic, communist totalitarian force, when the group was actually a rather broad coalition ranging from hard-core communists to mild, slightly left-of-center reformers. Likewise, opponents of the administration's policy saw the Contras as a monolithic, authoritarian far-right faction that had no internal support and existed only because it was on the U.S. payroll. A closer look would have shown them to be an uneasy coalition of varying political orientations with at least modest popular support among Nicaraguans who were disgusted with the Ortega regime's high-handed tactics. In fact, Pastora and a significant number of other armed fighters were disillusioned defectors from the ranks of the Sandinistas.

While both sides in the U.S. debate oversimplified matters, the anti-Contra camp had the better case on balance. At a minimum, the Contras had a serious image problem—and for good reason. Robert Kagan, a neoconservative scholar friendly to the Reagan administration, noted that "Reagan officials believed that the main weakness of the Contras was their lack of 'legitimate' leadership, which in American terms meant moderately progressive, anti-Somoza" figures.[44] National Security Advisor Robert McFarlane concluded that in order to get approval for further aid to the insurgents, "Congress had to find the Contra movement a more appealing, legitimate movement oriented toward political goals, pluralism and so forth."[45]

That comment indicated that even some administration officials harbored doubts about the official portrayal of the Contras as noble freedom fighters. And an examination of the group's top leadership certainly painted a different, less flattering, picture. As noted previously, an April 1985 report from the Arms Control and Foreign Policy Caucus found that 46 of the top 48 positions in the anti-Sandinista resistance were held by former members of Somoza's National Guard.[46] The composition of lower- and mid-level Contra forces was more diverse, but even so, the nature of the organization's leadership certainly did not fit with the Reagan administration's portrayal of the group as committed democrats fighting to restore freedom to their country.

Yet Reagan and his advisers flatly refused to concede that the insurgency was controlled by former Somoza regime officials. The president's belief, at least, seemed genuine. In a March 7, 1986, diary entry, Reagan describes a meeting with three top Contra leaders, [Alfonso] Robelo, [Adolfo] Calero, and [Arturo] Cruz. "They are here to help us persuade Congress to help the freedom fighters. They are an answer to the left wing propaganda that the freedom fighters are led by the former Somoza honchos. Two of these three were imprisoned by Somoza & the other one is a defector from the Sandinistas."[47]

A March 1985 report from the human rights organization America's Watch criticized both the Sandinista government and the insurgents for atrocities, but the report was especially critical of the Contras for engaging in "the deliberate use of terror."[48] The numerous incidents documented in the report added to the Contras' image problem in the United States and galvanized opposition to the Reagan administration's policy in Central America. Amnesty International, having made several fact-finding missions to Nicaragua since the 1979 revolution, reached similar conclusions. It documented a pattern of executions, torture, mutilations, and kidnappings by Contra forces. Some of the victims of those abuses included lay church workers and student teachers.[49]

Another very serious allegation made against the Contras was that they trafficked cocaine to fund their military and political activities. While evidence of such activities never was definitive, the allegations also never were convincingly debunked. Even worse, credible allegations were made that the CIA was aware of the Contras' activities and actually may have facilitated the trafficking to markets in the United States, thereby helping to fuel the crack cocaine epidemic.[50] The issue remains a matter of intense controversy, but all except the most extreme charges seem to have become more, not less, credible with the passage of time.[51] If true, the United States was guilty of supporting a truly odious client, and a powerful U.S. government agency operated utterly contrary to professed American values.

The Contra Issue Fades

As the Cold War faded in the late 1980s when Mikhail Gorbachev became leader of the Soviet Union and adopted a more conciliatory policy toward the West, even the modest strategic rationale for backing the Nicaraguan rebels diminished. Yet both the Reagan administration and its successor attempted to maintain solid support for the Contras. Baker later asserted that "abandoning the contras was morally and politically unconscionable to me."[52] By the time he became secretary of state under George H. W. Bush in 1989, however, congressional support for continuing to provide lethal aid to the insurgents was extremely weak. The Bush administration's fallback position was to ask Congress to maintain at least humanitarian aid to the Contras "to keep them intact as a credible deterrent in the event of a diplomatic stalemate" with the Sandinista regime.[53]

The denouement of the Nicaragua struggle demonstrated that Washington's portrayal of the Sandinistas as hard-core Leninists who were determined to maintain a dictatorship at all costs was simplistic and overwrought. Ortega's government agreed to elections in 1990, and outside observers later concluded that they were reasonably free and fair. Equally significant, Ortega and his followers relinquished power when voters elected a coalition of moderate opposition forces led by Violeta Chamorro.[54] The armed Contras, Washington's preferred clients, actually were a relatively small faction within that victorious coalition, and some of the Contras even would collaborate with the Sandinistas later.[55]

Ortega returned to power in 2006 following another free election and was re-elected in 2011. Ortega's rule during his second stint in office has been characterized by authoritarian populism, and the country's 2016 elections were tainted by serious incidents of voter fraud. Ortega is hardly a paragon of liberal democracy, but his behavior has not matched Washington's earlier caricature of him as a bloody-handed Leninist. Indeed, some disgruntled hardline leftists in the United States and elsewhere now argue that Ortega has moderated so much that he has betrayed the Sandinista revolution.[56]

BROADER IMPLICATIONS OF WASHINGTON'S SUPPORT FOR THE CONTRAS

Applying the Reagan Doctrine in Central America led to a variety of troubling actions. U.S. officials, and especially "movement conservatives" in Congress and elsewhere, exaggerated the political purity of the Nicaraguan Contras—sometimes to absurd lengths—to justify support for an anti-leftist insurgency. Such willful ideological blindness annoyed even Shultz, a major architect of the Reagan Doctrine. Shultz condemned some conservatives for a "fixation on the Contras." As the 1980s progressed, he contended, conservatives increasingly viewed the Contras "as an end unto themselves." Conversely, although he supported the Contras, Shultz insisted that he did so primarily "as a source of pressure to further our true objectives: democracy in Nicaragua and peace in Central America."[57] That was a surprisingly restrained objective that stood in contrast to his previous enthusiasm for so-called democratic freedom fighters around the globe.

Even the best of the Contras fell short of being the "moral equal" of America's founding fathers, and most of them were little more than corrupt, power-seeking political figures—a species that is all too common throughout the history of Central America. The fact that several Contra figures ultimately allied themselves with the Sandinistas after the Cold War reinforces such a conclusion.

Although a strategic rationale existed for backing anti-communist elements in the context of the Cold War—especially in a region so close to the U.S. homeland—it was a fairly modest one; it certainly never was sufficient to justify whitewashing the nature of the U.S. rebel clients in Nicaragua. At a minimum, the Reagan administration oversold both the necessity and the nobility of supporting the Contras.

CHAPTER TWO

THE AFGHAN MUJAHIDEEN:
HOLY WARRIORS, NOT FREEDOM FIGHTERS

In marked contrast to the bitter partisan controversies surrounding the wisdom of supporting rebel forces in places such as Nicaragua and Angola (Chapter 3), the policy of helping Afghan insurgents—the mujahideen—had strong bipartisan backing throughout the final decade of the Cold War. Liberals as well as conservatives expressed support for the plucky resistance forces who challenged the Soviet army of occupation. Such sympathy was understandable, because the public and Congress perceived that Afghanistan was the clear victim of Soviet aggression.

The reality was a bit murkier. Evidence later emerged that months *before* the Soviet invasion of Afghanistan, President Jimmy Carter's administration implemented National Security Adviser Zbigniew Brzezinski's proposal to back forces in Afghanistan who were opposed to the pro-Soviet government in Kabul.[1] The USSR intervened to occupy the country with its own troops only after the insurgents posed a serious threat to topple that regime. At the time, though, most Americans were totally unaware of that backstory.

AFGHANISTAN AS A PAWN IN THE U.S.-SOVIET STRATEGIC RIVALRY

U.S. support for Afghan insurgents thus began as an increasingly high-stakes geostrategic rivalry between the United States and the Soviet Union.

Washington had engaged in a variety of maneuvers to counter Moscow's growing influence in Afghanistan during the mid and late 1970s and to draw Afghanistan into the Western camp. Brzezinski later admitted that the administration hoped to bait the Soviets into establishing a heavier footprint that would antagonize the Afghan people and give the USSR a major geopolitical headache. Washington was helping to establish—and to provide at least some covert assistance to—resistance forces months before the full-scale Soviet invasion in December 1979.[2]

Nevertheless, U.S. officials seemed both surprised and alarmed at the scope of Moscow's escalation when the Red Army proceeded to occupy the entire country. Administration leaders feared that the move might be the first stage of a broad Soviet offensive to dominate Southwest Asia and to gain a stranglehold on the flow of oil coming out of the Persian Gulf. Hawks had warned for several years that communist forces around the world would exploit America's ignominious retreat from Vietnam, and the extent of the Soviet military intervention in Afghanistan seemed to confirm those warnings.

Ideology aside, Moscow's desire to establish a presence on the Indian Ocean, and, specifically, to gain control of a warm water port, predated the existence of the USSR. The takeover of Afghanistan could be interpreted as an initial move toward that objective and as maneuvering to establish a dominant position in the Persian Gulf. Carter sought to dissuade Moscow from even toying with such an idea. In his State of the Union address on January 23, 1980, Carter stated that "an attempt by an outside power to gain control of the Persian Gulf region [would] be regarded as an assault on the vital interests of the United States and [would] be repelled by any means necessary, including military force."[3] During a visit to India later that month, former Secretary of Defense Clark Clifford, serving as a special adviser to the president, issued an even more emphatic, saber-rattling warning to Moscow: "The Soviets must know that if part of their plan [in their occupation of Afghanistan] is to move toward the Persian Gulf, that means war."[4]

The Carter administration then began to increase its military assistance to anti-Soviet elements in Afghanistan; once the Reagan administration came into office, the scope of the assistance expanded substantially.

By the beginning of 1985, the United States already had provided some $625 million to the insurgents.[5] Congress ultimately approved more than $2 billion in covert assistance for the mujahideen.[6] That sum was greater than the funding for all other covert Central Intelligence Agency (CIA) operations in the 1980s combined. By 1987, Washington was providing nearly $700 million in assistance per year to the rebels. In marked contrast to the bitter partisan controversies over aid to Nicaragua's Contras and Angola's National Union for the Total Independence of Angola (UNITA), funding for Afghanistan was met with little congressional opposition. Support for the implementation of what ultimately became the Reagan Doctrine was strong across the political spectrum in this case.

In their support of insurgent forces that were resisting the Soviet occupation, American officials and opinion leaders habitually overlooked evidence about the actual nature of those insurgents. U.S. officials and members of the American news media frequently portrayed them not only as opponents of Soviet imperialism, but also as pro-Western freedom fighters. President Ronald Reagan routinely referred to the mujahideen as freedom fighters, not just publicly, but in private diary entries—sometimes even capitalizing the words.[7]

The use of that laudatory label to describe anti-communist insurgents occurred in every Cold War theater where the United States backed such forces, but never was it more awkward than with respect to Afghanistan. Contrary to the freedom fighter label—a term intended for those dedicated to overthrowing an oppressive regime in an effort to replace it with a democratic government—the reality regarding the mujahideen was far more complex, murky, and troubling. As noted in the introduction, even the word mujahideen is translated as "holy warriors," not freedom fighters—a very different connotation indeed. From the outset of Washington's support for the Afghan resistance, a plethora of evidence indicated that very few of the insurgents embraced even basic Western political values, much less a commitment to pluralistic democracy.

The decision to aid the Afghan mujahideen had extremely nasty long-term consequences for the United States. Indeed, the terrorist attacks on September 11, 2001, had some of their roots in that decision. Washington's assistance to the mujahideen helped train some fighters who later became significant figures in al Qaeda—especially the "foreign volunteers" from Arab countries. As James Scott, author of a comprehensive analysis of the Reagan Doctrine, points out, "the network of mujahidin trained by the United States turned against its benefactor."[8] Such blowback was nearly inevitable. Scott highlights a crucial defect in Washington's Afghanistan strategy during the 1980s: "The policy's success at organizing rebel resistance brought radical, committed fighters who despise[d] the United States as much as they hate[d] the former Soviet Union into contact with each other."[9]

At the time, though, assisting the Afghan resistance seemed not only strategically sound but also morally justified. The struggle in Afghanistan involved a clear case of Soviet aggression—although, given the Carter administration's meddling, it was not entirely unprovoked aggression. Moscow had been involved on the margins of the 1978 coup that had brought a Marxist government to power, and Soviet support and "guidance" of the new regime had been extensive throughout the following months.[10] And Moscow's intervention became massive once the USSR poured troops across the border in December 1979 to preserve that client regime's tenuous control. Ultimately, more than 120,000 Soviet troops occupied the country.

In retrospect, Moscow's actions may have been more a defensive response to Washington's policy foray into Afghanistan than a wider geopolitical offensive. Washington's apprehension that the Kremlin was attempting to reach the Indian Ocean and gain key leverage over Persian Gulf oil was not erroneous, but it was exaggerated. From Moscow's perspective, Washington appeared to be meddling in the Soviet Union's neighborhood, and such activity needed to be neutralized.

Another, less obvious motive for Moscow's intervention was its concern about the rise of Islamic radicalism on the USSR's southern flank and its potential destabilization of the predominantly Muslim Soviet republics in Central Asia and the Caucasus. (Later turmoil in Chechnya in the 1990s confirmed that Moscow's fears had not been unfounded.) The success of the 1979 Islamic revolution in Iran worried Soviet leaders at least as much as it worried their American counterparts. When the political grip of Moscow's communist dependents in Kabul began to slip,

Soviet officials worried that a successor government might be either a U.S. client or, perhaps even worse, an Iranian-style regime—fears that were heightened when recalling pro-Islamist riots that had taken place in the predominantly Shiite city of Herat in western Afghanistan in the spring of 1979.[11]

Either outcome was anathema to the Kremlin, so Leonid Brezhnev's government made the fateful decision to try to prop up its Afghan client through a direct military occupation. The Soviets also embarked on their own version of nation building. In an effort to "guide" their Afghan charges, Soviet administrators were put in charge of every department of Babrak Karmal's puppet government and that of his successor, former secret police chief Mohammad Najibullah. Moscow also conducted a concerted campaign to indoctrinate Afghans into the virtues of Marxism-Leninism, even going so far as to separate thousands of children from their parents to be educated in the USSR.[12]

WASHINGTON'S COMMITMENT TO AFGHAN REBELS GRADUALLY ESCALATES

Moscow's invasion and subsequent heavy-handed imperialism soon provoked a ferocious resistance. U.S. officials saw an excellent opportunity to foment trouble for America's Cold War adversary in the latter's backyard. At first, though, U.S. military aid was cautious and limited. From 1980 through 1981, the assistance amounted to $50 million. Peter Schweizer concludes that during the early years, the covert assistance program was just "marginally successful in sustaining the resistance."[13] *New York Times* correspondent Tim Weiner concludes that the initial goal of U.S. policy "was not to liberate Afghanistan. No one believed that the Afghans could actually win."[14] Instead, the goal was to help the insurgents harass the Soviets and give Moscow something to worry about close to home.

That limited goal may have been true for Carter administration officials and some members of the Reagan administration, but other policymakers seemed to harbor more ambitious objectives for the insurgency. Reagan CIA Director William Casey was dissatisfied with both the amount and quality of the weaponry being given to the mujahideen.

Schweizer noted that Casey was briefed in early 1981 about the assistance going "to the 'muj' as they were affectionately called at Langley [CIA headquarters]."[15] Casey was emphatic about increasing Washington's backing, telling his CIA subordinates: "Supporting the resistance—this is the kind of thing we should be doing—only more! I want this sort of activity in other places on the globe. . . . The captive nations are our best allies."[16]

Such comments were the early policy wellsprings of the Reagan Doctrine; after its inception, both the extent of the material assistance to and the magnitude of Washington's rhetorical embrace of the mujahideen increased markedly.

Additionally, some members of Congress and conservative activists outside the government wanted Washington to send more extensive and more sophisticated weaponry to the Afghan resistance. Sen. Paul Tsongas (D-MA) pushed through a bipartisan resolution in October 1984 calling on the administration to provide such increased aid. That resolution stated, "It would be indefensible to provide the freedom fighters with only enough aid to fight and die, but not enough to advance their cause of freedom."[17] Once again, American supporters of the mujahideen conflated the rebels' goal of expelling Soviet occupiers from their country with the goal of embracing "freedom."

Rep. Charlie Wilson (D-TX), chair of the House Appropriations Subcommittee on Defense, was an even more impassioned supporter of the mujahideen than Tsongas appeared to be. Wilson became an especially crucial figure in getting more substantial U.S. financial and military aid to Afghan insurgents.[18] Other influential members of Congress joined the campaign, including powerhouse Sens. Sam Nunn (D-GA) and Daniel Patrick Moynihan (D-NY). The last key convert to the cause of all-out support was Sen. Barry Goldwater (R-AZ), chairman of the Senate Intelligence Committee.[19]

Conservative and libertarian activists added to the pressure on the administration. An especially dedicated campaigner was author and world adventure traveler Jack Wheeler, president of the Freedom Research Foundation. Wheeler portrayed the Afghan mujahideen in the most glowing terms as true freedom fighters.[20] Although Wheeler justified the Reagan Doctrine on strategic grounds, because he believed the Soviet Union posed a dire threat to America's security and was using proxy regimes in the Third World to strengthen its position, he also emphasized the doctrine's moral aspect. During a symposium at the Reason Foundation, he cited both motives. Supporting "these freedom fighter organizations is the most cost-effective way that I can possibly think of to defend the interests of the U.S," Wheeler contended. But supporting them also would "do something which I would consider to be moral, and that is to make an effort to bring freedom to these peoples under Soviet colonial sway."[21]

Wheeler's underlying logic seemed to be that if the rebels were anti-Soviet and anti-communist, they also were proponents of freedom. In the Afghan setting—and in many other places—nothing could have been farther from the truth. But his perspective had a growing number of allies inside the government, both in Congress and the executive branch. One of the latter was Dana Rohrabacher, a speech writer for Reagan— and a future congressman from California. He had Reagan's ear, and he used that access to help shape the Reagan Doctrine, especially with respect to Afghanistan. Like Wheeler, Rohrabacher tended to equate rebels who were merely anti-communist with genuine advocates of freedom, and he presented a romanticized view of the former. After leaving his White House post in 1988, he even briefly fought alongside mujahideen units.[22]

The growing pressure from key members of Congress and outside activists who supported the mujahideen produced the desired result: Washington's support for the rebels increased inexorably, and so did America's identification with their cause.

Pakistan Channels U.S. Aid to Afghanistan's Radical Islamists

Afghanistan is a landlocked country. Given that geographical reality, Washington was compelled from the very beginning to work closely with the government of Pakistan to channel aid to rebel forces. A trickle of aid could be channeled through China's Wakhan Corridor, a tiny finger of territory that jutted into Afghanistan, but the logistics through the treacherous mountains of the Hindu Kush limited that alternative. Besides, Beijing had its own aid program directed toward its favorite insurgent clients,[23] and it was not especially motivated to support a U.S. effort. Iran was the only other neighboring country that could serve as an effective channel for the distribution of arms and other assistance, but once the Islamic revolution poisoned Washington's relations with Tehran, that was not a viable option. The reliance on the Pakistanis was most unfortunate, though, because it became a major factor in the resulting boost to the most radical Islamic factions among the mujahideen.

Pakistan had its own political agenda with respect to Afghanistan, and that agenda was only partially compatible with Washington's. Both governments wanted to bleed Soviet occupation forces and ultimately force Moscow to disgorge Afghanistan, but beyond that, the two countries' objectives diverged. Islamabad wanted above all a government in Kabul that was subservient to Pakistan. Pakistani leaders viewed the previous, pre-Soviet governments in Kabul as excessively receptive to the influence of Pakistan's archrival, India. Given that India was a de facto Soviet ally, that perception largely was true. Pakistani leaders believed that an Islamist regime in Afghanistan would be more likely to align with Pakistan than a secular one—even a secular government not under Moscow's domination. The strongly Islamist views of Pakistan's military ruler, Mohammed Zia ul-Haq, who had instituted Sharia law there, reinforced support for the most avowedly religious factions in the Afghan mujahideen.[24]

Zia was an exceedingly unreliable, self-serving partner for the United States, but U.S. leaders largely failed to grasp that point. Reagan's December 7, 1982, diary entry following his first meeting with the Pakistani leader illustrated a disturbing degree of trust: "We got along fine. He's a good man (cavalry). Gave me his word they were not building an atomic or nuclear bomb. He's dedicated to helping the Afghans and stopping the Soviets."[25]

At Zia's insistence, Pakistan's Inter-Services Intelligence (ISI) directorate was in charge of channeling U.S. aid to the Afghan insurgents.[26] The head of ISI was General Akhtar Abdul Rehman Khan. Schweizer describes Khan as "a secretive, serious man, cold and reserved with a granite-like face. Akhtar was, in effect, running the resistance in Afghanistan. He was determining which weapons to buy and which Afghan leaders would get them."[27] Weiner contends that the ISI "favored the Afghan factions who proved themselves most capable in battle. Those factions also happened to be the most committed Islamists."[28] Islamabad favored the radicals not only because they were generally better fighters but also because their ideological and political orientation tracked more closely to that of Zia and other leaders of the Pakistani government. In any case, Khan and the ISI made certain that most military hardware and financial aid provided by the CIA went to Afghan religious radicals.

Washington expressed few serious objections—even after the Soviet occupation army withdrew from Afghanistan in 1989 and the flow of aid continued disproportionately to extremist factions. One exception was Robert Oakley, the U.S. ambassador to Pakistan from 1988 to 1991. Oakley argued that the United States "should drastically reduce our assistance to the 'real radicals' in Afghanistan, and work to make the mujahideen more moderate." But Oakley recalled that "the CIA couldn't or wouldn't get its Pakistani partners in line." Consequently, "we continued to support some of the radicals."[29] Weiner contends that "no one dreamed that the holy warriors could ever turn their *jihad* against the United States."[30] If true, that was a case of astonishing blindness on the part of U.S. officials. Scott's observation is apt: noting Islamabad's insistence on targeting the most radical mujahideen factions as the primary recipients of aid. Scott concludes that "while Pakistani leaders bear the brunt of this responsibility, the United States endorsed or acquiesced and thus is accountable."[31]

U.S. AID AND POLICY GOALS BOTH EXPAND

The scope of U.S. aid increased steadily, and so did the underlying purpose of Washington's policy. Initially, both the Carter and Reagan administrations embraced the goal of harassing the Soviets and raising the costs of their occupation of Afghanistan.[32] By 1985, though, the goal had escalated to one of outright victory, partly in response to growing

congressional pressure. At a January 1985 meeting of the National Security Planning Group, Reagan admonished his subordinates: "Do whatever you have to [to] help the mujahedin not only survive but win."[33]
Aid promptly was doubled, reflecting the broad support the insurgency
enjoyed in Congress. By 1986, the CIA's Afghan operation cost
$700 million a year and accounted for nearly 80 percent of the CIA's clan-
destine service budget.[34] Supporting the Afghan insurgents had become
a top U.S. foreign policy priority. Secretary of State George Shultz concluded that "our policy of aid to the Afghan mujaheddin, who were
fighting fiercely against the Soviet occupiers and their Afghan collaborators, was paying off."[35] In addition to an overall increase in aid, the
Reagan policy team placed a much greater emphasis on providing the
insurgents with sophisticated, high-tech weaponry.[36]

An especially key change came in 1986, when Washington provided the mujahideen with anti-aircraft Stinger missiles that they soon
used to bring down scores of Soviet helicopters and transport planes,
neutralizing the Red Army's principal advantage in the war. Reagan
Doctrine proponents in the administration had to overcome objections
by the State Department and some portions of the Defense Department
who feared that those lethal weapons might fall into "hostile hands."[37]
Indeed, even most U.S. allies did not have access to Stinger missiles. The
combination of greater quantities of military aid, along with the shift to
more lethal weaponry, enabled the mujahideen to conduct large-scale
operations and score major victories over Soviet and Afghan government
forces.

Not only did Washington's more robust strategy entail helping the
mujahideen expel the Soviet occupation forces from Afghanistan, it now
included the goal of extending the insurgency into the Soviet Union's
predominantly Muslim republics in Central Asia and the Caucasus.
That meant encouraging Islamic insurgents inside the USSR itself.
Mujahideen forces began to conduct operations outside of Afghanistan.[38]
Casey stressed that "this was about throwing off the Russian yoke and
freeing the passions of millions of devout Muslims."[39] The CIA even
paid to have "tens of thousands" of copies of the Koran printed and dis-
tributed in Afghanistan and the Central Asian republics.[40] Casey and his

associates seemed oblivious to the possible wider adverse consequences of igniting the flames of religious fervor in that part of the world.

Despite the surge of U.S. aid, the mujahideen remained a loose coalition of seven major groups—and, occasionally, factional offshoots of them—based mostly in the Pakistani border city of Peshawar. In response to U.S. and Pakistani prodding,[41] the seven factions formed an official alliance, the Islamic Unity of Afghan Mujahideen—also known as the "Peshawar Seven"—ostensibly to coordinate political and military activities. Intense rivalries persisted, though, and little actual coordination occurred.

THE REAL NATURE OF THE AFGHAN "FREEDOM FIGHTERS"

The common storyline promoted by both U.S. policymakers and the Western news media tended to minimize the in-fighting and the odious nature of most of the mujahideen factions.[42] Schweizer, president of the conservative Government Accountability Institute, was a little more nuanced in his analysis, contending that "some were religious moderates and pro-Western, others fundamentalist and anti-American."[43] Other Western accounts and analyses concluded that the factions included three "moderate" or "traditional" groups and four "Islamic fundamentalist" groups. According to that breakdown, the moderate contingent consisted of the Movement for the Islamic Revolution, the National Islamic Front, and the Afghan National Liberation Front. The opposing fundamentalist factions consisted of the Islamic Society of Afghanistan, which was led by Burhanuddin Rabbani, who would become the country's new president once the Soviets withdrew; the Islamic Alliance; and two factions of the Afghan Islamic Party—one led by Mohammad Yunus Khalis, the other by Gulbuddin Hekmatyar.

The media's portrayal of a clear distinction between moderates and radicals did not reflect the political reality of the Afghan insurgency. Even the so-called moderates did not advocate a secular state, much less anything resembling a secular democratic state. Some of the factions clearly were worse than others, though, and the most stridently intolerant was Hekmatyar's organization. He openly sought to establish a theocratic

Islamic state similar to Iran's under the Ayatollah Khomeini, with the very important difference that it would be Sunni Muslim rather than Shiite.

Hekmatyar received not only U.S. financial and military aid but, thanks to the Pakistanis, he received the lion's share of that aid—and he showed no gratitude whatsoever toward Washington. Using rhetoric reminiscent of Khomeini's, he routinely denounced the United States as the Great Satan and castigated Western values—especially those of capitalism and democracy—as "social poisons."[44] As the Soviet occupation drew to a close, he wasted no time switching the focus of his wrath from the Soviet Union to the United States—as would younger mujahideen radicals, including a Saudi fighter named Osama bin Laden. In early October 1989, on the eve of the departure of Soviet troops from Afghanistan, Hekmatyar told an assembly of fellow militants, "My brothers, the Russians have been defeated. Now we are going to fight against the Americans."[45]

Given the political makeup of the Afghan "freedom fighters," U.S. policymakers should have been more than a little unsettled when the Pakistani ISI directed the bulk of its money and military hardware to the most extreme Peshawar exile groups, especially Hekmatyar's faction. At least 75 percent of U.S. aid to the insurgents went to the four fundamentalist groups—with some 50 percent of the total going to Hekmatyar's branch of the Afghan Islamic Party.[46]

Saudi Arabia also provided funds to the insurgency, and Riyadh was rigorous in making sure that Islamabad directed the bulk of the assistance to reliably Islamist elements. Saudi functionaries showed up in Peshawar to carry out supposedly charitable activities and to promote education through newly constructed madrasahs (Islamic religious schools).[47] What that really meant was that Saudi clerics were conducting extensive indoctrination campaigns to promote the same Wahhabi Sunni religious extremism that dominated Saudi Arabia itself. Western-style secular values found no place whatsoever in that campaign.

WASHINGTON'S CULPABILITY IN BRINGING RADICAL ISLAMISTS TO POWER

That Washington's Pakistani and Saudi allies were strengthening the most extreme Islamist factions in Afghanistan was just one appalling aspect of the situation; that U.S. officials were willing to court the radicals as though they really were freedom fighters was yet another. William Webster, who became director of the CIA in 1987, invited Afghan rebel leaders to lunch in Washington; one of the honored guests was Hekmatyar. Weiner recalled that when he met Hekmatyar in Afghanistan, the Afghan leader vowed "to create a new Islamic society, and if it took a million more deaths . . ., so be it."[48] U.S. leaders may not have been aware of the virulence of his Islamist orientation at the time, but ample evidence already indicated that this man was no warrior for freedom and democracy. Washington should have been far more cautious and realistic about the clients it was backing in Afghanistan. And basic prudence should have led the United States to steer more of its military and financial assistance toward less extreme factions, even if that meant confronting the Pakistani government about its perverse priorities. Unfortunately, little evidence indicates that the Reagan administration even made such an attempt.

Washington's myopic policy skewed the political composition of the Afghan resistance in two important ways. First, it greatly inflated the importance of the "Peshawar Seven," even though those organizations' popular following inside Afghanistan and among the 3 million Afghan refugees in Pakistan appeared to be quite modest. The favoritism that Pakistan and Saudi Arabia exhibited toward the extreme factions within the Seven (with U.S. tolerance, if not outright approval) also magnified the clout of Islamic radicalism as a political force in Afghanistan.

Rep. Donald Ritter (R-PA), a strong supporter of helping Afghans expel the Soviet invaders, nevertheless was horrified by the nature of some of the insurgents the United States had helped bring to power. Speaking in early 1990 shortly after the departure of Soviet troops, Ritter noted that Pakistan had handpicked the leaders of the Peshawar Seven and that those figures were utterly unrepresentative of the Afghan people. "Some of the moderate parties have a legitimate following among the Afghan people, whose brand of Islam has never been marked by fanaticism. The fundamentalist parties, on the other hand, were creations of Pakistan and in one case Saudi Arabia."[49] Those regimes, Ritter charged, "have sought to put Hekmatyar in power."[50] And they would soon succeed, much to the chagrin of those American supporters of the Reagan Doctrine who genuinely believed that Washington's ultimate goal in aiding the mujahideen was to bring freedom and a better way of life to Afghanistan's suffering people. American aid never would do anything of the kind.

U.S. policymakers' repeated attempts to whitewash both the extremist political orientation of the Peshawar Seven and Pakistan's role in strengthening radical Afghan factions came at the expense of more moderate elements. At a committee hearing in May 1989, Rep. Stephen Solarz (D-NY) asked Howard Schaffer, deputy assistant secretary of state for Near East and South Asian Affairs, about press reports that Islamabad had disbursed the bulk of U.S. aid to the most militant, anti-Western factions.

Schaffer's flat dismissal of those allegations[51] clearly was the official line, regardless of the facts. At a hearing before the same House committee in 1986, Robert Peck, Schaffer's predecessor, asserted not only that the Peshawar alliance "speaks for the Afghan people" but also that the alliance "embraces the spectrum of the resistance effort."[52]

Yet the evidence that U.S. aid was empowering some of the most fanatical Afghan political factions—who did not represent the views of most Afghans—was overwhelming. And no one could make the case that U.S. officials weren't repeatedly warned about the trend.[53] Speaking in early 1989, Selig Harrison, a prominent expert on Central and South Asian affairs at the Carnegie Endowment for International Peace, warned Congress that neither the Moscow-backed government in Kabul "nor the Peshawar government-in-exile represents the majority of Afghans."[54]

Shortly after the Soviet withdrawal, Ritter noted that most U.S. aid had gone to "resistance groups whose agenda is largely unappealing, if not downright frightening, to a majority of Afghans."[55] The fear of those groups was especially strong "among the more educated urban populations," and their fears had "contributed to the staying power of the communist regime."[56] In 1990, Peck, no longer at his State Department post, offered a view sharply different from his congressional testimony four years earlier. "By continuing to put massive amounts of arms and cash subsidies into Afghanistan," he conceded, "we undercut the ability of moderate Afghans to shape the political course of their country."[57]

Instead of heeding the many warning signs and listening to critics' cautionary messages, U.S. officials spouted platitudes about the supposedly representative characteristics of the Peshawar-based fighters. Perhaps most disturbing, the stonewalling tactics persisted long after the last Soviet troops departed Afghanistan, when U.S. national security justifications for maintaining strict secrecy lost any arguable validity.

In 1986, Sen. Gordon Humphrey (R–NH), who had been one of the strongest proponents of U.S. aid to the mujahideen,[58] provided an ironic indictment of Washington's policy in Afghanistan.

> The objective [of U.S. policy] is not to achieve any old settlement. Indeed, it isn't even to achieve any old peace, because real peace isn't just about the absence of war, it is also about the absence of oppression. Peace without freedom is hardly worth achieving, and no people on the face of this Earth cling to that belief more tenaciously than the brave people of Afghanistan.[59]

BLOWBACK

U.S. policy did not bring peace—much less peace with freedom—to Afghanistan. By supporting the mujahideen, Washington did inflict a humiliating geopolitical defeat on Moscow; in fact, Scott argues that the Reagan Doctrine "had its greatest success in Afghanistan. American assistance to the rebels was an important factor in the defeat of the Soviet Union and its subsequent decision to withdraw."[60] Indeed, according to Scott, the positive results went beyond Afghanistan. "As William Casey had predicted it would, the Afghan debacle contributed to internal changes within the Soviet Union."[61] Those internal changes and attempts at reform under Mikhail Gorbachev ultimately destabilized the USSR and led to its demise.

But gaining a geopolitical victory over the Soviet Union in Afghanistan came at an appalling cost to the Afghan people in both the short and long term. The destabilization of the country, the violent postwar factionalism of the mujahideen, and the disproportionate strength of Islamic radicals that Pakistan and the United States had empowered produced a bloody civil war. By the mid-1990s, a new radical movement, the Taliban, came to power, controlling a majority of Afghanistan's territory. That regime, in turn, provided sanctuary to an especially militant Arab faction, al Qaeda, led by a Saudi veteran of the Afghan war, Osama bin Laden. Washington's aid program, which had empowered Islamic militants and falsely portrayed them as freedom fighters, produced unintended adverse consequences that spread across the world. And with the 1993 bombing of the World Trade Center and the far more destructive terrorist attacks on September 11, 2001, the catastrophic blowback reached America's homeland.

The United States responded to the 2001 attacks by launching air strikes and an invasion of Afghanistan, seeking to crush al Qaeda and oust the Taliban regime for giving safe haven to al Qaeda. That offensive marked the opening phase of America's longest war, now in its 17th year. In addition to the military campaign, Washington has pursued an ambitious nation-building effort.[62] U.S. leaders still seem fixated on bringing freedom and democracy to Afghanistan; unfortunately, those goals seem no more realistic today than they did when the United States backed the mujahideen in the 1980s.

The Persistence of Wishful Thinking

Amazingly, architects of aid to the mujahideen in the Carter and Reagan administrations still seem oblivious to the nature of the faction they backed and ultimately empowered. In an appearance on CBS's *Late Night with David Letterman* in March 2014, Carter himself touted the decision "to arm the freedom fighters,"[63] and he continued to use that laudatory term throughout the interview.

Former Secretary of State Shultz likewise clung to the belief that the Afghan insurgents were noble freedom fighters. In his memoirs, Shultz noted that giving the mujahideen Stinger missiles was met with considerable controversy among national security agencies, with the Pentagon being especially wary. Shultz, however, exhibited no such reluctance. "I strongly disagreed" with the Pentagon's position, he recalled. "We should help the freedom fighters in Afghanistan to be as effective as possible," he insisted.[64] Throughout his memoirs, Shultz still repeatedly referred to the mujahideen as "freedom fighters," and as "our friends."[65] Yet that volume was published in 1993, when extensive evidence already had emerged about the extremist, anti–Western orientation of the Afghan factions Washington had supported. His denial of an increasingly evident reality was a classic example of a former official being stubbornly unwilling to admit that he and other policymakers had woefully misjudged the nature of Washington's "pro-freedom" clients.

Gregory Treverton provided a succinct verdict on Washington's policy in Afghanistan: "Support for resistance forces in Afghanistan," he contended, could "be justified as a way to put strategic pressure on Soviet occupation of that country." But "given the character of the resistance forces, it cannot be said to be a way to bring 'democracy' to Afghanistan."[66] Perhaps most telling, Treverton wrote those perceptive words in the mid-1980s. Even at that time, the fact that America's clients were not freedom fighters struggling to create a democratic Afghanistan should have been as apparent to U.S. policymakers as it was to him and other astute observers.

The comment of John McMahon, deputy director of the CIA during the Reagan years, is an appropriate epitaph for the U.S. policy of aiding the mujahideen. "In covert action," McMahon stated, "you always have to think of the endgame before you start it. And we don't always do that."[67] The decision to support the Afghan "freedom fighters" was a textbook example of such a failure.

Weiner's account is shocking and depressing. "The CIA's briefing books never answered the question of what would happen when a militant Islamic army defeated the godless invaders of Afghanistan." Weiner related the comments of Tom Twetten, the number two official in the CIA's clandestine service in the late 1980s, who in 1988 finally was given the task of figuring out what was likely to become of the Afghan rebels if they defeated the Soviet army of occupation. Twetten told Weiner that "it quickly became clear" that Washington had no postwar plan. Twetten recalled that the CIA simply decided that "there'll be 'Afghan democracy.' And it won't be pretty."[68]

Given the ongoing tragedy in Afghanistan, that assessment proved to be a considerable understatement. The United States' negligence is remarkable on two levels. First, astonishingly, officials apparently never considered the possible long-term consequences of the policy they were implementing. Second, nothing in Afghanistan's history or culture suggested that any form of democracy, pretty or otherwise, likely would emerge from the insurgency against the Soviet Union. Afghanistan was a preindustrial, tribal society—generally not the foundation for a democratic political system. U.S. officials' glamorization of the mujahideen as freedom fighters who would bring reasonably tolerant secularism (perhaps even secular democracy) to Afghanistan is an example of their seeing what they wished to see, not what was actually there.

The application of the Reagan Doctrine in Afghanistan was a case of dangerous, delusional thinking. Unfortunately, it would not be the last. Similar unrealistic endeavors would take place in several arenas during the post–Cold War era.

CHAPTER THREE

JONAS SAVIMBI: THE REAGAN
DOCTRINE'S BIGGEST EMBARRASSMENT

As defective as the strategies in Nicaragua and Afghanistan had been, far worse was the U.S. embrace of an insurgent faction despite a weak to nonexistent security rationale and despite evidence that its principal leader was a psychopathic charlatan. The country? Angola. The insurgent leader? Jonas Savimbi.[1]

Angola's very location 7,000 miles away should have counseled restraint on Washington's part. The United States had important security and other concerns in its own hemisphere—especially in Central America, a mere two-hour flight from Miami, as hawks never tired of pointing out. From a strategic standpoint, preventing the Soviet Union from establishing additional client states in the Western Hemisphere—thereby preventing the rival superpower from projecting its political influence and perhaps even military power in America's own backyard—made sense.

At the time, one even could have argued that significant American interests were at stake in Afghanistan. That country's proximity to the Indian Ocean and the Persian Gulf region's oil riches gave Afghanistan some strategic relevance, although not as much as U.S. policymakers reflexively assumed. However, even if American leaders overestimated not only the importance of that region's oil supply but also the extent of Moscow's expansionist agenda, an attempt to deny a Soviet bid for preeminence there was not completely irrational. If thwarting possible communist expansionist moves through the low-cost, low-risk policy of aiding indigenous fighters who were resisting Soviet aggression in Afghanistan was feasible, so much the better. Or so it seemed, as long as U.S. policymakers ignored the disturbingly radical nature of their chosen Afghan clients (Chapter 2).

But in the case of Angola, arguing that America had important interests there that warranted support for insurgents required a substantial stretch of the imagination. Sub-Saharan Africa was a strategic and economic backwater that merited little U.S. involvement. Angola did have some oil resources in its extreme northwest province of Cabinda, but the country was hardly a major factor in the world's oil supply. Moreover, Angola's leftist government had never given even the slightest indication that it intended to deny the United States or other Western nations access to its petroleum production. Quite the contrary—and despite their leftist orientation—Angolan officials were eager to do business with multinational oil companies.

American strategic and economic interests in the region certainly did not warrant embracing a nebulous, supposedly anti-communist rebel group and providing it with military assistance—yet that's exactly what Washington did, especially during the 1980s under the rubric of the Reagan Doctrine. Author and conservative political consultant Peter Schweizer contends that "Savimbi was a perfect test case for supporting anti-communist insurgents, a policy that [CIA Director William] Casey proposed in early 1981."[2] More accurately, the United States' support for Angola became a textbook example of the perils of assuming that foreign insurgents embody fundamental American values—or even vaguely democratic ones.

True, the extent of U.S. identification with Angolan insurgents and the extent of aid provided never reached the levels of the Afghan or Nicaraguan conflicts. But an important reason for that limitation was the pushback from a wary post-Vietnam Congress that was controlled by the Democratic Party during some of that time. Not only were Democrats of that era inclined to favor a less interventionist foreign policy than their Republican opponents, but also they had a natural partisan opposition to any policies pursued by the White House's GOP occupants. In all like-lihood, if the Ford and Reagan administrations could have charted their own policy without interference from Congress, an even more robust aid program to supposedly pro-Western Angolan rebels might have been put in place. Such an outcome would have been unfortunate, though, because the principal rebel movement in Angola was more than a little unsavory.

THE ANGOLAN TRIBAL STRUGGLE

The Angolan conflict began as a three-sided struggle for power during the waning days of Portuguese colonialism in the early and mid-1970s. When a new revolutionary government in Lisbon jettisoned Angola and the other remnants of Portugal's once-extensive empire, three competing left-of-center Angolan factions maneuvered for political and economic dominance. The tripartite division actually had more to do with Angola's tribal makeup than with ideological factors—a point that U.S. policymak-ers rarely acknowledged, much less fully appreciated. Instead, they tended to view the Angolan struggle solely through the lens of the Cold War.

Each of the Angolan political factions was dominated by a specific tribe, and each was geographically based. The Popular Movement for the Liberation of Angola (MPLA), led by Agostinho Neto and José Eduardo dos Santos, became the primary power throughout the western portion of the country—including the capital, Luanda, and the key oil-producing province, Cabinda. The MPLA was overwhelmingly made up of members of the Mbundu tribe. Moscow soon threw its support to that faction, ultimately providing some $6 billion in military sales and aid between 1976 and 1988, plus economic assistance.[3] The principal opposing faction was the National Union for the Total Independence of Angola (UNITA), which was most active in the southern and eastern portions of the country, the homeland of Savimbi's Ovimbundu tribe. Initially, both China and South Africa backed UNITA, although Beijing soon dampened its support.

The U.S. government, with all-too-typical bad judgment, initially backed the weakest of the three organizations, the National Front for the Liberation of Angola (FNLA). The FNLA was led by Holden Roberto,[4] a relative by marriage to long-time U.S. ally Mobutu Sese Seko, who was the dictator of neighboring Zaire, (now the Democratic Republic of the Congo).[5] Two months after the fall of Saigon in the spring of 1975, President Gerald Ford approved a new initiative to secure Angola against a communist takeover, with aid to the FNLA as the centerpiece of that effort. Roberto was a member of the Kongo tribe, which had a major presence on both sides of Angola's northern border with Zaire. The FNLA proved to be a significant force only in the provinces directly along that border, which was not surprising considering that more Kongo lived in Zaire than in Angola itself, and the FNLA was widely seen as a Zairian government surrogate.

Washington was slow to grasp just how weak the FNLA's domestic base of support was. Author Tim Weiner notes that when "the CIA-backed troops in Angola faltered, and their enemies, strongly supported by Moscow and Havana, took control of the capital, [Secretary of State Henry] Kissinger ordered another $28 million in support."[6] It was a classic case of pouring money into a doomed policy. Despite U.S. financial and logistical assistance, the FNLA never became a major player in Angola's post-colonial power struggle.

Because of congressional restrictions, Ford's administration could not openly provide military assistance to supposed pro-Western elements, although the Central Intelligence Agency (CIA) did covertly funnel money and arms to the FNLA (and, to a lesser extent, UNITA). However, in December 1975, Congress—fearful of another Vietnam-style quagmire—passed the Clark Amendment to the U.S. Arms Export Control Act. That amendment—named for Sen. Richard Clark (D-IA)—terminated all military and paramilitary aid to Angola. After that development, the administration focused on providing indirect help, channeling money and weaponry through President Mobutu to friendly Angolan forces. That decision made Zaire's tyrant a key player, a fact that he knew and exploited to the fullest. While Washington seemed inclined to support any Angolan faction that professed to be anti-communist and anti-Soviet, Mobutu wanted most of the aid to go to his ally and kinsman, Roberto.

Some U.S. officials harbored doubts about Roberto's popular appeal and military effectiveness from the beginning, believing that Savimbi's

UNITA forces were a better bet, but they ultimately bowed to Mobutu's preferences. In January 1975, the White House authorized $300,000 in aid for the FNLA but turned down the CIA's proposed $100,000 for UNITA. To senior Ford administration officials, "Roberto was a known quantity, clearly a member of the 'home team'; by contrast, UNITA appeared unreliable."[7] Because of the Clark Amendment's strictures, Washington and Kinshasa devised a type of arms-laundering scheme to allow the United States to support the Angolan militants unofficially.[8] That operation would continue throughout the 1980s, even after Congress repealed the Clark Amendment in 1985.[9] During the early portion of the joint effort, a disproportionate amount of the aid went to Roberto, as Mobutu insisted. Indeed, to Washington's acute frustration, evidence surfaced that Mobutu himself pocketed a large portion of the funds.[10] Evidence of Roberto's meager military capabilities and thin internal public support became irrefutable when MPLA forces routed his fighters and drove them back into Zaire in early 1976. Washington then began to shift the focus of its aid, and UNITA soon was the principal recipient.

External interference became the hallmark of Angola's emerging civil war. South Africa's apartheid regime not only backed UNITA with funds and military hardware but also sent its own military units into the struggle. The Soviet Union and its client, Cuba, more than matched that assistance. Moscow equipped MPLA forces with sophisticated weapons, and Cuba sent in 20,000 troops of its own, backed by tanks and rockets. The combined MPLA-Cuban force smashed the FNLA while driving back UNITA and its South African allies. The MPLA then was able to establish itself as the internationally recognized government of Angola. Over the succeeding decade, the USSR continued to pour aid into the country, and Cuba's troop contingent reached approximately 30,000. Yet with South Africa's help, UNITA was able to establish and maintain a semblance of control over roughly one-third of the country.

One cannot discuss the Angolan civil war without acknowledging the role that regional and tribal loyalties played. Left-wing analysts and much of the liberal media in both the United States and Europe tended to dismiss Savimbi and UNITA as South Africa's lackeys. Pretoria certainly provided important assistance to his cause, but such a dismissive assessment is too simplistic. As journalist Karl Maier notes, despite his ties to South Africa, as well as his opportunism and drive for personal power, "Savimbi had a domestic constituency among the central high-lands people traditionally regarded as Angola's second-class citizens. . . ."[11] Ignoring that significant base of domestic support from a mistreated underclass, and instead portraying Savimbi as nothing more than Pretoria's tool, was a serious distortion of reality.

Excessive American Optimism about Jonas Savimbi

Enthusiasm for Savimbi among American "movement conservatives" reached impressive heights during the late 1970s and throughout the 1980s. Prominent supporters included organizations such as the Heritage Foundation, Freedom House, the American Conservative Union, the Young Americans for Freedom, and the American Security Council. Various publications, including *Human Events, National Review, American Spectator,* and the *Wall Street Journal* amplified the pro-Savimbi cause. It was a sophisticated public relations campaign. Those and other backers arranged a major speaking tour for the Angolan leader in 1979 and facil-itated meetings with congressional leaders and administration officials in Washington in 1981, 1986, and 1989.

Their admiration for Savimbi remained intact even though trou-bling evidence of UNITA's harsh, autocratic internal practices and its collaboration with South Africa's apartheid government arose early on. To many American conservatives, Angola was the latest arena in the Cold War, and Savimbi was an effective leader capable of scoring important victories. Piero Gleijeses, the Christian A. Herter Professor of American Foreign Policy at Johns Hopkins University, contends that "Savimbi's champions—in the press and in Congress—did not care" about his rumored character flaws. "They knew what mattered to them: there were thousands of Cuban soldiers in Angola, and Savimbi had promised to defeat them." But Gleijeses concedes that Savimbi's support was more than simply a case of realpolitik calculation; according to him, "The pro-Savimbi forces seized the high ground; they argued in terms of both U.S. interests and morality."[12]

Glowing accounts of the Angolan rebel appeared throughout right-wing publications. William F. Buckley Jr.'s article in *National Review* was typical. He argued that "Savimbi fought for independence against Portugal" for years to secure "democratic government and civil liberties." And since the Marxist MPLA had hijacked the independence movement, Buckley insisted, Savimbi had been battling against Soviet-Cuban imperialism to achieve those same values.[13] Some Savimbi backers even implied that a failure to support UNITA reflected, if not outright racism, at least insensitivity to black Africans' aspirations for liberty. Rep. Mark Siljander (R–MI) stated, "It's time that we stood up for UNITA and black freedom fighters, just as we have stood up for the freedom fighters in Afghanistan."[14]

Washington Times correspondents Arnaud de Borchgrave and Roger Fontaine were noticeably upbeat about Savimbi after visiting his headquarters in rural Angola in May 1984. They described him as "the world's most successful anti-Marxist guerrilla fighter and one of Africa's most impressive leaders."[15] They also favorably relayed the boast he made in interviews with them that if the Cuban troops left, the MPLA government would collapse within three months, and that even if Cuban forces stayed, the regime would be finished in 12 to 18 months. That was an early example of American analysts vastly overrating the internal popular support and military prowess of supposedly democratic insurgents. A similar pattern would occur decades later in such places as Iraq and Syria.

In the meantime, American conservatives hated the restrictions that the Clark Amendment imposed, and the Reagan administration backed their drive to repeal the legislation, which Congress eventually did in July 1985. Leading conservatives continued to hail Savimbi as a charismatic, pro-Western political figure and a committed freedom fighter. Presenting Savimbi with an award from the American Conservative Union and the Young Americans for Freedom, U.S. Ambassador to the United Nations Jeane Kirkpatrick lauded him as "one of the few authentic heroes of our time."[16] She urged the administration, which was represented at the gathering by Vice President George H. W. Bush, to provide UNITA with "real assistance," which she emphasized meant "real helicopters" and "real ground-to-air missiles." And, "Whether that help is overt or covert"—the subject of a growing controversy over tactics between administration officials and more aggressive conservatives—"is a bureaucratic detail."[17]

Kirkpatrick's idealized portrait of Savimbi was the typical right-wing perspective in the United States. President Reagan shared it, at one point describing Savimbi in a diary entry as "a good man" and one who "has offered a plan for peaceful settlement in Angola."[18]

When Congress repealed the Clark Amendment in response to the Reagan administration's persistent pressure and a vigorous public lobbying effort, Sen. Steve Symms (R-ID) celebrated the vote and eagerly looked forward to providing official assistance to UNITA. Angola, he asserted, was a place in which the United States could "achieve victory, not only an actual victory on the field but a moral victory, psychological victory, which will give strength to free men all over the world."[19]

Gleijeses discerned a major difference in the cases presented by supporters and opponents of aid to Savimbi. UNITA's advocates insisted that assisting the insurgent movement not only was in America's strategic interests but also was justified on moral principles. Aid opponents made narrower arguments: they contended that greater U.S. involvement in Angola's struggle risked snaring America in yet another military quagmire; they also typically expressed worries about UNITA's relationship to South Africa and what Washington's indirect collaboration with that racist pariah state might do to America's reputation in sub-Saharan Africa and the rest of the Third World. According to Gleijeses, UNITA's critics, especially media critics, "did not, however, challenge the heroic portrait of Savimbi drawn by his admirers, or they did so only fleetingly." Most did not even highlight the group's human rights record, even though "UNITA's atrocities provided sufficient cause to oppose Savimbi's ambitions."[20] Such timidity by the anti-Savimbi camp ceded a major advantage in the debate to the pro-Savimbi factions.

Despite the soaring rhetoric and passionate advocacy that movement conservatives generated for Savimbi's cause, U.S. officials proceeded more cautiously than Kirkpatrick and other luminaries wanted. Among members of Congress, UNITA's admirers included Symms, Rep. Jack

Kemp (R–NY), and other key members. Sen. Orrin Hatch (R–UT) wrote, "I have had the privilege of meeting Mr. Savimbi and have been extremely impressed by his honesty, integrity, religious commitment." Insisting that Savimbi had been fighting for two decades "to liberate Angola, first from Portuguese control and later from the MPLA," Hatch contended that he deserved stronger U.S. assistance. Savimbi's ultimate goal, Hatch stated confidently, was not military conquest, but "free elections." The conflict in Angola was not a civil war, the Utah senator insisted. "It is a battle over ideologies: Soviet totalitarianism versus freedom, self-determination, and democracy." U.S. aid to Savimbi would "send a strong signal to the world that the Reagan doctrine is not mere words, that we are determined to help freedom fighters resist Communist hegemony."[21]

The enthusiasm for UNITA and its leader was increasingly strident and uncritical. One of the more embarrassing episodes in American conservatives' campaign to lionize Savimbi was an op-ed published in the *Wall Street Journal* under Savimbi's byline (but apparently with major portions written by a right-wing ghost writer). The piece hailed the virtues of capitalism and democracy and pledged to make Angola a model of both if the United States would help UNITA oust the pro-communist government in Luanda.

Savimbi's piece told conservatives exactly what they wanted to hear. Angolans, he wrote, had discovered that "there was something worse than [traditional] colonialism: Soviet colonial exploitation and imposition of socialism." He then outlined his movement's supposed objectives: "UNITA's first goal is to win the independence of Angola—to drive the Cuban and Soviet troops and 'advisers' from our shore." But that was only the start; the larger goal was to build a new, democratic country. Nor was that all. "In addition to UNITA's commitment to a democratic, multiparty Angola with religious tolerance and freedom of speech, it is vital that we recognize the importance of economic liberties."[22] Savimbi proceeded to express support for a "completely free market" in agriculture and the elimination of all trade barriers. It was as though economist Milton Friedman's intellectual disciple had shown up in southern Africa. *National Review* gushed about his "astonishing defense of freedom."[23]

What was so striking about Savimbi's op-ed in the *Wall Street Journal* was that UNITA did not actually practice any of those political or economic principles in the portion of Angola it controlled. Certainly no evidence of democracy existed, multiparty or otherwise; UNITA maintained a ruthless monopoly of power. And despite the pledge stated in the article that farmers would be exempted from all taxes (a rather difficult commitment in a heavily rural country, in any case), UNITA imposed heavy taxes on the agricultural sector. And trade was the nearly exclusive province of Savimbi and his close associates—a textbook example of crony capitalism.

Much of that information already was available when the *Wall Street Journal* published Savimbi's op-ed. In all fairness, information about Savimbi's shockingly brutal behavior was not yet so well known. But even a reasonable degree of due diligence would have encouraged conservatives to be more wary of endorsing him. Such prudent skepticism largely was absent.

AN INTRA-CONSERVATIVE QUARREL ABOUT U.S. POLICY TOWARD UNITA

Secretary of State George Shultz endeavored to restrain the growing enthusiasm among the administration's conservative allies for anticommunist insurgencies in southern Africa. In particular, he tried to draw a distinction between UNITA and the Resistência Nacional Moçambicana (RENAMO) insurgency in Mozambique—movements that right-wing members of Congress backed fervently. "RENAMO, from all the evidence I saw, did not at all possess the natural base of support of Savimbi and, a careful report confirmed, engaged in terror and cruelty on a large scale."[24]

Shultz was correct on the first point: because of its secure tribal base, UNITA had far more domestic support than RENAMO ever could have hoped to muster. But the secretary of state was wrong on the second point; he and other officials tended to ignore evidence that Savimbi and his UNITA colleagues were nearly as brutal as RENAMO. However, even the Reagan administration's support for UNITA seemed insufficient to Savimbi's passionate American backers. Norman Podhoretz, the neoconservative editor of *Commentary*, echoed Kirkpatrick's demand for "real assistance" to UNITA, not merely "empty expressions of pious support."[25] According to Podhoretz, providing such aid was an eminently worthy cause. Savimbi, Podhoretz stated, "has done nothing to forfeit his claim to good faith when he speaks of democracy and freedom."[26]

Shultz indicated that he even had to labor to keep his boss from pushing the Reagan Doctrine too far, especially in southern Africa. "President Reagan could be led to agree with the proposition that all freedom fighters—UNITA and RENAMO alike—deserved unquestioned support."[27] In addition, the secretary of state lamented the fact that CIA Director William Casey and other policy hardliners were more than happy to lead the compliant president in that direction, even if it meant undermining policymakers who favored a more moderate approach. Indeed, the State Department found its diplomatic initiatives subject to internal sabotage. During delicate negotiations to achieve a ceasefire and subsequent accord between dos Santos and Savimbi, Shultz fumed, "Right-wing staffers from Congress, fueled by information from the CIA, were meddling—visiting Savimbi, trying to convince him that [Assistant Secretary of State Chester] Crocker and I would sell him out by depriving him of South African support while leaving loopholes in the agreement regarding Cuban troop withdrawal."[28]

Some conservatives from both inside and outside the administration seemed more uncompromising than Savimbi himself about the underlying political objective. "Savimbi, too," Shultz contended, "could see that he could not overpower the dos Santos regime. While many of his supporters on the right in the United States wanted a military victory, Savimbi himself knew better."[29]

True believers in the Reagan Doctrine were in no mood for compromising the policy's ideological objectives for reasons of geopolitics in southern Africa. And Shultz, because of his relatively cautious posture regarding U.S. support for Savimbi, became a lightning rod for conservative anger. In his memoirs, Shultz recalled that "with the Clark Amendment out of the way, a debate began to rage: should the United States now provide aid to Savimbi's UNITA? Savimbi's supporters in both parties avidly desired to register American support in a public way."

Proponents introduced bills in Congress to do just that, but the secretary of state urged that they be rejected. It was not that he disliked
Savimbi: "I feel strongly about Savimbi's courageous stand against Soviet
aggression," Shultz wrote to House GOP leader Bob Michel, "but there
are better ways to help."[30] Specifically, he favored keeping aid to UNITA
both limited and covert, rather than providing lavish assistance in a public manner. Quiet, modest aid, Shultz believed, would be more effective
in creating the conditions for a negotiated settlement.

That stance infuriated many on the right. Representative Kemp
explicitly called for Shultz's resignation because of his allegedly insufficient support for Savimbi's cause.[31] "Conservatives in Congress, always
suspicious of me and the State Department," Shultz recalled, "went on
a virtual rampage." Kemp, in particular, "did not want to listen to the
realities; the conservatives wanted an open vote as a matter of thump-
ing their collective chests."[32] It was an all-too-familiar development.
In 1983, even as the Reagan administration was providing supposedly
covert (but widely known) assistance to UNITA, movement conservatives were grumbling that it was not enough. Howard Phillips, a leading
right-wing activist, even wrote to Shultz denouncing him for his "aban-
donment of Jonas Savimbi."[33]

The disagreement between Shultz and Kemp became intense and
personal. In his diary, Reagan described a November 8, 1985, meeting with the Republican congressional leadership that produced an
extremely candid exchange of views between the secretary of state and
his antagonist. "Things got hot for awhile," the president admitted.[34]

In fairness, although Reagan and Shultz (as well as other top administration officials) supported Savimbi, movement conservatives correctly
pointed out that some of Shultz's subordinates were far more ambivalent.
Jeff Davidow, director of the Office of Southern African Affairs, stated
later, "We all saw Savimbi as a charismatic figure who was extremely
brutal."[35] Another member of the Africa Bureau, Robert Cabelly, had a
similar impression of Savimbi, noting that, initially, the insurgent leader
"came across as very reasonable and a capitalist. But he was neither."
Cabelly conceded that although the UNITA leader was very smooth, he
also was "an extremely ruthless guy."[36] Gleijeses notes: "Charisma and

ruthlessness were the attributes U.S. officials most often used to describe Savimbi. They captured the essence of the man."[37] John Stockwell, who left the CIA after directing its operation in Angola during the 1970s, reached a similar conclusion. "Savimbi had no ideology," Stockwell contended. "He believes in nothing beyond his own ambitions."[38]

Despite such input, not much of a substantive policy dispute actually existed between top-level administration officials and their conservative allies outside the government. The Reagan administration was fully willing to provide aid, including lethal military aid, to UNITA. But Shultz and other officials wanted to limit identifying U.S. values and interests with Savimbi's agenda, because he was such a controversial figure internationally. Among other things, his close relationship with South Africa made him a suspect figure with most Third World governments and even some Western governments.

Savimbi's American admirers, though, did not want a covert aid program to their hero, even if the assistance package was a generous one. They wanted Washington to make an ostentatious display of support for a courageous freedom fighter. And they increasingly vilified Shultz because he advocated a more cautious policy. I was "tagged by congressional conservatives, as being soft on freedom fighters," he recalled.[39] That outcome was especially ironic for the man who had delivered the iconic Reagan Doctrine speech in February 1985.

Despite some manifestations of his own caution, Shultz was at heart a supporter of Savimbi's and believed that the Angolan rebel was a courageous anti-communist fighter. The secretary of state also believed that his affections were reciprocated. "Savimbi well knew that the United States would stand up for freedom and for those, like himself, willing to fight for it. As the Reagan administration and my own term in office neared its conclusion, I received a gift from him in thanks for America's support of his UNITA freedom fighters and their long struggle in the bush of southern Angola against the Communist regime in Luanda."[40] The gift was a captured Soviet Kalashnikov automatic rifle. "The gift symbolized one of the striking turnabouts in the history of the Cold War," Shultz contended—"The Reagan Doctrine replacing the now-retreating Brezhnev Doctrine. The image of Soviet-backed Communist guerrillas fighting from the bush to seize power had now been replaced by American-backed revolutionaries operating from jungle camps to oppose the Communist domination of their countries—and supplying themselves by capturing Soviet- and Chinese-made and supplied weapons!"[41]

The fact that movement conservatives could regard Shultz—an ardent supporter and prominent intellectual architect of the Reagan Doctrine—as insufficiently zealous in his support of Savimbi suggests just how detached they were from reality. Their view of the African insurgent leader was nothing short of hero worship—and hero worship makes an especially poor foundation for a wise U.S. foreign policy.

Delusions about Savimbi Persist

One especially powerful institutional cheerleader for Savimbi was the conservative Heritage Foundation. Heritage scholar Michael Johns had long been one of the most vocal advocates of support for Savimbi and other anti-communist insurgents, and the think tank had strongly endorsed the Reagan Doctrine in several publications. Such enthusiasm persisted even beyond the Reagan years, when the Cold War rivalry with the Soviet Union clearly was fading. A telling example was Heritage's decision to invite Savimbi to deliver a public lecture in October 1989. The Angolan leader was effusive in his thanks for the organization's support. In a lecture that Heritage hosted, he declared:

> When we come to the Heritage Foundation, it is like coming back home. We know that our success here in Washington in repealing the Clark Amendment and obtaining American assistance for our cause is very much associated with your efforts. This foundation has been a source of great support. The UNITA leadership knows this, and it is also known in Angola.[42]

Savimbi assured his audience, "UNITA is now stronger than ever militarily, politically, and diplomatically. We have spent the last fourteen years struggling for freedom. And we shall achieve it."[43] He expressed his gratitude for the U.S. government's continuing support. Speaking of his meeting that very morning with President George H. W. Bush, Savimbi affirmed that the meeting "went well because the President has reassured us that the U.S. will continue to give effective support to our struggle. Also, the President has stated very clearly that the [a]dministration stands for free and fair elections in Angola. This has pleased us very much."[44] He closed by stressing: "We are fighting for democracy, for a free market. We are fighting so our people can participate in the public life of their country."[45]

The 1989 visit was not the first time that a U.S. administration had given Savimbi VIP treatment. In February 1986, despite Shultz's retroactive expressions of caution in his memoirs about the insurgent leader, both the State Department and the White House received him. Officials also escorted him to meetings on Capitol Hill and to interviews with newspapers and television outlets, even to a luncheon at the Heritage Foundation.[46] Gregory Treverton observed that Savimbi's 1986 visit "received rave reviews, especially among American conservatives."[47]

Growing Signs Emerge about the Real Jonas Savimbi

Had Reagan Doctrine supporters of the 1970s or early 1980s succumbed to the illusion that Savimbi and UNITA stood for the values of democratic capitalism, one might understand. But by late 1989, a substantial body of evidence showed that Savimbi was a corrupt, thuggish individual and that UNITA had no serious commitment either to free markets or democracy. Some of Savimbi's worst crimes were not uncovered until the early 1990s, but others already were fully apparent in the mid- and late 1980s. One such example was a gruesome war crime in the village of Camabatela. Fighting between MPLA and UNITA forces had occurred there in February 1986, and the latter had emerged victorious. In the aftermath, UNITA soldiers slaughtered more than 100 civilians, hacking them to death with machetes.[48]

Writing in 1986 while still sympathetic to Savimbi's cause and on the verge of publishing a favorable biography, British author Fred Bridgland nevertheless had to concede that UNITA sometimes engaged in torture and coercive "re-education" measures against captured MPLA soldiers and other possible opponents. Relating a 1977 account about one such incident from *Washington Post* reporter Leon Dash—who spent seven months in southern Angola with UNITA soldiers—Bridgland described how a UNITA officer threatened to shoot two prisoners. Looking both men in the eyes, the officer stated: "I will keep you to see if you can be re-educated." He added: "If I do not think I can trust you or I feel you are too stupid to learn, then I will personally shoot you in the head." Not surprisingly, Bridgland noted dryly, the two men gave enthusiastic assurances that they would welcome the opportunity to be re-educated. When Dash protested about the barbaric spectacle, the guerrilla commander insisted the technique worked well: "I'll let them sit in jail for a month or two. Let them think a little."[49]

More disturbing evidence of Savimbi's brutality came to light in 1987, when accounts emerged that two high-level UNITA officials, Tito Chingunji and Wilson dos Santos, had suffered incredibly brutal treatment in Angola. Chingunji was UNITA's foreign affairs representative, and he had been effective in cultivating support for UNITA in the United States and throughout Western Europe. But his growing prominence may have posed a threat to Savimbi's dominance. Moreover, Chingunji also apparently had made "not for attribution" comments to friends, including Bridgland and other Western reporters, about increasingly troubling developments back home. Those developments included the mysterious disappearances of UNITA activists who were out of favor with Savimbi; incidents of torture; and even credible rumors that Savimbi ordered the burning of individuals he suspected of witchcraft.

For whatever reason, Chingunji was recalled to UNITA's capital, Jamba, in December 1988; while there, he and dos Santos disappeared. Two other prominent UNITA leaders soon defected and accused Savimbi of having ordered the executions of Chingunji, dos Santos, and other key figures.[50] Given Savimbi's repeated boasts that he was UNITA's sole leader, the assassination of two such high-level officials likely would not have taken place without his approval, if not direct order. The fates of Chingunji and dos Santos did not appear to be an aberration. According to UNITA dissidents, who were mainly students and professionals with family ties to party leaders, "Savimbi had been personally responsible for the elimination of party rivals by such means as detention, torture, witchcraft trials and assassinations."[51]

Credible allegations of such egregious behavior caused even a few of Savimbi's Western supporters to repudiate him. Bridgland, whose laudatory biography was first published in 1986, saw matters far differently by the end of the decade. The principal catalyst for that change was Savimbi's treatment of Chingunji and other UNITA leaders who had been candid sources for Bridgland's previous writings. During a December 1988 visit to Jamba, Bridgland received reports of horrific incidents of torture and murder, including witness accounts of hearing screams from a hut where Chingunji was confined.[52]

National Review also began to break ranks with Savimbi's supporters. The magazine's roving correspondent, Radek Sikorski, spent three months in Jamba and elsewhere in UNITA-controlled territory in early 1989. While there, he amassed information from defectors and his own observations that led him to conclude that the evidence of abuses was too extensive and persistent to ignore.[53]

Plenty of other disquieting signs surfaced about the right's Angolan hero. Contrary to his soothing, idealistic rhetoric, all indications were that the UNITA leader was not only a narcissistic autocrat but also a socialist. The organization's official seal proclaimed it to be socialist, and Savimbi started out as a loyal client of communist China.[54] Even as early as the late 1970s and early 1980s, evidence had already emerged that Savimbi fostered an effusive cult of personality and had no tolerance toward potential UNITA competitors who might challenge his dominant position in the organization. In his book *Angola: Promises and Lies,* Karl Maier notes that many commentators believed that Savimbi's original flirtation with China accounted for some aspects of his cult of personality. "Savimbi has always had an appetite for cultivating a Mao Tse-Tung–type reverence among his people." UNITA's radio broadcasts routinely referred to him as "the guide of the Angolan people." Savimbi even imitated Mao's fashion choices. "His favored style of dress, other than military fatigues, is a Mao suit," wrote Maier. "The rounded Mao cap is standard issue for UNITA soldiers."[55]

Later in the 1980s, even more damning revelations came to light, including accounts of torture, assassinations, and other human rights abuses. Allegations even surfaced along with evidence that—while not definitive—was credible that Savimbi had practiced cannibalism on occasion. Even if the most extreme charges were never proved, more than enough evidence of Savimbi's true nature existed to set off warning lights for U.S. officials and other American supporters of the supposed freedom fighter. Yet too many of those supporters embraced him and his cause uncritically—and some continued to do so long after the damning evidence had reached overwhelming levels.

Indeed, passionate backers sometimes went to great lengths to explain away blatantly troubling signs, including conservative journalist Peter Worthington, who had visited the UNITA camp at Jamba. He noted that Savimbi "has 'political officers' throughout his army," which Worthington admitted he initially found "disquieting." But that uneasiness persisted only "until I sat in on lectures." Why? Because those lectures "concentrated on the virtues of democracy, of multiple political choices, of free movement, of self-reliance, individual initiative, private property, free enterprise, fiscal accountability, balanced budgets, democracy, human rights, a humane and just judicial system, democratic institutions, rule by law and constitution," and other Western values.[56]

Stanford University Visiting Fellow Elaine Windrich criticized *Washington Post* correspondent Dash for similar insufficient skepticism about UNITA's political behavior in his multipart series of articles from rebel-held territory in Angola: "He did not think it amiss for armed guerrillas to preside over the ballot box while delegates to the party congress unanimously re-elected their leader by casting the 'right' colored ballot paper for a 'yes' vote."[57] Right-wing journalist Fred Reed even made the strange argument that "Savimbi would probably be a benevolent ruler if unopposed."[58] Left unsaid was what kind of leader Reed thought Savimbi would be if someone had the temerity to become an opponent.

Certainly by October 1989, given the amount of adverse information that was already publicly known about UNITA and its leader, the Heritage Foundation had no excuse for giving Savimbi a prominent lecture platform, and President Bush had even less of an excuse for meeting with him and expressing continued U.S. support for the

UNITA insurgency. Both actions suggest either an inability or an unwillingness to come to grips with reality.

Moreover, the already weak strategic rationale for the relationship no longer existed. James A. Baker III, Bush's secretary of state, conceded as much. In his memoirs, Baker notes, "At the start of the Bush administration, the Soviet-American proxy war in Angola was showing signs of fatigue."[59] Yet Washington continued to laud Savimbi as though the Cold War were still raging.

Baker would gain a sobering insight into the African leader's real agenda later in the Bush administration. On May 1, 1991, following protracted negotiations in Lisbon, the MPLA and UNITA reached a ceasefire accord and an agreement to hold free elections. All Cuban troops were to leave the country, as well. Baker attended the ceremony in Lisbon on May 6 of that year, where José Eduardo dos Santos and Savimbi signed the formal agreement. The secretary of state assured the latter in a private meeting that "the United States was firmly committed to continuing non-lethal aid to UNITA and would only recognize an Angolan government that emerged from the elections scheduled for September 1992."[60]

Those elections were held on schedule, Baker notes, "and by most accounts were fairly conducted." Four days later, though, Savimbi claimed election fraud. Baker continues: "On October 11, much to my disappointment, fighting resumed in Angola."[61] Violence would flare and subside several times in the succeeding months. Savimbi's repudiation of the outcome of a free and fair election should have dispelled any lingering notions that he was even slightly committed to democratic norms.

A Stain on America's Honor

Support for the likes of Jonas Savimbi is a stain on America's honor that will take time to erase. U.S. officials and their conservative allies not only supported Savimbi but also lionized him—and they did so long after evidence of his unsavory conduct emerged. To make matters worse, not even a modest security justification could be made for such a moral compromise, as could have been made in Nicaragua and Afghanistan.

Central and southern Africa were economic and strategic backwaters that warranted, at most, very modest U.S. attention.[62] Even former CIA Director Allen Dulles once conceded that Washington's fears of Soviet penetration of those regions had been excessive.[63]

The actions of U.S. administrations with respect to UNITA and Savimbi constituted an unnecessary trashing of America's moral principles, and they serve as a cautionary tale regarding the kind of initiative that American policymakers need to avoid in the future. Embracing a fraudulent democratic insurgent like Jonas Savimbi did little to enhance America's interests or values; to the contrary, it tarnished America's image as an advocate of democracy and human rights.

CHAPTER FOUR

WASHINGTON EMPOWERS A RUTHLESS KOSOVO FACTION

Washington's wishful thinking about the nature of so-called freedom fighters did not disappear with the end of the Cold War, a fact that became all too apparent with the Clinton administration's military interventions in the Balkans during the mid- and late-1990s. As Yugoslavia unraveled, the administration repeatedly oversimplified the country's complex ethnic and geopolitical struggle and, as a result, embraced a violent and morally dubious insurgent force, the Kosovo Liberation Army (KLA). By helping the KLA achieve Kosovo's secession from Serbia, Washington not only demeaned important American values but also violated important international norms. The Kosovo policies that Presidents Bill Clinton and George W. Bush pursued set extremely dangerous precedents for other world powers to follow; indeed, at least one major power, Russia, already has done so in places such as South Ossetia, Abkhazia, and Crimea.

PRELUDE: THE BOSNIA INTERVENTION

The adverse consequences flowing from the early phase of Yugoslavia's slow-motion disintegration affected all portions of the country, including Slovenia, Croatia, and Bosnia-Herzegovina.[1] The turmoil and human tragedy were especially pronounced in Bosnia, where three major ethno-religious groups—Catholic Croats, Eastern Orthodox Serbs, and Muslims—maneuvered for advantage. All three factions engaged in ethnic cleansing—the expulsion of ethnic groups other than their own— wherever they gained control of a geographic region. Fighters in all three armies also committed atrocities and other war crimes. Although Bosnian Serb forces seemed somewhat more inclined to engage in such abuses, the scope of their offenses, both in number and severity, was not hugely disproportionate to the other armies'. Yet, Western accounts focused almost entirely on Serb misconduct.

U.S. and North Atlantic Treaty Organization (NATO) officials and most of the Western news media painted a picture that was far from balanced. In their hands, Bosnia's murky, multisided struggle became a straightforward Serbian war of aggression aimed at innocent Croat—and especially Muslim—civilians. The supposed architect of this plot against Croats and Muslims in Bosnia was Slobodan Milošević, the leader of neighboring Serbia, another of the successor states of the disintegrating Yugoslavia. We now know that such a thesis was a grave oversimplification. Nearly two decades after the Balkan wars ended, the International Criminal Tribunal for the Former Yugoslavia (ICTY) issued a surprise ruling that Milošević was not responsible for war crimes committed during the 1992–1995 Bosnian civil war. Indeed, the ICTY found that Milošević tried to restrain Bosnian Serb leader Radovan Karadžić's efforts to split Bosnia and establish the independent Republika Srpska.[2]

Acting on the erroneous assumption that the Bosnian civil war was a stark struggle between good and evil, the Clinton administration ultimately induced its NATO partners to support a military intervention on behalf of the Muslim-led central government in 1995. Bosnian Serb forces up to that point had been quite successful, increasing the amount of territory that Serbs controlled from about 35 percent to nearly 50 percent of the country. NATO's air strikes against Serb military positions, in support of a Croat-Muslim ground offensive, reduced that control to some 30 percent. Washington then pressed all three factions to agree to a dictated settlement. Negotiated (or more accurately, imposed) by Assistant Secretary of State for European Affairs Richard Holbrooke, the Dayton Accords brought an end to the fighting in November 1995.

The agreement did not resolve Bosnia's intractable ethnic divisions, though, and two decades later, Bosnia is still a politically and economically dysfunctional entity.[3]

The disappointing aftermath of the Dayton Accords was obvious early on, as the three feuding ethnic groups consistently refused to cooperate on even the most routine political and economic matters. Increasingly, the United Nations (UN) high representative, the official whom the Dayton Accords tasked with supervising Bosnia's postwar governance, ended up ruling like a colonial viceroy, making nearly all significant policy decisions.[4]

The sobering outcome of the U.S.-led intervention in Bosnia, though, did not inhibit U.S. leaders from further intervention in the Balkans. Less than four years later, the United States and NATO intervened in another portion of the former Yugoslavia. And once again, the Western powers directed their wrath at the Serbs. A de facto alliance gradually developed between the United States and the KLA, an insurgent force seeking to gain independence for Serbia's predominantly Albanian province of Kosovo.

The Kosovo insurgency had complex and morally ambiguous origins. To the people of Serbia, Kosovo was extremely important both historically and culturally. Indeed, Serbs often referred to the area as the cradle of their civilization—their "Jerusalem." As late as the mid-1930s, Kosovo's population was about 38 percent Serbian and about 45 percent Albanian, with an assortment of other ethnicities making up the remaining percentage. Over the next five decades, that ethnic composition changed dramatically. After German and Italian forces defeated and occupied Yugoslavia in April 1941, the victorious Axis powers handed Kosovo over to neighboring Albania. Tens of thousands of Serbs then fled and were replaced by an influx of new Albanian residents. By the late 1980s, Kosovo was nearly 90 percent Albanian.[5]

Some of that shift was attributable to the substantially higher birthrate among Albanian families. But less savory elements also were at work, including the Axis occupation years and the Albanian majority's discriminatory rule—and sometimes outright harassment—in the post–World War II era,[6] when Yugoslav dictator Josip Broz Tito authorized the Albanian provincial authorities in Pristina (the capital of Kosovo) to exercise considerable autonomy. That was especially true after the implementation of a new Yugoslav constitution in 1974, which allowed Kosovo to establish its own parliament, school system, and other institutions. The Albanian Kosovars used that power as part of a campaign to eradicate Kosovo's Serbian heritage and, even more significantly, to discriminate against and harass Serb inhabitants in an effort to pressure them to leave the province. Those practices occurred to some extent even before the constitution's implementation in 1974, which was not surprising given Tito's generally anti-Serb attitude (partly a reflection of his Croat-Slovene heritage). However, the discrimination and insidious ethnic cleansing against Kosovo's shrinking Serbian population grew far worse once the new constitution took effect.

After Tito's death in 1980, ethnic nationalist sentiments grew among all of Yugoslavia's constituent republics. Serb nationalism produced an especially outspoken leader in Milošević, who gained control of Serbia's government in 1989. One of his first actions was to curtail Kosovo's political autonomy and exert greater control over the province's affairs from Belgrade (Yugoslavia's capital). That move intensified tensions in the province and ignited an Albanian Kosovar bid for outright independence.

In this classic case of civil unrest, both sides comprised villains as well as innocent parties. Unfortunately, as Washington deepened its involvement in Balkan affairs, the dominant narrative that drove U.S. policy was a simplistic, Manichean one.[7] Analyst James Jatras accurately summarizes Washington's one-sided narrative:

> Prior to 1989, the NATO mythology goes, Kosovo was at peace under a system of autonomy that allowed the ethnic Albanian majority a large degree of self-rule. That status quo was disturbed when the Serbs revoked Kosovo's autonomy and initiated an apartheid system of ethnic discrimination. After a decade of oppression by the Serbs, the ethnic Albanians of Kosovo were ultimately faced with a pre-planned program of genocide, similar to that undertaken by the Serbs in Bosnia. The rise of the KLA was an inevitable response to that threat.[8]

Jatras contends that Washington's Kosovo policy could not be justified "without recasting a frightfully complex conflict, with plenty of blame to go around, as a caricature: a morality play in which one side is completely innocent and the other entirely villainous."[9]

An early action taken by George H. W. Bush's administration became a template for Washington's biased policy. Administration officials warned Serb authorities in late December 1992 that the United States was prepared to respond militarily if Belgrade initiated an armed conflict in Kosovo. Just three weeks after the new Clinton administration took office in January 1993, the State Department reiterated that warning.[10] Those admonitions provided a green light to Albanian secessionists in Kosovo to press their agenda, confident that the United States was in their camp.

Initially that bid was predominantly political and nonviolent, marked by the creation of "shadow institutions." Ibrahim Rugova and his relatively moderate Democratic League of Kosovo led the effort. But as history has shown, secessionist bids rarely remain peaceful, and Kosovo's was no exception. A new, far more radical insurgent faction, the KLA, soon began to launch attacks on Serbian security forces in the province. As Yugoslavia disintegrated during the 1990s, the KLA stepped up its attacks on Belgrade's military and police units, and a simmering civil war developed. But KLA assaults were not confined to military targets; the insurgents also kidnapped, tortured, and killed Serbian and other ethnic civilians.[11]

WASHINGTON'S GROWING FONDNESS FOR THE KLA

Washington's bias in favor of Kosovo's Albanian community and its political agenda became ever more pronounced during the Clinton years. Secretary of State Madeleine Albright's attitude was typical. "Milošević was claiming that the Kosovars were violent, but the violence began with him," Albright wrote in her memoirs. "The Albanians had had autonomy under Tito, but Milošević had taken it away. There would have been no KLA had the Kosovars not been deprived of their rights."[12] That simplistic interpretation ignored, among other things, the

harassment and discrimination that the Kosovar authorities had perpe-
trated against Serbs and other minorities during the time the province
had enjoyed extensive autonomy.[13]

Washington's attitude toward the KLA itself underwent a dramatic
transformation. Initially, the KLA was met with pronounced wariness
mixed with some alarm, as U.S. officials clearly preferred the more moderate Democratic League of Kosovo led by Rugova. Robert Gelbard,
President Clinton's special envoy to the Balkans, stated in early 1998 that
the KLA "is, without any questions, a terrorist group."[14] Even more disturbing, evidence indicated that the KLA had significant ties to al Qaeda
and other extremist Islamic movements. Foreign mujahideen began
showing up in KLA ranks. Iran's Intelligence Ministry began moving
weapons (including grenades, machine guns, and assault rifles) into
Kosovo to strengthen the insurgents. In July 1998, Serbian border guards
shot a KLA fighter trying to cross into Kosovo from Albania; documents
found on his body indicated that he was guiding a 50-man force across
the border, including 1 Yemeni and 16 Saudi nationals.[15]

Nevertheless, the Clinton administration began to shed its skeptical view of the KLA, and U.S. involvement in the Kosovo struggle
on behalf of the Albanian Kosovar secessionists deepened. In February 1998, despite Gelbard's comments, the State Department officially
removed the KLA from its list of terrorist organizations, and over the
following year, the Clinton administration's criticism virtually disappeared. By early 1999, U.S. and German intelligence agencies apparently
were even training KLA fighters.[16]

Albright's view of the Kosovar cause and the emergence of the KLA
was a model of balance and caution compared to the laudatory comments
of some of the group's American admirers. The most wildly positive view
of the insurgents was held by Sen. Joseph Lieberman (D-CT), who stated
in April 1999: "The United States of America and the Kosovo Liberation
Army stand for the same human values and principles. . . . Fighting for
the KLA is fighting for human rights and American values."[17]

Washington's bias had important policy implications. U.S. and NATO
officials convened a conference at Rambouillet, France, in early 1999 for
the ostensible purpose of preventing war between the NATO alliance

and the Belgrade government. However, the positions that Western negotiators adopted seemed almost calculated to provoke a Serb rejection and create the justification for war—an outcome that served the KLA's purposes perfectly. David N. Gibbs, professor of history at the University of Arizona, observes, "The conference organizers, especially the United States, began with a strong predilection in favor of the Albanian perspective and against the Serbs." U.S. negotiators made it clear to the Serbs that they would be bombed if they rejected the proposed agreement. However, "If the KLA refused an agreement, the only danger to them was that the United States might undercut their international support; there was no threat of military action."[18]

Commenting in *NATO's Empty Victory,* Christopher Layne, the Robert M. Gates Chair in Intelligence and National Security at Texas A&M University's George Bush School of Government and Public Service, underscored the same NATO bias and its implication. When (much to the surprise of U.S. officials) the KLA initially refused to sign the Rambouillet document, Layne notes, "Washington used NATO's threat to bomb Serbia as a carrot. U.S. officials reminded the KLA that, unless it signed the Rambouillet pact, the alliance would be unable to carry out its threat."[19]

The diplomatic charade was even more evident from the stance the United States and its allies took toward Serbia. "Belgrade correctly believed that the Rambouillet settlement disproportionately favored the KLA," Layne writes. "Although the plan provided that Kosovo would nominally remain part of [what remained of Yugoslavia] for three years, Belgrade's actual control of the province would have been reduced to a nullity." The KLA "made it quite clear what would happen [at the end of the three-year period]: either Kosovo would become independent or the KLA would resume the war. Indeed, even as they agreed to sign the Rambouillet accord, KLA leaders expressed their intent to ignore its disarmament provisions and keep the KLA's military capabilities intact."[20]

Another provision of the Rambouillet pact ensured that Serbian authorities in Belgrade would never sign it. Not only did the United States and its NATO allies insist on deploying peacekeeping forces in

Kosovo, they included an appendix in the Rambouillet document that would have allowed NATO alliance forces to operate at will anywhere in Serbia. Layne concludes, "Belgrade hardly can be condemned for balking at the prospect of such a pervasive regime of military occupation. Few, if any, governments would willingly accept such onerous terms."[21]

NATO GOES TO WAR

Following the predictable failure to secure an agreement at Rambouillet, the United States led an air war against Serbia that lasted 78 days. According to a report from Human Rights Watch, the offensive killed at least 500 civilians;[22] the Serbian government estimated the toll at 2,500.[23]

Those air strikes ultimately compelled Belgrade to relinquish control of Kosovo to an international peacekeeping mission under the nominal auspices of the UN Security Council. That situation became a halfway house leading to full independence for Kosovo in 2008. KLA alumni dominated the new government in Pristina from the outset. In retrospect, whether the Clinton administration cynically backed the KLA for Washington's own purposes or got played by a shrewd political movement and its American backers is a little unclear. To her credit, Albright seemed to harbor some uneasiness about the KLA:

> My own view of the fighters was mixed. I sympathized with their opposition to Milošević, understood their desire for independence, and accepted that force was sometimes necessary for a just cause to prevail. On the other hand, there did not appear to be much Jeffersonian thinking with the KLA. Often indiscriminate in their attacks, they seemed intent on provoking a massive Serb response so that international intervention would be unavoidable. I wanted to stop Milošević from marauding through Kosovo, but I didn't want that determination exploited by the KLA for purposes we opposed. We therefore took pains to insist that we would not operate as the KLA's air force.[24]

Whether Albright's explanation of her stance was disingenuous or just slightly less naive than the Pollyannaish views of Lieberman and his camp is difficult to tell. In any case, it turned out to be a distinction without a difference. The United States and NATO did become the

KLA's de facto air force. At best, U.S. officials served as the organization's useful pawns in the drive for Kosovo's independence. At worst,
the policy was a deliberate and unnecessary interference in the internal affairs of a country that posed no threat whatsoever to America's
legitimate interests—and it was an interference that ultimately empowered some extraordinarily unsavory political elements.

The KLA's drive to secure Western military backing might not have
succeeded, though, without pervasive allegations that the Milošević government was committing genocide. The notion that Kosovo is saturated
with mass graves where Milošević's forces buried thousands of innocent
victims has become part of the Western lore surrounding the conflict
between Belgrade and Albanian Kosovars. In the prelude to NATO's
military intervention, U.S. officials and the American news media ped-
dled even the most inflated atrocity accounts with little skepticism or
reflection. Secretary of Defense William Cohen claimed that as many
as 100,000 Kosovar men of fighting age were missing and might have
been murdered by Serbian security forces.[25] His estimate was restrained,
though, compared to the allegations of David Scheffer, the U.S. special envoy for war crimes, who put the number of victims as high as
225,000.[26]

Despite cries of genocide in the Western media and repeated claims
that tens of thousands of Albanian Kosovars had been killed, postwar
investigators determined that only 2,000–3,000 people perished in the
years of fighting between Serb forces and Kosovar insurgents preceding
NATO's air war. And many of them were military fighters.[27] Carla Del
Ponte, the chief prosecutor for the International Criminal Tribunal for
the Former Yugoslavia—and no friend of Serbia's—told the UN Security
Council that investigators "had found 2,108 bodies" in some 195 sites.[28]

That more modest total included Serb victims, both military and
civilian. Indeed, British Defense Secretary George Robertson conceded
that up until January 1999, "The KLA were responsible for more deaths
in Kosovo than the Yugoslav authorities."[29] The actual number of
Albanian noncombatants who died was probably fewer than 1,000. If
that level of violence constitutes genocide, then virtually any conflict
between two or more groups involving different races, religions, or ethnic

backgrounds qualifies. If the term is thrown around so loosely, though, it debases the horror of true cases of genocide, such as the Ottoman Empire's treatment of Armenians during World War I, Stalin's systematic starvation of Ukrainians in the 1930s, the nightmare of the Nazi-era Holocaust during World War II, Pol Pot and the Khmer Rouge's mass exterminations in Cambodia, and the slaughter of Tutsis in Rwanda in the 1990s.[30]

Even some staunch defenders of the Kosovo intervention later grudgingly conceded that the tales of systematic killing by Milošević's Serbian forces had been exaggerated. Brookings Institution scholars Ivo Daalder and Michael O'Hanlon admit that the "levels of violence in Kosovo before March 23, 1999, were modest by the standards of civil conflict. . . . The violence had caused the deaths of 2,000 people in the previous year. This was not an attempted genocide of the ethnic Albanian people."[31] In the period leading up to NATO's air war, however, such admissions were virtually nonexistent.

Those who sought NATO's military intervention to achieve Kosovo's forced separation from Serbia did not shy away from exploiting the term genocide. When challenged after the fact about the modest casualty total, defenders of the U.S.–NATO action typically argue that the intervention prevented a genocide that the Milošević government intended to carry out and probably would have, absent Western military intervention. The alleged "intention" factor also played an important role in U.S. policymaking. Albright boasted that she "laid down a marker" in 1998, just a little more than two years after the Dayton Accords ended the fighting in Bosnia: "We are not going to stand by and watch the Serbian authorities do in Kosovo what they can no longer get away with in Bosnia."[32]

After the war, Radio Free Europe/Radio Liberty contended that substantive actions were not necessary to demonstrate the danger of genocide; mere inflammatory rhetoric was sufficient. "Milošević's aggressive intentions were clear from the rhetoric in the 1980s, just as Hitler's were in the 1930s. But it was not until Kosova [sic] in 1999 that the [North] Atlantic Alliance showed that the lessons of the previous decade had been learned."[33] Radio Free Europe/Radio Liberty's ideological bias was even evident from its choice to spell the name of the province as "Kosova," an unconventional spelling favored by the Kosovars and their international supporters. Again, defenders of the Western intervention were creating the image that the complex ethnic quarrel in Kosovo was a rerun of the Nazis' horrific campaign of genocide and the Kosovar insurgents were the moral equivalent of Jews and Hitler's other victims.

No credible evidence has emerged that Belgrade even had a plan for comprehensive ethnic cleansing, much less genocide. Yet the false image was extremely potent and served the objectives of those who favored Western intervention for the purpose of creating an independent Kosovo. Genocide, or the risk of genocide, supposedly justified support for the KLA and its secessionist agenda, even if that organization may have had some moral deficiencies. But such "anticipatory humanitarian intervention," as one may call it, was an exceedingly weak basis for launching a war against a sovereign state that posed no threat to the security of the United States. Such anticipatory intervention also was a dangerously open-ended precedent that, once set, could be used to justify aggressive war in almost any context. As Balkan analyst David Chandler notes, the belief that a situation would be even worse without international military intervention "provides a hypothetical *post facto* excuse that is difficult to disprove."[34]

Former State Department official George Kenney, at one time a strong proponent of Western military intervention in the Balkans, subsequently contributed to the debunking of the inflammatory accounts of genocide in Kosovo. Kenney cites an address delivered by Clinton administration National Security Advisor Sandy Berger to the Council on Foreign Relations in which he mentioned a purported mass grave in the village of Ljubenić, which supposedly contained "as many as 350 bodies." Kenney notes that the Italian general in charge of the site had told the press several days earlier that the exhumation had been completed and that only seven bodies had been found. Kenney observed acidly: "All press mention of Ljubenić ceases after that point."[35]

The fizzling of the Ljubenić genocide story was not an aberration. Kenney, citing an *El Pais* news report about a broader blow to the charges of genocide in Kosovo, writes: "Spanish forensic investigators sent to

Kosovo had found no proof of genocide. The team, which had experience in Rwanda, had been told to expect to perform more than 2,000 autopsies in one of the areas worst hit by the fighting, but it found only 187 bodies to examine. No mass graves and, for the most part, no signs of torture."[36] That outcome was typical of the inflated atrocity stories.

Chandler also notes, "The use of available facts to challenge the case for war found relatively little support or media space"; rather, actual facts ran up against the stifling climate of consensus based on a smug sense of moral superiority on the part of war proponents. "It seemed that the facts on the ground mattered less to Western advocates of intervention than the principle that a stand must be made on the side of the human rights cause."[37] During the year leading up to the NATO military intervention, the often emotional testimony at congressional hearings on Kosovo tended to confirm that conclusion.[38]

If U.S. officials and the news media had taken a more skeptical view of the genocide and ethnic cleansing allegations from the beginning, U.S. and NATO policy regarding Kosovo might have turned out differently; instead, they became a conduit for hyping inflammatory claims by one side in a complex internecine conflict.[39] Also, they might have spared Washington from forging a de facto partnership with the KLA, one of the more morally dubious organizations in that part of the world.

Aftermath: Reverse Ethnic Cleansing—and Worse

Perhaps most troubling of all was the West's inattention to, if not outright whitewashing of, atrocities that KLA forces committed in Kosovo, both before and after the expulsion of Serbian authorities. In the months following NATO's successful air war to end Belgrade's control of Kosovo, evidence emerged that the new authorities were pursuing systematic ethnic cleansing. A blatant double standard came into play. Despite the fact that NATO troops were occupying the province, the KLA proceeded to wage campaigns of terror and intimidation against non-Albanian inhabitants.

Over the course of the following months, some 240,000 people fled or were driven from Kosovo. And the victims were not just Serbs but also members of other minority ethnic groups, including Bulgarians, Romanians, Greeks, Roma, and Jews.[40] The Roma minority was hit especially hard, and the group's treatment at the hands of the KLA-led Kosovo regime has not improved much with the passage of time. Almost as soon as Milošević's troops began their withdrawal in early June 1999, Kosovar military units and auxiliary mobs launched a series of revenge attacks on the Roma. Although most Roma had tried to remain neutral in the war between Belgrade and the KLA, most Kosovars viewed them as Serb allies. As documented in a 2017 *Al Jazeera* article, such attacks "varied from harassment and theft to arson, rape and murder." As many as 1,000 Serbs and Roma were missing and unaccounted for in the months following the cessation of the war. "'Investigations, as far as I can remember were never done,' one Roma man, Hisen Gashnjani, who recalls the incidents, told *Al Jazeera*. 'There weren't even any arrests,' he says."[41]

If the Kosovar authorities or the general population regretted the KLA's barbaric actions, little evidence of it exists. Indeed, in the rare cases in which KLA leaders were prosecuted for their atrocities, large demonstrations erupted in Pristina in support of the accused. In mid-January 2017, Ramush Haradinaj, a former KLA senior commander and later Kosovo prime minister, was arrested in France on a war crimes warrant; thousands of Kosovar Albanians took to the streets of Pristina to protest his arrest. Similar protests had erupted in 2015 following the sentencing of Sylejman Selimi, another KLA commander.[42]

Yet U.S. and European Union (EU) officials said little about the KLA's massive ethnic cleansing campaign, which was taking place on NATO's watch. The Western news media—that during the mid- and late-1990s had reported multiple accounts of Serbian government abuses against Kosovo's Albanian population (whether real, exaggerated, or even fictional)—seemed strangely indifferent to the flip side of the story. News accounts and in-depth analyses of the persecution faced by non-Albanians were rare; even when they did appear, in most instances, the authors couched the accounts in such a way as to suggest that those incidents, while regrettable, had been the inevitable backlash to previous Serb abuses against Albanians.[43]

Western officials and news outlets showed a similar indifference toward the Kosovar Albanians' systematic desecration of Christian monasteries and other religious sites—some of which were hundreds of years old and were rife with historical as well as religious significance. In just five years after NATO took over the province, more than 100 Serbian Eastern Orthodox churches and monasteries were destroyed, culminating in an orgy of violence by Kosovar Albanian mobs in early 2004. Witnesses stated that NATO troops, supposedly there to protect inhabitants and property, did little or nothing to help.[44]

Balkan analyst Christopher Deliso contends that "although there were (and are) true believers in the rightness of the Albanian cause," such apparent indifference was not solely the result of Western moral hypocrisy.[45] "The international administration that set up shop in July 1999 had to deal with the hardened fighters of the KLA, most of whom were dangerous, and some of whom controlled powerful, clan-based organized crime networks, while moonlighting as politicians." According to Deliso, because such men "had the capability of causing everything from political liquidations to massed armed resistance," Western officials "quickly realized that it was better to come to an understanding with the ex-KLA than to cross it." Deliso quotes one former UN official who stated, "The deal was, you leave us alone, we leave you alone." The official added that the arrangement "had its benefits, mainly that we were allowed to live."[46] The cowardly response of the NATO and UN personnel involved suggests just how far removed the now-dominant KLA was from the beleaguered, pro-democratic freedom fighter image portrayed in Western media accounts and embraced by Western political elites.

The situation has improved marginally since the early postwar years. The pace of destruction directed against churches and monasteries has subsided since the culmination of violence in 2004, partly because few undamaged sites remain. Nevertheless, Kosovo still is far from being a model of religious tolerance. Indeed, incidents of desecration and persecution persist, as well as the overall negative atmosphere created by government-sanctioned intimidation of minorities.

Although the ethnic cleansing and the desecration of Christian sites were disturbing developments, they were not the worst consequences of Western support for the KLA. Some of the subsequent revelations involving that organization are truly horrific. Just before Christmas 2010, the Council of Europe released an investigative report that confirmed long-standing rumors that the KLA was involved in the trafficking of human body parts, including killing Serb prisoners to harvest their kidneys and other organs.[47]

Two aspects of the report were especially significant. First, the author and lead investigator was Swiss Senator Dick Marty, a highly respected champion of human rights. Second, the report specifically named Kosovo Prime Minister Hashim Thaçi as an accomplice in those atrocities and other criminal activities—including drug trafficking and politically motivated murders. Thaçi, of course, vehemently disputed the Marty report, but those who had followed Thaçi's career since his guerrilla days (when he was known as "The Snake") hardly considered such allegations far-fetched.

A subsequent international investigation in 2014, led by EU Chief Prosecutor Clint Williamson, reached conclusions similar to Marty's. Williamson, a former U.S. ambassador-at-large for war crimes, hardly could be accused of harboring pro-Serb or anti-Kosovar sentiments, because he had been one of the principal drafters of the indictment brought against Milošević by the UN war crimes tribunal in The Hague. Thus, Williamson's announcement that his team had procured enough evidence to support indictments against numerous senior KLA members was especially troubling. "[T]he evidence is compelling," he said, "that these crimes were not the acts of rogue individuals acting on their own accord, but rather they were conducted in an organized fashion and were sanctioned by certain individuals in the top levels of the KLA leadership."[48] Such revelations make a mockery of Lieberman's assertion that the KLA stood for the same values as America. However, Lieberman has yet to condemn the KLA for any of its actions.

Such an appalling aftermath to the NATO intervention is especially ironic given the fact that a key rationale for the intervention was to prevent ethnic cleansing and other human rights abuses in the first place. As related in the memoirs of both President Clinton and Secretary of State Albright, the principal justification for bombing a sovereign state and amputating one of its provinces was the Milošević government's alleged plans to ethnically cleanse Kosovo of its Albanian inhabitants. However, the record today suggests that those "we need to take action to prevent ethnic cleansing" and other justifications ring hollow. Not only was evidence of such genocidal intent by Belgrade skimpy at best, but the very faction that the NATO alliance supported later went on to commit an indisputable campaign of ethnic cleansing. And it all happened on NATO's watch.

Many of the inflammatory accounts of the Kosovo (and earlier Bosnia) conflict originated with, or were shaped by, sophisticated public relations campaigns conducted by heavyweight firms such as Ruder Finn, which wealthy Albanians and Albanian-Americans (as well as financier George Soros) helped fund.[49] The most important pro-KLA lobbying organization was the Albanian-American Civic League, headed by former Rep. Joe DioGuardi (R–NY), which worked closely with public relations firms.[50]

In addition to pushing their case with the news media, interest groups friendly to the KLA cultivated close ties with influential political figures. Albanian-American individuals and groups contributed generously to the political campaigns of Senate majority leader and 1996 GOP presidential nominee Robert Dole and Sen. John McCain (R–AZ), among others. When he was a senator from Kansas, Dole was a fierce critic of Belgrade's policy in Kosovo;[51] following his retirement from the Senate at the end of 1996, he became a staunch public advocate for the KLA, testifying at congressional hearings and giving numerous media interviews on behalf of the Kosovar cause.[52] He was an early advocate of U.S. military intervention against Belgrade. McCain likewise was an outspoken proponent of Kosovar independence.[53]

THE WEST FURTHER COMPOUNDS THE KOSOVO PROBLEM

McCain and others who favored an independent Kosovo eventually got their way. In February 2008, the United States and its allies bypassed the UN Security Council and recognized Kosovo's unilateral move to declare itself independent from Serbia as the Republic of Kosovo.

The KLA, with no small degree of help from the United States, had achieved its goal. Russia and China strenuously objected to Washington's orchestrated bypassing of the UN Security Council (and their veto rights as permanent members). Russian officials pointedly warned that the Western actions set a dangerous precedent in international affairs, even though U.S. leaders insisted that Kosovo was a special case. In a February 2008 State Department briefing, Under Secretary of State for Political Affairs R. Nicholas Burns made that argument explicitly.[54] Because the situation was unique, he insisted, the West's Kosovo policy set no precedent regarding other ethnic secessionist situations. Both the illogic and the hubris of the U.S. rationale were breathtaking.

Just months later, the extent of Washington's detachment from reality became clear: Russia exploited a provocation by Georgia's government and used military force to back the secession of two disgruntled Georgian regions, South Ossetia and Abkhazia (Chapter 5).[55] Secretary of Defense Robert Gates was one of the few U.S. officials to acknowledge the connection between the Kosovo episode and that later incident: "The Russians used Kosovo's declaration of independence . . . which the United States and the Europeans supported, as a pretext to turn up the heat on Georgia. The West's logic in supporting Kosovo's independence, said the Russians, ought to apply as well to Abkhazia and South Ossetia."[56]

Washington's support for the KLA, therefore, resulted not only in the empowerment of a dubious Balkan faction, but it created an alarming precedent that legitimized meddling by great powers on behalf of secessionist movements. U.S. policy was strategically myopic as well as morally suspect.

Western, especially American, leaders have little reason to be proud of their handiwork in Kosovo. Thaçi and other members of Kosovo's political elite have been named in Western intelligence reports as prominent organized crime figures.[57] Indeed, Kosovo has become a center of heroin trafficking, prostitution, and other organized crime activities.[58] *New York Times* correspondent Chuck Sudetic notes, "Gangland killings and intimidation of diplomats are hardly unusual in Kosovo, and the Kosovars' traditional practice of blood vengeance, which demands retaliation even against family members of a violator, still trump Western-style rule of law."[59] Also, for years Thaçi—first as prime minister and later as foreign minister, deputy prime minister, and president—systematically stalled attempts to establish a special international tribunal to deal with the allegations made against him in the Marty and Williamson reports.

In addition to the troubling allegations of human rights abuses, Kosovo has become a pit of economic despair. A third of its workforce is unemployed, and some 40 percent of its 1.8 million people live in dire poverty.[60] The country's desperation was underscored by the surge of Kosovar refugees—numbering in the tens of thousands—trying to immigrate to EU countries in 2014 and early 2015.[61] The flow of refugees through Serbia into Hungary became so large that the Hungarian government erected a fence on its border with Serbia in defiance of EU rules that promote the free movement of individuals.[62] The tide of Kosovar refugees largely predated the even more unpopular tsunami of refugees from war-torn Arab countries in the Middle East and North Africa.

Additionally, the KLA-controlled regime in Pristina and its supporters once more began to pursue a "Greater Albania" expansionist agenda, much as they had during the period immediately following the 1999 NATO war. In neighboring Macedonia, in provinces with Albanian majorities or even pluralities, trouble has surfaced. For years, Washington and other Western capitals have pressed Macedonia's government to make more and more political concessions to the country's Albanian minority, yet their demands keep escalating.[63] It appears that Macedonia's president has finally had enough and is firmly resisting those demands, despite continuing Western pressure for more appeasement.[64] The drive for a Greater Albania is gaining new momentum, and that creates major problems with multiple neighboring states.

What is more, Thaçi and the current roster of KLA alumni might not even be the worst of the ethnic forces that the United States and its allies have helped to unleash. In early September 2016, hardline Albanian nationalist members of parliament forced the Kosovo government to postpone a vote on a draft agreement that would have settled a border dispute with Montenegro. The decision to postpone the vote came after numerous, increasingly violent demonstrations from Albanian nationalist zealots. The demonstrations to protest both the border proposal and measures that might have given even the slightest autonomy to Kosovo's Serbian remnant sometimes shut down the parliament.[65] Such developments did not bode well for the Western-cultivated goal of a multi-ethnic, democratic Kosovo at peace with its neighbors. Frustrated Western leaders still were prodding Pristina to ratify the border agreement in April 2017.[66]

Nearly two decades after NATO's military intervention, Kosovo remains an economically and politically dysfunctional international ward. And ethnic animosity is alarmingly intense on multiple fronts. In mid-January 2017, Serbia attempted to restart train service to the northern, predominantly Serbian portion of its former province. Kosovar police and paramilitary units (as well as a civilian mob) forcibly prevented the first train from crossing the de facto border between Serbia and Kosovo.[67] Furious Serbian leaders branded the move "an act of war," and already worrisome tensions spiked.[68] Belgrade promptly severed the diplomatic dialogue that the EU—with more than a little prodding directed at both capitals—had sponsored since 2011.

Matters became so tense that even Senator McCain, a long-time vocal supporter of Kosovo independence, begged Kosovar officials to resume the dialogue with the Serbian government, contending that it was "the only way to a prosperous future."[69] NATO Secretary General Jens Stoltenberg issued a similar plea.[70] President Thaçi apparently had different ideas, though, wanting to create a full-fledged army instead of the existing, lightly armed security force. According to Kosovo's constitution, the drafting of which had been heavily influenced by Western officials, taking such a step required a formal amendment. Thaçi bypassed that obstacle—and the opposition of the Serb minority in parliament— and simply authorized internal security forces to acquire heavy weapons.[71] At the same time, he asked for U.S. and NATO support to legitimize an official army.[72] In a move that was particularly telling of how nervous both U.S. and NATO leaders had become about the growing tensions in the Balkans and Pristina's sometimes abrasive behavior, they firmly rebuffed Thaçi's request.[73] Underscoring Kosovo's continuing subservient status as a Western protectorate, Thaçi promptly retreated.[74]

And as if all of those headaches weren't enough, the growing threat of Muslim extremism in the region is yet another, and again, the Kosovar client state that Washington backed is a significant source of the problem. Jihadist fighters from both Bosnia and Kosovo are showing up in greater and greater numbers in Syria, Iraq, and other combat arenas, and the jihadi influence in Kosovo itself is surging.[75] Ethnic Albanian terrorists even have been implicated in plots directed against targets in the United States.[76] By all measures, Washington's nurturing of Kosovo has reaped a bitter harvest.

Washington's Gratuitous Sponsorship of an Unsavory Faction

What was especially galling about Washington's support for the KLA and its agenda was the dearth of bona fide American security interests at stake in the Balkans. Slobodan Milošević was undoubtedly a nasty ruler, and Serb forces in both Bosnia and Kosovo clearly committed atrocities. But such events are typical in warfare, especially in the course of civil wars, and (while not justifying Serb atrocities) Belgrade's opponents also committed atrocities against Serbian civilians. Neither side could make a credible, much less a compelling, moral case for U.S. intervention to support their cause. To be blunt, the United States did not have a dog in that fight, neither morally nor strategically.

The government that KLA alumni created is certainly no model of liberal, democratic rule. Indeed, it has been marked by corruption, ethnic intolerance (often including outright ethnic cleansing), and pervasive economic mismanagement. Once again, the "freedom fighters" that American supporters touted fell far short of that standard. U.S. officials stubbornly refuse to concede that point, however. In an early 2016 interview, Victoria Nuland, assistant secretary of state for European and Eurasian Affairs, lauded Kosovo's "considerable progress" toward political stability and voiced her expectation that it would become "a multi-ethnic country where Kosovo Serbs, Kosovo Albanians, all ethnicities can live in peace, because not only does the region need that but the planet needs it and Kosovo has an opportunity to set that example."[77]

Nuland's description bore little resemblance to the actual Kosovo, where unemployment rates hovered near 35 percent, corruption was rampant, and ethnic tensions continued to boil. Aidan Hehir, a scholar at the University of Westminster, provides an insight into why Nuland and other advocates of humanitarian crusades like the Kosovo intervention feel compelled to defend the results despite the contrary evidence:

> As a consequence of the massive investment of economic and political capital, perpetuating an image of Kosovo as "multi-ethnic," "democratic," and "peaceful" has become vital to liberal internationalism's image. Preserving this image, however, has led to the imposition of a national identity which simply does not equate with the reality on the ground in Kosovo. More damagingly, the determination to artificially contrive a façade of peace and stability with Kosovo has led external actors to tolerate, and at times support, corruption and intimidation perpetrated by Kosovo's powerful criminal network. Paradoxically, therefore, Kosovo's people have been forced to endure profoundly illiberal practices orchestrated by the various "internationals" who micromanage the country so as to maintain its image as their success.[78]

The United States and its NATO allies have been at the forefront of the "illiberal practices" that have helped empower the KLA alumni and have made the remnant Serbian population a terrorized victim. Those actions would have been bad enough even if vital American interests had been at stake, but U.S. policymakers did not even have that justification—not that they didn't attempt to make it. Both at the time and subsequently, advocates of U.S.-led intervention have habitually overstated the relevance of the Balkans to the United States.

Holbrooke, Clinton's assistant secretary of state for Europe and later ambassador to the UN, was typical, asserting that the bloodshed in the Balkans was taking place "in the heart of Europe."[79] Although developments in the Balkans might be painful and annoying, they are hardly critical to the continent's future—much less to America's. Otto von Bismarck, chancellor of the German Empire from 1871 to 1890, aptly observed that the Balkans were not worth the bones of a single Pomeranian grenadier. That was true for continental Europe's leading power then, and it is even more so for a distant power like the United States now. Yet U.S. officials and opinion leaders have acted like the region is

central to America's security and well-being—so much so that they have
been willing to make common cause with a ruthless political movement
that has committed especially repulsive war crimes, even willing to then
whitewash those abuses.

The KLA's lobbying efforts certainly have paid off regarding its
narrow, nationalistic agenda. And the Kosovars understand all too well
that without having manipulated the Clinton administration, they never
would have achieved their secessionist agenda. Indeed, in Pristina,
"A three-meter tall, gold-sprayed statue of Bill Clinton stands on a cor-
ner of the long boulevard that also bears his name."[80] And the wooing
of Washington has continued since independence. As of spring 2017,
nine years after the 2008 declaration of independence, only a little more
than half of UN member states (114 of 193) had recognized Kosovo's
independence. Kosovar leaders are relying on the United States to deliver
the rest, despite opposition from Russia, China, and other influential
states. Agron Demi, a scholar at the Kosovar think tank GAP, states:
"We relied heavily on U.S. lobbying a lot to get more recognitions. We
still have only 113 [sic] countries on our side, but we need a lot more."[81]

Unfortunately, there is little indication that U.S. leaders have learned
from their failed Kosovo policy. Indeed, despite its professed commitment to a foreign policy firmly based on substantive American national
interests, even the Trump administration shows signs of having been
sucked back into the Kosovo quagmire. In July 2017, the administration
announced that it would deploy 500 U.S. troops as part of a strengthened
international peacekeeping force to dampen rising tensions in Kosovo.[82]

Sadly, Kosovo would not be the last case of U.S. involvement in supposedly democratic insurgent movements. Although the Cold War had
long been over, concerted public relations campaigns to get the United
States to back questionable causes would become prominent again during
the so-called War on Terror following the 9/11 attacks. That was especially true of the successful manipulation woven by the Iraqi National
Congress and its American supporters in the lead-up to the Iraq War
(Chapter 6).

Washington's embrace of groups such as the KLA, the Iraqi National
Congress, Ukraine's Maidan demonstrators, and the so-called "moderate"

Syrian insurgents seeking to unseat dictator Bashar al-Assad affirms the depressing reality that a new generation of American political leaders, journalists, and policy analysts has learned very little from the earlier embarrassing episodes of U.S. support for bogus democratic insurgencies. And despite the Trump administration's professed lack of enthusiasm for those policies and the regime-change wars they tend to generate, U.S. association with unsavory contingents is a recurring theme that threatens to create problems in the future.

CHAPTER FIVE

COLOR REVOLUTIONS
PRODUCE BLEAK OUTCOMES

Washington's response to the ostensibly democratic upheavals that erupted during George W. Bush's presidency revealed that U.S. policymakers once again lacked a healthy skepticism toward self-proclaimed democratic insurgencies. The so-called "Color Revolutions" took place in diverse countries ranging from Ukraine to Lebanon to Kyrgyzstan (now the Kyrgyz Republic). Robert Legvold, the Marshall D. Shulman Professor Emeritus at Columbia University, notes in *Foreign Affairs* that more of the movements actually were named after flowers than colors (notably, Georgia's Rose Revolution and Kyrgyzstan's Tulip Revolution), and Lebanon's Cedar Revolution was named after a tree, but nevertheless, Color Revolutions became the umbrella term for all of these movements.[1]

The West's pervasive hope that such movements would produce stable, lasting democratic governments is puzzling in retrospect. None of the countries had a significant heritage of political pluralism or strong civil societies. Lebanon's prospects were best, but the country had only meager, intermittent, and fragile experience with democratic governance; the other countries (including former Soviet republics) didn't have even that. Despite regularly scheduled elections in Ukraine and Georgia following the collapse of the USSR, their political systems were rigged and corrupt.[2] And neither of those two former Soviet states had meaningful civil societies with strong nongovernmental organizations that could become the foundation of a liberal democratic order.[3] Kyrgyzstan's background was even less conducive to the emergence of a pluralistic system. Its entire history—before, during, and after its inclusion in the Soviet Union—was one of thoroughgoing autocracy.[4] Prospects of fragile shoots of democracy growing in the soil of such countries were not good.

Nevertheless, Western governments exuded optimism. American officials and opinion leaders were especially enthusiastic about the 2003 Rose Revolution in Georgia, led by Mikheil Saakashvili, and the 2004 Orange Revolution in Ukraine, led by Viktor Yushchenko and Yulia Tymoshenko. Bush and his advisers tended to oversimplify both the origins and the nature of those two political transformations. The president described Georgia's Rose Revolution as "a bloodless coup" that reflected a surge of popular sentiment to oust incumbent President Eduard Shevardnadze, who supposedly held office solely as a result of a corrupt election.[5]

Bush's account of Ukraine's Orange Revolution was even more laudatory and one-sided:

> In November 2004, a similar wave of protests broke out after a fraudulent election in Ukraine. Hundreds of thousands braved freezing temperatures to demonstrate for opposition candidate Viktor Yushchenko. At one point during the campaign, Yushchenko suffered a mysterious poisoning that disfigured his face. Yet he refused to drop out of the race. His supporters turned out every day clad in orange scarves and ribbons until the Ukrainian Supreme Court ordered a rerun of the tainted election. Yushchenko won and was sworn in on January 13, 2005, completing the Orange Revolution.[6]

Such accounts were not entirely wrong. The incumbent regimes in both countries were notoriously corrupt, and the elections in question were hardly models of free and fair balloting. But Bush ignored evidence that other important factors were at play; for example, the campaign in Georgia reflected both mundane factionalism and Saakashvili's intense personal political ambitions in addition to popular disgust over financial corruption and electoral fraud.[7]

The situation in Ukraine was even more complex. Yushchenko and his followers tended to be more democratic—and certainly more free market—than President Leonid Kuchma and the other entrenched former communist apparatchiks they opposed and managed to displace in 2004. However, the differences were not as stark as Western admirers seemed to believe. After all, Yushchenko had once served as Kuchma's prime minister.[8] The Orange Revolution also was the product of a bitter rivalry between the western and eastern portions of Ukraine, a rivalry that transcended ideological differences. Most of Yushchenko's support came from the western region, and the bulk of his opponents were centered in the east. That geographic chasm would become more evident as time passed, culminating in the 2014 Maidan Revolution (Chapter 9) and Ukraine's subsequent civil war.

Instead of recognizing such ambiguities and the problems they could cause, the U.S. government supported the new Georgian and Ukrainian regimes without reservation. In April 2005, Yushchenko paid a state visit to Washington and was accorded the honor of addressing a joint session of Congress. In a joint press conference with the Ukrainian president, Bush described the Orange Revolution as "a powerful example of democracy for people around the world" and asserted that the ideals of the new Ukraine were the ideals of Western civilization. Moreover, he declared that Washington and Kiev "share a goal to spread freedom to other nations."[9]

That praise was relatively restrained, though, compared to his later assessment of the achievement in Georgia. Bush exhibited great personal admiration for Saakashvili, describing him in his memoirs as "a charismatic young democrat,"[10] and the president was equally enthusiastic about Saakashvili's political handiwork. In a May 2005 speech in Georgia's capital, Tbilisi, Bush hailed Georgia as "a beacon of liberty" and praised that country's self-styled democrats for creating the template for the Color Revolutions. "Before there was a Purple Revolution in Iraq or an Orange Revolution in Ukraine or a Cedar Revolution in Lebanon," the president intoned, "there was a Rose Revolution in Georgia." Georgians deserved special recognition, he believed. "Your courage is inspiring democratic reformers and sending a message that echoes around the world: Freedom will be the future of every nation and every people on Earth." Georgia itself was "building a democratic society where the rights of minorities are respected; where a free press flourishes; where a vigorous opposition is welcomed and where unity is achieved through peace."[11]

Other American leaders shared in the Saakashvili hero worship. Both Sens. John McCain (R-AZ) and Hillary Clinton (D-NY) nominated him (along with Yushchenko, the new Ukrainian president) for the Nobel Peace Prize in January 2005,[12] although what exactly Saakashvili had done to promote global peace was unclear. Apparently, the assumption was that the democratic transformation of a small country was sufficient in and of itself to advance the cause of peace. That assumption was especially ironic with respect to Georgia; from the outset, Russia had been wary of, if not hostile to, Saakashvili and his policy agenda. The American tendency to treat Saakashvili as a democratic champion and cherished U.S. ally intensified the Putin government's suspicions that Washington intended to surround Russia with obedient military clients. The Bush administration's concerted campaign to give Georgia and Ukraine membership in the North Atlantic Treaty Organization (NATO) only validated the Kremlin's suspicions.

GEORGIA'S ROSE REVOLUTION: A TEMPLATE FOR DISILLUSIONMENT

By 2005, the bloom of the Rose Revolution already was fading. In retrospect, even from its outset, serious questions existed about just how democratic the movement actually was.[13] The Saakashvili government seemed more quasi-democratic than fully democratic in its overall behavior. The admiration expressed by Bush, McCain, Hillary Clinton, and other American cheerleaders was overblown, at the very least. Mounting evidence implicated Saakashvili and his associates in political corruption and human rights abuses. Some political opponents already languished in his jails. The wave of repression grew worse in subsequent years. A detailed December 2007 report by Human Rights Watch (HRW) documented how Saakashvili's administration harshly suppressed peaceful street demonstrations, jailed dozens of political critics, and harassed or even shut down opposition media outlets, including the main television station.[14]

The HRW report noted that one protest rally in Zugdidi, a city in western Georgia, "turned violent after a group of unidentified men, believed to be security officials, attacked the protestors and severely injured two members of parliament as they were leaving the demonstration site."[15] Regarding a later incident, the HRW report detailed additional disturbing evidence of the government's intolerant behavior:

[T]he fragility of Georgia's commitment to human rights and the rule of law was revealed on November 7, 2007, when government forces used violent and excessive force to disperse a series of largely peaceful demonstrations in the capital, Tbilisi. In the course of breaking up the demonstrations, law enforcement officers hastily resorted to the use of tear gas and rubber bullets. Police and other law enforcement personnel, many of them masked, pursued fleeing demonstrators of all ages, kicking and punching them and striking them with truncheons, wooden poles, and other objects.[16]

HRW investigators were especially critical of the regime's treatment of Imedi Television, the principal opposition media outlet:

Heavily armed special troops raided the private television station Imedi, threatening and ejecting the staff and damaging or destroying much of the station's equipment. Outside the studios, Imedi staff and their supporters found themselves set upon by riot police again using tear gas and rubber bullets and pursuing those who fled. Extensive photographic and video evidence captured that day by journalists and others illustrates these incidents.[17]

The report concluded bluntly, "The raid on and closure of Imedi television was a violation of Georgia's commitments to guaranteeing freedom of expression."[18] The Saakashvili government's contention that the raid and closure were necessary because Russia was fomenting a military coup in which Imedi was deeply involved did not impress investigators: "The legal basis for the decision to raid and close Imedi has been seriously called into question, and there is evidence to suggest that the legal basis was established after-the-fact and backdated."[19] In other words, HRW concluded that Saakashvili's regime was using a probably fictional Russian coup plot as a pretext for silencing its media critics.

The Saakashvili government's increasing authoritarianism and brutality were the reaction to growing public discontent with his rule. A
stream of revelations about corruption (and worse) exacerbated the public's discontent. For example, in September 2007, Irakli Okruashvili,
a former defense minister in Saakashvili's administration, detonated a
major domestic and international political bombshell when he charged
that the president had instructed him to have a Georgian economic oligarch assassinated. More generally, Okruashvili confirmed widespread
accusations that the government was guilty of "immorality, injustice,
and repression."[20] Georgian authorities responded by arresting him
on highly questionable charges of extortion, money laundering, and
"negligence."[21] Okruashvili then requested—and received—political
asylum in France.[22] Apparently, French political leaders did not share
the Bush administration's view that Georgia was a model Western-style
democracy or even that it would give a political opponent a fair trial.
When Okruashvili fled Georgia and refused to return, the Saakashvili
regime tried him in absentia and convicted him.

Even if lurid tales of assassination plots never were substantiated,
independent analysts did confirm other abuses. A December 19, 2007,
report by the International Crisis Group concluded that Saakashvili's
government had "become increasingly intolerant" of any dissent.[23]
The 2007 HRW report accused the regime of "taking serious steps" to
undermine human rights and the rule of law.[24] International observers
refused to certify the May 2009 parliamentary elections as either free
or fair. Even Freedom House, an early admirer of the Rose Revolution, conceded in its 2009 report that Georgia ranked as only "partly
free," and that the trend was signaling further deterioration.[25] The reason for Freedom House's rating downgrade was clear: "Georgia received
a downward trend arrow due to flaws in the presidential and parliamentary election processes, including extensive reports of intimidation and
the use of state administrative resources, which resulted in a marked
advantage for the ruling National Movement party."[26]

Such developments mocked the breathless enthusiasm that American
officials and journalists had displayed for the Rose Revolution.

Indeed, HRW had some caustic words for the United States and others who admired Saakashvili and the Rose Revolution:

> Georgia's international partners, including, most prominently, the United States and the European Union, have provided unwavering support for President Mikheil Saakashvili and his government since the Rose Revolution brought it to power.
>
> Georgia has been seen as a small but crucial bulwark to counter Russian dominance in the region and as an important ally for the United States. It has also been held up as an example of a successful transition to democracy in the former Soviet Union region. As a result, the US and EU have refrained from criticizing Saakashvili in public and from engaging in robust discussion of the country's human rights problems. They have relied on the Georgian government's repeatedly-stated good intentions and promises of reform, ignoring warning signs that the government was not only failing to live up to the principles of the rule of law and human rights it espoused during the Rose Revolution, but taking many serious steps to undermine these principles.[27]

Columbia University research scholar Lincoln Mitchell reaches a similar critical judgment regarding Washington's stance. According to Mitchell, if Georgian government leaders had learned soon after the Rose Revolution "that they would be held to their words regarding their democratic intentions, they might have been less likely to move away from democracy. Instead, they learned the opposite lesson—that moving away from democracy, whether through restricting media, rewriting the constitution, or pressuring judges, would bring about no consequences from their American patrons."[28]

Western enabling behavior was not confined to reticence about the Saakashvili regime's worsening conduct. Instead, praise from U.S. officials and journalists barely diminished, and the flow of aid to Georgia actually increased. Whether Washington's passivity toward Saakashvili's domestic abuses flowed from a refusal to give credence to the growing evidence that his rule was deeply flawed, from a belief that the geopolitical benefits of having a pawn to contain Russian power trumped worries about the future of Georgian democracy, or simply from an all-too-human reluctance to admit an error in judgment is not clear. But whatever the reason (or reasons), there was little evidence of a chill in U.S. policy toward Tbilisi.

Regardless of Washington's support, domestic irritation with Saakashvili and his faction increased steadily during the years following the 2007 demonstrations and the violent government crackdown. Saakashvili did win reelection in early 2008, but allegations of voter fraud and other election abuses soared. The subsequent parliamentary elections in May seemed even more tainted. Freedom House succinctly summarized the worrisome situation: "President Mikheil Saakashvili won reelection in January 2008, having called an early poll after a controversial crackdown on the opposition in late 2007. His National Movement party also handily won parliamentary elections in May, but international monitors noted an array of irregularities."[29]

By 2012, public discontent with Saakashvili boiled over. In October elections, his party lost control of parliament to the Georgian Dream Alliance, led by billionaire businessman Bidzina Ivanishvili. The election also marked the start of the country's transition from a presidential system to a parliamentary one, with far more power and responsibility placed in the post of prime minister.[30] That change was another reflection of concern among the Georgian people that the presidency was too powerful and that Saakashvili had abused his authority. The total repudiation of Saakashvili culminated the following year when one of his staunch opponents was elected president.[31] (Georgia's constitution bars a president from running for a third term, and although Saakashvili flirted with trying to change that provision, he ultimately abided by it.)

The opposition did not seem inclined to forgive or forget the excesses of Saakashvili's presidency. In the months following the 2012 and 2013 balloting, the new government indicted dozens of former officials on charges of corruption and abuses of authority. In July 2014, prosecutors charged Saakashvili himself with those offenses.[32] Several charges were related to abuses that had occurred during the government's authoritarian crackdown in 2007 and which were highlighted by HRW and other international organizations. When the former president denounced the proceedings as a "witch hunt" and remained outside the country, the government unsuccessfully sought Interpol's assistance to apprehend him.[33] In any case, it was an ignominious development for a political leader whom a multitude of influential friends throughout the West had hailed as a model democrat.

Yet neither Saakashvili nor his American allies appeared willing to accept his disgrace. He went into what *New York Times* correspondent Jason Horowitz described as a "genteel exile" in the posh Williamsburg neighborhood in New York City. Prominent U.S. boosters, including Senator McCain, Assistant Secretary of State Victoria Nuland, and former Central Intelligence Agency (CIA) Director David Petraeus, were Saakashvili's frequent visitors. Horowitz concluded that he was "plotting a triumphant return, even as his steep fall from grace serves as a cautionary tale to many American government officials who had hoped he would be a model exporter of democracy to former Soviet republics."[34]

Saakashvili's international conduct, as well as his autocratic tendencies at home, should have been a warning signal to his American sponsors. Secretary of Defense Robert Gates aptly described him as "an impetuous Georgian nationalist" who went out of his way to push the envelope on sensitive issues.[35] However, other U.S. leaders and Western news media accounts largely ignored any signs of Saakashvili's risky behavior. That was true even in 2008, six years earlier, when his actions helped trigger a war between Georgia and Russia. Instead, Saakashvili's boosters portrayed the Russo-Georgian armed conflict that broke out in August of that year as a case of blatant Russian aggression. President Bush concluded: "It was clear that the Russians couldn't stand a democratic Georgia with a pro-Western president."[36]

The reality was more complex than that, and responsibility for the war was mixed. Indeed, Saakashvili took the fatal aggressive step when he launched a military operation into the secessionist region of South Ossetia in northern Georgia. Russian peacekeeping forces had been deployed in South Ossetia since disorder erupted there following the 1991 dissolution of the Soviet Union. On the heels of Georgia's declaration of independence earlier that year, South Ossetia and another region, Abkhazia, sought to break away from Georgia to establish their own independent states. Influential Russians, especially those who owned

estates on Abkhazia's Black Sea coast, encouraged such secessionist sentiments. The simmering violence in Georgia escalated to civil war, which
would not subside until late 1993. Russian peacekeeping forces were
deployed to South Ossetia and Abkhazia during the conflict, ultimately
making both regions de facto Moscow protectorates.

Saakashvili fumed at having two significant portions of Georgia lie
beyond his government's authority. In early August 2008, he responded
to one of the periodic cross-border shelling incidents with Ossetian units
by initiating a major incursion, apparently for the goal of re-establishing
control over the breakaway region. Unfortunately for Saakashvili, his
offensive also inflicted casualties on the Russian peacekeeping force;
Moscow responded with a full-scale counteroffensive that soon led to
the occupation of several Georgian cities and brought Russian troops to
the outskirts of the capital.

Even when the evidence confirmed that Saakashvili had initiated
the conflict, his American boosters still blamed the Russians. Vice President Dick Cheney offered a typical rationale, asserting that Saakashvili's
order to use force in South Ossetia "seemed to give Russian President
Vladimir Putin the excuse he had been looking for to launch an aggressive military action against the Georgians."[37]

In retrospect, Saakashvili acted rashly, even irresponsibly.
Apparently, he expected NATO—and especially the United States,
as the alliance's leader—to come to Georgia's aid militarily. Such an
expectation was not entirely irrational, given that Washington had
incessantly praised Saakashvili, had supplied Georgia with millions of
dollars in weaponry, and had provided training for Georgian troops.[38]
Nevertheless, any hopes that such support would culminate in direct
U.S. involvement in the resulting war were unfounded. When Bush
called Saakashvili just hours after the commencement of the Russian
offensive, the Georgian president urged him not to abandon a fellow democracy. Bush assured him of Washington's commitment to
Georgia's territorial integrity but tellingly stopped short of pledging
military backing.[39]

For all of Washington's previous expressions of support for a friendly
democratic country, the United States and its European allies were not

willing to risk a dangerous, unpredictable confrontation with a nuclear-armed power over an obscure territorial dispute. In a telephone call to Saakashvili, McCain would intone, "Today, we are all Georgians."[40] But U.S. and NATO forces were not deployed. Secretary of Defense Gates recalled that he was "blunt with my Georgian counterpart. I told him, 'Georgia must not get into a conflict with Russia that it cannot win.'"[41] Confronted with unyielding U.S. restraint, Georgia had to settle for a humiliating ceasefire and de facto peace with its large neighbor. It was a peace that saw Abkhazia and South Ossetia slip even farther away from Georgia's control and become part of the Russian Federation in all but name.

The conduct of America's political elite toward Georgia after the Rose Revolution was deficient in nearly every respect. Members wildly overestimated prospects for a stable and democratic capitalist future and overlooked Saakashvili's flaws. They irresponsibly led Georgians to believe that Washington's commitment to their security was far greater than it actually was—fostering such expectations was a factor in Tbilisi's ill-considered decision to attempt to reassert its sovereignty over the secessionist regions, despite clear signs that Moscow would never tolerate such a change. For Washington, jettisoning any notion that it would back Saakashvili's impetuous military offensive certainly was preferable to risking war with Russia, but it also likely triggered feelings of betrayal among Georgians who had placed their trust in U.S. support.

Still, the situation could have turned out even worse. It is sobering to consider what might have happened had the Europeans acquiesced to Washington's wishes and given Georgia membership in NATO. Under the terms of Article 5 of the North Atlantic Treaty, the United States and its allies would have been obligated to consider an attack on Georgia as an attack on them all. Because the allied governments accused Russia of aggression (despite conflicting evidence), they would have had little choice but to come to Tbilisi's aid, regardless of the risks. Even the mere possibility should have been a cautionary tale to Washington about the perils of backing a client state like Georgia merely because that country professes to be democratic.

U.S. enthusiasm for the Rose Revolution is a textbook example of the defective policies that unrealistic expectations often produce. Given its long legacy as a satrapy of the Russian empire and a constituent part of the totalitarian Soviet Union, Georgia had no history of democratic rule. The first president of Georgia after the republic became independent in 1991 was the former Soviet foreign minister Shevardnadze, who ruled for the next decade in the autocratic fashion typical of most ex–Soviet politicians. Saakashvili talked a good game, denouncing Shevardnadze for undemocratic behavior and mouthing all the right clichés about the importance of genuine democracy and capitalism for Georgia. Once in power, though, his conduct did not differ all that much from Shevardnadze's—or mundane autocrats in numerous other countries. Even his commitment to free-market economics was inconsistent and marred by extensive corruption. Worse, in his handling of foreign affairs, especially delicate relations with Russia, Saakashvili was a loose cannon. Still, as they had so many times before, American officials saw Saakashvili as the democratic, responsible ideal they wanted him to be rather than the man he actually was.

Ukraine's Orange Revolution: Sad Prelude to a Later Tragedy

Ukraine's Orange Revolution did not turn out significantly better than its Rose counterpart. At its outset, expectations were high not only among pro-Western Ukrainian reformers but also among their supporters in the United States and Europe. Bush administration officials clearly hoped that demonstrators' ability to overturn the results of Ukraine's tainted 2004 election and the subsequent victory of Viktor Yushchenko in the election's rerun signaled both the political and economic transformation of the country.[42] Washington's long-term goal was to see Ukraine join both the European Union and NATO—thus becoming a full-fledged member of the democratic West.

The United States did more than hope for a Yushchenko electoral victory. For several years, the federal government used the Freedom Support Act[43] and other programs to put millions of dollars into the hands of pro-Western political factions, and that effort accelerated in the lead-up to the rerun election. In addition to direct funding, nongovernmental organizations that were closely associated with the U.S. government—such as Freedom House and the Carnegie Endowment—added additional millions to the cash flow.[44] Although such aid ostensibly was for the generic goals of "promoting democracy" and ensuring election transparency, it constituted an indirect subsidy to political factions that Washington favored.

The U.S. support fueled allegations (as well as opposition campaign posters and literature) that Yushchenko was an American puppet.[45] Washington's role even made some American critics very uneasy. Rep. Ron Paul (R-TX) quoted President Bush's statement that any election in Ukraine "ought to be free of any foreign influence." Paul stated that he agreed "with the president wholeheartedly." However, he went on, "It seems that several U.S. government agencies saw things differently and sent U.S. taxpayer dollars into Ukraine in an attempt to influence the outcome."[46] How much of an effect U.S. financial subsidies had on the electoral result is open to question, but Paul was correct that the Orange Revolution's parentage was not entirely domestic.

International human rights organizations at first assessed the regime quite favorably. In its 2006 report, HRW stated, "Under the Yushchenko government, state manipulation of television and other media rampant in previous years appears to have ceased."[47] Likewise, the report noted that the Ukrainian justice and prison systems already had improved. That same year, Freedom House upgraded Ukraine's freedom status from "partly free" to "free."[48]

Those hopes soon faded. Richard Sakwa, professor of Russian and European Politics at the University of Kent in Canterbury, England, succinctly describes the rapid unraveling of the Orange Revolution: "Despite the mass mobilization and the enthusiasm attending Yushchenko's victory, his administration stumbled from crisis to crisis amid bitter personal conflicts, confused policy making and corruption."[49]

Indeed, Yushchenko's administration got off to an ethically dubious start with his appointment of Yulia Tymoshenko as prime minister. Tymoshenko was popularly known as "the gas princess"[50] for her often questionable acquisition of energy futures in the 1990s. Working in close cooperation with then–Prime Minister Pavlo Lazarenko, she amassed an enormous fortune in the natural gas business. Journalist Christopher Dickey summarizes the judgment of most analysts: "She was helped by the sweetheart deals Lazarenko allegedly sent her way."[51]

Dickey notes that Lazarenko later was convicted in the United States of money laundering and other crimes. Although Tymoshenko was not prosecuted, the indictment of Lazarenko explicitly cited her involvement in the criminal conspiracy:

> Lazarenko received money from companies owned or controlled by Ukrianian [sic] business woman Yulia Tymoshenko . . . in exchange for which Lazarenko exercised his official authority in favor of Tymoshenko's companies, and . . . Lazarenko failed to disclose to the people and government of Ukraine that he was receiving significant amounts of money from these companies.[52]

Despite such ominous signs, Washington offered enthusiastic backing to Ukraine's new leaders. U.S. Assistant Secretary of State for European and Eurasian Affairs Daniel Fried rushed to Kiev with an important message of U.S. support. He lauded Ukraine's transformation into a full-fledged democracy, but the country's democratic bona fides were not the only thing on his mind. Fried also stressed Washington's commitment to Ukraine's sovereignty and "its future as a free nation." Kiev had every right to make its own choices about its place in the world free from Russian intimidation, he asserted: "The Poles and the Balts had successes in asserting such rights in the face of Russian pressure and opposition, and Ukraine would as well, as long as its leaders were strong enough to continue reform."[53] Fried also emphasized U.S. support for Ukraine's aspirations for involvement in Euro-Atlantic institutions, including NATO.[54] Sakwa concludes that Ukraine's democratic aspirations were thus "inextricably bound up with geopolitical contestation, a fateful combination that would have devastating consequences in 2014."[55]

The United States' enthusiasm for Yushchenko's government seemed motivated at least as much by a perception that he would make a strong push for his country's inclusion in NATO as by confidence in his apparent commitment to democratic values and a market economy.

An October 2008 State Department cable to the embassy in Kiev lauded Yushchenko primarily for his views on NATO membership:

> President Yushchenko has a reputation as a visionary. Even his critics concede that his commitment to seeing Ukraine in NATO is sincere and unwavering. He has been the driving force behind Ukraine's request for a MAP [Membership Action Plan] and tireless in making the case both at home and abroad. In Yushchenko's view, NATO membership is the only thing that can guarantee Ukrainian sovereignty and territorial integrity for the long run.[56]

Unfortunately for both U.S. policy and the aspirations of the Ukrainian people, the democratic Orange coalition rapidly degenerated into a nearly comic opera rivalry between Yushchenko and Tymoshenko. That feud culminated with Yushchenko's dismissal of the prime minister and her entire cabinet in September 2005.[57] The bitter termination of their political partnership also led to the resignation of several other senior officials and produced pervasive public disenchantment with both leaders.

In the March 2006 parliamentary elections, a coalition of opposition parties, including the pro-Russian Party of Regions headed by Viktor Yanukovych, significantly outpolled Yushchenko's Our Ukraine party and won 129 seats to the latter's 85.[58] The president then had little choice but to appoint Yanukovych prime minister with a mandate to form a new government. Yanukovych served as prime minister from July 2006 until December 2007, a tenure marked by constant tensions with Yushchenko. Yanukovych already had his eyes set on the 2010 presidential election, seeing a golden opportunity to be Yushchenko's successor.

Tymoshenko had other ideas, however. Adopting an increasingly populist message, she was able to stage a modest political rebound, primarily by cutting into the support that Yanukovych and his allies enjoyed in eastern Ukraine (the aging industrial heart of the country). Meanwhile, she had declared a temporary truce with Yushchenko; in December 2007, Yushchenko, bowing to the Tymoshenko party's rebound in the most recent parliamentary elections, removed Yanukovych as prime minister and once again appointed Tymoshenko to the post. This time she held the post until the 2010 presidential and parliamentary elections. Despite the official re-establishment of the alliance between the president and new prime minister, their personal and political animosity continued to simmer. Especially bitter economic policy disputes broke out, with Tymoshenko's populist positions—expanding social welfare benefits, imposing increased taxes on the wealthy, and tightening some regulations on the economy—largely winning the day.[59]

Beyond the political problems and policy disagreements, Yushchenko's presidency was continuously plagued by corruption charges. His 19-year-old son's ostentatious lifestyle (which included tooling around the streets of Kiev in a new BMW sports car worth $120,000) did nothing to improve Yushchenko's image.[60] And as media accounts of apparent financial improprieties proliferated, Yushchenko exacerbated the public relations problem by lashing out at the press. On one occasion, he crudely branded a respected journalistic critic as a political "hitman."[61] As *BBC News* observed, such abrasive behavior outraged journalists, who accused the president of returning Ukraine to the climate of censorship experienced under his predecessor, Kuchma. A public letter signed by more than 100 journalists stated: "We don't think that the vocabulary and the tone that you used while answering a question about your son's lifestyle are worthy of a leader of a democratic European country."[62]

By the end of Yushchenko's first year in office, public disillusionment with the Orange Revolution was extensive and growing.[63] Unfortunately, the country's problems continued to fester—as did the bitter rivalry between Yushchenko and Tymoshenko. U.S. officials clearly were more favorable toward the former than the latter. Tymoshenko's growing allegiance to populism—especially, favoring policies that would place greater restrictions on foreign investment in Ukraine—and the mounting evidence of her longstanding corruption (some going back to her days as the country's "gas princess" in the 1990s) stirred suspicions in Washington. Also, Bush administration policymakers regarded Yushchenko as a far more reliable partner on geopolitical issues, especially NATO. Secretary of State Condoleezza Rice recalled Yushchenko's enthusiasm to join NATO's Membership Action Plan (MAP), an interim participation program for nations aspiring to join the

Alliance and the first stage in the process of becoming a NATO member. When Rice told him in 2008 that such a step was unlikely in the near future, "The Ukrainian president almost cried. 'It will be a disaster, a tragedy, if we don't get the MAP,' he pleaded."[64]

As in the case of Georgia, Washington held out the tantalizing prospect of NATO membership to Ukraine and encouraged Yushchenko to sell that prospect to his people. But the United States could not deliver such a prize, because NATO's leading European members were so reluctant. The Russo-Georgian war had demonstrated the limits of U.S. security backing for an ostensibly democratic Georgia; the aftermath of the Maidan Revolution would do the same regarding such backing for Ukraine (Chapter 9). Supposed "democratic solidarity" went only so far.

U.S. leaders saw Tymoshenko as a much less predictable actor than Yushchenko, and she was being especially cagey about Ukraine's policy toward NATO. Rice notes, "Tensions among the 'Orange forces' were extremely high. Tymoshenko had been coy about her support for MAP, but Yushchenko had managed to make MAP a litmus test of his ability to deliver his Western friends."[65] Given that difference, it was unsurprising that Washington liked Yushchenko much better than his domestic sometimes ally, sometimes rival Tymoshenko.

A 2009 Freedom House report still listed Ukraine in the "free" category, but the report also included some ominous negative comments. It cited the exceptionally bitter feud between Yushchenko and Tymoshenko and its adverse impact on Ukraine's politics and economy. "[R]elations between the two remained hostile at year's end. The sharp deterioration of the economy in the fall [of 2008] highlighted the politically divided state's inability to carry out fundamental reform." The report also took note of Yushchenko's increasing flirtation with undemocratic measures, stating that "the president continued to interfere with the courts, and corruption remained a severe problem."[66]

The situation did not improve significantly during the final years of Yushchenko's term, and the chronically languishing Ukrainian economy did not help the president's sagging political fortunes. Yushchenko's popularity plummeted steadily, falling so low that he became a nonfactor as the 2010 presidential election approached. Voters spurned his candidacy in the first round of that balloting, giving him a paltry 5 percent of the vote.[67] Even Western admirers of the Orange Revolution, such as Radio Free Europe/Radio Liberty, conceded that Yushchenko's presidency had been a huge disappointment. In a story marking his departure, the news organization concluded: "Yushchenko has left office with Ukraine in economic crisis and paralyzed by a bitter political standoff that has Ukrainians disillusioned and wondering what the Orange Revolution was all about."[68]

Prime Minister Tymoshenko showed somewhat better survival instincts than the hapless president. By altering her political message to stress populist themes, she confirmed suspicions that her commitment to the professed capitalist democratic values of the Orange Revolution was superficial at best. Notably, her platform for her 2010 presidential campaign rejected liberal economic policies. Instead, she embraced populist principles even more vigorously and emphasized a strong role for the state in both economic and social issues.[69] A milder version of that opportunistic switch had helped her in 2007, but the more robust application would not be enough to propel her to the presidency in 2010. She finished second, with 25 percent of the vote. Disgruntled voters spurned both Yushchenko and Tymoshenko in the 2010 balloting, electing instead Yanukovych—an old-style authoritarian politician whom U.S. officials viewed as a Kremlin stooge—with 35 percent of the vote. That result effectively marked the Orange Revolution's ignominious end.

The aftermath for Tymoshenko was even more painful than it had been for her one-time political ally Yushchenko. The new Yanukovych government soon prosecuted her for corruption, and the court sentenced her to seven years in prison.[70] The extent to which the verdict reflected pure political vengeance as opposed to genuine evidence of Tymoshenko's lawbreaking is difficult to determine. The trial certainly was not the model of impartial justice, but neither had her behavior over the years been the model of financial or political propriety. In any case, Tymoshenko remained behind bars until angry demonstrators overthrew Yanukovych in February 2014.

Once again, an American-lauded democratic revolution failed spectacularly to live up to Washington's expectations. The failure of the

Orange Revolution also set the stage for the domestic political upheaval that took place in Ukraine in 2014, the so-called Maidan Revolution against Yanukovych that brought a new pro-Western government to power. That development, which both the United States and the European Union celebrated and assisted, would in turn trigger a secessionist crisis in eastern Ukraine and a deep chill in Washington–Moscow relations following Russia's annexation of Ukraine's Crimea Peninsula.

THE COLOR REVOLUTIONS UNDERSCORE U.S. WISHFUL THINKING

Ironically, the Rose and Orange Revolutions were linked not only by politics and economics but also by personal relationships. Saakashvili and Yushchenko were close friends, so much so that Yushchenko was the godfather to Saakashvili's child.[71] And their once promising, liberalizing revolutions ultimately would share similar fates.

The connection between the Ukrainian and Georgian "democratic" movements remained extremely close even after the demise of the Rose and Orange Revolutions. In the year following Ukraine's Maidan Revolution, Ukraine's new pro-Western president, Petro Poroshenko, appointed Georgian Saakashvili as governor of Ukraine's Odessa region. Even some pro-Poroshenko Ukrainians were uneasy about Saakashvili's appointment. Giving a foreign national such a high post was controversial in and of itself; giving one to a foreign national facing criminal charges in his home country was even more so.[72] Saakashvili sought to neutralize objections about the first issue by acquiring Ukrainian citizenship (which Poroshenko quickly granted), but the overall controversy never dissipated.

Also, the two leaders soon began to clash badly. Under a growing cloud of graft and other allegations, Saakashvili resigned in November 2016 and left the country. But his quarrel with Poroshenko was just getting started. It culminated when the Ukrainian government stripped Saakashvili of his newly granted citizenship in June 2017 and the now-stateless Saakashvili illegally reentered Ukraine later that September.[73] Poroshenko then tried to have him arrested on corruption charges and for illegally entering the country. Saakashvili resisted arrest, at one point apparently threatening to commit suicide by jumping from the roof of a building in Kiev, thus raising questions about his mental stability. In a series of murky circumstances that included the assistance of supporters, he managed to escape capture, only to be rearrested a few days later.[74]

The gap between the democratic models that George Bush and other Western admirers of the Color Revolutions held up for display when promoting Georgia and Ukraine and those nations' actual democratic performance was massive. Yushchenko—and especially Tymoshenko— had not been very different from the corrupt politicians they displaced. Indeed, corruption in Ukraine remains pervasive following the 2014 Maidan Revolution, the second supposedly democratic upheaval in that country. The notion that the Orange Revolution would usher in an era of Western-style liberal governance was wishful thinking, at best.

The eventual outcome in Georgia was even more disappointing. The financial corruption was as at least as pronounced as it had been in Ukraine, and the violation of democratic norms was far more blatant and pervasive. After all, at least Yushchenko's government did not employ heavy-handed authoritarian tactics in an attempt to squelch political opposition. As documented by HRW, Freedom House, and other international monitors, Saakashvili and his associates repeatedly resorted to such police-state measures. By the time angry Georgians forced him from office in 2012, Saakashvili had amassed a record of repression not much different from those of other garden-variety tyrants. He never was the great democratic symbol that Bush and others had hailed. Once again, Washington was guilty of self-deception about an unscrupulous foreign political leader professing to embrace democratic values.

One thing that is not entirely clear is how much Washington's support for Yushchenko and Saakashvili stemmed from the desire to display the former Soviet Union states as models of the transition to democracy and how much stemmed from Washington's desire to take advantage of those states' perceived geopolitical value. The latter certainly was not an irrelevant consideration. Even HRW noted that U.S. leaders viewed Georgia "as a small but crucial bulwark to counter Russian dominance in the region and as an important ally for the United States."[75]

American policymakers saw Ukraine as an even more essential asset in the effort to contain Moscow's power.

President Bush enthusiastically embraced both countries' ambitions regarding NATO membership,[76] but for France, Germany, and most of Washington's other long-standing Alliance partners, giving Tbilisi and Kiev membership was too ambitious. When Bush formally proposed MAP for both Georgia and Ukraine at the NATO summit in April 2008, those Alliance members were opposed.[77] Rice recalls that German Chancellor Angela Merkel was especially negative. Merkel "did not trust the Georgians, whom she still saw as corrupt." The German leader also observed that the coalition governing Ukraine since the Orange Revolution "was a mess."[78]

When war broke out between Georgia and Russia in August 2008, the European allies were even more wary of provoking the Kremlin by adding Georgia and Ukraine to NATO. As evidence emerged that Tbilisi had made the first military move in the crisis, initial condemnations of Russian aggression began to fade.

By all appearances, though, U.S. enthusiasm for the Color Revolutions was not merely a cynical excuse for backing movements and regimes that might be useful in a new containment policy against Russia. At the outset, at least, Bush and other officials seemed genuinely convinced that the new Ukrainian and Georgian leaders were committed to Western political and economic values. Such a belief was not outrageous in the beginning, but as the new regimes engaged in a mounting list of misdeeds, clinging to such illusions should have been increasingly difficult for American leaders. Instead, Washington's commitment to its ostensibly democratic clients never expired. Indeed, little evidence suggests that it ever even wavered—a sad commentary on the wisdom and ethics of U.S. foreign policy.

CHAPTER SIX

THE IRAQI NATIONAL CONGRESS
CONS WASHINGTON INTO WAR

Following the 1991 Persian Gulf War, as relations between the United States and its former Iraqi client Saddam Hussein continued to deteriorate, influential American pressure groups mounted a lobbying campaign to "finish the job" and overthrow Saddam's regime. An open letter from Project for the New American Century (PNAC) to President Bill Clinton on January 26, 1998, explicitly set out that case, urging the president "to turn your Administration's attention to implementing a strategy for removing Saddam's regime from power. This will require a full complement of diplomatic, political and military efforts." The missive concluded: "The only acceptable strategy is one that eliminates the possibility that Iraq will be able to use or threaten to use weapons of mass destruction. In the near term, this means a willingness to undertake military action as diplomacy is clearly failing. In the long term, it means removing Saddam Hussein and his regime from power. That now needs to become the aim of American foreign policy."[1]

The list of signatories to the PNAC letter reads like a "who's who" of mainly neoconservative political and foreign policy activists, all of whom became famous for their strident advocacy of an interventionist foreign policy, both during the latter years of the Cold War and into the post–Cold War era. They include Elliott Abrams, William Bennett, John Bolton, Paula Dobriansky, Francis Fukuyama, Robert Kagan, Zalmay

Khalilzad, William Kristol, Richard Perle, Peter Rodman, Donald Rumsfeld, Paul Wolfowitz, R. James Woolsey, and Robert Zoellick; eventually, they all would successfully lobby for the United States to invade Iraq in 2003. Indeed, Bolton, Dobriansky, Perle, Rumsfeld, and Wolfowitz all would have high-level posts in George W. Bush's administration to drive U.S. policy regarding Iraq. Crucially, Rumsfeld would be the secretary of defense and Wolfowitz, the deputy secretary.

Advocates of "liberating" Iraq typically insisted that George H. W. Bush's administration made a major error at the conclusion of the Gulf War when it did not follow the expulsion of Iraqi forces from Kuwait with an offensive to achieve total victory—the overthrow of Hussein's Baathist regime—and they thought it imperative to correct that mistake.[2] Staunch neoconservatives were the most vocal about the need to right the wrong, but even some prominent Democrats subscribed to that view. Just months after the Gulf War, Sen. Al Gore (D-TN) said the same thing in an interview on ABC's *Nightline:* "I think that we ought to clearly set our objective as the removal of the Baathist regime from power." Furthermore, "We ought to start a war crimes tribunal, we ought to support groups within Iraq who are intent on overthrowing Saddam," Gore said.[3]

Anti-Iraq hawks scorned the view shared by more orthodox foreign policy practitioners that Washington's Middle East policy should be one of "dual containment" against both Iraq and Iran. Instead, they pushed a "dual rollback" policy of overthrowing Saddam in Iraq and eliminating the Islamic Republic in Iran. A vital tool in obtaining their objective in Iraq, they contended, would be the reservoir of internal opposition to Saddam and his regime. Another PNAC letter to President Clinton dated February 19, 1998, stressed that aspect:

> Saddam has an Achilles' heel: lacking popular support, he rules by terror. The same brutality which makes it unlikely that any coups or conspiracies can succeed, makes him hated by his own people and the rank and file of his military. Iraq today is ripe for a broad-based insurrection. We must exploit this opportunity.[4]

American proponents of forcible regime change held out the ideal of a democratic Iraq that would be friendly to the United States and its

economic and strategic interests throughout the Middle East. Their idealized government in Baghdad also would be willing to forge a cooper-
ative relationship with Israel, along the lines of that between the Jewish
state and Iran under the Shah in the mid-1900s or between Israel and
Turkey since relations were formalized in 1949.

The events that occurred between the end of the Persian Gulf War in
1991 and the onset of the Iraq War in 2003 are a textbook example of how
ambitious foreign activists can manipulate well-meaning American leaders. Because many portions of the U.S. political, foreign policy, and news
communities wanted to believe so badly that such a scenario was possible
(even those who were not allied with the neoconservatives), they were ripe
for the picking by determined Iraqi exiles. Hawkish types in the United
States thought they had a reliable, pro-democratic, Iraqi client to help oust
Saddam Hussein—the Iraqi National Congress (INC); in reality, though,
that client was exploiting American hawks to serve its own parochial
agenda of overthrowing Sunni strongman Saddam to replace him with a
Shiite leader of their own. As a result, the United States waged an unnecessary war that cost nearly 4,500 American lives and at least $2.2 trillion by
the time U.S. troops withdrew at the end of 2011.[5] With the resumption
of Washington's military involvement in 2013 to halt the growing menace
posed by the Islamic State, that total began to rise again. It also destabilized
Iraq, producing adverse consequences that still plague the United States
today. The conflict was bloody, counterproductive, and triggered by false
information fed to credulous U.S. officials, members of Congress, journalists, and foreign policy professionals by self-serving Iraqi exiles.

THE RISE OF THE IRAQI NATIONAL CONGRESS

As the agitation for a formal U.S. policy to overthrow Saddam grew,
so too did the enthusiasm for the INC, the most significant exile group
opposed to the Iraqi dictator. The leader of the INC was Ahmed Chalabi, whose family fled Iraq when he was a teenager. Longstanding evidence indicated that Chalabi and his associates were corrupt political
operators; indeed, the Jordanian government sought to prosecute Chalabi for various alleged financial crimes committed by his Petra Bank,
which collapsed in 1989.[6] In 1992, Chalabi was convicted in absentia by a

Jordanian court of having embezzled $230 million, and he was sentenced to 22 years in prison. In addition to allegations of financial illegalities, Chalabi also allegedly maintained disturbingly close ties to Iran's clerical regime—ties that began almost immediately after the overthrow of the pro-Western Shah in 1979.[7] More disturbing evidence: Chalabi's Petra Bank channeled money to Lebanon's Amal militia, one of Tehran's most prominent clients.

Despite such warning signs, the Central Intelligence Agency (CIA) funded the INC from its formation in 1992. Indeed, the agency—through a public relations front, the Rendon Group—even gave the organization its name.[8] Former CIA deputy of operations Thomas Twetten credits Rendon with virtually creating the INC. "The INC was clueless," Twetten said. "They needed a lot of help and didn't know where to start. That is why Rendon was brought in."[9] Chalabi's supporters in the United States, either unaware that the INC was a creature of the CIA or indifferent to that fact, portrayed him as the George Washington of Iraq. Chalabi assiduously cultivated political support in the United States. Francis Brooke, a close associate of Chalabi's in the 1990s, was candid about that goal: we "realized there were only a couple of hundred people in Washington who were influential in shaping policy toward Iraq."[10] Journalist Jane Mayer noted that Brooke and Chalabi

> set out to win these people over. Before long, Chalabi was on a first-name basis with thirty members of Congress, such as [Sen.] Trent Lott [R-MS] and [Speaker of the House] Newt Gingrich [R-GA], and was attending social functions with Richard Perle, a former assistant secretary of defense, who was now a senior fellow at the American Enterprise Institute, and Dick Cheney, who was CEO of Halliburton. According to Brooke, "From the beginning, Cheney was in philosophical agreement with this plan [to back the INC against Saddam]."[11]

Referring to the failure to overthrow Saddam during the Persian Gulf War, Cheney said, "Very seldom in life do you get a chance to fix something that went wrong."[12]

Chalabi's cultivation of powerful friends in Washington paid off. The January and February 1998 PNAC letters were major milestones. The latter pressed President Clinton to take nine policy steps that the signatories deemed essential to securing America's vital interests in the Middle East. The first recommendation was to "recognize a provisional government of Iraq based on the principles and leadership of the Iraqi National Congress (INC) that is representative of all the peoples of Iraq." Another proposed policy urged the president to release frozen Iraqi assets (totaling an estimated $1.6 billion in the United States and Britain), which then would be placed under the control of an INC-led provisional government "to fund its insurrection."[13]

In the months following the PNAC missives to Clinton, the authors and their political allies (especially Kristol, former chief of staff for Vice President Dan Quayle and founding editor of the influential *Weekly Standard* magazine) waged a focused campaign to ensure that the proposals set forth in the February PNAC letter were enacted into law. House Speaker Gingrich enthusiastically supported the effort, as did other members of the GOP's congressional leadership, but it was not merely a partisan venture: prominent Democrats also backed the idea of providing U.S. moral, organizational, and financial assistance to Iraqi exiles seeking to overthrow Saddam. The bipartisan effort paid off later that year with the passage of the Iraq Liberation Act of 1998. And both Congress and the Clinton administration clearly wanted the INC to be the principal financial beneficiary of that measure.

The Iraq Liberation Act passed with overwhelming bipartisan majorities: House Republicans voted in favor the measure 202 to 9, as did Democrats 157 to 29. The Senate passed the act without a single dissenting vote. Rumsfeld observed with satisfaction, "Regime change in Iraq was now the official policy of the United States."[14] President Clinton's signing statement confirmed that point:

> Today I am signing into law H.R. 4655, the "Iraq Liberation Act of 1998." This Act makes clear that it is the sense of the Congress that the United States should support those elements of the Iraqi opposition that advocate a very different future for Iraq than the bitter reality of internal repression and external aggression that the current regime in Baghdad now offers.
>
> Let me be clear on what the U.S. objectives are:
>
> The United States wants Iraq to rejoin the family of nations as a freedom-loving and law-abiding member. This is in our interest and that of our allies within the region.

The United States favors an Iraq that offers its people freedom at home. I categorically reject arguments that this is unattainable due to Iraq's history or its ethnic or sectarian makeup. Iraqis deserve and desire freedom like everyone else.

The United States looks forward to a democratically supported regime that would permit us to enter into a dialogue leading to the reintegration of Iraq into normal international life.[15]

Despite Clinton's statement and the pro-INC lobbying campaign, deep divisions existed within the defense, foreign policy, and intelligence communities about the wisdom of backing the "Iraqi externals" (as those agencies typically called the exile factions). Those divisions deepened once the Bush administration took office. By then, the CIA had pretty much stopped working with Chalabi after he botched some joint Kurdish-INC military offensives against Saddam's forces in 1995.[16] Rumsfeld recalls that the Defense Department "encountered strong resistance from [the Department of] State and the CIA to the idea of working with the Iraqi expatriates"; within those bastions, "Particular animus was directed against Ahmed Chalabi."[17] Rumsfeld did not share those misgivings in the least: "I couldn't quite understand why the idea was controversial," he said, noting that Chalabi had worked closely with the CIA during the 1990s, thus making the agency's hostility toward him even more puzzling.[18] Yet CIA leaders were wary of Chalabi precisely because they were familiar with him.

In his memoirs, Rumsfeld denies allegations (most notably, those of then-CIA Director George Tenet) that the Defense Department was engaged in "thinly veiled efforts to put Chalabi in charge of a post-invasion Iraq."[19] Rumsfeld contends that Chalabi "struck me as one of a number of bright Iraqis looking to do what they could for the country"; but, he insists, "No one in the Department of Defense urged that Chalabi be 'anointed' as the ruler of post-Saddam Iraq."[20] However, Rumsfeld issued that denial years later—after detrimental revelations about Chalabi had become commonplace. Looking back, though, Defense Department officials certainly appear to have pushed for a leadership role for Chalabi and the INC. And the Iraqi expatriate had his ardent admirers elsewhere in the U.S. foreign policy and political communities. Robert Blackwill, former U.S. ambassador to India, reportedly described Chalabi as "the Michael Jordan of Iraq"—a true superstar, indeed.[21]

George W. Bush was sworn in as president in 2001, and right-wing advocates for the INC watched as many of their ideological compatriots were appointed to high-level policy posts in the administration; the time to push their agenda to "liberate" Iraq was now. *New York Times* correspondent Judith Miller (who later would be at the center of a whirlwind storm concerning her role in disseminating faulty INC intelligence), points out that neoconservative activists wasted no time in promoting Chalabi and his organization to the new administration: "The day after President Bush's inauguration in January 2001, Richard Perle, an influential defense expert whom I had known for many years, . . . hosted a brunch for Chalabi and a small group of neocons who would soon occupy key national security posts . . . to discuss how best to persuade the new president to overthrow Saddam."[22]

Other analysts (even Chalabi himself) have confirmed Miller's account of that meeting. Attendees included Deputy Defense Secretary Wolfowitz; Under Secretary of Defense Douglas Feith; Khalilzad, who soon would become the administration's ambassador-at-large for Iraqi exiles; and John Hannah, Vice President Cheney's national security adviser. A centerpiece of the discussion was how to get the administration to provide more vigorous backing to the INC and its agenda.[23]

Interagency squabbling about Chalabi and the INC persisted up to and during the 2003 invasion, and CIA and State Department officials were not the only members of Bush's administration who felt uneasy about him. Condoleezza Rice, Bush's national security adviser, observed that, while there was "no doubting his intelligence," she also found Chalabi to be a "somewhat manipulative" figure.[24] Deputy Secretary of State Richard Armitage seemed even more suspicious about Chalabi and the INC. On a March 2008 segment of PBS's *Frontline,* he described the source of his misgivings:

When I got into the Department of State and I saw that we were required by congressional action to actually fund the INC, I started to look into his activities. I looked into trying to get some receipts, as a steward of the national funds, from him, not down to the penny, not down to the dollar, not even down to the hundred dollar. I just wanted to [sic] an idea of where the money was going. And when I couldn't get it, I couldn't get any receipts from him and he seemed upset about this, I no longer had the State Department fund him. The funding went to the Department of Defense. So it didn't take me long to come to the belief that Mr. Chalabi was a charlatan.[25]

For the most part, however, the administration's skepticism of Chalabi and the INC centered in the CIA. Rumsfeld fumed, "CIA officials opposed our efforts to constitute a force of Iraqi exiles to fight and act as interpreters and translators alongside our troops in the invasion." Once again, he considered the CIA's stance wrongheaded. "While not large in size, I believed the Free Iraqi Forces, as they were called, could be a useful corrective to the perception that the United States was invading Iraq to occupy the country rather than liberate it."[26] Because of the continuing opposition from the State Department and the CIA, he added, "We were unable to recruit and train enough Free Iraqi Forces to show that Iraqis were involved in the military campaign to rid their country of Saddam."[27]

A more likely explanation is that the INC and other exile groups lacked the credibility and popular support needed to attract a sufficient number of recruits to create an Iraqi nationalist façade for a U.S. invasion. U.S. officials would encounter similar obstacles a decade later when they sought to recruit, fund, and train "moderate" insurgents in Syria as an alternative to Bashar al-Assad's dictatorial regime and the radical Islamist insurgents of the Islamic State (Chapter 10).

Bush administration policymakers and other INC boosters could not admit the possibility that the group had weak support inside Iraq. To make such an acknowledgment would be to contradict the entire narrative that the administration had been pushing. Moreover, the fighters the INC *did* recruit showed very little competence. *Washington Post* lead reporter Bob Woodward concludes that, although the group received American-sponsored training, "Everything about the military group had been a bust. Besides training only a tiny fraction of the number that was supposed to be armed and ready, there had even been a fight over what the group should be called. Chalabi's band was eventually given the alliterative but redundant name Free Iraqi Freedom Fighters."[28]

LURING THE UNITED STATES INTO WAR

The INC superbly exploited Defense Department officials' trust, as well as the trust of members of Congress and other centers of support. Chalabi continuously fed the U.S. government and key news media outlets—in particular the *New York Times*—bogus information about two developments that were certain to alarm the American people and generate public pressure for war. One line of faulty intelligence highlighted Saddam's alleged ties to al Qaeda—the group responsible for the September 11, 2001, terrorist attacks.

The INC's "intelligence" linking Saddam to al Qaeda included knowledge of clandestine meetings between Iraqi officials and leaders of the terrorist organization. On October 27, 2001, the *New York Times* published a key story by Patrick Tyler and John Tagliabue alleging that an Iraqi intelligence agent met with 9/11 ringleader and hijacker Muhammed Atta and other al Qaeda operatives in Prague shortly before the attacks.[29] Additionally, the article reported "new information" to suggest that "Hussein was actively training terrorists to attack American interests throughout the 1990's," citing a PBS *Frontline* interview in which an Iraqi army captain and defector described terrorist training camps where non-Iraqi Arabs were trained "on assassinations, kidnapping, hijacking of airplanes . . . and all other kinds of operations related to terrorism."[30] When Miller met with Chalabi at Reagan Washington National Airport in November 2001, he confirmed the role he had played in that story and another *Times* piece:

> I mentioned to Chalabi two *Times* stories that seemed to have his fingerprints all over them. The more explosive was about a defector: an Iraqi general who had allegedly seen his officers train Arab fighters to hijack airplanes without weapons at a camp near Salman Pak in Iraq. The story suggested a link between Iraq and Al Qaeda—and, hence, between Iraq and 9/11. Had he been responsible for that story? Yes, Chalabi confirmed that he had connected my *Times* colleagues and others to the general, as well as other defectors.[31]

Later, when administration policymakers and their political allies were called to account for intelligence that they claimed proved Saddam possessed weapons of mass destruction—and which ultimately led the United States to invade Iraq—Chalabi's previous meddling cast serious doubts on their claims that the intelligence came neither from him nor the INC. David Wurmser, one of the most hardline analysts in the Office of Special Plans within the Department of Defense, which critics accused of being especially guilty of cherry-picking intelligence data to "prove" the case against Saddam, offered precisely that testimony in his posthumous tribute to Chalabi published in the *National Review* after Chalabi's death in 2015: "I and my colleagues (one of whom later became a Democratic congressman) in this period had absolutely no information from Chalabi and instead relied on pre-existing intelligence collected by our intelligence agencies in official channels." Wurmser insisted that instead, "What we did import from Chalabi was his optimism and faith in a better future for his people. . . ."[32]

While Bush administration officials denied that Chalabi had been the source of the "weapons of mass destruction" intelligence, they eagerly accepted the INC's intelligence about alleged Iraqi collaboration with al Qaeda, especially about the purported meeting between Atta and the Iraqi intelligence agent in Prague less than five months before the 9/11 attacks. Yet the administration was receiving information from its own intelligence agencies that cast grave doubt on whether such a meeting ever took place. In 2012, the National Security Archive released a declassified CIA briefing paper that was issued to the White House on December 8, 2001. That document included the finding that the alleged meeting between Atta and the Iraqi official did not happen.[33] Yet the following day, Cheney appeared on NBC's *Meet the Press* and used the phantom Prague meeting to incriminate Iraq in the 9/11 attacks.[34] In other words, the White House had received disconfirming information about the Atta meeting from its own intelligence community as early as December 2001, but they basically ignored it, choosing instead to rely on Chalabi's claims.

The CIA was not the only agency that was skeptical about the information flow from the INC. Appearing on the PBS program *Frontline* in

2008, Mark Garlasco, an official with the Defense Intelligence Agency from 1997 to 2003, stated, "We had INC constantly shoving crap at us. You know, they were providing information that they thought that we wanted to hear. They were feeding the beast."[35]

And the beast ate it up. BBC and *al Jazeera* analyst Muhammad Idrees Ahmad describes the progression of the narrative. He notes that the *New York Times* was not the only major news outlet to break stories alleging that Iraq and al Qaeda were close allies who had colluded in the 9/11 attacks. *Washington Post* columnist Jim Hoagland did the same in an article on October 12, 2001, again relying heavily on information supplied by Iraqi defectors. The incestuous nature of the East Coast's elite news community became clear, Ahmad contends, when *Times* columnist William Safire then cited Hoagland's story as "evidence" of Baghdad's culpability in the terrorist assault.[36] Safire repeated and amplified the allegations about collusion between Atta and the Iraqi government in a column the following May.[37] Ahmad observes caustically, "Safire would harp on this theme well into 2003, long after it had been discarded by others."[38] In November 2001, PBS's *Frontline* gave a platform to prominent American advocates of war with Iraq (including Perle, former CIA director Woolsey, and former ambassador to Israel Dennis Ross), along with Chalabi and a bevy of INC-supplied Iraqi defectors who pushed the narrative of Saddam's link to al Qaeda.[39]

In December of that year, British journalist David Rose joined the fray with a long article in *Vanity Fair* highlighting Iraq's alleged role in 9/11. His article was based on testimony from a defector furnished to him by the INC. Rose showed no signs of skepticism about the accuracy of the defector's information; indeed, he appeared on CNN and NBC to repeat the unsupported allegations. At one point he told NBC's Chris Mathews that 9/11 was a "joint operation between al Qaeda and Iraq." The thesis seemed to become an obsession with Rose. Ahmad points out that in the time leading up to the U.S. invasion of Iraq in March 2003, Rose "would produce three more equally fantastic reports, all referencing INC defectors."[40]

The second intelligence stream featured alleged defector Adnan Ihsan Saeed al-Haideri, who provided "evidence" that Saddam's government was vigorously expanding its arsenal of "weapons of mass destruction" (WMDs)—specifically, chemical and biological weapons.[41] Most worrisome, Haideri contended that Baghdad was actively pursuing a nuclear weapons program and had already made substantial advances. INC operatives filled in the holes in Haideri's story, embellished the allegations, and concealed the meager extent of Haideri's expertise regarding WMD issues.[42] Chalabi put Haideri in touch with his good friend Judith Miller, who broke the story in a *New York Times* exclusive.[43] Investigative reporter and Chalabi biographer Aram Roston notes, "The story splashed across the newspapers of the world like a can of paint. Reuters, the AP, and other wire services picked it up. Newspapers from Australia to Austin, Texas, ran the story. Network news anchors read terse accounts of it."[44]

As longtime national security writer James Bamford concludes: "It was damning stuff—just the kind of evidence the Bush administration was looking for." If the charges were true, they gave the White House a compelling reason to invade Iraq and depose Saddam. There was only one problem, Bamford notes: "It was all a lie."[45] Indeed, the CIA suspected as much and gave Haideri a polygraph test, which he failed.

Nevertheless, Chalabi and his INC associates continued to peddle the allegation that Saddam was developing WMDs that posed a grave danger to both regional peace and U.S. security. Haideri became the first in a series of "helpful sources" that the INC offered to Bush administration officials and major media outlets. The most prominent individual was a man with the code name "Curveball," who elaborated on some of the allegations first made by Haideri and others. Curveball was a crucial source of bogus information to American journalists about the WMD threat in the period leading up to the U.S. invasion; and, as it turned out, he was the younger brother of a close Chalabi aide,[46] which at least should have generated some caution among both U.S. intelligence officials and journalists. Curveball's accounts of Baghdad's supposed alliance with al Qaeda ultimately proved to be as bogus as the other defectors'.

Miller was an especially useful conduit for the INC's disinformation campaign. Miller was a close confidant of White House aide L. Lewis (Scooter) Libby and other leading neoconservatives in the Bush administration, and she had been a trusted outlet for INC propaganda for years.[47]

Given her repeated assertions that she had high-level contacts within the intelligence community, Miller certainly should have been aware that the CIA had already determined that Haideri's information was unreliable. Instead of exercising caution, though, beginning in December 2001, she published a series of articles hyping the WMD allegations. Bamford notes, "For months, hawks inside and outside the administration had been pressing for a pre-emptive attack on Iraq." Now, thanks to Miller's stories, "They could point to 'proof' of Saddam's 'nuclear threat.'"[48]

Despite extended search efforts after the successful U.S. invasion of Iraq, the United States and other international inspectors never found any caches of Iraqi weapons of mass destruction. What few WMD stocks they did find consisted of obsolete, decaying weapons from the 1980s or earlier—items that were useless for any military purpose. All but the most stubborn defenders of the Bush administration had to accept the fact that the information the INC had so generously provided was exaggerated at best and utterly fictitious at worst. When the evidence became undeniable, Chalabi shrugged off charges that he and his colleagues had deliberately misled the United States. "We were heroes in error," he told reporters. And he was surprisingly candid in his "ends justify the means" rationale: "As far as we're concerned, we've been entirely successful. That tyrant Saddam is gone and the Americans are in Baghdad. *What was said before is not important.*"[49]

Miller and other journalists who circulated the INC's disinformation have gone to great lengths to wash their hands of the policy disaster that ensued. In an April 2015 *Wall Street Journal* op-ed, Miller denied all responsibility for helping build a false case for war.[50] She protested, "Relying on the mistakes of others and [making] errors of judgment are not the same as lying." Miller would repeat and amplify her denials of culpability in her subsequent memoir.[51]

Her point is a valid one: relying on faulty sources and making errors in judgment are not the same as lying. But critics justifiably point out that Miller treated the information fed to her by INC operatives with a naiveté unworthy of a serious journalist—especially one writing for the most prestigious and influential newspaper in the United States, if not the world. Only days after Miller's memoir was published, a group of U.S. intelligence veterans that included former United Nations weapons inspector Scott Ritter responded to Miller's defense of herself: "It's almost as though she is saying that if Ahmed Chalabi told her that in Iraq the sun rises in the west, and she duly reported it, that would not be 'the same as lying.'" The rebuttal went on to say that "Judith Miller will be judged" for "authoring stories for the 'newspaper of record' that were questionably sourced and very often misleading." The Ritter et al. memo concludes that Miller "played a pivotal role in building the public case for an attack on Iraq based on shoddy reporting that even her editor at the *New York Times* has since discredited—including overreliance on a single source of easy virtue and questionable credibility—Ahmed Chalabi."[52]

The fact that Miller's employer was the *New York Times* was especially crucial to her role in helping to lead the United States to war. To a great extent, the *Times* sets the news agenda for television, radio, and print coverage—especially on international issues—because media outlets throughout the country and around the world routinely reprint its articles. *Times* stories are widely circulated, and, not surprisingly, panicky accounts of Iraq's alleged WMDs were quickly amplified worldwide. In her memoirs, Miller bristles at suggestions that she and other members of the media pushed America into a disastrous war, noting that none of them had the authority to set policy.[53] That argument is true technically, but it is disingenuous. She and other pro-war journalists helped to shape—rather, distort—public opinion to support a crusade to depose Saddam. Miller was, therefore, an enabler of a disastrous, avoidable war. To be blunt, she served as one of the INC's most valuable "useful idiots."

The impact that the INC's misinformation had on the direction of U.S. policy cannot be overstated. The culmination of the INC–neoconservative propaganda campaign came during Secretary of State Colin Powell's presentation to the United Nations (UN) Security Council in February 2003. There he laid out the administration's case on both Saddam's alleged cozy relationship with al Qaeda and Iraq's WMD arsenal. Powell later would describe the speech as a major failure on the part of America's intelligence community and as a "blot" on his own record.[54] His own culpability in selling the bogus case for war is considerable. He was an extremely useful—perhaps even essential—tool for pro-war forces. If Rumsfeld or any other notoriously hawkish administration official had delivered the presentation, the public likely would have received it with more skepticism, because Rumsfeld and those like him were pushing hard for war. But Powell was widely respected across the political spectrum and had a long-standing reputation for sober policy views. Having his imprimatur on the case against Iraq legitimized the INC-supplied propaganda and solidified both elite and public support for military action.[55]

Confronting Troubling Political Realities in War-Torn Iraq

Pro-intervention lobbyists got what they wanted in March 2003, when the United States launched a full-scale invasion of Iraq to overthrow Saddam Hussein. To the surprise of very few, it was a thoroughly one-sided conflict. Within weeks, "coalition" (overwhelmingly U.S.) forces entered Baghdad, and the Iraqi dictator fled the capital, only to be captured later that December when he was discovered hiding in a crude underground shelter near his birthplace of Tikrit. But the military phase of the mission to overthrow Saddam proved to be the easy part of Washington's regime-change war.

Not only did Chalabi and the INC's reliability as intelligence assets prove illusory, so too did their alleged political support inside Iraq. A few weeks after the war began, Chalabi and his allies in the administration pressured the U.S. military to fly the tiny group of Free Iraqi Freedom Fighters into Iraq. Although the United States finally acquiesced, the exile force did not receive a warm welcome. Their conduct was hardly exemplary, either; reports of reprisals and looting immediately began to circulate.[56]

Divisions persisted within the Bush administration about how to facilitate the political transition in post-Saddam Iraq. The Pentagon established the Office for Reconstruction and Humanitarian Assistance and appointed Jay Garner, a retired U.S. Army lieutenant general, who had ably directed the civilian relief effort in Iraq's Kurdish region following the 1991 Persian Gulf War, to head the operation. With respect to his new mission, Garner advocated a restrained role for the United States and other outside powers. Foreign policy scholar Andrew Bacevich, author of *America's War for the Greater Middle East*, concludes that Garner "saw his role as akin to that of a midwife. Garner and his team would encourage and coach, but Iraqis themselves would do the hard work of birthing. It was, after all, their country."[57] Rumsfeld soon desired a more activist approach, though, and he replaced Garner with L. Paul Bremer at the head of a renamed entity, the Coalition Provisional Authority.

Bacevich observes correctly that the stark contrast between Garner's and Bremer's approaches reflected a continuing division within the highest levels of the administration. Officials were "of two minds about how best to bring the 'new' Iraq into existence. In one camp were those favoring an approach akin to the Allied liberation of France in 1944: Vanquish the occupiers, hand over military authority to an Iraqi version of General Charles de Gaulle, and have done with it."[58]

Chalabi's biggest fans in the administration were usually members of that camp, who saw him as the Iraqi de Gaulle and the INC as the equivalent of the Free French Forces. But as Bacevich observes caustically, both assumptions were "absurd." De Gaulle had a well-earned reputation for integrity, and as the most prominent leader of the resistance in exile, he had become a hero to most French during their country's painful foreign occupation by Germany. None of those features applied to Chalabi's situation. Nevertheless, the Chalabi hero worship in some administration circles remained very strong. According to Dov S. Zakheim, a senior official in the Pentagon, Under Secretary of Defense Feith wanted Garner simply to "declare Chalabi president."[59]

But in other administration circles, resistance to a rapid transition to Iraqi self-rule—whether under Chalabi or any other figure—was growing. Bacevich notes that in this camp "were those who saw the problem as analogous to liberating Nazi Germany after 1945: Only after those implicated in the crimes of the previous regime had been identified and punished could the creation of a new order go forward. Bremer leaned toward the second approach."[60] Chalabi wanted a combination of the two policies: an instant transfer of authority to Iraqi leaders (first and foremost, himself), but with the ultimate objective of thoroughly purging Iraq of personnel who had been involved in Saddam's rule.

Washington's pro-INC faction generally prevailed, although not quite to the extent that they had hoped and expected. Chalabi did not become Iraq's U.S.-designated political leader, but the Bush administration did make sure that he had a high-level position in the country's transitional ruling body, which was overseen by the Coalition Provisional Authority. Specifically, Chalabi was put in charge of the de-Baathification program to purge the Iraqi political system of Saddam Hussein's supporters.[61]

That proved to be a dreadful and fateful choice. Chalabi used his post not only as a lucrative sinecure to provide jobs for relatives and political followers, but he also worked with Shiite zealots to make the purge as broad and deep as possible. He also kept personal custody of the files of Iraq's now defunct intelligence service. As the *Washington Post*'s Woodward writes, "Those files were a prime source of information on who had been a true believer" in Saddam's regime and who had been functionaries just going through the motions. As a result of Chalabi's hoarding, it was "almost impossible" for either U.S. military leaders or other officials in Iraq's interim government "to determine levels of involvement."[62]

Even civil servants who had been little more than perfunctory members of the Baath Party—a basic requirement if one had any hope of career advancement in Iraq during Saddam's rule—now found themselves out of work. Moreover, a disproportionate percentage of the purge targets were Sunnis, which exacerbated the already surging resentment Sunnis felt toward the new Shiite- and Kurdish-dominated government in Baghdad. That resentment would explode into civil war in 2006 and 2007. Chalabi's rigorous de-Baathification campaign was hardly the only factor to produce that outcome, but it certainly played a role.

Chalabi's influential post in the transition authority did not translate into meaningful voter support. Public opinion surveys taken in 2005 showed Chalabi only modestly more popular than Saddam Hussein. The latter had a 22 percent favorable rating and 78 percent unfavorable; Chalabi's approval rating was 34 percent favorable, 66 percent unfavorable.[63]

Even most Iraqi Shiites seemed to prefer other candidates. When parliamentary elections were held in December 2005, Chalabi's party garnered barely 0.5 percent of the vote. So much for the political superstar—the Iraqi Michael Jordan—that U.S. officials and American pro-democracy activists believed would be the popular leader of a new Iraq.

Rumsfeld notes that President Bush "often expressed his belief that freedom was the gift of the Almighty. He seemed to feel almost duty bound to help expand the frontiers of freedom in the Middle East."[64] Indeed, Bush at one point asserted that the desire for freedom and democracy was universal: "Muslims desire to be free just like Methodists desire to be free," he said at one point during an interview with friendly and mostly conservative journalists.[65] Bush's statement was an explicit rejection of the notion that cultural factors play any role in popular attitudes toward government, democracy, or respect for individual rights, and it failed to appreciate the historical chasm that existed between the experiences of Middle East societies and those of the West, especially the United States.

Rumsfeld now insists that he had always been skeptical of the prospects for democracy in Iraq and elsewhere in the Middle East. "Emphasis on Iraqi democracy invited critics of the war to find the innumerable instances in which Iraq would inevitably fall short," he writes.[66] Whether Rumsfeld actually held those views at the time, and not just with 20/20 hindsight, is unknown. But even if he had been a cautious skeptic from the outset, many of his Defense Department deputies who lobbied for a leadership role for Chalabi were not.

Vice President Cheney's office also was deeply involved in those lobbying efforts. Cheney himself met with a delegation of Iraqi exiles in August 2002, but that meeting was simply another in a series of initiatives to demonstrate that the administration supported their goal of overthrowing Saddam. Cheney later admitted that "since January 2002, [vice presidential aide] Libby had been urging the State Department to get the major Iraqi opposition groups together for an international conference to begin planning for a post-Saddam government." But that idea encountered resistance, Cheney recalled to his disgust. "Secretary Powell and Deputy Secretary Armitage warned about too much engagement with

Saddam's opponents. They were 'externals,' or so the argument went, who left Iraq during Saddam's reign and would not have credibility with Iraqis who had stayed."[67]

Cheney, like Rumsfeld, sneered at such reasoning. "I think we would have done a better job in the wake of Saddam's ouster if we had had a provisional government, made up of externals and internals, ready to take over as soon as Saddam fell. This would have put Iraqis in charge of Iraq and helped avoid the taint of occupation that we began to experience under the Coalition Provisional Authority."[68] Of course, Chalabi and the INC would have been the single strongest, most influential component of such a coalition—something that would not have displeased Chalabi's admirers in the Defense Department and the vice president's office in the slightest.

The belief that the INC would be the vanguard of a democratic Iraq was a crucial factor driving U.S. policy. After all, installing the INC to head the provisional government theoretically would neutralize, or at least soften, Iraqis' perception that Saddam's overthrow was the product of a foreign invasion and occupation. But, at least for some American backers, the hope that post-Saddam Iraq actually would become a democratic, well-governed country seemed genuine. Logically, Iraqis should lead such a transformation, with only some assistance from the United States.

That point came through rather clearly in Cheney's August 26, 2002, speech to the Veterans of Foreign Wars. Although he warned that Saddam was determined to "acquire the whole range of weapons of mass destruction" (implying that a nuclear arsenal was one of the Iraqi dictator's goals), Cheney put great emphasis on a different, much broader, goal than neutralizing that threat: "With our help, a liberated Iraq can be a great nation once again." Washington's goal was nothing less than "an Iraq that has territorial integrity, a government that is democratic and pluralistic, a nation where the human rights of every ethnic group are recognized and protected." Such a country would know "they have a friend and ally in the United States of America."[69]

Cheney's vision bore almost no resemblance to the reality of a bitterly divided Iraq riven by sectarian animosity. Of course, Chalabi and the

INC did nothing to alert the Bush administration to those impending dangers, nor did the INC's collaborators in the United States. Kristol summarily dismissed warnings that a serious risk of sectarian violence existed in Iraq, asserting in an April 2003 National Public Radio interview that the notion that "somehow the Shia can't get along with the Sunni" in Iraq was nothing more than "pop sociology."[70] Events later would prove his complacent assessment spectacularly wrong.

AFTERMATH: MOST HAWKS STILL REFUSE TO ADMIT THEY WERE CONNED

As evidence accumulated that Chalabi's supposed support among the Iraqi people was a mirage and that he and his organization seemed to be reaching out to Tehran, the Bush administration began to distance itself from its onetime client. In spring 2004, Iraqi police, backed by U.S. troops, raided Chalabi's home, as well as offices in the INC's new headquarters in Baghdad. The Iraq government's investigation produced allegations of embezzlement, theft, and kidnapping against high-level INC officials. Even before the raid, several of Chalabi's lieutenants had fled Iraq, and more would do so now.[71]

One of those top aides, Aras Karim Habib, the INC's chief of intelligence, already was under intense scrutiny by Iraqi and U.S. investigators for allegedly passing along classified U.S. documents to Iran. He escaped Iraq just before being served a warrant for his arrest. U.S. officials asserted that Habib had been a paid agent of Tehran's for years.[72] Some members of the intelligence community even began to express suspicions that Iran had orchestrated a sophisticated disinformation campaign, using its allies in the INC, precisely for the purpose of getting the United States to invade Iraq and depose Saddam, Tehran's longtime nemesis.[73] In any case, given the mounting evidence of INC wrongdoing, the Bush administration finally cut off funding to the organization.[74]

Chalabi was not about to acknowledge any wrongdoing, however. "It's customary when great events happen that the U.S. punishes its friends and rewards its enemies," he told New Yorker staff writer Jane Mayer.[75] In this case, the "great events" were mounting signs that Washington's occupation effort was going badly, including violent incidents that heralded the rise of an insurgency. Bush officials needed a scapegoat, Chalabi charged, and apparently he was it.

Disillusionment with the INC was slower to develop outside the Bush administration, but eventually a few staunch conservative supporters concluded that they had been duped. Establishment types, especially on the liberal side of the political spectrum, were more inclined to admit error. The *New York Times* even published an editorial in 2004 conceding that its reporters had relied too heavily on information from "a circle of Iraqi informants, defectors, and exiles bent on 'regime change.'"[76] The disillusionment accelerated once it became clear that there were no "weapons of mass destruction" to be found in Iraq, and that instead of being welcomed as liberators, American forces were becoming the target of angry insurgents. "Ahmed Chalabi is a treacherous, spineless turncoat," stated L. Marc Zell, former law partner of Under Secretary of Defense Feith: "He had one set of friends before he was in power, and now he's got another."[77] Zell was referring to evidence of Chalabi's increasingly close ties to the Iranian government.

Yet the Iraqi politician's tilt toward Tehran should not have come as a surprise. Chalabi was, after all, a Shiite political luminary, and it was logical for him to seek support among his coreligionists in Iran. Indeed, Iranian backing seemed crucial to preventing any chance of a restored Sunni domination in Iraq. The last thing that Iraqi Shiites wanted to risk was the emergence of a new government that amounted to little more than continued Sunni Baath party rule, just without Saddam Hussein. Iraq's Shiite majority had been marginalized and oppressed for decades, and now they intended to rule. A friendly Iran could facilitate that goal, while a hostile Iran could undermine it. Beyond that consideration, Chalabi had already shown himself to be a rank opportunist. Robert Baer, a former CIA field officer who was in charge of covert operations to undermine Saddam in the mid- and late-1990s, notes that Chalabi "was willing to ally with anyone to get where he is now, whether it was the neocons, the Israelis or the Iranians. He wanted back into Iraq and nothing was going to stop him."[78]

Zell's disillusionment must have been painful. Chalabi had met with Zell, Feith, and other leading American neoconservatives numerous times between the mid-1990s and the 2003 invasion. Zell recalls what Chalabi had promised his American supporters: "He said he would end Iraq's boycott of trade with Israel, and would allow Israeli companies to do business there. He said the new Iraqi government would agree to rebuild the pipeline from Mosul [in the northern Iraqi oilfields] to Haifa [an Israeli port and the location of a major refinery]."[79] As it turns out, Zell concluded glumly, Chalabi delivered on none of his promises.

In retrospect, the only surprise was the extent of the naiveté among Chalabi's neoconservative supporters. The reality was, no Iraqi government could develop cozy links to Israel and hope to survive the ensuing domestic political firestorm. *Financial Times* correspondent John Dizard puts it well: "Had the neocons not been deluded by gross ignorance of the Arab world and blindsided by wishful thinking, they would have realized that the chances that Chalabi or any other Iraqi leader could deliver on such promises were always remote."[80] Israel is widely hated in Iraq, just as it is in most Muslim (especially Arab) countries. The notion that an Iraqi regime would welcome Israeli investment was preposterous, and the prospect of a pipeline was a pipe dream. Chalabi simply told his American neoconservative backers what he knew they desperately wanted to hear. Playing that cynical game assured that their financial and political support for his ambitions would continue. And with dedicated neoconservative backing, more skeptical types during the Clinton and Bush years either were intimidated into acquiescence or swept along in the current of enthusiasm for the INC.

TRUE BELIEVERS CONTINUE TO SING CHALABI'S PRAISES

Amazingly, despite the mounting evidence of Chalabi's perfidy, many of his American admirers, especially on the right, continued to support him. Richard Perle lauded Chalabi's alleged capabilities and values: "He's effective in bringing groups of Iraqis together," Perle told CNN in March 2004. "He believes in democracy. I have complete confidence in him, and I hope that the people of Iraq are wise enough to see his benefits."[81] Perle's assessment—particularly his implication that he and other American policymakers understood the kind of leadership Iraq needed

better than the Iraqis did—was incredibly patronizing. It was also astonishing, considering that Chalabi, in his behavior, came nowhere close to
matching that idealized image.

Perle was not the only leading neoconservative to persist in wishful thinking on the subject. Some of Chalabi's supporters were enraged
when the Bush administration began to distance itself from him.
Danielle Pletka, vice president of the conservative public policy think
tank the American Enterprise Institute, blasted Chalabi's critics: "The
recent reports detailing the alleged perfidy of Ahmad Chalabi actually
say much more about his accusers in the U.S. government than they
do about Chalabi himself," she wrote in a June 2004 *Los Angeles Times*
op-ed. "They reveal Washington as a faithless friend and its agencies as
more concerned with carrying out vendettas than with pursuing the real
enemies of the United States."[82] Chalabi's real sin, according to Pletka,
was that he "never accepted the premise that it was better to accept a
tyrant in Iraq than risk destabilizing the Middle East. In so doing, he
earned himself the undying hostility of a variety of Washington players."

Pletka's admiration of Chalabi clearly remained intact; she gushed:
"There were all too few Iraqis who were willing to risk life and limb
to topple Hussein, and there were even fewer who believed in Western
democratic values. Chalabi was one." And she offered a prediction: "In
the end, little of this storm over Chalabi will matter to the man himself.
As a target of American harassment, he has renewed his credibility in the
eyes of his people."[83]

She was wrong. Chalabi's dismal performance in Iraq's elections—
that took place just a few months later and in which his party garnered
less than 1 percent of the popular vote and did not win a single seat
in parliament—demonstrated that Pletka's predictions about his alleged
enduring domestic popularity had been just as wrong as her previous
belief that the U.S. invasion would bring stability and democracy to Iraq.

Even a decade later, some neoconservatives, including American
Enterprise Institute scholar Michael Rubin, still refused to repudiate
Chalabi.[84] Wolfowitz and Chalabi's other hard-core American admir-
ers even tried to generate a boomlet of support for his candidacy as
Prime Minister Nouri al-Maliki's hold on power faded.[85] Wolfowitz

acknowledged Chalabi's close ties to Iran, but he seemed to place much of the blame at the door of the United States. Noting that the United States cut ties with Chalabi in 2004, Wolfowitz stated, "We've put him in a situation where, in my view, he's much too close to Iran."[86] The clear implication was that if an ungrateful Washington had not spurned him, Chalabi wouldn't have turned to Iran. That statement exceeded even the typical tendency of democracy promoters to overlook their chosen clients' flaws and to deny irrefutable evidence regarding foreign policy realities.

In David Wurmser's 2015 eulogy of Chalabi, he gushed that Chalabi had been nothing less than "an evangelist for Middle East reform."[87] To the extent that Chalabi had any weakness, Wurmser contended, it was a noble one: having too much faith in the ability of Arab political systems (and, more broadly, Arab culture) to overcome decades of authoritarian corruption and embrace freedom and democracy. Such comments underscore that Wurmser and others like him who view democracy as an American export product persistently fail to acknowledge that their supposedly honorable foreign partners often are not what they seem.

ASSIGNING BLAME

Washington's support of the INC was yet another case of misplaced hopes and erroneous expectations, with policymakers in two administrations ignoring pervasive warning signs. The CIA acted as the midwife for the birth of the INC in 1992; Iraqi police and U.S. troops raided Chalabi's Baghdad offices in 2004. In the intervening years, the United States had given the organization more than $100 million.[88] In exchange, Washington was the recipient of a propaganda campaign and a deluge of bogus intelligence information designed to entice the United States to carry out the INC's goal of overthrowing Saddam Hussein. Vincent Cannistraro, a former CIA counterterrorism specialist, provides a succinct verdict regarding the fruits of Washington's INC sponsorship: "With Chalabi, we paid to fool ourselves. It's horrible. In other times, it might be funny. But a lot of people are dead as a result of this. It's reprehensible."[89]

Excoriating Chalabi and his cronies for a campaign of deception that ultimately entangled the United States in a counterproductive war whose adverse consequences continue to reverberate even today is easy and, to some extent, justifiable. But more blame accrues to policymakers in the Clinton and Bush administrations who failed to do their due diligence. Former ambassador Peter Galbraith's blunt assessment rings true. Galbraith, a one-time supporter of Chalabi's, states that, as early as the 1980s, Chalabi figured out "that the road to Baghdad ran through Washington. He cultivated whom he needed to know. If he didn't get what he wanted from State, he went to Capitol Hill. It's a sign of being effective. It's not his fault that his strategy succeeded. It's not his fault that the Bush Administration believed everything he said. Should they have? Of course not. They should have looked critically"; after all, Chalabi's clear goal from the beginning "was to get the U.S. to invade Iraq."[90]

Galbraith's observations are rather cynical, but they also have considerable validity. Chalabi and his associates may have engaged in persistent and pervasive deception, if not outright lies. But American officials and journalists allowed the INC to manipulate both them and U.S. policy. Ultimately, they bear primary culpability for the resulting mess in Iraq.

CHAPTER SEVEN

MORE SUSPECT FREEDOM
FIGHTERS: IRAN'S MEK

Many of the same opinion leaders that pushed both the Clinton and Bush administrations to support Ahmed Chalabi and the Iraqi National Congress (INC) during the lead-up to the Iraq War also pushed the Obama administration to support the People's Mujahideen or Mujahideen-e-Khalq (MEK) in Iran. Even now, they are enlisting support from within the Trump administration to pursue the same goals in Iran that they had for Iraq: forcible regime change aided by Iranians in exile who hate that country's governing clerical regime.

While abundant evidence indicates that the MEK has meager support inside Iran, little evidence indicates that the organization has any respect for either democratic values or human rights, even when applying generous definitions of those concepts. The MEK's conduct is depressingly different from the image of a tolerant, secular democratic faction that it and its American supporters have fostered. Instead, the movement is a weird political cult built around the husband and wife team of Massoud and Maryam Rajavi—although Massoud has not been seen in public for more than a decade. The MEK is guilty of numerous terrorist acts, and until February 2012, the U.S. government formally listed it as a terrorist organization. Once again, the enthusiasm that some American opinion leaders have shown for foreign, so-called democratic insurgents appears to be misplaced.

Americans who express their support for the MEK display a disturbing degree of self-deception. Yes, the MEK is supposedly dedicated to ousting Iran's extremist clerical regime and bringing freedom and democracy to Iran, but its American admirers tend to ignore or dismiss evidence of the organization's terrorist roots and ongoing autocratic internal governance. They also typically dismiss evidence of the group's cultish, pseudo-religious nature and its record of human-rights abuses—including its mistreatment of group members who fail to exhibit rote conformity to the leadership's demands.

The MEK's Curious—and Troubling—History

The Mujahedeen-e-Khalq did not start out as an enemy of Iran's clerical regime; in fact, it began long before the mullahs came to power at the conclusion of the 1979 Iranian Revolution, and its original orientation seemed strongly Marxist. The MEK was founded in 1965 by leftist Iranian students opposed to Mohammad Reza Pahlavi, Shah of Iran, who at the time was one of Washington's major diplomatic and strategic allies.[1] The United States was in the MEK's crosshairs during those early years: in the late 1960s and throughout the 1970s, the MEK directed terrorist attacks that killed several Americans working in Iran. The organization now denies a connection to those attacks, claiming that they were committed by a breakaway faction that emerged after the Shah's security forces jailed MEK leader Massoud Rajavi.[2] However, those denials occurred only after the MEK began its campaign to win support from Washington.

When the Islamic revolution broke out against the Shah in late 1978 and early 1979, the MEK was an avid participant. The U.S. government claims that the MEK also was involved in the November 1979 raid on the U.S. embassy in Tehran, during which the diplomatic staff were taken hostage. MEK leaders now deny involvement in the embassy assault, but contemporary accounts contradict those denials. A 2011 State Department report on terrorism concluded: "Though denied by the MEK, analysis based on eyewitness accounts and MEK documents demonstrates that MEK members participated in and supported" the embassy takeover. Moreover, "The MEK later argued against the early release [of] the American hostages."[3]

The MEK's odd blend of Marxism, feminism, and Islamism soon brought it into sharp conflict with the Islamic Republic of Iran, the new, staunchly Islamist clerical regime established by Ayatollah Ruhollah Khomeini after his successful 1979 ouster of the Shah. Khomeini's regime soon began to crack down on its erstwhile allies, including the MEK, but the group did not fade away quietly. In July 1981, the MEK established a parallel parliament, the National Council of Resistance of Iran. It also struck at the Ayatollah by assassinating dozens of senior Iranian government officials.[4] The most high-profile attack was an August 1981 bombing that killed Iran's president, Mohammad Ali Rajai, and the country's prime minister, Mohammed Javad Bahonar.[5] Soon after the dual assassination, the MEK's top leadership fled Iran to escape the wrath of the Islamic Republic's security forces. Hundreds of MEK activists, including most of the top leadership, went into exile in France, where they remained until President Jacques Chirac's government officially expelled the group in 1986. Despite that order, dozens of MEK members stayed in France until the early 2000s.

Following its expulsion from France, the MEK leadership joined forces with Iraqi dictator Saddam Hussein. From new bases in Iraq and in conjunction with Iraqi forces, MEK fighters launched attacks against Iranian military units and other targets. Indeed, the MEK's military arm became a significant player in Saddam's bloody war of aggression against Iran throughout the 1980s. Western authorities noticed that many of the MEK's attacks were against civilian targets. European governments began to pay more attention to the organization's behavior, and they did not like what they saw. The European Union (EU) declared the MEK a terrorist organization in 2002; the following year, French authorities conducted a new crackdown, arresting more than 150 MEK members for allegedly plotting and financing terrorist attacks outside of France.[6]

Washington's initial attitude toward the MEK was equally unfavorable. The State Department added the MEK to its list of terrorist organizations in 1997; during the 2003 U.S.-led invasion of Iraq, U.S. forces attacked MEK targets along with those of Saddam's government, despite the MEK's protestations of neutrality. As Washington consolidated its occupation of Iraq, U.S. military leaders negotiated a ceasefire with the MEK that required MEK fighters to give up their arms and be confined to Camp Ashraf, a massive former Iraqi military base.

Signs of a Weird Political Cult

In addition to the strong evidence that the MEK was a terrorist group that made common cause with Hussein, other revelations should have inclined democracy proponents toward giving the organization a wide berth. Besides its terrorist activities, the MEK has the hallmarks of a strange—and likely dangerous—cult of personality built around the Rajavis.

In 1993, the MEK's National Council of Resistance of Iran, which considers itself Iran's legitimate government in exile, officially elected Maryam Rajavi as "Iran's future president."[7] Spokesmen insist that the MEK will supervise a six-month democratic transition in Iran once the clerical regime is removed and President-elect Rajavi is installed in power. The organization's platform pledges support for human rights, equal status for women, capitalism, religious freedom, and protections for the rights of minorities.[8] Some of those platform planks are more credible than others. Given the dominant role that Maryam Rajavi and other women play in the MEK, the pledged commitment to equal rights for women seems plausible. Former Council on Foreign Relations press fellow Elizabeth Rubin observes that the MEK may be "the only army in the world with a commander corps composed mostly of women."[9] However, as we shall see, considerable doubts surround the MEK and its actual views and practices regarding gender.

Considering the group's Marxist roots, Westerners ought to view the MEK's alleged commitment to free markets with intense skepticism. And given that loyalty to the Rajavis is not only enforced but also central to the organization's doctrine, the MEK's vows to implement democracy in Iran carry little weight.[10] A 2009 Rand Corporation report provides disturbing details. It notes that MEK members swear an oath of devotion—not to democratic political principles but "to the Rajavis," and they do so on the Koran. Divorce and celibacy are mandatory, lest any personal emotions or obligations interfere with a member's commitment to the MEK. The Rand report emphasizes that "love for the Rajavis was to replace love for spouses and family."[11]

The MEK's conduct belies its superficial façade of gender equality and tolerance. For example, Rand investigators note that at Camp Ashraf, lines were painted down the middle of hallways to separate them into men's and women's sides. At an MEK-run gas station, there were separate hours for men and women. Such practices are more akin to those of Saudi Arabia and other repressive medieval cultures than to modern democratic societies.

The organization's public optics in the United States are a bit jarring and serve to bolster suspicions that the MEK is a cult. MEK members typically attend congressional hearings dealing with Iran policy en masse wearing garish, bright yellow jackets or vests (akin to uniforms).[12] Members sit in tight ranks and, whenever possible, occupy the front rows of the spectators' section in the hearing room. Their behavior, combined with their compulsory devotion to the Rajavis, does little to refute perceptions that the MEK is a political cult. Yet once again, as American officials and opinion leaders go about touting MEK activists as democratic freedom fighters who may one day unseat Iran's Islamist regime and bring democracy to that country, they seem oblivious to the various warning signs.

WASHINGTON'S EVOLVING ROMANCE WITH THE MEK

During George W. Bush's administration, U.S. policy toward the MEK underwent a seismic shift. In 2004, in spite of the State Department's objections, Secretary of Defense Donald Rumsfeld declared the MEK detainees at Camp Ashraf as "protected civilian persons."[13] So designated, American conservatives and others vehemently opposed to Iran's government have worked steadily to refashion the MEK's image into one of idealistic freedom fighters and potential allies of the United States. Their campaign had a gradual but ultimately decisive influence on the United States' official stance toward the MEK.

Iraq's post-Saddam government essentially quarantined the MEK detainees at Camp Ashraf (or Camp Liberty as the MEK and its American admirers renamed it), and pro-Iranian Shiite militias allied with the new Iraqi government treated the exiles at Camp Ashraf with a noticeable lack of trust. But influential Americans campaigned to boost U.S. support and protection. Indeed, the concerted efforts of such figures to promote the MEK's interests and agenda continue to this day.[14]

In late 2015, Sen. John McCain (R-AZ) criticized Washington's policy toward the MEK, especially the Obama administration's stance regarding the Camp Ashraf detainees: "The U.S. government and military made a commitment to protect thousands of people who surrendered their weapons and came under our protection as a result," McCain argued. "Clearly this commitment has not been sustained." He added, "This is not just a matter of our ideals, but also our interests. . . . The group to which the residents of Camp Liberty belong has provided some very useful intelligence on Iran's nuclear program, specifically, revealing the existence of covert Iranian nuclear activities."[15]

For American hawks in both the Bush and Obama administrations, the claims that the MEK had unique and extremely valuable access to information about Tehran's nuclear program became one of their favorite refrains and was the carrot that shifted U.S. policy toward the organization in 2012.[16] Both before and after an accord was made between the P5+1 countries (the five permanent members of the United Nations [UN] Security Council—China, France, Russia, the United Kingdom, and the United States—plus Germany) and Iran regarding its nuclear program, the MEK's admirers were pushing that argument. Retired Lt. Gen. David Deptula was typical, asserting that "the most secretive information" about Tehran's nuclear weapons program "has to a large extent come from the Iranian opposition."[17]

The reliability and accuracy of intelligence gathered by the MEK must be considered at least as suspect as the intelligence provided by the Iraqi National Congress in the period before the Iraq War (Chapter 6). The similarity should surprise no one, given that one of the MEK's highest priorities is to enlist Washington's assistance in overthrowing the Iranian regime. A 2015 incident illustrates the need for great wariness about MEK-provided intelligence. Journalist Eli Clifton points out that in February of that year, "Right-wing media outlets leapt at the MEK's claim that it had evidence of a secret underground nuclear site. The MEK exhibited photos allegedly showing a tunnel leading to the facility and a steel door." As Clifton notes, "That's where the story fell apart." Skeptical analysts and journalists at the *Daily Kos* "matched the photo to a safe company's website. The full, uncropped image showed windows and sunlight, refuting the MEK's claim of having acquired evidence of a nuclear facility, but also revealing that the group had intentionally cropped a catalog image of a safe in a warehouse to look like a surreptitious photograph of an underground bunker."[18]

The MEK, of course, has an obvious interest in hyping Iran's alleged nuclear threat and in shading any evidence presented to U.S. intelligence agencies. It is no coincidence that leading American proponents of using the MEK as a key intelligence source on the nuclear issue (and other subjects) are rabid hawks regarding Iran, including the American Israel Public Affairs Committee and former U.S. ambassador to the UN (and now national security adviser to President Trump) John Bolton. Indeed, Bolton and other advocates (including the Center for Security Policy headed by former assistant secretary of defense Frank Gaffney) are even considered to be on the fringe of the militant anti-Iran contingent.

The parallels between the MEK and the INC are striking and unsettling. After having been burned by the INC's false information about Saddam Hussein's alleged weapons of mass destruction, one would think that government officials, members of the foreign policy community, and journalists would be doubly cautious about the accuracy and reliability of information they received from an Iranian exile organization pursuing the goal of regime change. Unfortunately, as Deptula and McCain's comments indicate, such skepticism once again was in short supply.

Instead, extensive warning signs about the MEK's undemocratic nature and unscrupulous conduct regarding intelligence information have never deterred its American admirers, which may or may not reflect gullibility. It is notable that many of the MEK's supporters have received generous financial payments from the organization. Whatever the underlying motives, the well-funded, well-coordinated lobbying effort of MEK proponents achieved a major objective in September 2012.[19] Three high-powered Washington lobbying firms—DLA Piper, Akin Gump Strauss Hauer & Feld, and diGenova & Toensing—were paid nearly $1.5 million to press the Obama administration and key congressional players to support removing the MEK from the State Department's list of foreign terrorist organizations.[20] With noticeable reluctance, the State Department ultimately took that step. The change unfroze the MEK's financial assets in the United States and enabled it to open an office in Washington, DC, the following April.

Delisting the MEK was a crucial development. Journalists Ali Gharib and Eli Clifton note that "since being legitimized, the Mojahedin's influence on Capitol Hill spread from the fringes of Congress to include more mainstream and respected Republicans and Democrats."[21] Rep. Brad Sherman (D-CA), a senior member of the House Foreign Affairs Subcommittee on Terrorism, Nonproliferation, and Trade, made comments during an April 2015 hearing that tended to confirm Gharib and Clifton's observation. Sherman stated categorically that the MEK should no longer be vilified, since it was no longer on the U.S. list of foreign terror threats. "Former is former," Sherman concluded.[22]

Rep. Dana Rohrabacher (R-CA) had earlier adopted a similar "let bygones be bygones" view. He said that the MEK's past attacks on Americans, its bombing campaign in Iran that killed top politicians and civilians, and its support of Saddam Hussein were history, and that the group had long since turned its back on violence. "This isn't a bad group." Rohrabacher stated. "A long time ago, in their history, they certainly had a questionable time—20, 30, 40 years ago. But I don't know of any evidence they've engaged in terrorism for many, many years. They're not a terrorist group simply because some bureaucrats in the State Department say so."[23] On another occasion, Rohrabacher stated confidently that the MEK seeks "a secular, peaceful, and democratic government."[24]

The State Department's decision came despite a palpable uneasiness about the MEK. Even the department's official announcement of the decision conveyed considerable ambivalence. "With today's actions, the

Department does not overlook or forget the MEK's past acts of terrorism, including its involvement in the killing of U.S. citizens in the 1970s and an attack on U.S. soil in 1992," the announcement of the decision emphasized. "[T]he Department also has serious concerns about the MEK as an organization, particularly with regard to allegations of abuse committed against its own members."[25] Georgetown University scholar Ariane Tabatabai—at the time, a fellow at the Kennedy School's Belfer Center for Science and International Affairs at Harvard University—documents some of the abuses directed at the MEK's own members. "The MEK controls every aspect of its members' lives and tortures them. Some of these human-rights abuses include: mass, compulsory divorces; beatings and torture, costing some members their lives; and solitary confinements so extreme that some members preferred to take their own lives than be subjected to them."[26]

Ambassador Daniel Benjamin, who served as coordinator for counter-terrorism policy at the State Department during President Obama's first term, reaches similar conclusions in a 2016 article about the MEK's disturbing internal conduct.[27] Benjamin stresses the group's "cult-like" behavior, as well as "the abuses and even torture it commits against its own members." He points out that "more than 70 percent of the MEK members in Camp Ashraf in Iraq are held there against their own wishes, according to a RAND Corporation study."

Yet the MEK's worrisome record never has deterred a surprising roster of prominent Americans from endorsing the organization. In the months preceding the State Department's decision, dozens of well-known advocates—primarily, but not exclusively, conservatives—lobbied on behalf of the group. Vocal supporters included former CIA directors R. James Woolsey and Porter Goss, former FBI director Louis J. Freeh, as well as Tom Ridge and Michael Mukasey, both cabinet secretaries in George W. Bush's administration. Several prominent House members, including Rohrabacher, Ted Poe (R-TX), Ileana Ros-Lehtinen (R-FL), and Bob Filner (D-CA) also were outspoken advocates. Other proponents included former New York City mayor (and now presidential adviser) Rudy Giuliani, former House Speaker Newt Gingrich, and Sen. McCain.[28]

Gingrich has been especially enthusiastic about the MEK over the years, describing it as the vanguard of "a massive worldwide movement for liberty in Iran."[29] Following his appearance at a June 2017 MEK gathering in Paris, Gingrich equated Maryam Rajavi to George Washington and to American Revolutionary hero Marquis de Lafayette.[30] That comparison is even more absurd than Reagan's assertion that the Nicaraguan Contras were the moral equal of America's Founding Fathers (Chapter 1). But Gingrich's extreme hero worship of the MEK is typical among major American political figures. Giuliani boasted on one occasion that he was going to Berlin to meet with the group, asserting confidently that MEK members "believe in a constitutional democracy. They fought for constitutional democracy."[31]

That affection is widespread on Capitol Hill. In the months before the 2012 State Department decision, dozens of members introduced and signed a resolution that advocated taking the organization off the terrorist list. Among the sponsors were arch-conservative House members Darrell Issa (R-CA) and Spencer Bachus (R-AL).[32]

Even modestly prudent individuals ought to be cautious about blindly accepting the MEK's self-portrait as a democratic vanguard. As British journalist Mehdi Hasan points out, the group's name in Farsi translates as "Holy Warriors of the People."[33] Assuming that a group with that chosen label is fighting for Western-style freedom and democracy replicates the blunders that U.S. administrations made in the 1980s and early 1990s when they assumed that the Afghan mujahideen were "freedom fighters." Hasan is right that the MEK "has all the trappings of a totalitarian cult."

Although conservatives, especially neoconservatives, seemed to be the MEK's biggest fans, some significant liberal names have made the list of supporters as well. And a few conservatives are quite critical of their ideological brethren who favor the MEK. Michael Rubin, a scholar at the American Enterprise Institute, is especially caustic. Using the alternative acronym "MKO" for the People's Mujahedeen, Rubin stressed, "The enemy of my enemy is not always my friend." Moreover, Rubin emphasizes, "Iranians despise the MKO for siding with Saddam Hussein as he murdered Iranians. After the liberation [of Iraq], the MKO embraced America, not because it loves liberty and apple pie but because it is an ideological chameleon." Rubin warned American MEK supporters that "embracing the MKO is the surest way to make anti-American the 65 million Iranians who dislike the government and dislike theocracy."[34]

Left-of-center proponents of the organization include Clarence Page, syndicated columnist and senior member of the *Chicago Tribune* editorial board; Gen. James Jones, President Obama's first national security adviser; former Vermont governor and onetime presidential hopeful Howard Dean; Sen. Robert Menendez (D-NJ); Eleanor Holmes Norton, Washington, DC, congressional delegate; Rep. Sheila Jackson Lee (D-TX); Rep. Judy Chu (D-CA); and Pennsylvania Governor Ed Rendell.[35] Rendell seemed determined to equal Gingrich in expressing praise for the MEK, contending that it is "a force for good and the best hope we have."[36] Dean even urged U.S. officials to recognize Rajavi as Iran's president in exile.[37]

Such attitudes have not faded to any significant extent. In May 2015, a new MEK front group, the Organization of Iranian American Communities, held a briefing on Capitol Hill for interested members of Congress and their staffs. Among the prominent attendees were newly elected GOP senators Tom Cotton (R-AR) and Thom Tillis (R-NC). They were joined by Marc Ginsberg, former U.S. ambassador to Morocco; Robert Joseph, former under secretary of state for arms control and international security; and other prominent hawks opposed to any improvement of U.S. relations with Tehran. The MEK ingratiated itself to such figures by staunchly opposing the P5+1 nuclear agreement with Iran—the Joint Comprehensive Plan of Action.[38]

Perhaps most troubling, many of the MEK's American supporters have accepted fees of $15,000 to $30,000 to give speeches to the group. They also have accepted posh, all-expenses-paid trips to attend MEK events in Paris. Rendell confirmed in March 2012 that the MEK had paid him a total of $150,000 to $160,000, and it appeared that other "A-List" backers had been rewarded in a similar fashion.[39] Needless to say, accepting such largesse from a highly controversial foreign political organization—and one that was still listed as a terrorist organization at the time—should raise justifiable questions regarding the judgment, if not the ethics, of the recipients. Rubin was correct when he argued that in order to have an honest debate on the issue of U.S. policy toward the MEK, American defenders "should acknowledge the honorarium or consulting fees that they receive from the group."[40]

Enthusiasm for the MEK among its American proponents has increased since its delisting as a terrorist organization. The House Foreign Affairs Committee even invited Maryam Rajavi to testify at a hearing on strategies for defeating the Islamic State. That invitation infuriated some Middle East experts.[41] Robert Ford, former U.S. ambassador to Syria, spoke for many of his colleagues when he fumed: "What the f—k do the MEK know about the Islamic State?"[42] But the committee's decision to give Rajavi a platform was not that surprising. Many of the members (especially the GOP members) are staunch advocates of a regime-change strategy toward Iran. The MEK serves the same function for such hawks as Chalabi and the Iraqi National Congress did in the lead-up to the U.S. invasion of Iraq.

A significant percentage of American hawks do not make distinctions between Sunni extremists and Shiite radicals, even though both factions are mortal enemies. To proponents of forcible regime change, the two factions are simply part of a monolithic Great Islamic Menace. Ted Poe, the chairman of the subcommittee that held the hearing for Rajavi, epitomized that implicit assumption. He defended the decision to invite Rajavi, arguing that she was qualified to discuss the Islamic State because she was a Muslim woman who "knows the prejudices inherent in radical Islamic ideology."[43] Raymond Tanter, who served on the National Security Council in Ronald Reagan's administration, expressed a similar perspective, asserting that she was a most logical choice as a witness because "as a pro-democracy woman with a moderate view of Islam, Rajavi represents the opposite of the misogynistic Iranian regime's rulers; they are authoritarian, suppress women, and hold an extreme view of Islam."[44] For Poe, Tanter, and other hawks, the MEK provides the image (although not likely the substance) of an indigenous democratic alternative to the Iranian clerical regime—an opposition movement that hawks believe Washington should support.

But in a testy exchange with Rajavi at the House Foreign Affairs Committee hearing in April 2015, Rep. Danny K. Davis (D-IL) underscored the danger of idealizing the MEK and similar groups.

"Over the past 30 years," Davis stated, "the United States has been drawn into some serious diplomatic and military dead-ends in the Mideast by mistakenly backing individuals and organizations claiming popular support, which turned out to be exaggerated and somewhat manufactured."[45] Davis was clearly referring to Washington's unfortunate enthusiasm for the Iraqi National Congress, and he challenged Rajavi to show why the situation with the MEK was not similar. Despite a valiant effort, her response amounted to little more than unsupported allegations that her organization enjoyed widespread support among the Iranian people. Those who recalled similar confident claims from the INC were hardly reassured. Ariane Tabatabai contends that the MEK "is merely manipulating the West, hoping that it will rush to it for fear of the greater enemy: the Islamic Republic."[46]

ULTERIOR POLICY MOTIVES OF SOME AMERICAN BACKERS OF THE MEK

When advocates of an extremely hardline U.S. policy toward Iran also want "vigorous support for Iran's opposition, aimed at regime change in Tehran," as Bolton recommended,[47] one should be wary. Given his vocal cheerleading for the MEK over the years, Bolton most likely was not referring to the moderate, anti-clerical "Green coalition" inside Iran, which conducted street demonstrations after the disputed re-election of hardline Islamist President Mahmoud Ahmadinejad in 2009;[48] Bolton had the MEK in mind, instead.

American Conservative columnist Daniel Larison cites Bolton's earlier support for the INC and suggests that the outspoken hawk was using the same approach to gain American backing for the Iranian exile group. "When Bolton or someone else with this record talks about 'vigorous American support for Iran's opposition,' we can be fairly sure that he means that the U.S. should be backing the MEK in its quest for seizing power in Iran." Larison warns, "Once again we have a hawkish demand for U.S. support for an exile group that has absolutely no support in its own country in order to achieve regime change. Indeed, the group that Bolton has been helping to promote is widely loathed in Iran for good reason and has no credibility at all with the domestic political opposition."[49]

In a subsequent article, Larison reiterates his alarm at the widespread support for the MEK among key American opinion leaders. "One of the more troubling things about American MEK supporters is their willingness to whitewash the group's past as well as its present-day behavior. They aren't content to work with an avowedly bad group against a common enemy, but feel compelled to pretend that the group is upstanding and noble. At an appearance in Paris last year, [Rudy] Giuliani called the cult leader Maryam Rajavi a 'hero,' which either suggests that his understanding of heroism is extremely poor or that he will say anything to get paid."[50]

Although American MEK supporters express confidence that the organization is a credible democratic alternative with extensive support inside Iran, many Iran experts echo Larison's assessment. The MEK is still "a fringe cult with very limited appeal among Iranians," contends Karim Sadjadpour, a foreign policy scholar at the Carnegie Endowment for International Peace.[51] Tabatabai is even more categorical. Noting pervasive Iranian anger at the MEK because of the organization's active support of Saddam Hussein's war against Iran in the 1980s, she concludes, "The MEK has no viable chance of seizing power in Iran. If the current government is not Iranians' first choice for a government, the MEK is not even their last—and for good reason."[52]

Writing in the *American Prospect*, Jeremiah Goulka offers a pertinent warning to American backers of the MEK. He cautions, even hawks "who insist on wanting regime change in Iran need to understand that . . . the MEK is a bad ally." Aligning ourselves with that movement "would undermine any attempt at credibility among Iranians because it would make us look like dupes."[53]

Yet some American supporters identify with the MEK to an alarming extent. Addressing an MEK conference in Paris in the summer of 2014, former Rep. Robert Torricelli (D-NJ) proclaimed that he was "a soldier in the liberation of Iran." He continued, "First we gathered in Frankfurt, in London, and Paris and New York in the hundreds. Then we came to Paris in the thousands. Hear me well, Mullahs: soon we will come to the streets of Tehran by the millions, and take back the future of the people of Iran."[54]

Torricelli's comments might have set a new standard for conflating his interests (and by extension, America's interests) with those of a foreign exile group. It was precisely what George Washington, John Quincy Adams, and other early American leaders feared and warned against.

Unfortunately, as Gharib and Clifton point out, the MEK's burgeoning influence in the United States, especially on Capitol Hill, is "a classic story of money, politics, and the enduring appeal of exile groups promising regime change."[55] A similar pattern was seen with respect to the Nicaraguan Contras, the Afghan Mujahideen, Angola's National Union for the Total Independence of Angola (UNITA), the Kosovo Liberation Army, the Iraqi National Congress, and other groups—usually to the detriment of America's best interests.

Donald Trump's election as president led to some speculation that the United States would opt out of the regime-change business as a significant feature of its foreign policy. During his 2016 campaign, the GOP nominee not only articulated an "America First" approach to global affairs, but he specifically condemned the regime-change wars that the Bush and Obama administrations had waged in Iraq and Libya (Chapter 8). Trump correctly concluded that those ventures had produced disastrous results, making both previously stable countries dangerously unstable and a playground for radical Islamist forces.

However, any hope that Trump's newly installed foreign policy team might truly have internalized the lessons of those policy failures soon faded. Trump's first secretary of state, Rex Tillerson, not only signed on to the Obama administration's demand that Syrian dictator Bashar al-Assad leave office before a settlement of that country's bloody civil war could be negotiated (Chapter 10), but he also embraced regime change in Iran.

Testifying before the House Foreign Affairs Committee in mid-June 2017, Tillerson was explicitly asked by Representative Poe whether the United States supported a policy of regime change in Iran. Poe argued, "There are Iranians in exile all over the world. Some are here. And then there's [*sic*] Iranians in Iran who don't support the totalitarian state."[56]

Tillerson replied that the administration's policy toward Iran was still "under development" but that Washington would work with "elements inside Iran" to bring about the transition to a new government.[57] Although he did not explicitly mention the MEK, any U.S. promotion of domestic dissidents would almost certainly have to include that faction. More moderate reformers in Iran have repeatedly rejected such an American embrace, justifiably concerned that such an association would destroy their credibility within Iran. Indeed, a significant segment of Iranian moderates endorsed President Hassan Rouhani and were a major factor in his decisive re-election victory over a hardline opponent in the 2017 election.

The Trump administration faces mounting congressional pressure to come out solidly in favor of regime change in Iran. The ultra-hawkish Senator Cotton urges the administration to declare that goal as Washington's policy. "The policy of the United States should be regime change in Iran," he stated bluntly during a Senate hearing in June 2017. He specifically called for support of Iranian groups committed to "domestic dissent."[58]

Having such staunch advocates of regime change in Iran—and long-time supporters of the MEK—as Bolton and Giuliani become members of President Trump's inner circle of policy advisers is particularly ominous. Cato Institute Vice President for Defense and Foreign Policy Studies Christopher A. Preble notes that "John Bolton sits a few doors down from the President of the United States. Ahmed Chalabi would have lusted after the level of access that the MEK's Maryam Rajavi now has."[59]

Recently, the MEK has intensified its campaign against the Iranian government, possibly with the hope or expectation of gaining aid from the Trump administration. The MEK endorsed anti-government demonstrations that erupted in several Iranian cities in late December 2017 and early January 2018, and the organization's operatives sought to infiltrate them.[60] Although a few MEK banners were visible at some of the demonstrations, little support for the group was evident from the vast majority of protestors.[61] Indeed, having the MEK's imprimatur on the demonstrations primarily served to give greater credibility to the clerical regime's predictable allegation that the CIA had orchestrated the marches as part of another regime-change operation—just as the agency had overthrown Iran's democratic government in 1953 and reinstalled the Shah in power.[62]

The Trump administration and other proponents of regime change moved quickly to exploit the protests. In a speech before the UN Security Council, Ambassador Nikki Haley officially pledged U.S. support for the dissidents. After highlighting some of the slogans chanted by Iranian protesters, she stated that Iran is "on notice." Haley continued, "The Iranian regime's contempt for the rights of its people has been widely documented for many years," and she added that the United States has stood "unapologetically with those in Iran who seek freedom for themselves, prosperity for their families, and dignity for their nation. We will not be quiet."[63]

Representative Rohrabacher, who had so enthusiastically supported the Reagan Doctrine during the 1980s, has revived that approach with respect to Iran. In a *National Interest Online* article, Rohrabacher asserted, "Just as the dissidents behind the Iron Curtain knew Ronald Reagan was a true ally and sincere believer in human rights, so in Iran today the Iranian people sense that President Trump is on their side."[64] John Bolton was equally outspoken, urging the United States to give vigorous support to the protesters, including providing financial aid and communications gear to help them coordinate their activities.[65]

Although neither Rohrabacher nor Bolton specifically advocated making the MEK the major recipient of such aid, both men have been avid supporters of the organization. Indeed, Bolton, along with Senator McCain, visited the new MEK military training center in Albania just a few months before demonstrations in Iran broke out. Also relevant is the fact that *Fox News* repeatedly featured Maryam Rajavi as a guest analyst regarding the demonstrations.[66] Lobbyists for regime change in Iran may hope to broaden the opposition by including other factions, but, by all appearances, they have not changed their minds about wanting the MEK to be a leading—if not the leading—player in any effort to unseat the clerical regime.

U.S. leaders are playing a dangerous and morally untethered game by once again interfering in Iran's domestic affairs, and especially by flirting with the likes of the MEK. *American Conservative*'s Larison highlights the problem with their approach: "I have marveled at the willingness of numerous former government officials, retired military officers, and elected representatives to embrace the MEK. There's no question that they are motivated by their loathing of the Iranian government, but their hostility to the regime had led them to endorse a group that most Iranians loathe."[67]

That is precisely the danger. Most of the MEK's American admirers so hate the Tehran regime that they are making common cause with a repulsive faction that is corrupt, brutal, and utterly undemocratic. It is essentially the same myopic strategy that America's political and policy elites adopted with respect to insurgent movements in other countries. Mehdi Hasan is correct that hawkish supporters of the MEK seem to "long for a bad sequel to the Iraq war. And Maryam Rajavi's MEK is auditioning for the role of Ahmed Chalabi's Iraqi National Congress."[68]

America's record of adopting such an approach certainly has not bathed her in glory, and nothing indicates that she will fare any better by supporting the MEK. President Trump should learn from the follies of his predecessors; they pursued regime-change wars that only made matters worse for citizens of those countries. In particular, Trump should avoid the blunders of other administrations that backed supposedly democratic foreign groups who then turned out to be nothing of the sort. A glut of signs warns about the real nature of the MEK. U.S. leaders need to eschew their regime-change agenda in Iran and avoid the MEK like the plague.

CHAPTER EIGHT

THE OBAMA ADMINISTRATION'S CALAMITOUS CRUSADE IN LIBYA

The Obama administration's decision to intervene militarily in Libya in 2011 was implicitly based on the "responsibility to protect" (R2P) doctrine,[1] the notion that individual governments—and, ultimately, the international community—have an obligation to protect populations from humanitarian abuses such as genocide and ethnic cleansing. Enthusiasm for the R2P doctrine had been on the rise in liberal internationalist circles for some time. After all, the logic underlying R2P had been a major driver of the U.S.-led military interventions in both Bosnia and Kosovo in the 1990s, the rationale in both cases being that if the Western powers did not take proactive military action against Slobodan Milošević's Serbian forces, civilian suffering would be widespread. Proponents of intervention invoked the specter of genocide (even a repeat of the Holocaust) and kept that nightmare front and center in media coverage and official statements (Chapter 4).

Libya appeared to be another laboratory for testing the R2P doctrine. Libya's longtime dictator Muammar Qaddafi ruled with an iron fist, imprisoning or executing his opponents with little semblance of due process or even basic mercy. Once again, the desire to protect Libyan innocents from nasty treatment dovetailed with the goal of helping supposed democratic insurgents overthrow an odious dictatorship, as it had in other U.S. military interventions during the post–cold war era.

The Western case against Qaddafi was built on R2P and the promotion of democracy.

Despite his harsh, authoritarian rule, however, Qaddafi posed only a modest security threat to neighboring countries and no credible security threat to the United States whatsoever. Indeed, in December 2003, Washington and its allies scored a major diplomatic coup when they induced Qaddafi to relinquish his embryonic nuclear program in return for the removal of sanctions and readmission into Western diplomatic and economic circles.[2] Nonetheless, the ruthless nature of the Libyan strongman's rule did not change significantly, and deep domestic divisions continued to plague the country.[3]

As with most "nations" created throughout the Middle East and Africa by outside imperial powers in the late 19th or early 20th centuries, Libya was an extremely artificial entity. Primarily between 1910 and 1920, Italy cobbled Libya together as a colony from three regions of the decaying Ottoman Empire—although some portions were not securely under Italian rule until 1931. Those three regions had very little common history or culture, and when the victorious Allies stripped Rome of its colonial possessions in World War II, the United Nations (UN) preserved the defective handiwork and kept Libya intact. The principal centers of political and economic influence were Tripolitania in the west and Cyrenaica in the east. The southern Fezzan region was more sparsely populated—largely by the Tuareg and Tebu tribes that sought to maintain an independent existence there.[4]

Since the beginning of his rule in the late 1960s, Qaddafi's political power structure had always been centered in the western Tripolitania region. He relied on support from tribes—especially in the area around Tripoli—to stay in power. Tribes in the southern Fezzan region were far less inclined to support him. Most important, though, the eastern tribes in Cyrenaica, especially near the city of Benghazi, were overwhelmingly hostile to Qaddafi. Indeed, rebellions had broken out in the east several times during his rule. Columbia University scholar Rajan Menon notes that eastern Libya "housed the political base of the Senussid monarchy that Gaddafi had overthrown in 1969 and of those elites who regarded the onetime colonel as a parvenu and usurper from society's lower ranks."[5]

In late January and early February 2011, yet another uprising began in a number of eastern Libyan towns and villages, with demonstrations focused mainly on the government's incompetent economic policies. But the rebellion reached critical mass on February 15, when Qaddafi's security forces fired on demonstrators in Benghazi. The insurgency spread rapidly, and on February 27, rebels formed the National Transitional Council (NTC) as a competing government to Qaddafi's regime.

WASHINGTON AND ITS ALLIES EXPLOIT LIBYA'S DOMESTIC CRISIS

Given the lengthy history and deep roots of Libyan regional and tribal factionalism, the events of 2011 were not unusual and cast doubt on this confident assertion made by Rand Corporation scholar Christopher Chivvis in his book *Toppling Qaddafi*: "Although tribal, regional, and other cleavages do exist in Libya, there was near unanimous opposition to Qaddafi's rule."[6] However, support for the rebellion was far from unanimous, and it was heavily concentrated in the traditional anti-Qaddafi east. Indeed, Chivvis seems to contradict himself later when he concedes, "Without NATO's intervention, [the rebels'] uprising would most likely have been snuffed out." If opposition to Qaddafi's rule truly had been "near unanimous," both his political base and army would have evaporated, leaving the dictator bereft. That did not happen.

U.S. and other Western officials did not see the rebellion as just the latest in a series of bloody manifestations of Libya's fractious tribal and regional politics. Instead, they reacted to the disorder as though it were yet another theater in the Arab Spring democratic uprisings that were beginning to sweep portions of the Middle East and North Africa. The wave of political upheavals that were sometimes violent and sometimes not, began in Tunisia at the end of 2010 and quickly caught fire in Bahrain, Egypt, Syria, Yemen, and now, by all appearances, Libya. Sen. John Kerry (D-MA), chairman of the Senate Committee on Foreign Relations, made that connection explicitly in mid-March. Describing the growing turmoil in the Middle East as a "new Arab Awakening" and a "huge blow to extremism," Kerry asserted that Washington's reaction to developments in Libya and other countries would determine "how

Muslims around the world see us going forward, probably for decades to come."[7]

And, reminiscent of their prevailing attitudes before and during the conflicts in the Balkans and the war in Iraq, high-ranking elected officials and members of the media once again portrayed the struggle in Libya as a stark morality play: on one side, a vicious, murderous dictator; on the other, rebels seeking greater freedom for their country and protection for civilians from the dictator's security forces. The assumption of well-meaning Westerners, based on little more than faith, was that a successor government would be a great improvement over the current one.[8] Sen. John McCain (R–AZ), ranking Republican on the Senate Armed Services Committee, ridiculed arguments that the United States didn't know enough about the NTC to arm them. "That is ridiculous. They have been organized for weeks," he said in a March 14 statement on the Senate floor.[9] A month later, after North Atlantic Treaty Organization (NATO) airstrikes to support the insurgents had begun, McCain visited rebel-held territory in eastern Libya and described the insurgents fighting Qaddafi's troops as his "heroes."[10]

Sen. Joseph Lieberman (I–CT), the Democratic Party's nominee for vice president in 2000 (and now officially an independent), was equally passionate in his advocacy of U.S. support for the forces opposing Qaddafi. As Kerry did, he tied the events in Libya to the ongoing Arab Awakening. Unless Washington backed the Libyan rebels, Lieberman warned in a Senate speech, "This peaceful democratic revolution in the Arab world ends here. If Qaddafi survives this, he is going to cause no end of trouble for the United States and anyone else in the world who supported the freedom fighters."[11] Once again, the assumption that insurgents were "freedom fighters" was all too prevalent. Liberal MSNBC commentator Ed Schultz referred to the Libyan rebels by that effusive term and called for arming them to the hilt, as did other members of the media.[12]

As the congressional pressure on the Obama administration suggests, lobbyists for a "humanitarian military intervention," both in the United States and in key European members of NATO, were in full offensive mode by early 2011.[13] They accused the Qaddafi government of war crimes and even crimes against humanity, calling for a detailed UN probe into the allegations.[14] As time went on and the rebellion against his authority spread, Western activists insisted that Qaddafi's military offensive against the insurgency in Benghazi and its environs would culminate in a genocidal bloodbath. Dennis Ross, a senior Obama administration adviser, warned that 100,000 people would be killed in Benghazi if Qaddafi succeeded in conquering the city.[15] Such a horrific total would have been one-seventh of Benghazi's population, but as Menon points out, Ross made that allegation "without a shred of evidence."[16] Ross was not alone, though, in his inflammatory speculations. In her memoirs, Hillary Clinton—secretary of state at the time—stated flatly: "We were looking at a humanitarian catastrophe, with untold thousands at risk of being killed."[17]

Intervention proponents twisted statements Qaddafi had made, thereby "proving" that he intended to kill innocent civilians and not merely armed rebels who resisted his government's authority.[18] Although Qaddafi's comments may have been taken out of context, he gave some credence to their charges by threatening to "annihilate" the rebel forces and vowing to hunt them down "like rats"—door to door if need be. But as David Bromwich, frequent foreign policy author and Yale University Sterling Professor of English, points out, "Qaddafi had marched from the west to the east of Libya, in command of an overwhelming force, without the occurrence of any such massacre, and the Pentagon and U.S. intelligence assigned low credibility to the threat."[19] Menon also observes that during the military offensive that brought Qaddafi's forces to the outskirts of rebellious Benghazi, the regime had not massacred civilians en masse, despite a golden opportunity to do so. And for what it's worth, Qaddafi pledged that rebel fighters who laid down their arms would not be punished, and no convincing evidence has shown that he did otherwise.[20]

Although only the most trusting souls would give much credence to promises of mercy from a dictator like Qaddafi, no compelling evidence of an ongoing or impending holocaust ever emerged. As Alan Kuperman, chair of the Graduate Studies Committee in the LBJ School of Public Affairs at the University of Texas, noted at the time, "Despite ubiquitous cellphone cameras, there are no images of genocidal violence, a claim that smacks of rebel propaganda."[21] Yet as Harvard University professor Stephen Walt observes, pro-intervention voices perpetuated the myth that extensive atrocities had already occurred and that a blood-bath was nearly certain if the West did not intervene quickly.[22]

Even the normally cautious and skeptical Secretary of Defense Robert Gates exhibited some susceptibility to the fear of a looming humanitarian catastrophe. Gates recalls that by March 14, there was "a real danger" that Qaddafi's forces would move into Benghazi itself, and "few doubted that the city's capture would lead to a bloodbath."[23]

The rebels continuously hyped atrocity stories and blared their horns, warning that Qaddafi would conduct a mass slaughter if the United States and its allies did not intervene militarily. At one point only weeks into the uprising, the insurgents falsely claimed that Qaddafi's forces had already killed 30,000 civilians.[24] That figure was equal to the one the NTC eventually gave as the upper estimate for all deaths (military as well as civilian) during the entire nine-month civil war that finally overthrew the Qaddafi regime. Yet, Menon notes acidly: "Apparently no American official thought it worth asking how Gaddafi's small and lackluster army, fighting an armed rebellion on multiple, widely sepa-rated fronts, could have managed such a feat in only two weeks."[25] The rebel political leadership issued other outlandish statements and received little to no pushback. On March 10, for example, prominent opposition leader Mustafa Abdul Jahil asserted that the Qaddafi regime would kill 500,000 people unless the UN or Western powers promptly imposed a no-fly zone.[26] Western officials and media outlets typically took such predictions at face value and then regurgitated them to an ambivalent but generally credulous public.

Within the Obama administration, Secretary of State Clinton was an outspoken proponent of an armed intervention in Libya—ostensibly for humanitarian purposes, but more fundamentally to achieve regime change.[27] On March 14, 2011, Clinton met with Mahmoud Jibril—chair of the NTC and the most visible leader of the anti-Qaddafi insurgents—and a few of his associates at a hotel in Paris.[28] She was attempting to assess not only the strength and cohesion of the rebels, but also their degree of commitment to human rights and democratic principles.

In her memoir, Clinton is candid about her motive for the meeting: "Who were these rebels we would be aiding, and were they prepared to lead Libya if Qaddafi fell? What was the endgame here? I wanted to meet Mahmoud Jibril face-to-face to discuss these questions."[29]

When the secretary of state met with Jibril, she apparently conducted a lengthy inquiry into those and other issues. "She was asking every question you could imagine," Jibril later recalled.[30] Clinton describes her alleged wariness upon going into the meeting: "As Jibril spoke, I tried to take his measure." She realized that the stakes were high: "If the United States agreed to intervene in Libya, we would be making a big bet on this political scientist and his colleagues."[31] Jibril clearly passed her tests. If she had harbored any doubts about backing the rebel cause, the Paris meeting erased them.

From the standpoint of Clinton and other proponents of U.S. military involvement in Libya, Jibril made an appealing insurgent leader. He was articulate and American educated, with a doctorate in political science from the University of Pittsburgh. There seemed to be little question about his commitment to democracy and other Western values— and, indeed, his commitment may have been sincere. But, true to the real political environment in Libya, hardliners quickly edged out Jibril as interim prime minister in the post-Qaddafi government; he resigned amid growing pressure in October 2011, after only seven months. Later, Jibril would blame the international community for the chaos that engulfed Libya in the aftermath of Qaddafi's ouster. He insisted that the intervening powers could have done much more to maintain order, especially by disarming the plethora of armed militias that sprung up.[32]

Even at the outset of the NTC's insurgency, there were indications that Jibril was not a typical rebel figure. Most of the other influential players in the Libyan insurgency had decidedly authoritarian tendencies. For example, the leading military commander of the rebellion was Abdel Fatah Younes, who, according to Chivvis, "had been a key figure in the coup that brought Qaddafi to power, a member of his inner circle, and a one-time interior minister." Younes's position as interior minister should have been particularly concerning to Western backers, because the interior ministry was responsible for implementing the

Qaddafi regime's repressive security measures. Indeed, Younes's agents brutally extinguished a revolt in the city of Derna in the 1990s. After the 2011 rebellion against Qaddafi broke out, Younes "defected and quickly established himself as an important rebel commander."[33]

His quick defection immediately should have alerted everyone that he was much more likely an opportunist than a committed democrat—not only an opportunist, but one with more than a little blood on his hands who saw the chance to retain his power and save his hide at the same time. But Younes's troubling past did not seem to bother U.S. and European supporters of the insurgency.

In her campaign for military intervention in Libya, Clinton received strong support from both National Security Council staffer Samantha Power (a longtime advocate of the R2P doctrine) and U.S. Ambassador to the UN Susan Rice. However, at a crucial March 17, 2011, meeting of the president's national security advisers, intense divisions were evident within the administration. Secretary of Defense Gates succinctly identified the factions: "Clinton, Rice, Power and [Deputy National Security Adviser Ben] Rhodes argued that we had to get involved." Among those opposed to U.S. military action were Vice President Joseph Biden, Chairman of the Joint Chiefs of Staff Michael Mullen, Central Intelligence Agency (CIA) Director John Brennan, and Gates himself. And although President Obama "said it was a close call," he ultimately "came down on the side of intervention."[34]

At the same time, the European allies (especially France) and the Arab League were putting growing pressure on Washington to take action. The Arab League's involvement should have been a warning sign to the Obama administration, because, as Menon emphasizes, leaders of the Libyan opposition had close connections to Saudi Arabia, Qatar, and the United Arab Emirates.[35] Those countries, as well as other members of the Arab League, were pressing not only for a Western military intervention but also for immediate recognition of the NTC in Benghazi as Libya's legitimate government. And given that the Arab League is an association of thoroughly authoritarian regimes, they most likely weren't backing the Benghazi insurgents for their ardent advocacy of democracy. More likely, the Arab tyrants saw the Benghazi rebellion as an opportunity to install a reliably authoritarian alternative to the habitual loose cannon Qaddafi.

Clinton conceded that the Arab League policy declarations of support for the NTC were "major steps by an organization previously known as a club for autocrats and oil barons," but rather than being skeptical of their motives, she concluded that the Gulf monarchs wanted to "show their own restive populations that they were on the side of change."[36] Yet at the same time that the Arab League was backing "democratic" rebels in Libya, Saudi Arabian tanks and troops were invading neighboring Bahrain to crush demonstrations against the autocratic, pro-Saudi monarchy.[37] That episode, along with a dearth of democratic reforms and improvements in human rights policies among the various Gulf powers, should have at least raised questions with Clinton and other Obama administration officials about why those governments really were backing the Libyan NTC; friends like those should have generated some uneasiness about the NTC's democratic bona fides.

ANOTHER REGIME-CHANGE WAR

Despite the misgivings harbored by more realistic types like Gates, proponents of humanitarian intervention soon prevailed, both in the United States and internationally. During the March 17 meeting of the UN Security Council, members adopted Resolution 1973, laying the legal foundation for military intervention into Libya's civil war.[38] The resolution deepened U.S. involvement in two ways: first, it imposed a no-fly zone throughout the entire country, and the United States and its NATO allies were tasked with enforcing it; the no-fly zone effectively grounded Qaddafi's air force, including his helicopter fleet—a major source of his military advantage over the rebels. Second, and even more significant, Resolution 1973 empowered UN members to "take all necessary measures" to protect "civilians and civilian population centers under threat . . . ."[39]

The language of Resolution 1973 was crucial. Indeed, Russia and China withheld their vetoes precisely because of its emphasis on protecting civilians, casting abstentions instead. Neither government would have endorsed another Western-orchestrated war for regime change. They were already worried and annoyed about the interventionist precedents set in the Balkans and Iraq. The day after the resolution was adopted, President Obama approved military intervention; soon thereafter, air and missile strikes began. The "protect civilians" provision proved to be nothing more than a cynical fig leaf. Almost immediately, the United States (with NATO nominally at the helm) launched strikes on Libyan air defenses and other targets that posed no threat to civilians, but that had everything to do with which side eventually would win the war. Yet U.S. leaders from President Obama on down clung to the official humanitarian rationale, even when it became obvious that the goal was far broader.[40]

Russian officials had a very different reaction to the quick transformation of the mission, as Gates recalls all too clearly:

> The Russians later firmly believed they had been deceived on Libya. They had been persuaded to abstain at the UN on the grounds that the resolution provided for a humanitarian mission to prevent the slaughter of civilians. Yet as the list of bombing targets steadily grew, it became obvious that very few targets were off-limits, and that NATO was intent on getting rid of Qaddafi. Convinced they had been tricked, the Russians would subsequently block any such future resolutions, including against President Bashar al-Assad in Syria.[41]

How advocates of so-called humanitarian military intervention managed to steer policy so easily toward something altogether different is especially surprising given the brutally disillusioning experience of the Iraq War, which was still fresh in everyone's minds. Yet there was very little public or congressional resistance to the intervention. Even before Obama's final decision to approve U.S. military involvement on March 18, the Senate had already passed a resolution on March 1 urging the UN Security Council to impose a no-fly zone and take other measures to protect civilians in Libya. Gates notes that when the president gathered with congressional leaders at the White House to inform them of his decision to launch a military intervention, "There was no real disagreement."[42]

U.S. leaders were on autopilot to repeat many of the same errors that the Bush administration had committed in Iraq. Once again, the United States was leading an effort to overthrow the longtime secular dictator of a very fragile, artificial country based on little more than a hope that the aftermath would be more stable and democratic.

Former Cato Institute Research Fellow in Defense and Homeland Security Studies Benjamin H. Friedman summarizes the pro-intervention case that was presented at the time:

> Secretary of State Clinton, along with President Obama made three major arguments for supporting Libya's rebels in 2011. One was that a rebel victory over the Gaddafi government would make Libya a liberal democracy. Another was that by supporting Libya's rebellion, the United States and other outside powers would show willingness to stand up for other rebels and Arab Spring protests against Middle Eastern dictators. Convinced of U.S. resolve, those dictators would give ground to the democratic movements rather than crush them. The third argument was humanitarian: by aiding the rebels, we would protect civilians, especially in Benghazi.[43]

As with the Iraq war, most policymakers seemed blissfully unconcerned about what might follow the ouster of the incumbent government, a pattern that is extremely troubling. Launching military missions that have potentially far-reaching consequences without first developing a serious strategy for the aftermath is unprofessional, if not outright malpractice. Such flippancy on the part of U.S. leaders would seem to be a violation of policymaking 101. Yet time and again, Washington has embarked on humanitarian interventions or regime-change enterprises without such considerations. Libya would become yet another prime example.

Sen. John Cornyn (R–TX) spoke for at least a few congressional figures when he expressed uneasiness about the intervention's "ill-defined endgame" and lack of a "post-Qaddafi" plan, but such reservations were the exception.[44] Gates was especially worried about the same thing and even admitted to his staff that he had considered resigning over the Libya decision. He also confided to them that he had tried to raise a variety of those issues with the president—"an open-ended conflict, an ill-defined mission, Qaddafi's fate, and what came after him"—but, to Gates's frustration, the president "had not been interested in getting into any of that."[45]

Clinton, Rice, and other administration officials especially underestimated the prospects for chaos. As it had in Iraq, the United States linked itself to insurgents with extremely murky ideological pedigrees. Instead of assessing those prospective clients soberly, U.S. officials convinced themselves that they were backing democrats of the desert. Such an assumption did not turn out well in Iraq, and it wouldn't turn out well in Libya, either.

With Resolution 1973 in hand, the United States and its NATO allies openly assisted the insurgents. NATO bombings and missile strikes were the centerpiece of that aid, but Sunni Arab powers (especially Egypt and Qatar) and several European powers also shipped arms to rebel forces. Senator McCain expressed hope early on that the United States and other countries would assist the rebels in that fashion.[46] On March 30, Reuters reported that, according to confidential sources inside the Obama administration, the president had signed a secret order authorizing covert military aid to the Libyan insurgents.[47] However, strong evidence indicated that CIA agents had already been in eastern Libya for weeks, training and otherwise assisting militia forces in that region.[48] Operatives from the British and French intelligence services had been doing the same. And in a worrisome omen, keeping the various militias from running amok was proving difficult.[49]

Indeed, for all the warnings about Qaddafi's actual or planned war crimes, the insurgents were committing plenty offenses of their own[50]—a point that defenders of the U.S.-led intervention habitually overlooked (both at the time and retrospectively).[51] Menon succinctly describes the extent of such abuses during the rebel assault on Sirte, a city on Libya's central Mediterranean coast and a pro-Qaddafi stronghold:

> To the anti-Gaddafi fighters firing the heavy weapons, the safety of Sirte's trapped civilians, many of whom lacked the basic necessities for survival, was an afterthought. Once they entered the city, they shot bound prisoners, tortured others and looted freely. This was not an isolated incident. Even prior to the NATO intervention, regime

supporters, soldiers, and their relatives were shot or hanged—notably in Benghazi, Bayda, and Derna—and others were abducted. . . . [Such] incidents became more frequent as the conflict escalated.[52]

Yet these were the very people that the Obama administration believed would found a new, tolerant, and democratic Libya.

Relations between the Western powers and the insurgents were tense, even as they collaborated to overthrow Qaddafi's regime. At one point, two British MI5 intelligence agents and six Special Service soldiers were captured and held prisoner, not by Libyan government forces, but by the West's supposed Libyan militia allies.[53] Such ill-disciplined behavior (combined with the barely concealed cynicism or animosity those fighters sometimes exhibited toward their Western patrons) seemed to foreshadow the September 2012 attack on the U.S. consulate in Benghazi.[54]

Rather than a limited humanitarian intervention to protect vulnerable civilians, the U.S.–NATO operation in Libya was quickly outed as yet another regime-change war. With the help of the U.S.-led air and missile barrage against Libyan government forces and the influx of military hardware, the insurgents were able to topple Qaddafi a mere five months after strikes began. Obama administration officials believed that their policy had been vindicated. When rebel forces captured Qaddafi at the end of August and then tortured and executed him in an especially gruesome fashion later that October, Hillary Clinton responded with the flippant observation, "We came, we saw, he died."[55]

Persistent U.S. Illusions

President Obama was less crude and insensitive, but he clearly shared his secretary of state's assumption that the new Libya would be a decided improvement over Qaddafi's rule. "Tripoli is slipping from the grasp of a tyrant," the president stated in August. "The people of Libya are showing that the universal pursuit of dignity and freedom is far stronger than the iron fist of a dictator."[56] Senators McCain and Lindsey Graham (R–SC) were equally gratified and optimistic: "The end of the Gadhafi regime is a victory for the Libyan people and the broader cause of freedom in the Middle East and throughout the world," they insisted.[57]

The two senators, along with Senate colleagues Mark Kirk (R–IL) and Marco Rubio (R–FL), proclaimed during a visit to "liberated" Tripoli that the rebels had "inspired the world."[58]

In his remarks regarding the dictator's death in October, Obama asserted that "the dark shadow of tyranny has been lifted" from Libya. He urged the citizens of that country to "build an inclusive and tolerant and democratic Libya that stands as the ultimate rebuke" to the former oppressor.[59] Ivo Daalder, the U.S. ambassador to NATO, and Admiral James Stavridis, NATO supreme allied commander, Europe, were equally euphoric. Describing the intervention as "an extraordinary job, well done," they called it "an historic victory for the people of Libya who, with NATO's help, transformed their country from an international pariah into a nation with the potential to become a productive partner with the West."[60]

Much of the American foreign policy community and news media chimed in about the glorious outcome of the U.S.–NATO intervention. Anne Marie Slaughter, Princeton University professor and an outspoken advocate of R2P in general and the Libya mission in particular, asserted that skeptics of that intervention were "proved badly wrong."[61] *New York Times* columnist Nicholas Kristof gushed about how the people he encountered in Libya loved America. "Americans are not often heroes in the Arab world, but as nonstop celebrations unfold here in the Libyan capital I keep running into ordinary people who learn where I'm from and then fervently repeat variants of the same phrase: 'Thank you, America!'" Unlike some supporters of the intervention, Kristof at least made the pro forma admission that things could still go wrong, but he definitely saw the Libya intervention as an attractive model for future missions. "[T]o me Libya is a reminder that sometimes it is possible to use military tools to advance humanitarian causes. This was an exceptional case where we had international and local backing." The Libyans, Kristof contended, "overwhelmingly favored our multilateral military intervention."[62]

Only a few voices dissented from the celebration. Journalist Glenn Greenwald expressed his astonishment and dismay at the lack of realism or even minimal skepticism on the part of policymakers:

> I'm genuinely astounded at the pervasive willingness to view what has happened in Libya as some sort of grand triumph even though

virtually none of the information needed to make that assessment is known yet, including: how many civilians have died, how much more bloodshed will there be, what will be needed to stabilize that country and, most of all, what type of regime will replace Gadhafi?[63]

Washington's hopes for an orderly transition to democracy in Libya proved just as illusory as they had in Iraq. Just weeks after Qaddafi's fall, the insurgents began to fragment, largely along tribal and regional lines. The western tribes started to coalesce around a power center in Tripoli, whereas the eastern tribes generally supported a rival faction headquartered in Benghazi. The southern portion of Libya was characterized more by generalized disorder.

None of that should have come as a surprise. Even Chivvis, a supporter of the intervention, had to admit that "beyond ridding themselves of Qaddafi, rebels fought for different ideals. Meanwhile nefarious groups have taken advantage of the situation to pursue their own interests."[64] During the war against Qaddafi, the insurgents put on a unified face and managed to play down overt manifestations of their underlying factionalism. Even then, though, there were signs that trouble was brewing. The fate of Abdel Fattah Younes, for example, signaled the potential for serious instability in post-war Libya.

In perhaps the biggest blow to the insurgency, assassins killed the rebel military commander on July 28, 2011. What was especially disturbing was the uncertainty surrounding who was responsible for the assassination. The number of diverse suspects was alarmingly large, as Chivvis highlights: "It is difficult to say who killed Younes. Possibilities included death at the hands of Qaddafi loyalists, murder by untamed militias of Benghazi, retribution from Islamists for his suppression of their revolt in Derna in the 1990s, and execution by the rebel leadership themselves."[65]

Following Qaddafi's overthrow and death, the factionalism that had barely been concealed during the war boiled over completely. According to Chivvis:

> The unity the *thuwwar* [armed insurgents] displayed during the fight against Qaddafi did not endure after he was gone. The fissures evident when Younes was assassinated persisted and were in many ways

compounded after the war, when security in Libya fell into the hands of a wide variety of armed groups with varying allegiances and often conflicting agendas. Many of those groups were simply rebel *kata'ib* [militias] that stayed mobilized after the war, but some were in fact groups that formed after Tripoli fell, either out of fear of what the *thuwwar* might do to them (as in the case of towns perceived to have been insufficiently loyal to the cause) or for more nefarious purposes.[66]

Those divisions rapidly translated into political dysfunction. There were open, bitter disagreements about the extent of federalism, the role of Islamic law, and the overall design of the country's post-revolution political system. Meanwhile, "concerns about Salafi [Saudi-backed Sunni] extremists, relegated to the background during the intervention itself, resurfaced."[67] Most troubling of all was the dominant role that the competing militias were playing. They had supplied the personnel in the campaign to overthrow Qaddafi, and now they were refusing to disband or even to submit to control by a central government.

The newly empowered but highly splintered insurgents also were selling weapons from Qaddafi's military depots to questionable customers in already nasty battle zones such as Chad, Nigeria, and Syria.[68] Despite having played midwife to the birth of a "new" Libya, Washington proved either unable or unwilling to protect its new offspring by stemming the destabilizing flow of arms into the hands of uncontrolled militias.

And the loose weapons that were flooding the black market weren't only destabilizing Libya. The demise of Qaddafi's regime had effects that rippled into several neighboring countries. In Mali, fighting broke out between ethnic Tuaregs (many of whom had served in Qaddafi's security forces) and government troops; in turn, Mali's military overthrew the country's democratically elected government.[69] Apologists for the Libya intervention insist that more than just Qaddafi's fall played a role in Mali's turmoil.[70] True enough, economic malaise, ethnic divisions, and official corruption also contributed to the country's troubles. But the chaos in Libya and the ensuing migration of fighters and weapons out of that country into neighboring ones also was a crucial factor, whether or not supporters of the Obama administration's regime-change war will admit it. Sadly and ironically, the U.S.-NATO military intervention to bring regime change and democracy to Libya ended up undermining a pre-existing, albeit fragile, democratic system in Mali. Fighting among the Tuaregs and several other—mainly Islamist—factions still continued in late 2017.

Instead of being allied with fledgling democrats in Libya, the United States now found itself in an increasingly uncomfortable association with tribal militias—many of whom were decidedly Islamist in their orientation. The parallels between America's sobering experience backing the Afghan mujahideen and the situation that was unfolding in Libya should have given Obama administration officials more than just a small sense of déjà vu. The perils of trying to cooperate with such factions became all too apparent on September 11, 2012, when an extremist militia attacked the U.S. consulate in Benghazi, killing Ambassador Christopher Stevens and three other Americans.

Much has been written and said about the Benghazi attacks, most of it focused on the narrow questions of whether Hillary Clinton's State Department provided adequate security for the consulate and whether the Obama administration's initial accounts of the attacks given to Congress and the news media were deceptive. But both Clinton's defenders and her (mostly GOP) critics failed to address the broader question of what exactly was the nature of the United States' relationship with various militias in eastern Libya, including with the militia that executed the raid. Those very forces appear to have been an integral part of the insurgency that Washington backed against Qaddafi. Not only that, but Ambassador Stevens had been the liaison between the U.S. government and the Benghazi-based insurgents in the months leading up to Qaddafi's overthrow.[71]

Such a background begs several questions: did U.S. officials vet those groups to try to exclude extreme Islamist elements? If not, why not? If so, why did the process fail so spectacularly that we ended up with a burned out consulate and a dead ambassador? And more broadly, were Washington's expressed hopes for a democratic post-Qaddafi Libya sincere, if naive? Or were they a cynical façade for another U.S. power play in the Greater Middle East? A serious congressional investigation into the Benghazi tragedy would have explored all of those issues, but instead, a shallow, largely partisan, spectacle of an investigation is all that ensued. Andrew Bacevich, author of *America's War for the Greater Middle East*, is on the mark regarding the Benghazi episode: "The ill-conceived U.S. intervention in Libya demanded serious reflection, perhaps even contrition. Instead, Washington opted for crude partisanship."[72]

IRAQ FIASCO REDUX: LIBYA IN CHAOS

In any case, the aftermath of the U.S.-led intervention has been a mess. Libya has become a playground for both rival militias and rival governments. Writing in 2012 shortly after the Benghazi attacks, Greenwald asked perceptively: "How much longer will it be before we hear that military intervention in Libya is (again) necessary, this time to control the anti-U.S. extremists who are now armed and empowered by virtue of the first intervention? U.S. military interventions are most adept at ensuring that future U.S. military interventions will always be necessary."[73]

With respect to Libya, Greenwald's prediction proved to be devastatingly accurate. Less than four years after the Benghazi incident, the United States conducted a new round of airstrikes to prevent the establishment of an Islamic State of Iraq and Syria (ISIS) beachhead in Libya. But by that point, the Islamic State infiltration already was quite evident. Indeed, in early 2015, the terrorist group had carried out a mass beheading of 21 Egyptian Coptic Christians who had migrated to Libya to find work.[74]

The ISIS presence was hardly the only problem. Writing in June 2013, Andrew Engel, a scholar at the Washington Institute for Near East Policy and currently an analyst with the Navanti Group, documented the growing Libyan chaos. Engel contends that "to make up for its weakness following the revolution, the nascent central government cultivated semiofficial militias" to "project state authority." Many rebel brigades joined one such militia, the Libya Shield, as intact units, and "Libya Shield has become an army unto itself." The would-be government dispatched Libya Shield forces to the Kufra district of Libya in April 2012 to halt clashes between Zwai Arabs and the minority Tebu tribe there. Numerous bloody incidents followed, and the Tebu accused the militia of atrocities bordering on "an extermination policy."[75] Noting a June 8, 2013, clash in Benghazi between the Libya Shield and protestors demanding its dissolution, Engel emphasizes that the protests targeted "an Islamist militia that, despite its semiofficial government imprimatur, largely oversees its own agenda and is led by figures with loose ties to al-Qaeda."[76] That statement applies just as well to other militias that have overrun Libya.

The insurgents that the United States helped bring to power have been no more pleasant in their dealings with Libya's Coptic Christian minority. Coptic leaders accuse Libya Shield of running a torture center and targeting people with cross tattoos.[77] It appears that ISIS is not the only bane to the dwindling Christian community in Libya.

Despite the dismal results of the Western intervention, Hillary Clinton and her political and ideological allies continued to portray the mission as a success.[78] During an October 2015 Democratic primary debate, Clinton insisted that the Libya intervention was "smart power at its best." She put a positive gloss on the war's outcome, stating that "the Libyan people had a free election for the first time since 1951. And you know what, they voted for moderates, they voted with the hope of democracy." She conceded that because "of the Arab Spring, because of a lot of other things, there was turmoil," but she insisted that the long-term outlook remained encouraging.[79]

Secretary of Defense Leon Panetta, Gates's successor, echoed Clinton's assessment. He boasted how the United States and its NATO allies played "a decisive role in knocking out Qaddafi's air defenses, clearing the way for the rebels to take the lead."[80] Panetta emphasized that such a strategy proves that not every U.S. military intervention is doomed to become a quagmire with thousands or tens of thousands of American boots on the ground.

The mission's defenders in the media and academic establishments adopted a similar optimistic tack. Writing in early 2014, Chivvis expressed the caveat that it "will be many years before we know the extent to which the operation achieved its longer-term political objectives. More than two years after the revolution, Libya is still very unstable."

Nevertheless, he insisted, "The situation is on many accounts better than it was when Qaddafi was there, and as long as Libya does not collapse into widespread internecine slaughter, the intervention will have improved life for most Libyans."[81]

Given the extent of the armed turmoil in Libya and the massive outflow of refugees in the years since Chivvis wrote those words, it would be hard to make such a case any longer. Human Rights Watch (HRW) estimates that by the end of 2016, there were nearly 400,000 internally displaced Libyans, and that's in addition to the nearly 1 million refugees that had fled the country entirely—some 400,000 in 2016 alone. Moreover, the pace of that desperate migration to Europe had tripled since 2013.[82] In other words, the situation was getting worse, not better. Additionally, the massive refugee flow into Europe was causing serious societal tensions within some of Washington's most important strategic European allies—yet another unforeseen, inadvertent consequence of the Libya intervention.

A 2017 HRW report on the overall situation is uniformly depressing and underscores how the West's expectations for post-Qaddafi Libya have become a mockery:

> The United Nations-backed, internationally recognized Government of National Accord (GNA) struggled in 2016 to assert itself in the capital Tripoli, as two authorities—one also based in Tripoli and another in eastern Libya—continued to compete for legitimacy and control over resources and infrastructure.
>
> Forces aligned with all governments and dozens of militias continued to clash, exacerbating a humanitarian crisis with close to half-a-million internally displaced people. The civilian population struggled to gain access to basic services such as healthcare, fuel, and electricity. Militias and armed forces affiliated with the two governments engaged in arbitrary detentions, torture, unlawful killings, indiscriminate attacks, abductions, and forcible disappearances. Criminal gangs and militias abducted politicians, journalists, and civilians—including children—for political and monetary gain.[83]

Along with their continuing claims of success, the underlying justifications that proponents use for having launched the Libya intervention

remain largely unaltered. Panetta put the growth of anti-Qaddafi sentiment in Libya within the larger context of the Arab Spring phenomenon
sweeping the region, and asserted that, "A reasonably coherent group of
insurgents sought Western aid."[84] He conceded that with the removal of
Qaddafi, "Libya's fate was now in uncertain hands, but the country had
at least cast off a murderous and deranged dictator."[85]

Given that Panetta wrote those words in late 2013 or early 2014,
they were a feeble attempt to put a favorable spin on an increasingly
ugly situation—by then a bloody, multisided struggle that included several militant Islamic factions—turning Libya into an arena of anarchy.
Pitched battles occurred in Tripoli and several other cities, causing the
United States to evacuate its embassy there in July 2014.[86] The country's
history of warfare between rival tribes, which proved to be a major
factor in Libya's bloody 1936 civil war, also resurfaced, especially in
the northwest.[87] Indeed, the parallels with the aftermath of George W.
Bush's Iraq intervention were uncomfortably close for Clinton, Panetta,
and other leading Democrats.

In numerous respects, matters have grown steadily worse since
Panetta's attempt to apply a gloss of optimism. In addition to the burgeoning humanitarian tragedy there, ISIS began to see Libya as a possible area of opportunity for establishing a presence. By the spring of
2016, Obama administration officials were discussing the need for a new
military intervention in Libya—this time to root out ISIS. In July 2016,
the United States launched the airstrikes against Sirte, at this point an
ISIS-held city, and Greenwald's depressing prediction from 2012 came
to pass.

The new intervention came at the behest of the so-called "unity
government," a splicing together of two previously feuding regimes
that, as mentioned in the 2017 HRW report, had received official UN
backing. The reality was that, despite its name, the "unity government"
or Government of National Accord still was just one of several factions jockeying to govern post-Qaddafi Libya—indeed, at the time the
United States commenced its new air campaign, three rival governments
were seeking control.[88] One competitor, the General National Congress
(GNC), also called Libya Dawn, was closely allied to Islamist fighters,

especially the powerful Misrata militia.[89] Given its geographic base in Tripoli in northwestern Libya, the GNC drew support from western Libyan tribes that had previously backed Qaddafi; also, the GNC received important outside backing from Turkey and Qatar.

A third key rival was the Libyan House of Representatives, sometimes called the Council of Deputies, led by Field Marshal Khalifa Haftar (or Hiftar) and based in Tobruk in the eastern part of the country. Haftar was the de facto leader of the House of Representatives primarily because he led a rebel armed faction that was highly effective in the effort to unseat Qaddafi.[90] Haftar was a former CIA asset, and he once lived just a few miles from the agency's headquarters in Langley, Virginia; indeed, the United States had backed him with financial and logistical support in a failed coup attempt against Qaddafi in 1988.[91] Haftar's history as a tool of U.S. foreign policy likely did not help his credibility with the Libyan people. In spite of his previous CIA ties, by 2016, U.S. officials no longer regarded Haftar as a worthwhile asset; in fact, they viewed him as an impediment to their overall Libya policy. Although he was reliably anti-Islamist and commanded a significant contingent of armed fighters, U.S. policymakers concluded that his actions were dangerously divisive and primarily motivated by a drive for personal glory.[92] So instead of backing Haftar and his troops, the Obama administration linked its fortunes, for better or worse, to the GNA.

Nevertheless, Haftar became (and remains) a major—and highly controversial—player. He insists that his goal is to push Libya's democratic process forward and to neutralize extremist elements; he called for new elections to be held in late 2018, and attained an agreement to that effect. However, Haftar's opponents note both his autocratic bearing and the often brutal conduct of the military forces under his control. They fear that his real goal is to establish a personal dictatorship.[93]

As noted, the UN anointed the GNA as the legitimate government of Libya, despite the fact that it lacked any electoral standing, and Washington hopped on board. However, things started to fall apart quickly after U.S. airstrikes on Sirte began. Within days, Martin Kobler, the UN's point man for Libya, conceded that domestic support for the GNA was crumbling, although how he had measured that support in the first place remains unclear.[94] In areas with at least tenuous GNA control, the modest backing that the regime did enjoy was being undermined by electric power outages and rampant currency inflation. Washington's quest for reliable democratic clients seemed no closer to fulfillment in 2016 and 2017 than it had in 2011.

Former congressional aide Daniel McAdams contends that it is a bit of a stretch for the United States and the other Western powers to bless the GNA as the legitimate Libyan government. He observes acidly that it is "a governing body that was not selected by the Libyan people, but rather created by the UN and sent into Libya on a ship from Tunisia." That's not to say that the GNA has no domestic support, but the extent of that support is unknown, and the government is very much a creature of external power brokers. McAdams skewers the hypocrisy at the root of U.S. policy: "The U.S. is bombing Libya to consolidate the power of a non-elected government that the U.S. installed because the previous government was not elected."[95]

The tripartite governmental feud that still simmered into 2018 does not capture the full extent of the chaos. An October 2017 incident illustrates just how fractured post-Qaddafi Libya remains and how convoluted the political and military rivalries have become:[96] An air strike in the besieged city of Derna, about 165 miles west of the Egyptian border, killed at least 15 civilians, including a dozen women and children. At the time of the attack, Derna was controlled by a coalition of Islamist militants and rebel veterans known as the Derna Mujahideen Shura Council (DMSC), one of the numerous political and religious factions in the country. The source of the airstrike was unclear. The coastal city had long been under siege by Egypt and the eastern-based, Egyptian-backed Libyan National Army (LNA) that was Haftar's armed wing. Egypt and the LNA had previously conducted air strikes against Derna in an effort to wrest the city from the DMSC.[97] However, both Egypt and the LNA denied carrying out the raid; indeed, Egypt's foreign ministry issued a statement condemning the strikes, which it said had killed innocent civilians. One Egyptian television station with close ties to the Cairo government insisted that Libyan planes had conducted the attack, but the LNA denied that assertion and said there had been a "terrorist attack" in the area. The Tripoli-based, UN-backed GNA government, which opposes the LNA and maintains very loose ties with the DMSC, denounced the air strikes and announced three days of mourning.

That was hardly the extent of the murky, complex, multisided struggle, however. The DSMC had controlled Derna only since 2015. It came to rule by expelling ISIS, which had established a foothold in the city the previous year. In other words, one militant Islamic group drove out a rival militant Islamic group. Such is the nature of political and military affairs in post–Qaddafi Libya.

And still more extremist groups are exerting greater leverage in Libya, including the increasingly prominent faction made up of groups influenced by the Madkhali-Salafist movement. Writing for the Atlantic Council, Middle East scholar Ahmed Salah Ali notes that the Madkhali-Salafists "are slowly gaining ground via both the al-Tawhid Brigades in the east under Field Marshal Hafter's umbrella and the Rada forces in the west that support the UN-sponsored Presidential Council (the executive arm of the GNA). Both strands adopt an ideology that grants the ruler unquestioned authority, is intolerant to opposing views, and encourages the use of force against opponents."[98] The presence of such a pernicious influence in two major political camps—the GNA and Haftar's faction—does not bode well for the overall prospects of secular, democratic values in Libya.

Given the multiple players vying for dominance, Libya's continuing strife is a surprise to no one. Despite an official cease fire agreement in 2017, fighting occurred as recently as early 2018.[99] Mohamed Eljarh, a Libyan scholar with the Rafik Hariri Center for the Middle East, soberly observes that progress toward democracy and good governance "will require a level of stability and security hard to imagine in Libya today."[100] Engel even fears that the country could be headed for all-out civil war.[101]

Recently, a few encouraging developments have taken place. In late May 2018, Haftar and his rivals reached an accord to conduct nationwide elections on December 10.[102] The mediation effort was headed by French President Emmanuel Macron, who helped facilitate the accord's signing.[103] (Macron's role may have been appropriate national penance, because one of his predecessors, Nicolas Sarkozy, had been a vocal proponent of the

2011 NATO military intervention that helped bring about Libya's current tragic situation.) Additionally, at an earlier Macron-hosted meeting outside Paris in July 2017, feuding Libyan factions reached a cease-fire agreement[104] that continues to be at least sporadically effective at dampening the overall level of violence. Between the cease-fire and the election accord, we now have at least a glimmer of hope that the country's long, violent nightmare might be drawing to a close.

However, a great deal of uncertainty remains, especially about whether the target December 10 election date will hold.[105] The cease-fire agreement negotiated in July 2017 contained a provision promising elections in early 2018; clearly, that did not happen. Skeptics also argue that any agreement to hold early elections is putting the cart before the horse.[106] They doubt whether a free and fair election can be held without first achieving a marked improvement in Libya's overall stability. They contend that holding elections in the current fractured, volatile environment is a recipe for voter intimidation, ballot box stuffing, and other forms of electoral fraud. They predict that the losing party will almost certainly reject the outcome of such a tainted election—and perhaps the losing outcome of any election—and resume full-scale fighting. At that point, they warn, Libya will be even worse off than it has been since the 2011 NATO-assisted revolution. And even if such a meltdown can be avoided, they remind us that Libya still has a long way to go toward becoming a functional democracy. Neither Haftar nor his opponents show signs of being committed to democratic norms.

One point is clear: if the situation in Libya is to improve on a lasting basis, it will need to be the result of more prudent actions adopted by the various Libyan factions themselves. Democracy and stability, if they come to Libya at all, must be a self-help project. The chaos sown by Western powers with their ill-considered meddling demonstrates that even well-meaning outsiders cannot implant the values and institutions necessary for democracy to flourish.

Despite the awful results of the Libyan regime-change strategy to date, defenders urge the United States to stay the course (proving that some people just never learn). Ben Fishman of the Washington Institute for Near East Policy contends that bringing stability and liberty to

Libya warrants even greater Western intervention;[107] David Mack of the Middle East Institute makes a similar argument.[108] The already suffering Libyan people may not withstand additional tender ministrations from the West's aggressive democracy exporters.

CONCLUSION: ANOTHER FAILED DEMOCRACY-PROMOTION MISSION

Benjamin Friedman puts it well: upon reflection, he says, none of the main arguments for the original Libyan intervention "made sense at the time, and they have aged poorly. Today Libya is illiberal and chaotic."[109] Once again, U.S. policymakers invested excessive hopes in insurgent allies about whom they knew very little. And once again, most of the rebels turned out to be something other than Western-style secular democrats. Among the various parliaments, cabinets, and militias competing for power in post-Qaddafi Libya, their one common feature is a lack of commitment either to secularism or democracy, much less to both values. Instead, they display a pronounced trend toward various types of authoritarianism, often with a distinctly Islamist overlay. Hillary Clinton and her ideological allies may describe the 2011 intervention as a victory, but their arguments strain believability well past the breaking point.

In his 2013 policy brief for Harvard's Belfer Center, Kuperman gives a far more accurate assessment of the Libya intervention: "NATO's action magnified the conflict's duration about sixfold and its death toll at least sevenfold . . . while also exacerbating human rights abuses, humanitarian suffering, Islamic radicalism, and weapons proliferation in Libya and its neighbors."[110]

New York Times reporter Mark Landler contends that Libya "has descended into a state of *Mad Max*–like anarchy." Post-Qaddafi Libya is now "a seedbed for militancy that has spread west and south across Africa." Beyond those problems, Libya has "become the most important Islamic State stronghold outside of Syria and Iraq," and it sends out "waves of desperate migrants across the Mediterranean, where they drown in capsized vessels."[111] Yale's Bromwich concurs, stating that the U.S.-NATO action to overthrow Qaddafi with the hope of a democratic replacement "has turned out to be a catastrophe with strong resemblance to Iraq—a catastrophe smaller in degree but hardly less consequential in its ramifications, from North Africa to the Middle East to southern Europe."[112]

The Libya episode is yet another case in which U.S. leaders allowed foreign activists to play them like a violin. A passage in a 2016 *New York Times* story about Clinton's central role is revealing and disturbing.

> Mrs. Clinton was won over. Opposition leaders "said all the right things about supporting democracy and inclusivity and building Libyan institutions, providing some hope that we might be able to pull this off," said Philip H. Gordon, one of her assistant secretaries. "They gave us what we wanted to hear. And you do want to believe."[113]

American Conservative writer Daniel Larison points out what is so terribly wrong about Gordon's defense:

> "Wanting to believe" in dubious or obviously bad causes in other countries is one of the biggest problems with ideologically-driven interventionists from both parties. They aren't just willing to take sides in foreign conflicts, but they are looking for an excuse to join them. As long as they can get representatives of the opposition to repeat the required phrases and pay lip service to the "right things," they will do their best to drag the U.S. into a conflict in which it has nothing at stake.[114]

The Obama administration's venture in Libya was yet another amid the growing list of tragic outcomes for the U.S. regime-change foreign policy and the multitude of victims left in its wake. As with most earlier interventions (with the notable exception of Iraq), Washington's democracy-promotion war in Libya attracted little opposition from the American public at the time or since. Clinton may have inadvertently revealed the probable reason for the lack of public opposition when she emphasizes that the United States did not lose a single soldier in the conflict. Bacevich argues that, in Libya, "The absence of U.S. troops enabled Americans to avert their gaze from what intervention had wrought."[115] What it wrought was vastly different from the stable, harmonious, democratic polity Washington envisioned. It instead grew into another chaotic arena featuring bloody pitched battles among competing authoritarian factions.

CHAPTER NINE

WASHINGTON BACKS UKRAINE'S MURKY MAIDAN REVOLUTION

Ukraine President Viktor Yanukovych was hardly an admirable character. After his election in 2010, he used patronage and other instruments of state power in a flagrant fashion to give an advantage to his Party of Regions. State-controlled media outlets devoted roughly 50 percent of their coverage to that party's candidates in the 2012 parliamentary elections.[1] Given the number of parties and candidates on the ballot, 25–30 percent would have been a much more reasonable portion. Yanukovych also displayed a vindictive streak, prosecuting former Prime Minister Yulia Tymoshenko for corruption. Although the case against her had merit, Ukrainian corruption was so rampant and pervasive that most political figures, including the president himself, could have been charged with similar offenses.

His government's high-handed behavior and legendary corruption alienated large portions of Ukraine's population, a trend that was exacerbated as the Ukrainian economy languished and fell further and further behind those of Poland and other East European neighbors who had implemented significant market-oriented reforms. In 2013, Ukraine was one of only two countries emerging from the wreckage of the Soviet empire that had an economy smaller than it did when the USSR dissolved at the end of 1991 (the other was Kyrgyzstan, now called the Kyrgyz Republic).[2] Reflecting the growing anger toward Yanukovych in western Ukraine, Tymoshenko's Fatherland

Party came in second in the 2012 balloting for parliament (winning 101 of the 450 seats), despite the fact that Tymoshenko was languishing in prison.

Richard Sakwa, professor of Russian and European Politics at the University of Kent, Canterbury, England, states that "it was clear that Yanukovych would face an uphill struggle to win the 2015 presidential election. His support plummeted from 46 percent to 26 percent by the end of his first year in power, and never recovered." Indeed, Yanukovych's backing "had faded even in his home turf in the Donbas" in eastern Ukraine, and public opinion polls indicated that Vitali Klitschko, leader of the Ukrainian Democratic Alliance for Reform (UDAR) party, would handily defeat Yanukovych in the next presidential election.[3]

Nevertheless, despite his leadership defects and character flaws, Yanukovych had been duly elected in 2010 balloting that international observers considered reasonably free and fair[4]—about the best standard one could hope to achieve outside of the mature democracies of the West. Yet staunch supporters of Ukraine's 2004–2005 Orange Revolution (Chapter 5) immediately denounced Yanukovych's victory as a coup d'état, a stance that confirmed the view of diehard nationalists in western Ukraine that a pro-Russian president from eastern Ukraine would never have legitimacy. The tumultuous events of 2013 and 2014 must be viewed in that context.

Given a decent respect for democratic institutions and procedures, Yanukovych ought to have been able to serve out his lawful term as president, but that's not the way his political enemies saw matters. The fatal crisis began on November 21, 2013, when the Yanukovych administration, under considerable pressure from Russian President Vladimir Putin's government, rejected an Association Agreement (AA) that would have increased Ukraine's ties with the European Union (EU). That agreement had become very important to former Orange Revolution adherents who wanted maximum economic (and eventually, military) ties with the West. From her prison cell, Tymoshenko embraced the AA and urged her followers to pressure Yanukovych's government to sign it.[5]

When Yanukovych spurned that option, political restlessness among the president's critics mounted. Some of those opponents were ardent Europeanists who looked forward to the day when their country could achieve membership in the EU and become a full-fledged member of the democratic, capitalist West. They saw the AA as a crucial initial step toward that goal, one that also would create important incentives and pressures for badly needed domestic reforms to reduce corruption and undermine the oligarchs who had dominated Ukraine's economy and politics since the dissolution of the Soviet Union. Other Yanukovych critics were not pro-European liberals, however, but strident Ukrainian nationalists who believed that rejecting the EU's offer would lock Ukraine even more tightly into the economic and political orbit of the hated Russians. Despite their other differences, the Europeanists and the nationalists rallied around the EU's AA as a focal point of their opposition to the Yanukovych government.

In addition to the unhappy Europeanists and nationalists in Ukraine, EU leaders did not react well to Yanukovych's decision. When last-ditch negotiations at the EU Partnership summit in Vilnius, Lithuania, on November 28–29, 2013, "could not deliver Yanukovych's signature, European leaders browbeat him during the evening reception, with the cameras rolling. Those awkward moves not only humiliated and angered Yanukovych, they created the distinct impression that motives other than Ukrainian reform and economic integration were driving EU policy."[6] Now, both Yanukovych and Putin were even more suspicious that the West was determined to wrest Ukraine out of the Russian sphere of influence.

Following the failure of the EU negotiations, a resentful Yanukovych arrived in Moscow for talks on a competing agreement. Those talks proved reasonably successful. Ukraine agreed to increase cautious links with the Russian-led Eurasian Economic Union (EEU), although Kiev would not officially join that body. In exchange for that modest commitment, Moscow rewarded Kiev with abundant concessions; among others, Putin agreed to purchase $15 billion in Ukrainian Eurobonds and to slash the price of natural gas exports to Ukraine by more than $130 per thousand cubic meters—or roughly one-third.[7]

The reasoning behind Kiev's decision to reject the AA was complex. Russian pressure, both subtle and not, certainly inclined Yanukovych to tilt toward Moscow and away from the EU. Putin's government had reached the outer limits of its tolerance for the expansion of Western institutions (both the EU and the North Atlantic Treaty Organization [NATO]) into

Russia's immediate neighborhood—a sore point among Russian officials ever since NATO's eastward expansion began in the late 1990s[8] (and which intensified in 2004, when the Alliance admitted the former Soviet republics of Estonia, Latvia, and Lithuania as members). East-West tensions increased further when officials in George W. Bush's administration began to push for both Georgia and Ukraine to have NATO membership.[9]

If the AA and the road it paved toward EU membership had been a stand-alone proposition for Ukraine, it's uncertain how adamant Putin would have been against it—although Moscow certainly did not welcome increased competition for economic and political influence in Eastern Europe. But Russian leaders were alarmed because they viewed EU membership as merely a prelude to NATO membership, and they were determined to prevent Ukraine (and Georgia) from becoming Western (meaning, primarily U.S.) military bastions on Russia's border. In some respects, Russia's 2008 war against Georgia (explored briefly in Chapter 5) was designed to send a message to Washington and other NATO capitals: further eastward expansion of the Alliance would not be tolerated. The prospect of closer ties between Kiev and the EU was deeply threatening to Russia's interests, so Putin and his subordinates were adamant about preventing Ukraine from becoming a Western client state, even more so than they were with Georgia.[10]

Putin had various sources of leverage he could use to keep Ukraine under Moscow's influence. A key factor was that Russia provided the bulk of Ukraine's natural gas supply—and at heavily subsidized prices; after the EEU agreement with Yanukovych was signed, they would become even more so. Kiev's deepening its association with the EU meant risking the stability of that gas supply—or at the very least created the likelihood that gas prices would spike sharply. Not only did Yanukovych want to avoid antagonizing Moscow, he also apparently concluded that the financial incentives Moscow was offering were superior to the EU's.[11] And most crucially, Russia was not pressing for the expensive domestic economic reforms that the EU was demanding of Kiev. Given the state of its moribund economy, Ukraine was not in a good position to absorb those reform costs. To Yanukovych and other officials, closer economic ties with Russia must have seemed a much more affordable option.

What was on the surface a mundane decision about which economic offer to accept became the catalyst for a major political and diplomatic upheaval. EU leaders acted as though the rejection was an intolerable insult, and Yanukovych's domestic opponents took to the streets in protest. At first, the gatherings were relatively small and mostly peaceful. However, on November 30, 2013, Ukraine Interior Ministry police units cracked down on demonstrators who had camped out in Kiev's Maidan (Independence Square). After that point, the size of the gatherings exploded. The next day, some 500,000 demonstrators converged on the square.

The location for the start of what became known as the Maidan Revolution was hardly coincidental. Kiev, located in the western, intensely anti-Yanukovych part of the country, had been the epicenter of the pro-Western Orange Revolution in 2004, in which the ex-Soviet, quasi-communist oligarchy running the country was forced to relinquish political power, at least temporarily; the oligarchs' entrenched economic power remained largely intact, though. By late 2013, huge and increasingly rowdy demonstrations in the Maidan highlighted the extent of the new burgeoning political crisis.

Some experts argue that if Yanukovych's security forces had not dealt so harshly with protestors during the initial demonstrations that were largely peaceful, they likely would have faded away.[12] It is a plausible argument—after all, the esoteric issue of an excruciatingly boring, 2,100-page economic association agreement would not typically galvanize sustained popular opposition to a regime, especially an elected one. Yet subsequent developments suggest that much more was at stake in the dispute than simply which economic agreement the Ukrainian government should accept. Sakwa argued that a "growing gulf between an irresponsible elite and the mass of the people was the precipitating factor for the protest movement from November 2013. The 'European choice' acted as a proxy for blocked domestic change."[13]

But a growing frustration with corruption, although quite understandable,[14] was not the only factor in the rising public discontent. The choice between two competing economic agreements was merely the top layer covering deep ideological and regional fissures in Ukraine.

Those cleavages went far beyond economic policy or even a widespread desire for cleaner and more responsive government. Ukraine was a fragile entity with a thin veneer of national unity; U.S. and EU actions soon made those serious flaws even worse.

Between November 30, 2013, and mid-February 2014, the situation in Kiev grew inexorably more tense and violent. The Western news media reprised the role they had played in so many other foreign political confrontations. They put the fault for the crisis and the resulting violence almost entirely on one side. In this case, the dominant narrative in the Western press made the Yanukovych government the designated villain, while the Maidan demonstrators were aggrieved citizens simply trying to secure democracy and justice.[15] Tim Judah, writing in the *New York Review of Books*, even argues that the confrontation was a fight "for the very soul of Ukraine."[16] In a subsequent article, Yale professor and pop historian Timothy Snyder typified the pro-Maidan analysis:

> On January 16, the Ukrainian government, headed by President Yanukovych, tried to put an end to Ukrainian civil society. A series of laws passed hastily and without following normal procedure did away with freedom of speech and assembly, and removed the few remaining checks on executive authority. This was intended to turn Ukraine into a dictatorship and to make all participants in the Maidan, by then probably numbering in the low millions, into criminals. The result was that the protests, until then entirely peaceful, became violent.[17]

Authors Samuel Charap and Timothy Colton point out that political struggles are rarely that clear cut, and the Ukraine situation certainly was not. Among other factors, there was strong evidence to indicate that far-right elements among the demonstrators bore a significant share of the blame for the rising violence:

> [T]he government and a far-right nationalist vanguard among the protesters, who unlike the peaceful majority of the diverse crowd, had taken up firearms, Molotov cocktails and improvised weapons, escalated the violence. As pandemonium unfolded in Kyiv, Russia and the West, reverting to type, sought to influence events to gain advantage in their contest over Ukraine, with both geoeconomics and geopolitics now in play."[18]

Even Assistant Secretary of State for European and Eurasian Affairs Victoria Nuland reluctantly conceded in testimony before a House committee in May 2014 following the revolution that the demonstrators contained some unsavory elements. During Nuland's testimony, Rep. Dana Rohrabacher (R–CA) asked her if she was aware that neo-Nazis had participated in the street violence that led to Yanukovych's removal. When Nuland was evasive, Rohrabacher asked her if, in addition to the popular Maidan images of mothers and grandmothers holding flowers, the demonstrators had also included very dangerous street fighters and neo-Nazi groups. Nuland responded, "Almost every color of Ukraine was represented, including some ugly colors." Rohrabacher said he took that as a "yes."[19]

Two far-right parties, Svoboda and Right Sector, were especially prominent in the ranks of the armed demonstrators, and both were highly unsavory organizations. Svoboda emerged in 1991 as the Soviet Union disintegrated. Its original name, the Social-National Party of Ukraine, evoked Adolf Hitler's National Socialism; the connection was hard to miss once the party adopted a *Wolfsangel* (wolf's hook)— eerily reminiscent of the Nazi SS symbol—as its emblem. Sakwa observes that Svoboda "was distinguished by its openly revolutionary ultranationalism." It also was intent on blaming Russia for all of Ukraine's ills. Perhaps most ominous, the party openly advocated using violence to overthrow an objectionable government and recruited "Nazi skinheads and football hooligans" as enforcers.[20]

In 2004, the party changed its name to Svoboda and replaced the wolf's hook with a trident (the national symbol of Ukraine). Despite those superficial changes, though, there was little evidence that the organization's ideology had moderated (notably, the party militia retained the wolf's hook as its emblem). Moreover, according to Sakwa: "Until 2013, they were happily distributing Ukrainian versions of Nazi tracts." Ugly anti-Semitism was a prominent feature of the party's speeches and literature. But as prominent as anti-Semitism was in Svoboda's ideology, "The intensity of its Russophobia was far greater."[21]

Even before the onset of the Maidan Revolution, unfortunately, Svoboda was a serious factor in Ukrainian politics. In the country's October 2012 parliamentary election, the party garnered more than

10 percent of the vote, resulting in 35 seats. Once in office, those representatives transformed many a session into a fight against what they termed, "*Yids*, Russkies, and other filth."[22] As the Maidan demonstrations dragged into 2014, Svoboda and its neo-fascist allies began to overshadow the more numerous and more moderate demonstrators. The extremist faction's disproportionate clout in the demonstrations was the product of its superior organization, its ideological intensity, and the fact that its members were armed.

While Svoboda had been in existence for more than two decades, Right Sector was formed on November 26, 2013, during the early stages of the anti-government demonstrations. It combined a number of smaller extreme-right factions, including All-Ukrainian Organization "Tryzub," the Ukrainian National Assembly, White Hammer, and the openly fascist Social-National Assembly. The name "Right Sector" came about because the group assumed responsibility for guarding the right-hand portion of the Maidan against government security forces.[23] In terms of nationalist ideology, some of the factions within Right Sector made even Svoboda seem moderate; in militance and violence, some of the Right Sector factions clearly eclipsed Svoboda.

The Kremlin prodded Yanukovych to get tougher on the demonstrators. Initially, the Ukrainian leader refrained from going that route, but in mid-January, he pushed new legislation through the parliament to suppress even peaceful demonstrations and mild criticism of the government.[24] Those anti-sedition laws were modeled on measures adopted by Putin in Russia, and they had done much to strangle the embryonic democratic system there.

Still, a glimmer of hope for compromise persisted, especially after Yanukovych tried to placate the Maidan demonstrators by inducing parliament to rescind the offensive new anti-protest laws.[25] By mid-February, indications were that reasonable figures on both sides of the barricades were growing weary of the confrontation, especially after unusually bloody clashes on February 18–19, 2014, left dozens dead. On February 21, Yanukovych and the three key opposition leaders who had commenced negotiations three days earlier signed a settlement agreement. In a major concession, Yanukovych agreed that within 48 hours he would restore constitutional provisions enacted in 2004; those provisions placed stringent limits on the powers of the president but were repealed in 2010 shortly after Yanukovych was elected president. He also agreed to the formation of a national unity government within 10 days. In exchange, the demonstrators were to end their occupation of government buildings and relinquish all illegal weapons. Despite the major concessions required of the Yanukovych administration, Putin reportedly urged the beleaguered president to sign the deal.[26]

Unfortunately, the agreement collapsed almost immediately, largely because of actions taken by the Maidan demonstrators. Just hours after crowds withdrew from occupied government buildings and police moved in to make an effort to secure them, the occupiers returned. Those demonstrators, most of whom were Svoboda and Right Sector shock troops, renewed their demand that Yanukovych resign immediately—despite the provisions of the just-signed agreement. The next day, the president and much of his inner circle fled Kiev. The rump parliament, shorn of pro-Yanukovych legislators, voted 328–0 to impeach and remove Yanukovych and to call for new elections. That action exemplified the extra-constitutional nature of the Maidan Revolution: the Ukraine constitution contained no impeachment provision.

The successor government's makeup should have set off alarm bells for democracy proponents in the United States and among U.S. allies. Most of the ministers came from the intensely nationalistic, anti-Russian, western part of Ukraine, with almost no representation from the eastern regions; additionally, right-wing extremists had a disturbingly large presence.[27] Svoboda and Right Sector held 6 of the 21 ministerial posts, including a deputy minister post in the interior ministry that was responsible for maintaining internal order.[28] Svoboda and Right Sector's armed militias also continued to have a heavy presence on the streets of Kiev. In another gratuitous slap at eastern, pro-Yanukovych regions, one of first actions the new parliament took was to repeal a 2012 law that allowed the oblasts (provinces) to use Russian in addition to Ukrainian for official business. To the large Russian-speaking population in the eastern portion of the country, the law's repeal was a clear signal that they were now second-class citizens.

Despite such obviously vindictive and foreboding steps, Charap and Colton note that, "Western leaders neither voiced concern about these developments nor sought a new accord to replace the 21 February agreement . . ." Rather, behind the scenes, "Western officials were celebrating the change in government."[29] Michael McFaul, the U.S. ambassador to Russia, later admitted that he had received numerous "high-five emails" from colleagues in the days following the revolution.[30] Those colleagues apparently assumed that Washington had played a major role in the rebellion's success—an assumption that was not all that far-fetched. The day after the change in power, "The U.S. declared its 'strong support' for the new authorities."[31] Indeed, Washington had been giving strong support to the opposition forces while Yanukovych was still in power.

THE U.S. ROLE IN UKRAINE'S DISORDERS

The United States and the leading EU powers were very clear that they supported the demonstrators' efforts to force Yanukovych to reverse course and approve the EU Association Agreement or remove him as president before his term expired.[32] Rebecca Harms, leader of the Green Party in the European Parliament, aptly captured the dominant sentiment of the continent's political elites: "We cannot afford to be indecisive about those who are standing on the Maidan," she insisted during a floor debate in December 2013. Referring to a series of peaceful protests by East Germans that took place on Monday evenings in 1989 and 1990, Harms said, "That would be . . . as if, at the time of the Monday demonstrations in East Germany, we had clarified our interests with Moscow before taking sides."[33] Equating the Maidan demonstrators' grievances with peaceful popular resistance to decades of Soviet imperial oppression in East Germany was more than just a little over the top, but such exaggerations were typical in European countries regarding the events in Ukraine.

Among American political and business figures, sentiments were equally in favor of the demonstrators. In a January 3, 2014, *National Review* article, Robert Zubrin, the head of Pioneer Energy, urged the U.S. government specifically and Americans generally to provide tangible aid to the Maidan demonstrators. "The brave men and women at the barricades in Kiev are fighting for freedom and the rule of law," he stated. "The events unfolding in Ukraine right now are of global historic importance."[34]

Far more important than the lobbying efforts of a business leader like Zubrin was the role that key administration policymakers and U.S. elected officials played in the Ukrainian turmoil. Sen. John McCain (R-AZ), ranking Republican on the Senate Armed Services Committee, went to Kiev to show solidarity with the Maidan activists. McCain dined with opposition leaders, including Svoboda members; later, during a mass rally in the Maidan, he stood on stage shoulder to shoulder with Svoboda leader Oleh Tyahnybok. As previously noted, Svoboda had an appalling track record of authoritarian, racist nationalism, and Tyahnybok himself displayed an especially odious ideological orientation. In 2004, he gave a speech attacking "the Moscow-Jewish mafia ruling Ukraine," and in another speech, he excoriated "the *Moskali* [Russians], Germans, Kikes [Jews], and other scum who wanted to take away our Ukrainian state."[35]

Appearing on the same stage with the likes of Tyahnybok would have been poor form in any setting, but to do so at an anti-government rally was doubly poor. Indeed, for an influential United States senator to appear at an anti-government rally in a foreign country and inject himself into a volatile internal political dispute was completely inappropriate. And yet, just as he had done in Libya, that's exactly what McCain did once again—this time to back the opponents of an elected government. "We are here to support your just cause, the sovereign right of Ukraine to determine its own destiny freely and independently," McCain said. Having given a perfunctory nod to Ukraine's sovereignty while also taking an implicit shot at Russia's attempts to influence Kiev's decision on economic ties, McCain did not mince words when he told the Ukrainians that they had only one correct choice to make: "The destiny you seek lies in Europe." And in the unlikely event that anyone missed the thrust of his message, he added, "Ukraine will make Europe better, and Europe will make Ukraine better."[36]

But McCain's actions were the model of diplomatic restraint compared to those of Nuland, the assistant secretary of state. As Ukraine's political crisis deepened, Nuland and her subordinates became more active in favoring the anti-Yanukovych demonstrators. In a speech to the U.S.-Ukraine Foundation on December 13, 2013, Nuland noted that she had traveled to Ukraine three times in the weeks since the demonstrations began. Visiting the Maidan on December 5, she handed out cookies to demonstrators and expressed America's support for their cause.[37]

In an especially embarrassing episode, Russian intelligence intercepted and leaked to the international media a telephone call between Nuland and U.S. Ambassador to Ukraine Geoffrey Pyatt in which they expressed their clear preferences for personnel in the post-Yanukovych government.[38] The U.S.-favored candidates included Arseniy Yatsenyuk, the man who eventually did become prime minister after Yanukovych was ousted from power. In the phone call, Nuland said, "Yats is the guy who's got the economic experience, the governing experience."

What is startling about Nuland and Pyatt's phone call is that it took place while Yanukovych was still Ukraine's lawful president. Diplomatic representatives of a foreign country—a country that routinely touts the need to respect the democratic process and the sovereignty of other nations, no less—were mulling about the removal of an elected leader and replacing him with someone they believed merited U.S. approval. Unfortunately, this episode was just the latest in a lengthy list of similar U.S. behavior toward other countries—even democratic ones—over the decades.[39]

Washington's conduct in Ukraine constituted not only meddling bordering on outright subversion, but it also reflected a poor attempt at micromanagement. At one point, Pyatt mentioned the complex dynamic among the three principal opposition leaders, Yatsenyuk, Tyahnybok, and Klitschko. Both Pyatt and Nuland wanted to keep Tyahnybok and Klitshko out of an interim government. With respect to the former, they worried about his extremist ties; respecting the latter, they wanted him to wait and make a bid for office on a longer-term basis. Nuland told Pyatt, "I don't think Klitsch should go into the government. I don't think it's necessary." About Yatsenyuk, she said, "What he needs is Klitsch and Tyahnybok on the outside."[40]

But she wasn't saying that Washington's chosen candidate should seek to exclude Tyahnybok and Klitschko from influence; quite the contrary. "He needs to be talking to them four times a week," she told Pyatt. Concerned that Klitschko might harbor resentment about Yatsenyuk's getting the top post instead of him, Pyatt urged Nuland to contact Klitschko: "I think you reaching out directly to him helps with the personality management among the three and it gives you also a chance to move fast on all of this stuff and put us behind it before they all sit down." The overarching goal, Pyatt stressed, was to "keep the moderate democrats together."

The two diplomats also were prepared to escalate the extent of U.S. involvement. Pyatt stated bluntly, "We want to try to get somebody with an international personality to come out here and help to midwife this thing [the political transition]." Nuland clearly had Vice President Joe Biden in mind. Noting to Pyatt that she had already been in direct contact with the vice president's national security adviser to discuss a Biden visit, Nuland relayed to Pyatt that she and the adviser had agreed, "Probably tomorrow for an atta-boy and to get the [details] to stick. So Biden's willing."[41]

The Maidan Revolution: Fascist Coup, Democratic Uprising, or Something in Between?

The intercepted phone call is a disturbing, behind-the-scenes glimpse into Washington's role in the Ukrainian turmoil. The late journalist Robert Parry opined that the conversation between Nuland and Pyatt "sounded like two proconsuls picking which Ukrainian politicians would lead the new government. Nuland also disparaged the EU's less aggressive approach with the pithy put-down: 'F—k the E.U.!'"[42] At a minimum, the Nuland-Pyatt phone call openly reveals Washington's gratuitous meddling in the political affairs of another democratic country. And if the situation weren't embarrassing enough, Washington's sympathy and support for the demonstrators' cause also made a compromise solution more difficult.

Both the Obama administration and most of the American news media portrayed the Maidan demonstrations as a spontaneous, popular uprising against a corrupt and brutal government. When government security forces shot down demonstrators—so the dominant narrative went—it underscored the thuggish nature of the Yanukovych regime. The demonstrations then grew in size until they eventually forced the beleaguered autocrat from office on February 22, 2014. And thus, an indigenous popular uprising had produced a new, more democratic, and decidedly more pro-Western government. A *Washington Post* editorial cheered on the Maidan demonstrators and their successful campaign to oust Yanukovych from office, saying, "The moves were democratic," and "Kiev is now controlled by pro-Western parties."[43]

But as James Carden and Jacob Heilbrunn point out in a subsequent *National Interest* article, "Missing from the editorial was the fact that Kiev was now also controlled by a cabinet that included some unsavory far-right characters."[44] Indeed, the selective blindness exhibited by the *Washington Post* and other admirers of the Ukrainian uprising toward the ideological makeup of the supposedly pro-democratic forces has only intensified with the passage of time.

Yanukovych's followers and Russian allies tell a very different version of the narrative than the Western one. They portray the events in Kiev as a pro-fascist coup orchestrated by the United States and its EU allies; to support such claims, they point right to the role that Svoboda and Right Sector played in the demonstrations. The revolution's Western supporters dismiss such allegations as transparent Russian propaganda. Timothy Snyder sneers at the notion that Yanukovych's forced departure was either fascist or a coup. Instead, he asserts that it was a "classic popular revolution."[45] Neoconservative writer James Kirchick is equally scornful of the Russian allegations, mocking "Putin's imaginary Nazis."[46]

Yet, as is so often the case with complex world events, the reality appears to lie somewhere in between the two extreme narratives. Moscow's take is a grotesque oversimplification that regards all of the Maidan demonstrators as fascist conspirators and seeks to absolve Yanukovych and his associates from responsibility for the onset of violence and the collapse of his hold on power. But the Ukraine president brought much of the grief on himself. His regime was pervasively corrupt, and he was stubbornly unwilling to deal with the demonstrators and their desire for a more pro-Western orientation in the nation's economic and political policies—until it was too late. Also, the president's security forces reacted to the burgeoning demonstrations with a heavy hand. Even before the February shootings of demonstrators caused a major escalation of the crisis, the Yanukovych government's behavior seemed to validate many of the harshest accusations leveled by critics.

Conversely, too many Western admirers of the Maidan Revolution portray the episode as a spontaneous, nearly bloodless triumph by idealistic, pro-Western democrats who justifiably had become fed up with the Yanukovych government's corruption and other abuses.[47] They conveniently ignore or minimize the extent of U.S. and EU meddling or the role that Svoboda, Right Sector, and other extremist elements played in the uprising. The majority of Maidan demonstrators were not anti-Semites, much less committed fascists, and the extremists constituted a relatively small percentage of the insurgents. However, those extremists were usually armed, and they played an outsized role as shock troops in confrontations with government security forces.[48]

Indeed, evidence that includes photographs shows that at least some of the demonstrators who were killed and wounded in the February bloodshed were victims of attacks by militant right-wing contingents, not security forces.[49] Svoboda and Right Sector injected a sizable element of extremism into the demonstrations and made a peaceful settlement between the government and its opponents nearly impossible. The role that radical nationalists and outright fascists have continued to play in the post-revolution government and especially in Kiev's military offensive against separatists in the east as recently as 2017 also prove troubling, even to observers who are not even arguably tools of Russian propaganda.[50]

Portraying the events in Ukraine as a purely indigenous popular uprising is an oversimplification as misleading as the "fascist coup" depiction. The Nuland-Pyatt phone call substantiates that the United

States was considerably more than a passive observer to the turbulence. Instead, Washington was meddling—and meddling extensively—in Ukraine's politics, and it had been since long before the onset of the Maidan demonstrations. In 2004, Washington openly favored and tried to boost the fortunes of Viktor Yushchenko's presidential candidacy[51] and actively backed his "Orange Revolution" government between 2004 and 2010 (Chapter 5). In her December 2013 remarks to the U.S.-Ukraine Foundation, Nuland boasted that, since 1991, the United States had spent $5 billion to promote democracy in Ukraine, underscoring the extent of Washington's continuing involvement. Moreover, those were not politically neutral expenditures. Washington spent $5 billion to support those political factions that wished to steer Ukraine on a pro-Western course. Nuland clearly assumed that Ukraine's "European future" was the only appropriate option.[52]

Washington's influence sprang from sources other than just the Nuland–Pyatt backstage maneuvering, though. Other American democracy promoters clearly favored certain factions in Ukraine and saw the domestic political struggle there as a key front in the growing geostrategic rivalry between Washington and Moscow for influence throughout Eastern Europe. Carl Gershman, president of the Washington-based National Endowment for Democracy, expressed such an objective in inescapably candid terms. Two months before the November demonstrations erupted, Gershman declared that winning Ukraine for democracy meant winning "the biggest prize" in Eastern Europe. But beyond Ukraine lay an even greater prize: the opportunity to put Putin "on the losing end not just in the near abroad but within Russia itself."[53] Gershman was suggesting in no uncertain terms that the United States should pursue a regime-change strategy in Russia, as well.

Washington's conduct during the Maidan uprising may have been consistent with its goal of spreading democracy to Ukraine, but it was utterly improper. Trying to orchestrate political outcomes in a foreign country—especially one on the border of another great power—is inherently provocative. No wonder Russia reacted badly to the unconstitutional ouster of an elected pro-Russian government—an ouster that occurred not only with Washington's blessing but also with its assistance.

A Troubled Aftermath

Celebrations of the Maidan Revolution as a nearly bloodless victory for Western values and a geopolitical setback for Vladimir Putin were short-lived. If U.S. and European officials thought Russia would sit idly by and watch as the government in Kiev changed hands, they were disastrously wrong—as they would soon find out. Within days, Moscow greatly reinforced its limited military presence in Crimea (an autonomous region of Ukraine on the northern coast of the Black Sea), ostensibly to protect its naval base at Sevastopol. Russia's concern for the fate of that vitally important installation should not have surprised anyone, because the prospect of losing it had come up once before. In 2008, then-president Yushchenko announced that he intended to terminate Russia's basing rights at Sevastopol when the existing agreement expired in 2017.[54] As Yushchenko's domestic popularity plummeted and he became a political nonfactor, Russian leaders relaxed; they relaxed further still when the relatively compliant Yanukovych became president. But now they faced the near certainty that a new, rabidly nationalistic government in Kiev would terminate Moscow's access to the base, which Russians across the political spectrum considered critical to the country's security. Putin made clear by his actions that he would not allow the new government in Ukraine to make such a move.

Indeed, Putin was determined to go far beyond simply protecting Russia's continued basing rights at Sevastopol. The Kremlin orchestrated a hastily called referendum in Crimea for residents there to vote on whether to secede from Ukraine. The vote was overwhelmingly in favor of secession. In turn, the new Crimean government made an immediate decision to join the Russian Federation. Even in a free and fair election, Crimean voters might have chosen such a course; after all, a large portion of Crimeans are Russian speakers, and even those who are not tend to be suspicious of the anti-Russian political figures who dominate the new government in Kiev. But considering what Crimean voters might have done in a free and fair election is a moot point, because balloting was held under a de facto Russian military occupation and can't be considered either free or fair.

As a result of the maneuverings in Crimea, tensions between Russia and the Western powers increased sharply—and the aftereffects of the Maidan Revolution didn't stop there. In another tragic outcome, the already worrisome political and economic divide between eastern and western Ukraine deepened. The divide long predated the events of February 2014, and its roots were cultural, religious, political, and economic. The western regions were predominantly Catholic, the eastern areas largely Orthodox. In much of the eastern part of the country, Russian was a crucial second language, and, in some cases, Russian was the primary tongue used by the population. Western Ukrainians, however, frequently and ostentatiously flaunted their separate language and eschewed all manifestations of Russian culture.

In the post-Soviet era, western Ukraine developed expanded economic ties with Central and Western Europe and clearly sought to expand those ties even more. Eastern Ukraine was an aging center of "smokestack" industries, and it lagged behind its western counterpart not only technologically but also economically, with its economic orientation pointing heavily in Russia's direction. Politically, the gap between east and west was even more pronounced. Western Ukraine was the country's nationalistic heartland, and the population there usually exhibited a barely concealed Russophobia and, often, blatant hostility. The eastern regions, by contrast, generally were pro-Russian. In both the 2004 and 2010 elections, the country's deep political divide was evident. Nationalistic, pro-Western parties dominated in western Ukraine, and the pro-Russian Party of Regions dominated throughout the east. Indeed, the political dividing line running down the middle of the country was stark in both elections, with very little deviation on either side of the line.

Consequently, Yanukovych's 2014 ouster by extra-constitutional means did not sit well with most eastern Ukrainians. With Moscow's assistance, discontented elements in the Donbass region of eastern Ukraine rebelled against the new government in Kiev. The resulting secessionist struggle still goes on, as Kiev has not been able to re-establish control over its discontented eastern territories. A shaky cease fire has dampened the pace of fatalities, but by late 2017 the armed conflict still had claimed more than 10,000 lives.[55]

A CORRUPT, QUASI-DEMOCRATIC UKRAINE

The Maidan Revolution not only deepened Ukraine's regional divides and threatened the country's viability, but it also brought to power allegedly democratic insurgents who then displayed some troubling authoritarian tendencies once elected. Right-wing thugs attacked the few remaining Yanukovych supporters in Kiev and other portions of western Ukraine, and they targeted Jews, gays, and other minorities, as well.[56]

The Maidan revolutionaries actually did keep their commitment to hold elections as soon as possible. Yatsenyuk, Washington's favorite to lead the country, had served as Ukraine's interim leader following the upheaval, and most U.S. and European observers seemed to assume that either he or Klitschko would be elected president—but Petro Poroshenko won instead. Poroshenko was one of the country's most prominent economic oligarchs, having a leading and lucrative role in numerous enterprises. If Yulia Tymoshenko had been Ukraine's gas princess, Poroshenko was its "chocolate king" for the huge Roshen confectionary corporation he owned. Like most post-communist oligarchs in Ukraine and other East European countries, Poroshenko came with corruption allegations. He also had intense—and often very public—feuds with both Tymoshenko and Yanukovych. The extent of Poroshenko's enmity toward the former, along with the long shadow of corruption that followed him, impelled the U.S. ambassador to Ukraine, John Herbst, to dismiss the chocolate king in 2006 as nothing more than "a disgraced oligarch."[57]

Such an assessment proved to be faulty. Poroshenko threw his support to the Maidan uprising at a key moment and subsequently emerged as the leading political figure in the post-revolution period. He won the May 2014 presidential election handily, with 55 percent of the vote; his nearest competitor, Tymoshenko, received a meager 13 percent.[58] Now president, Poroshenko inexorably eclipsed Yatsenyuk, although the latter did stay on as prime minister. In the months following the October 2014 parliamentary elections, the public grew increasingly dissatisfied with the corruption scandals that continuously surrounded Yatsenyuk and with the constant feuding within his parliamentary coalition. With his political position weakening, the Nuland-Pyatt favorite resigned as prime minister in April 2016.[59]

Under President Poroshenko and Prime Minister Yatsenyuk, the Ukrainian government adopted a number of ugly autocratic policies. To wage the burgeoning civil war against separatists in the eastern Donbass region, Kiev instituted military conscription and arrested anyone who criticized that action. On February 7, 2015, authorities jailed television journalist and blogger Ruslan Kotsaba and a month later charged him with treason for making a video denouncing the conscription law.[60] Kotsaba become Amnesty International's first "prisoner of conscience" in Ukraine since the Maidan Revolution.[61] In a trial devoid of adequate standards for due process, a Ukrainian court convicted Kotsaba of a lesser charge of obstructing the armed forces and sentenced him to three and a half years in prison. He would not be released until an appeals court finally overturned his conviction in July 2016—and even then only after sustained pressure from international human rights organizations.[62]

The Poroshenko-Yatsenyuk government also harassed the media and sought to curb dissenting views. In July 2015, Ukraine's State Commission for Television and Radio Broadcasting suggested new measures that would ban books, magazines, and movies that it said were "promoting war, racial, and religious strife" and "threatening the territorial integrity of Ukraine." The law also prohibited "humiliating and insulting a nation and its people."[63]

Censorship powers of any kind are always suspect, but the vagueness of the provisions—and the absence of any meaningful independent review or right of appeal—was especially alarming. Indeed, soon thereafter, anyone who disputed the government's version of developments surrounding the Maidan Revolution or the conflict in eastern Ukraine was silenced. Ukrainian authorities even banned movies starring French actor Gerard Depardieu, who had been critical of Kiev's policies.[64]

Bogdan Ovcharuk, a spokesperson for Amnesty International's Kiev office, summed up the concerns of many free expression proponents: "This is a very slippery slope, indeed," he told the BBC. "It's one thing to restrict access to texts advocating violence, but in general banning books because their authors have views deemed unacceptable to politicians in Kiev . . . is deeply dangerous."[65] The consequences of such a "culture war," he warned, were certain to damage the fabric of liberty.

Yet Kiev's policies became even more restrictive. In September 2015, Ukrainian authorities issued an order banning 34 journalists and 7 bloggers from even entering the country. The Committee to Protect Journalists reported that the newly publicized list was just part of a much larger blacklist that contained the names of 388 individuals and more than 100 organizations that had been barred from entry on the grounds of "national security" and for allegedly posing a threat to Ukraine's "territorial integrity." Foreign journalists reacted with fury when one German and two Spanish writers were listed among the banned individuals, as well as three BBC reporters; the government retreated slightly in response, and those names were then removed.[66] The others remained on the blacklist, however, and in September 2017, Human Rights Watch criticized the Kiev government for imposing yet more restrictions on journalists.[67]

Other incidents were even more alarming: opposition politicians suffered a rash of mysterious deaths—particularly in Kiev, but also in other parts of the country. Victims included prominent pro-Russian journalist Oles Buzina and two former regional governors, Oleksandr Peklushenko and Oleksiy Kolesnyk.[68] Strangely, American and other Western media outlets that were quick to blame Putin for the suspicious deaths of opposition figures in Russia said very little about the equally suspicious cases in Ukraine. The double standard was blatant.

What's more, the Kiev government's overall human rights record leaves a great deal to be desired. In May 2014, nationalist activists, along with the aforementioned football hooligans, attacked pro-Russian demonstrators in the Black Sea port of Odessa. Forty-eight pro-Russian demonstrators perished in that clash, most of them after they barricaded themselves in a building to try to escape from the assaults by the nationalist activists, who then set their refuge on fire. As the months passed, Poroshenko's administration seemed uninterested in investigating the atrocity. A Council of Europe panel report issued in November 2015 sharply criticized the Ukrainian government for its continuing indifference.[69]

The Maidan Revolution had an especially troubling aspect: manifestations of ugly ultranationalism. In February 2016, French journalist and documentary filmmaker Paul Moreira (who has published other well-regarded documentaries on Iraq, Burma, and Argentina) released a documentary about the Maidan Revolution and its aftermath. Author Gilbert Doctorow points out the troubling evidence revealed in the documentary, including the extensive presence of neo-Nazi symbols and flags that were a discordant feature of scenes from the Maidan during the 2013–2014 demonstrations.[70] In the documentary, Moreira interviews leading Svoboda and Right Sector activists and also documents that the commandant of the Maidan "self-defense forces" was Andriy Parubiy, a well-known neo-Nazi who had founded the Social-National Party of Ukraine in 1991—not a piece of information to be found in Western news accounts of the Maidan Revolution. Parubiy was also a major influence on the post-Yanukovych government's attempt to rehabilitate and honor the memory of Stepan Bandera, a controversial Ukrainian nationalist leader who collaborated with the German invaders in World War II and whose paramilitary forces killed thousands of Poles and Jews.

Even more troubling than Parubiy's role in the Maidan demonstrations was his behavior as deputy in the Interior Ministry for the transitional government. He integrated right-wing militias, including the infamous Azov Battalion, into the National Guard and sent them into eastern Ukraine to crush the separatist rebellion there.[71] Such units were responsible for several atrocities, including the attack in Odessa.

Following the October 2014 parliamentary elections, Western officials breathed a sigh of relief when none of the far-right parties cleared the 5 percent vote threshold needed to gain seats in parliament.[72] However, that was primarily because Svoboda, Right Sector, and the others all ran separate campaigns. If they had coalesced, their vote total easily could have cleared the threshold. But even if the far right factions never join ranks to get the critical mass necessary to become an organized political force in parliament, the ultranationalist problem goes beyond mere voting power. On several occasions, Right Sector activists have besieged the parliament building and conducted violent demonstrations in an effort to intimidate and radicalize the government[73]—because even the post–Maidan, staunchly nationalistic government is not nationalistic enough to satisfy them. Moreover, the violence and intimidation extend well beyond the usual issues, such as internal security or policy toward Russia; right-wing thugs even attacked a gay pride parade in Kiev.[74]

Perhaps even more worrisome than street violence and other muscle flexing, the Azov Battalion and other far-right militias continue to play a sizable role in the government's overall military and national security capabilities.[75] Apparently, the Poroshenko government either is unwilling or unable to dispense with those troublesome associates in such roles.

As they review the results of the Maidan Revolution and consider the strength of the far-right parties and, especially, their well-armed militias, the United States and its Western allies should worry.[76] Those problems, along with the Poroshenko government's authoritarian practices and Ukraine's continuing corruption, lead to the unavoidable conclusion that the Maidan Revolution created something less than a model democratic government, although the outcome was less appalling than in other arenas where the United States backed supposedly democratic insurgent movements. Although the conflict in eastern Ukraine is tragic, thus far, we do not witness the horrific chaos that Washington helped unleash in Iraq, Libya, and Syria. U.S. leaders did not try to empower utterly corrupt human rights abusers as they did in Angola, Afghanistan, and Kosovo. Instead, Ukraine's Maidan demonstrations produced mixed results, as did the earlier Orange Revolution there and Georgia's Rose Revolution.

Today's Ukraine is quasi-democratic with a sketchy—albeit, not terrible—human rights record. The continuing power enjoyed by ultra-right militias and their political allies remains a worrisome factor. And the Kiev government's fondness for authoritarian measures to curb

dissent is not an encouraging sign. Also not encouraging is the flirtation of the Poroshenko administration and its supporters with extreme
nationalist figures, especially those with dubious symbolic significance
like Stepan Bandera.[77] The government even pushed through legislation barring criticism of Ukraine's past, including the role that Bandera
and his followers played in World War II.[78] Finally, Ukraine's continuing, pervasive economic corruption does not bode well for the goal of a
stable, democratic state. Some of the corruption even seems to implicate
Poroshenko and his inner circle.[79] Indeed, evidence suggests that the
president's high-level appointees have harassed and sought to impede the
work of the government's own anti-corruption bureau, as well as nongovernmental organizations that try to support the bureau's mission.[80] At
best, the jury is still out on whether Ukraine will become—much less
deserves to become—a member of the democratic, capitalist Western
community.

To assess the Maidan Revolution properly, one must go beyond
Ukraine's post-revolution performance and the country's future polit-
ical, legal, and economic prospects to consider Washington's behavior.
The Obama administration and key congressional leaders clearly med-
dled in Ukraine's political affairs and encouraged dissidents to bypass the
electoral process to unseat an elected president via mass demonstrations.
Moreover, instead of ushering in a stable Ukraine oriented toward the
West, the Maidan Revolution paved the way for a deep chill in the
West's relations with Russia; provided Moscow with a justification (or at
least a pretext) to annex Crimea; and exacerbated Ukraine's political,
religious, and regional fissures, thus leading to a bloody secessionist war
in the pro-Russian east.

For America's ethical standards and its enlightened foreign policy
interests, one could certainly argue that supporting efforts to remove
Yanukovych from office before the expiration of his term was ill advised.
Although Western officials were pleased that their clients ousted a
pro-Russian president and brought Kiev into the West's orbit, achieving
those goals must be measured against such disturbing costs. Washington's
role in Ukraine's revolution may not have been America's worst hour in
terms of policy, but it also was far from the republic's best.

CHAPTER TEN

INTO THE SYRIAN MAELSTROM AND
ANOTHER FRUSTRATING SEARCH FOR
ELUSIVE FREEDOM FIGHTERS

Many of the same opinion leaders that pushed both the Bill Clinton and George W. Bush administrations to support Ahmed Chalabi and the Iraqi National Congress during the prelude to the Iraq War also lobbied President Barack Obama to support Syrian rebels in their war to unseat strongman President Bashar al-Assad. Indeed, that campaign had been well underway even before Syria's tensions escalated to civil war in 2011. During the Bush years (2001–2009), the State Department established a "freedom and democracy promotion" initiative, directed by Elizabeth Cheney (Vice President Dick Cheney's ultra-hawkish daughter). Syria was one of her top-priority targets, and she channeled millions of dollars to opposition groups there. One of her favorite Syrian exiles—who also was a favorite of neoconservative Iraq War activist David Wurmser and his wife Meyrav—was Farid Al-Ghadry, a man that some cynical observers dubbed "Chalabi's mini-me."[1] When all was said and done, Ghadry did not turn out not to be a major player in the Syrian insurgency, but his lobbying for an explicit U.S. policy to overthrow Assad eventually won Washington's increasing backing and laid the foundations for a regime-change mission.

Hostility toward Assad and enthusiasm for his opponents hardened during the Obama administration. Emboldened by the late 2010, early 2011 Arab Spring uprisings taking place throughout the Greater

Middle East, Assad's adversaries (demanding political reforms and the restoration of civil rights) took to the streets to call for his removal. Anti-regime demonstrations erupted in several Syrian cities in early 2011 and quickly exploded into full-blown civil war. Syrian authorities soon took things too far in their violent suppression of the protests and that created revulsion in the United States and Europe.

By January 2012, U.S. officials were pushing the United Nations (UN) Security Council to authorize yet another "humanitarian" mission in the greater Middle East. Secretary of State Hillary Clinton's address to the Security Council embodied the same stark, black-and-white reasoning that the United States had used in its previous policies. "We all have a choice," Clinton told the Council, "Stand with the people of Syria and the region or become complicit in the continuing violence there."[2] A few days later, as Security Council members convened to consider whether to pass a resolution condemning Syrian authorities for "grave and systematic human rights violations" and for their "use of force against civilians,"[3] Clinton repeated her strident rhetoric: "Are we for peace and security and a democratic future," she asked, "or are we going to be complicit in the continuing violence and bloodshed?"[4]

As she had in Libya (Chapter 8), Clinton once again conflated the objective of humanitarian action to prevent atrocities and save innocent lives with the belief that outside intervention also would promote democracy in the target country. But the two goals, while related, are not necessarily congruent or equally attainable in any setting. Democracy promotion in Syria was especially impractical, yet Clinton's implicit assumption was that Assad's opponents wanted a "democratic future" for Syria, despite little or no evidence to support such an assumption.

When both Russia and China vetoed the UN resolution for fear that it would become the pretext for another U.S.-led regime-change war (as it had in Libya), the Obama administration worked through other channels to assist the rebels. In February 2012, Washington helped organize the Friends of the Syrian People, an ad hoc collective of some 60 nations (primarily Western and Sunni Muslim powers) that met in Tunis later that month to formulate aid plans, including the provision of "emergency" supplies to refugees and "increased training" for Syrian opposition leaders. Among the Friends of Syria, the Saudi Arabians and their Gulf allies proposed additional aid to arm the rebels—a lobbying effort that grew as the year went on. In her memoir, Clinton states that, although the United States was "not prepared to join such efforts to arm the rebels," she did tell the Saudi-led coalition that Washington would supplement their efforts by providing nonlethal assistance.[5] Her memoir account of U.S. restraint is more than just a little disingenuous: by this point, Washington was already collaborating with Saudi Arabia and other Sunni powers to provide arms to the rebels and soon would provide direct lethal assistance. By September 2013, the Central Intelligence Agency (CIA) was unquestionably providing weapons to insurgent forces, and some covert lethal aid had been flowing even before then.[6]

WASHINGTON BLENDS STARRY-EYED OBJECTIVES WITH GEOPOLITICAL HARDBALL

Despite Russian and Chinese vetoes of the February UN Security Council resolution and others in late 2011 and early 2012, the United States continued its push for council approval to deepen external involvement in Syria's escalating civil war. Knowing that a binding resolution would never make it past Moscow and Beijing's vetoes, Washington ultimately had to be content with a "statement" negotiated by former UN Secretary General Kofi Annan. The language of that statement is telling: it called for a ceasefire and "a transition to a democratic, plural political system . . . including through commencing a comprehensive political dialogue between the Syrian government and the whole spectrum of the Syrian opposition."[7] A yawning chasm existed between such idealistic sentiments and the political realities in Syria. In particular, the notion that the jihadist factions—who were growing ever-stronger within the insurgency—would be interested in creating a "democratic, plural political system" was laughable.

Yet that goal embodied official Obama administration policy. Clinton recalls, "I welcomed Kofi's plan to pave the way for a democratic transition and a 'post-Assad future.' The United States shared his goal of a democratic, pluralistic Syria that would uphold the rule of law and respect the universal rights of all of its people and every group, regardless of ethnicity, sect or gender."[8] Such beliefs, if sincerely held, suggest that U.S. officials were operating in their own fantasy world. Neither Syria nor other countries in the authoritarian, religiously intolerant, notoriously misogynistic Middle East were going to embrace political systems based on Western pluralistic values. Even the nominal democracies in the region, places like Lebanon and Turkey, had weak and severely flawed political systems. Indeed, under the leadership of President Recep Tayyip Erdoğan, Turkey was on a trajectory to become a barely disguised dictatorship. And most important, the majority of Syrian rebels showed no signs of having an allegiance to liberal, democratic values.

Nevertheless, as the Syrian civil war intensified in 2012 and 2013, so too did American praise for the rebel cause. Senators Joseph Lieberman (I-CT) and John McCain (R-AZ) met with representatives of the Free Syrian Army (FSA), at the time, the principal opposition group. "If America still stands for the cause of oppressed people who are fighting for their freedom, and justice, and deliverance from tyranny, we cannot abandon the people of Syria," they said in a joint statement. "We cannot shirk our responsibility to lead. Our deepest values and interests compel us to act in Syria, and we must do so before it is too late."[9]

Of course, Washington's backing for the insurgency was motivated by more than simple revulsion at Assad's treatment of his people. After all, the U.S. government had a long track record of siding with repressive regimes around the world when it benefited Washington's more tangible economic and geostrategic interests.[10] Indeed, even as it sought to oust Assad for the violence being committed on his watch, the Obama administration looked the other way while it maintained close relationships with Saudi Arabia and Riyadh's Gulf allies, some of the most brutal, autocratic governments on the planet. Given such history, something more than just humanitarian instincts was driving the administration to aid the rebellion seeking to overthrow Assad—it was Washington's hatred of Assad's patron, Iran. If Assad's ouster meant dealing a critical blow to Iran's clerical regime—who would lose its main regional ally—so much the better. Weakening Iran was a major reason (probably the principal reason) Washington signed on to the Turkish-Saudi policy of supporting the insurgents. Turkey, Saudi Arabia, and the United States all shared an intense hostility toward Tehran, and they all wanted to curb, if not fatally undermine, Iran's regional influence. Assad had run afoul of their larger goal for the region. Shortsighted yet again, Washington's support for the anti-Assad insurgency instead would help destabilize another country in the Middle East and strengthen some highly questionable political and ideological forces there.

America's Sad Quest for Syrian Moderates

During the initial stages of the Syrian uprising, the insurgents did seem to be a reasonably moderate lot. The principal armed opposition force was the FSA, a coalition of several factions committed to bringing down the Assad government.[11] The opposition's political leadership was in the hands of the Syrian National Council (SNC), a coalition that claimed to be the legitimate government of Syria from its base in Istanbul. Both the military and civilian branches of the insurgency maintained at least the image of secularism and a pro-democratic orientation. The United States and other Western powers barely hesitated before backing the rebellion against Assad's repressive, pro-Iranian regime.

Western analysts and pundits exhibited a widespread tendency throughout the Syrian civil war to dismiss or minimize the role of jihadism among anti-Assad forces. Brian Sayers, director of government relations at the Syrian Support Group, vehemently denied that a significant portion of the insurgents were Islamic extremists. Instead, he contended that they were committed to pluralistic, democratic values for post-Assad Syria.[12] Secretary of State John Kerry, Hillary Clinton's successor, offered similar reassurances. Speaking in September 2013, Kerry stated that the armed opposition to Assad "has increasingly become more defined by its moderation, more defined by the breadth of its adherence to some . . . democratic process and to an all-inclusive, minority-protecting constitution."[13] Reuters correspondents Mark Hosenball and Phil Stewart noted that Kerry's optimistic assessment of the rebel forces' moderate political composition was at direct odds with the conclusions emerging from U.S. intelligence agencies.[14]

Chatham House and Queen Mary University of London scholar Christopher Phillips also disputes the complacent view of Kerry and others like him who did not consider Islamists to be significant players during the initial stages of Syria's civil war. He says, "There was an Islamist presence from the start"; moreover, "its influence and power grew substantially as the conflict progressed." He notes, "By mid-2012, only half of the active militias had sworn allegiance to the FSA, and by the end of that year many disillusioned former FSA brigades had broken off to form independent bodies, mostly with an Islamist bent. By mid-2013, radicals who rejected the FSA controlled large swaths of Syrian territory."[15]

From the outset, extensive Sunni domination within the FSA (with strong hints of an Islamist orientation) was clearly evident. Phillips notes that the FSA "was never explicitly secular and, despite a spine of nationalist former military figures in its leadership, boasted a large number of Islamist militias within its fold." That situation was unsurprising, in his view. "Many of the rebels were already pious Sunnis, and the life and death experience of combat further increased religiosity." There was one other important factor; namely, "the search for external funds and weaponry offered further incentives to adopt Islamist identities."[16] The last point had considerable validity, because Saudi Arabia, Qatar, and other hardline Sunni powers were, by far, the principal sources of both funding and weapons. In spring 2012, David Enders, a reporter for McClatchy newspapers, spent a month with rebel forces in northern and central Syria. He found that while the early anti-Assad demonstrations were sometimes multiethnic and multireligious, "the armed rebels are Sunni to a man."[17]

SYRIA'S COMPLEX SOCIETAL DIVISIONS PLAY OUT IN WAR

That the armed rebels were almost all Sunni was no trivial factor. In a society with deep ethnoreligious divisions, domination of the insurgency by one sect—and an increasingly Islamist one at that—was bound to provoke greater resistance on the part of religious rivals. Contrary to the bipolar melodrama that the Obama administration and much of the news media portrayed, the Syrian civil war had multiple layers of complexity lying atop a foundation of shifting allegiances. The war was much more than just a run-of-the-mill fight between an evil dictator and his brutalized population trying to cast off the chains he had placed on them. Such a simplistic narrative ignores the bitter, intractable internal divisions afflicting Syria.

Syria was and is a fragile ethnoreligious tapestry. The predominant Arab ethnic population is subdivided among Sunnis (about 60 percent of the Arab population); Christians (10–12 percent); Alawites, a Shiite offshoot (also 10–12 percent); and Druze, a sect combining elements of Shia Islam, Christianity, and Judaism (about 5 percent). The remainder of the population comprises various (mostly Sunni) ethnic minorities, primarily Kurds (about 10 percent of the total Syrian population), Turkmen, and Armenians.[18]

For more than four decades, the Assad family—which is Alawite—has remained in power because of the loyalty of its Alawite bloc and its loose alliance with Christians, Druze, and other smaller ethnic groups. What erupted in 2011 quickly became a largely Sunni Arab bid to overthrow Assad's "coalition of religious minorities" regime; even Clinton, a staunch supporter of the rebellion, concedes that "the rebels were predominantly Sunnis."[19]

Veteran U.S. diplomat Chas W. Freeman Jr. captures a key reason why most non-Sunnis rallied around Assad, despite his many character flaws and ugly policies: "After seeing what followed Saddam Hussein's removal from power in Iraq, a lot of Syrians with no love for Mr. Assad had formed a well-founded fear of who and what might succeed him."[20] The Sunni Arab hatred of the apostate Alawites was especially virulent and had exploded into violence on several occasions in the past.[21] Yet, Washington would end up supporting several rebel organizations that pursued vehemently anti-Alawite agendas.

The various factions in the civil war each received support from their respective regional sponsors. The competing external players in Syria's civil war underscored the role that religion played in the conflict. The major Sunni powers—especially Turkey, Saudi Arabia, the United Arab Emirates, and Qatar—backed the insurgency; the region's principal Shiite power, Iran (along with Lebanon's Shiite militia, Hezbollah), moved to assist Assad.[22] The Syrian civil war was thus both an internal power struggle and a regional one.

However, the religious schism was not the only factor at play in the war's internal and regional dimensions; geopolitical and geostrategic considerations also played a role. After all, even if the bitter Sunni-Shia rivalry didn't exist, Iran and, in particular, Saudi Arabia might have used the Syrian civil war to maneuver for preeminence anyway. If a new Syrian regime that was hostile to Iran were to emerge victorious from the fighting, the regional balance of power would shift dramatically against Tehran. Having Syria wrenched out of its orbit not only would create serious security problems for Tehran on the country's western border, but it also would sever the logistical routes between Iran and its Hezbollah clients in Lebanon. Those changes would greatly benefit Saudi Arabia, Turkey, and Israel, and the Iranian regime was deeply threatened by that prospect.

The geopolitical factors influencing the conflict in Syria cannot be ignored; nevertheless, the fervor surrounding Islam's ancient Shia–Sunni split make the religious aspect of the conflict the most important one.[23] Regrettably, though, Western officials tended to ignore or minimize the significance of the dangerous religious undercurrents in Syria's civil war and in the wider regional power struggle.

WASHINGTON'S DEEPENING SUPPORT FOR SYRIAN REBELS

Most U.S. officials displayed a disturbing and persistent naiveté about such factors. They constantly sought out their elusive "moderates" who would eschew sectarian animosities and become a strong alternative to both Assad's regime and the Islamic extremists that ultimately formed the Islamic State of Iraq and Syria (ISIS). A few officials were a bit more cautious, though. Secretary of Defense Leon Panetta, for example, recalled that the Syrian rebels "posed a more difficult problem than had the forces that rose up against [Libyan dictator Muammar] Qaddafi. In Syria, there was little coordination between the opposition groups, and some had unsavory ties to terrorist groups." Those factors, he stated, "made us wary of committing to their cause, so our initial support was nonlethal—training, for the most part, as well as supplies, but not weapons."[24] In reality, Washington's backing was more extensive than Panetta described, but the warning signs he cited were very real and should have induced extreme caution. Unfortunately, that did not happen.

U.S. leaders tended to back—almost reflexively—any Syrian client that its Middle East allies Turkey and Saudi Arabia favored, even though those nations had religious and political agendas of their own that often were not compatible with America's values or best interests. As noted previously, with the Obama administration's blessing, Syrian rebel forces were receiving extensive financial aid and weaponry from leading Sunni powers in the Middle East, including most notably Saudi Arabia, Turkey, and Qatar. Such autocratic, sectarian powers would never give their backing to non-Sunni forces, nor would they likely support a campaign to implant secular democracy in Syria. Even Clinton recalls that, with respect to the flow of Sunni arms assistance, "a troubling amount of materiel was finding its way to extremists."[25]

Despite Panetta's assertion that U.S. support for the rebels remained limited, evidence suggests otherwise. Already in late 2011, mere months into the internecine fighting, the United States was assisting its Turkish and Saudi allies in supplying weapons to their clients in Syria. The following year, Washington began a covert program to provide arms directly to rebel forces.[26]

The CIA was in charge of that program; apparently, the agency had gained the weapons after victorious insurgents looted them from Qaddafi's military depots when they overthrew his regime.[27] As journalist Gareth Porter notes, CIA shipments from Libya "came to an abrupt halt in September 2012 when Libyan militants attacked and burned the embassy annex in Benghazi that had been used to support the operation."[28] Such timing might be purely coincidental, but that seems unlikely.

The halt in U.S. arms shipments from Libya was largely cosmetic, in any case. Through Washington's continuing cooperation with the government of Saudi Arabia (and its Gulf allies), U.S. leaders made certain that weapons shipments to the Syrian insurgents continued unabated from other sources. One U.S. official termed the overall extent of deliveries to the rebels as a "cataract of weaponry."[29] Yet in the summer of 2012, major administration figures, including CIA Director David Petraeus and Secretary of State Clinton, were feverishly lobbying for even more robust and direct U.S. military support to Syrian insurgents.[30]

So too was GOP presidential nominee Mitt Romney. Even more than some pundits and administration officials, Romney seemed to believe that the rebels were largely a moderate, pro-Western force. Criticizing Obama for insufficient boldness in providing arms to the insurgents, Romney pledged: "I will work with our partners to identify and organize those members of the opposition who share our values and ensure they obtain the arms they need to defeat Assad's tanks, helicopters, and fighter jets."[31]

THE RADICALS' GROWING DOMINANCE OF THE SYRIAN INSURGENCY

By early 2013, Islamists of various stripes had thoroughly eclipsed secular figures as the leading players in the Syrian rebellion. Christopher Phillips identifies three Islamist ideological strands within the insurgency—moderate, Salafist, and jihadist. Significantly—and testifying to the political realities in Syria at the time—his examples of "moderate" Islamists are militias affiliated with the Muslim Brotherhood—hardly a moderate organization in any normal context.[32] Whereas the so-called moderate Islamists were willing to accept at least a nominal separation of religion and state, the Salafists insisted on establishing an overtly religious state in Syria—not surprising, considering that the rebel groups' Salafist beliefs would have coincided with Saudi Arabia's and its ultra-conservative Sunni Gulf allies'.

What separated the Salafist rebels from outright jihadists, according to Phillips, was that the former confined their agenda to Syria, whereas the latter pursued global jihad. The most militarily successful Salafist militia was Ahrar al-Sham, which refused to profess allegiance to the FSA and instead formed—and became the leading member of—the Syrian Islamic Front. Ahrar al-Sham remained flexible in its tactical alliances, however, showing a willingness to fight alongside at least some

FSA militias, even as it formed increasingly close ties with the virulently jihadist militia Jabhat al-Nusra (also called Nusra or the al-Nusra Front).[33]

Indeed, Nusra shared common roots with the slightly more extreme ISIS.[34] Both originally were projects of the Islamic State in Iraq (ISI), which was a descendent of al Qaeda in Iraq. Both Nusra and ISI, along with Ahrar al-Sham, participated in the siege and capture of the city of Raqqa in March 2013. Charles Lister, formerly a visiting fellow at Brookings' Doha Center in Qatar, documents Nusra's string of military victories over Syrian government forces between the summer of 2012 and March 2013. Those victories, Lister emphasizes, played a crucial role in the group's rise as a leading player in the anti-Assad insurgency.[35] But following the joint victory at Raqqa, when ISI leader Abu Bakr al-Baghdadi claimed that Nusra had been formed on his orders and would merge with ISI to form ISIS, Nusra leaders balked; denying Baghdadi's account, they announced their decision to make Nusra's informal affiliation with al Qaeda official.[36]

Even by the end of 2012, contrary to Washington's initial expectations, it was apparent that Assad was not headed for a rapid departure from power. Equally daunting, the existing rebels—especially the supposedly moderate variety—seemed habitually disorganized and often militarily ineffectual. Clinton admits ruefully that "despite efforts by the Europeans, Arabs, and the United States," the opposition "remained in disarray."[37] Lister documents that such infighting and disarray were still pervasive in 2014.[38]

The forces that did display battlefield competence were mostly made up of radical Islamist fighters. Jabhat al-Nusra was especially effective on the ground, but its links to al Qaeda were unsettling to many Western officials. Not only was Nusra serving as al Qaeda's affiliate in Syria, but also by 2016, it would become the largest formal al Qaeda affiliate in history.[39]

Obama administration officials did not want to see such a faction control the direction of the Syrian rebellion. On December 11, 2012, the United States officially declared Jabhat al-Nusra a terrorist group, and the Treasury Department moved to block the group's financial transfers.[40] In a clear indication of Nusra's influence and the overall strength of radical sentiment within the Syrian insurgency, other supposedly more moderate factions protested Washington's move.[41] Indeed, as Phillips notes, "even after Nusra's declared al-Qaeda affiliation, most rebels fought alongside it at some point."[42]

Moreover, despite the Obama administration's official repudiation of Nusra as a terrorist organization, some of the other factions the United States supported, either directly or indirectly, were nearly as bad. Gareth Porter emphasizes the following:

> A major recipient of Turkish funding and arms was Ahrar al-Sham, which shared its al Qaeda ally al-Nusra Front's sectarian Sunni view of the Alawite minority. It considered the Alawites to be part of the Shiite enemy and therefore the object of a "holy war." Another favorite of the U.S. allies was Jaish al-Islam, the Salafist organization in the Damascus suburbs whose former leader Zahran Alloush talked openly about cleansing Damascus of the Shiites and Alawites, both of whom he lumped together as "Majous"—the abusive term used for pre-Islamic non-Arabic people from Iran.[43]

Given such sentiments, it was not surprising when extremist Sunni militias pursued the ethnic cleansing of Alawites as part of their agenda. In Tartous, a province in western Syria's Alawite heartland, the population was 90 percent Alawite before the war. By July 2012, following the initial rounds of combat, that figure dropped to 75 percent. After intensified fighting later that year, the level dropped again to 60 percent.[44]

Western Excuse-Making about the Insurgency's Extremism

To the extent that American and other Western supporters of the rebels grudgingly acknowledged the growing Islamist presence, they typically placed most of the blame on Assad. Clinton made that argument explicitly, pointing out that the Assad regime's shelling of civilian population centers was provoking a harsh, uncompromising response. As a result, she said, "The rebels' determination to resist at all costs was hardening; some were becoming radicalized, and extremists were joining the fight."[45]

Steven Heydemann, a professor of Middle East Studies at Smith College, expressed that view even more categorically. Writing in August 2014 following the sudden emergence of ISIS and its initial, breathtaking military victories in both Syria and Iraq that achieved control of roughly one-third of the territory of each country, including Iraq's second largest city, Mosul, and Raqqa, the Syrian city that ISIS proclaimed the capital of its new caliphate, Heydemann asserted that the Obama administration could have averted such a tragedy:

> Arming Syria's moderate armed opposition might pose political problems for the White House, but doing so two years ago would have had a more significant positive impact than Obama suggested. At that time, the armed opposition in Syria had not yet been radicalized. It was dominated by trained officers and soldiers who were among the tens of thousands who defected from the regime's military. Because military service in Syria is compulsory, civilians who did take up arms had been through basic training. Extremists constituted a tiny minority of opposition fighters. With little external support, this largely moderate armed opposition achieved notable success in "liberating" large swaths of Syria from the Assad regime.[46]

A 2014 report from scholars at the liberal Center for American Progress made a similar argument that a key reason for the continuing weakness of moderate forces in Syria was the lack of consistent, robust U.S. support. The authors insisted that they had identified a classic catch-22: "Potential U.S. partners are weak, causing the Obama administration to hold back additional meaningful support. But these 'third way' forces—moderate alternatives to Assad and ISIS—remain weak because they do not have organized and well-coordinated assistance."[47]

Both arguments were a combination of wishful thinking and excuse making. Little evidence suggests that moderates ever dominated the rebellion or that the main reason radicals gradually took full control was because of Washington's failure to provide adequate backing to the moderates fast enough. Instead, the bulk of the evidence suggests that radical elements were a major component of the insurgency from the beginning, and that even supposedly moderate Syrian rebel factions typically have turned out to be staunchly Islamist.

THE TRAIN AND EQUIP CHIMERA

Faced with such problems and growing frustration regarding the existing rebel factions, Obama administration officials began to shape a new
strategy. The United States would identify and train its own contingent of "moderate rebels." U.S. officials actually flirted with that option
early on. Clinton recalls, "I and others on the Obama national security
team began exploring what it would take to stand up a carefully vetted
and trained force of moderate Syrian rebels who could be trusted with
American weapons." If such a program worked, "it would be helpful in
a number of ways." A key benefit was that "even a small group might
be able to give a big psychological boost to the opposition and convince
Assad's backers to consider a political settlement."[48]

Although covert efforts to train and equip vetted moderate rebels
appear to have been underway in 2013, the administration formally
embraced that policy in June 2014, asking Congress to authorize
$500 million for the effort.[49] Officials would spend all of those funds
over the next 14 months.

Brookings Institution scholar Kenneth Pollack had an even more
extensive and robust effort in mind that would produce an insurgent army
capable of achieving "a decisive victory" in the war. To do that, he emphasized, "The United States would have to commit itself to building a new
Syrian army that could end the war and help establish stability when the
fighting was over. The effort should carry the resources and credibility of
the United States behind it and must not have the tentative and halfhearted
support that has defined every prior U.S. initiative in Syria since 2011."[50]

The Obama administration's program proved to be a total flop. Contrary to administration expectations that the Pentagon's new train-and-equip
venture would produce thousands of loyal fighters for a democratic Syria,
only 54 graduates emerged to create a moderate bulwark of the anti-Assad
rebellion.[51] And by September 2015, administration officials informed the
Senate that only "four or five" graduates remained actively in the field.[52]
The effort was even more wasteful than most government programs.

But advocates of stronger U.S. backing of the Syrian rebel cause
refused to abandon the "train and equip" chimera. A year after the
administration announced the program's termination, proponents were

still pressing for a renewed effort. A Washington Institute for Near East Policy study contended that the basic idea was sound. The failure, it argued, was caused by the tardiness in launching the program and by poor execution, especially the lack of "strategic vision."[53] Moderate Syrian insurgents still could become serious players, the authors insisted.

Attempting to create a new, moderate armed force from scratch was not the only component of the Obama administration's policy toward Syrian rebels, however. Despite mounting signs about the dubious nature of the anti-Assad resistance, the administration's overall support for the insurgency actually grew stronger. In June 2013, Deputy National Security Advisor Ben Rhodes proudly announced that Washington would provide increased assistance, including for the first time lethal aid to the Syrian National Council, a rebel umbrella group.[54] Washington's covert arms program had come out into the open.

Such activism produced more than a little confusion and sometimes outright incoherence. Components of Washington's national security bureaucracy even ended up at cross purposes in their efforts to assist Syrian insurgent factions. As journalist Eric Margolis observes caustically, "The U.S. military launched and supported its own rebel groups in Syria. The CIA did the same."[55] Those forces ultimately battled each other about as often as they battled either the Assad regime or ISIS.[56]

RED LINES AND A BLUNDER NARROWLY AVERTED

In 2013, the Obama administration took a stance that nearly led to full-scale U.S. military involvement on the side of the insurgents. In response to some small-scale incidents earlier that year that may have involved chemical agents, Obama warned Assad's government that any further use of such weapons would cross a "bright red line" that would not be tolerated. But on August 21, 2013, Syrian government forces appeared to have done just that and crossed the line with a chemical attack in Ghouta, a Damascus suburb. At least several hundred people—and perhaps more than 1,400—died from the effects of sarin gas.[57]

The administration moved to make good on its threat. But it soon discovered that public opposition to U.S. entanglement in Syria's civil war was much stronger than anticipated. White House e-mail and call centers—and those of House and Senate members—lit up with warnings from angry constituents. To make good on his threat to Assad, President Obama would be leading a manifestly reluctant country into yet another Middle East war.[58] Help came from an unlikely source when Russian President Vladimir Putin bailed Obama out of his political dilemma by prevailing on Assad (a longstanding Russian client) to accept a diplomatic deal to give up his arsenal of chemical weapons.[59] With that concession in hand, calls for cruise missile attacks and other military measures were muted, except among those members of the American political and policy communities who wanted to use the sarin gas incident as a justification for a full-fledged U.S. regime-change war against Assad.

In backing away from war, Obama made a wise decision. A quagmire similar to Iraq was looming. Moreover, despite the certainty expressed by administration officials and outside proponents of intervention, none could say with certainty exactly which faction—the Assad government, pro-Assad allies, or a rebel group—in Syria's civil war was guilty of the sarin gas attack. Even the pro-intervention *New York Times* reluctantly conceded that ascertaining the pertinent facts was difficult.[60] The investigations that followed only intensified the uncertainty, but U.S. officials would not acknowledge that they may have rushed to judgment about the culprit.

POSSIBLE REBEL INVOLVEMENT IN CHEMICAL WEAPONS ATTACKS?

As certainty about the Assad government's guilt withered, evidence emerged that rebels may have been complicit in the attack. Skeptics, including former CIA analyst Ray McGovern, suggest that the attack may have been a "false flag" operation—one in which a rebel faction conducted the attack for the explicit purpose of drawing the United States into the fighting as a full-fledged belligerent against Assad. Writing in the April 2014 *London Review of Books*, veteran investigative journalist Seymour Hersh echoes that thesis and specifically implicates both extremist Syrian rebels and Turkey's intelligence service.[61] To bolster their theories, Hersh, McGovern, and other dissenters present evidence that raises troubling questions about the episode.

In April 2017, a new chemical weapons attack on the village of Khan Sheikhoun intensified allegations that Assad's government was committing war crimes. The new Donald Trump administration reacted to the April incident as if there could be no doubt of the culprit, and it launched cruise missile strikes against the Syrian air base that U.S. officials identified as the source of the chemical weapons attack. Yet prominent critics, including MIT professor emeritus of Science, Technology, and International Security Theodore Postol—a longtime distinguished expert on intelligence issues—raised major questions about this episode as well—along with doubts about the quality of Washington's intelligence assessment.[62]

And there was yet another reason to be at least a little skeptical that the Syrian government was guilty of the attack: just days before the incident, U.S. Secretary of State Rex Tillerson and other officials announced that Washington would no longer demand that Assad leave office before a peace settlement could be achieved.[63] That was a major change in the U.S. position, and one that Assad's government had been seeking for years. Given that the Damascus government had just achieved such a diplomatic breakthrough, for it to commit the one act that was most likely to bring about a full-scale U.S. military intervention would have been the height of folly.

Conversely, the rebels were reeling from several recent military defeats at the hands of Syrian forces and their Russian allies who had commenced their intervention in 2015. Now, rebel factions were faced with an adverse change in Washington's diplomatic stance regarding Assad's departure. They had every motive in the world to get the United States to escalate its military involvement. When assessing any incident (or policy), the first question wise investigators ask is, "*Cui bono?*" (Who benefits?) Unfortunately, neither the Trump administration nor most members of the news media bothered to ask that question.

Of course, the Assad regime, in a foolish, self-defeating move, might have ordered the attack—or perhaps a trigger-happy military commander did so. A subsequent special UN commission investigation concluded that the Syrian government was responsible for the chemical attack, although some independent experts have disputed that conclusion.[64] The UN report also contains another troubling revelation: in a brief passage that was ignored in many media accounts, the commission concluded that ISIS had used sulfur mustard gas in a September 2013 assault.[65] With ISIS clearly having chemical weapons capabilities, guilt for the Khan Sheikhoun attack was muddied further.

The most reasonable conclusion is that the evidence was mixed and inconclusive. Although the Assad government may have been guilty, the possibility of a false flag operation from ISIS—a group that had already used chemical weapons—cannot, and should not, be dismissed. Even non-ISIS Sunni forces might have gained access to chemical weapons, perhaps from Syrian government stocks captured during the fighting. Obviously, ISIS obtained its mustard gas weapons from somewhere, and it is naive to assume that Jabhat al-Nusra or another extremist group couldn't have gotten chemical weapons of their own. Much of the evidence from the 2013 and 2017 chemical attacks had been gathered by rebel sources, and uncritically accepting their findings virtually invited manipulation by Syrian factions who had their own, often unsavory, political agendas. At the very least, U.S. policymakers should have exhibited greater caution before assigning responsibility for the chemical attacks with such certainty.

DELUSIONS ABOUT SYRIAN "MODERATES" PERSIST

Years before the Trump administration's cruise missile strikes against Syria, the United States and its Sunni allies had boosted rebel military capabilities. As noted previously, Washington, Riyadh, and Ankara provided a flood of armaments to insurgent forces, even during the early stages of the civil war. Moreover, the aid did not just strengthen those forces in general, but it specifically empowered the most extreme and unscrupulous Islamist factions. It was a déjà vu experience reminiscent of how the aid program to the Afghan mujahideen in the 1980s ended up with the U.S. arming radical Islamists.

Yet even in 2016 and 2017, much of the American media and political establishment still tried to convince the public that a moderate Syrian faction was a serious alternative to Assad and the Islamic radicals of ISIS. Former Assistant Secretary of State Elliott Abrams, a vocal advocate of U.S. support for the Syrian rebel cause and of forcible

Middle East democracy promotion in general, remained optimistic about a democratic outcome in Syria. He asserted that an "encouraging insight into the possibilities for Arab democracy is provided by what happened in parts of Syria when the hand of the repressive Syrian state was removed."[66] Abrams then quoted extensively from a July 2016 article in the English-language newspaper *The National*, published in the United Arab Emirates (UAE), which argued that numerous democratic local councils had sprung up in villages throughout "liberated" Syria.[67] Apparently, Abrams never considered the possibility that the UAE is not exactly a haven for free, independent journalism or that the article might be propaganda to alleviate Westerners' concerns about the growing evidence of autocratic behavior on the part of the Sunni forces that the UAE and other Persian Gulf powers were backing.

Contrary to Abrams and *The National*, evidence for the allegedly impressive spontaneous growth of democratic local governments was thin to nonexistent. Instead, developments like the one that took place in rebel-held areas of the northern city of Aleppo were far more typical. When Islamist rebel groups captured roughly half of that metropolitan area in late 2012, one of the coalition's first actions was to establish a Sharia Authority to compel all residents to comply with the strictures of Sharia law. Phillips points out that the situation in Aleppo was not unique; similar conservative enforcement bodies were established in many rebel-controlled territories.[68]

American enthusiasts of the Syrian rebellion exhibited great reluctance to acknowledge rebel abuses and the extremist nature of some insurgent factions. Journalist Stephen Kinzer excoriated the media for their coverage of the Syrian civil war, especially the fighting around Aleppo, and for their negligence in covering those facts. According to Kinzer, "For three years, violent militias have run Aleppo. Their rule began with a wave of repression. They posted notices warning residents: 'Don't send your children to school. If you do, we will get the backpack and you will get the coffin.' Then they destroyed factories . . . [and] trucked looted machinery to Turkey and sold it."[69]

In early 2016, the Syrian army, backed by Russian air support, launched an offensive to push the militant rebels out of Aleppo.

But according to Kinzer, "Much of the American press is reporting the opposite of what is actually happening. Many news reports suggest that Aleppo has been a 'liberated zone' for three years but is now being pulled back into misery." He notes that Washington-based reporters used terminology that attempted to portray even the staunchly Islamist faction Jabhat al-Nusra as being composed "of 'rebels' or 'moderates,' not that it was the local al-Qaeda franchise."[70] Georgetown University senior fellow Paul Pillar likewise is critical of much of the Aleppo coverage, finding it excessively emotional and one-sided.[71] British journalist Patrick Cockburn contends that far more propaganda than genuine news came out of Aleppo. Noting that the area had become far too dangerous for Western reporters to operate there, he points out that most outlets were relying on locals to provide information, which guaranteed a blatant pro-rebel bias: "The foreign media has allowed—through naivety or self-interest—people who could only operate with the permission of al-Qaeda-type groups such as Jabhat al-Nusra and Ahrar al-Sham to dominate the news agenda."[72]

ABC correspondent Martha Raddatz seems to follow the model highlighted by Kinzer and Pillar. While moderating the second presidential debate of the 2016 campaign, Raddatz asked: "Just days ago, the State Department called for a war crimes investigation of the Syrian regime of Bashar al-Assad and its ally, Russia, for their bombardment of Aleppo. So this next question comes through social media through Facebook. Diane from Pennsylvania asks, 'If you were president, what would you do about Syria and the humanitarian crisis in Aleppo? Isn't it a lot like the Holocaust when the U.S. waited too long before we helped?'"[73] Framing the Aleppo issue in that fashion certainly did not contribute to a balanced discussion, and it implied that the rebels in eastern Aleppo were innocent victims of Russian and Syrian savagery.

Adding credence to the criticisms raised by Kinzer and Pillar, the *Washington Post* published an op-ed by Brookings Institution fellow Leon Wieseltier that was yet another, even more blatant example of the over-the-top treatment the Aleppo situation was receiving. Wieseltier's piece began with an allegation about "the extermination of Aleppo and its people." He invoked Holocaust survivor Elie Wiesel and his teachings that one simply cannot stand by while another Auschwitz or Rwanda takes place.[74] As Pillar notes in his blog, the article proceeds "in a comparably black-and-white and overwrought vein" interspersed with disparagements of Obama for not having taken more decisive action to back the anti-Assad forces.[75]

A July 2016 report from Amnesty International paints a rather different picture than the stark, simplistic ones composed by Raddatz, Wieseltier, and others. The report also validates many of Kinzer's assessments of Aleppo. Amnesty confirmed that Nusra and allied "armed groups operating in Aleppo, Idlib and surrounding areas in the north of Syria have carried out a chilling wave of abductions, torture and summary killings."[76] Strangely, while Amnesty investigators were able to uncover an entire "wave" of such incidents, Western journalists operating in the same area apparently saw nothing but well-behaved insurgents resisting the brutal bombing and shelling campaign waged by Syrian government forces.

Rebel war crimes hardly were limited to Aleppo. Human Rights Watch (HRW) documents another episode of rebel atrocities in autumn 2013. A coalition of Islamist forces—including Jabhat al-Nusra, Ahrar al-Sham, and ISIS—launched an offensive into the Alawite heartland near the Mediterranean coast. At one point, the militias came within 20 kilometers of Assad's hometown (Qardaha) before being driven back by loyalist forces. HRW reports that some 190 civilians were killed during that campaign, at least 67 of whom were summarily executed; almost all of those atrocities took place during the first days of the rebel offensive.[77] Although the three militant groups all denied responsibility, the HRW report makes it clear that they were the perpetrators. Their denials eroded badly and finally lost all credibility when Nusra publicly executed a prominent Alawite sheik who had been captured by another Islamist faction, Harakat Sham al-Islam.[78]

Despite the biased and sanitized media accounts, which echoed Secretary Kerry's sunny assessments of the rebel cause, portions of the Obama administration had their doubts about the nature of some of Washington's clients in Aleppo and elsewhere. The split between the Pentagon and the CIA, which earlier had led to the two agencies' backing rival rebel factions in northern Syria, surfaced again. A news report in the *Daily Beast* succinctly explains the policy dispute between the agencies and the reasons for it: "Two Department of Defense officials told *The Daily Beast* that they are not eager to support the rebels in the city of Aleppo because they're seen as being affiliated with al Qaeda in Syria, or Jabhat al Nusra. The CIA, which supports those rebel groups, rejects that claim, saying alliances of convenience in the face of a mounting Russian-led offensive have created marriages of battlefield necessity, not ideology."[79]

Throughout the Syrian civil war, U.S. officials and their media allies have tended to be vague about what exactly constitutes a "moderate." Both Obama administration officials and American journalists gave Syrian rebel groups a great deal of latitude with respect to their ideological orientation and their behavior on the battlefield, and that was true of other Western governments as well. British Prime Minister David Cameron asserted in January 2016 that there were fully 70,000 "moderate" fighters in Syria. When pressed to substantiate that number, though, both he and his supporters seemed to be including almost any Syrian faction that was not explicitly allied with either Assad or ISIS. Pressed further about the 70,000 figure, Cameron responded, "Are all of these people impeccable democrats who would share the view of democracy that you and I have? No, some of them do belong to Islamist groups and some of them belong to relatively hardline Islamist groups. . . ."[80] Such an empty standard raises the question: just what did U.S. and other Western officials actually mean when they said they favored a "moderate" alternative to both Assad and ISIS?

Some prominent members of the U.S. foreign policy community appeared willing to skirt right around the official goal of supporting only moderates (however defined) and sell out for the insurgents completely. Former CIA Director Petraeus, for example, even urged Washington to make common cause with Jabhat al-Nusra, al Qaeda's affiliate in Syria.[81] He argued that at least some of the jihadists in Nusra's ranks could be "peeled" away from Nusra and used to fight both ISIS and the Assad regime. His proposal to use al Qaeda acolytes to fight the Islamic State smacked of wishful (even deluded) thinking, as well as utter desperation to salvage a failing policy. After all, ISIS and Nusra didn't have significant ideological differences with respect to the nature of their cause or the kind of future regime they thought should govern Syria; they simply disagreed about which organization was the legitimate vessel to lead the Islamist cause.

Other supposedly moderate insurgent groups that Washington supported also turned out to be horrifyingly bad. One such group, Harakat Nour al-Din al-Zinki, received U.S. arms and other assistance before American officials concluded that the group might be too extreme. That concern was borne out in July 2016, when a video surfaced showing group members beheading a child.[82] Apparently the gap between Syrian "moderates" and ISIS was not all that large.

Secretary of State Kerry and other Obama administration officials, though, remained focused on trying to identify and mobilize a group of moderates that were not tainted by a connection with either ISIS or Nusra. The issue came to a head in 2016 when Russian planes were continuing to bomb rebel targets. The Russians claimed that they were striking terrorists, but the United States contended that many of the targets were in fact moderate, pro-Western insurgents, or as Secretary Kerry termed them, "legitimate opposition groups."[83] His implicit definition of legitimate or moderate, though, didn't appear to be any more specific than Prime Minister Cameron's. Moreover, Kerry's insistence that such groups were separate from ISIS and the Nusra front, both organizationally and ideologically, had very little supporting evidence.

Kerry's assertion certainly failed to convince skeptics like Gareth Porter. In at least two key provinces, Porter wrote, the reality "is that there is no such separation." Indeed, "information from a wide range of sources, including some of the groups that the United States has been explicitly supporting, makes it clear that every armed anti-Assad organization unit in those provinces is engaged in a military system controlled by Nusra. All of them fight alongside the Nusra Front and coordinate their military activities with it."[84] Lister likewise cites the willingness of other insurgent groups to conduct joint military operations with Nusra—and often as junior partners.[85]

There is little doubt that Nusra usually was the dominant player in those joint operations. For example, one of the allegedly moderate groups Washington backed was the Syrian Revolutionaries Front (SRF). The Obama administration even supplied the SRF (and other moderates) with "TOW" anti-tank missiles.[86] When a combined force of Nusra and SRF rebels captured a major Syrian army base at Wadi al-Deif in December 2014, the power relationship among the various groups soon became quite clear: only Nusra and Ahrar al-Sham were allowed to enter the base. The non-jihadi SRF and other less radical types were excluded.[87]

Yet that treatment was relatively mild compared to what Nusra administered to another U.S.-supported group, Harakat Hazm. In April 2015, before launching a campaign against government-held Idlib province, Nusra forced Harakat Hazm to disband; Nusra then confiscated all of the TOW missiles Washington had given the group.[88] A year earlier, Jeffrey White, a defense fellow at the Washington Institute for Near East Policy, was one of several experts who lauded Harakat Hazm for its alleged values and its organizational and fighting capabilities.[89] His first argument was questionable, but given the ease with which Nusra disarmed the group, the second proved to be wildly unrealistic.

The bottom line is that Islamist elements continue to make up the strongest faction in the rebel insurgency against Assad.[90] Jabhat al-Nusra has renamed itself Tahrir al-Sham, but that move, along with its official severing of ties with al Qaeda, is purely cosmetic. The group's new name has done nothing to alter its rabidly Islamist nature or its controlling position in the Syrian insurgency. Islamists clearly continue to dominate the Syrian rebellion.

The optimism and trust that American and other Western supporters of the Syrian insurgency exhibit has remained tenacious, however. In mid-2016, the Center for a New American Security issued a report titled "From the Bottom, Up: A Strategy for U.S. Military Support to Syria's Armed Opposition." The report was a triumph of hope over experience, concluding, "The primary U.S. effort in Syria should be a bottom–up strategy to build cohesive, moderate, armed opposition institutions with a regional focus."[91]

Writing in the May 24, 2016, issue of *Foreign Affairs*, Middle East Institute scholar Ehud Ya'ari urged more extensive U.S. assistance to rebels in southern Syria. His belief in the potential beneficial effect of such aid was nearly boundless:

> A relatively modest assistance program from Washington could help the local factions expel ISIS from its small enclave in the region and gradually dissolve the local al Qaeda affiliate, Jabhat al-Nusra. Building up the military capabilities of the rebel forces and improving their fragile system of governance could ultimately transform them into a credible threat to the forces of Syrian President Bashar al-Assad in Damascus.
>
> What's more, strengthening the rebels' position in the south may convince the half million Druze in the southwestern city of Sweida to turn away from the Assad regime.[92]

More than 18 months later, though, the Druze still seemed firmly committed to Assad; and to the extent that Nusra and its allies' position had weakened, it was the result of military actions by the Syrian government and Russia, not pressure from phantom moderate rebels.

In late July 2017, the Trump administration announced that it was ending the CIA's covert program of support for "moderate" Syrian rebel forces.[93] Daniel DePetris, a fellow with the think tank Defense Priorities, concludes bluntly that the move was "an admission of failure."[94] The administration's statement might raise some hopes that U.S. officials finally were learning from their many policy blunders. However, the CIA support program was only one component of Washington's larger strategy to back Syrian insurgents. It remained unclear whether the administration would rescind the other measures to overthrow Assad's government. The Pentagon's deployment of 400 additional U.S. military "advisers" to Syria at roughly the same time that the covert support effort ended strongly suggests that the overall strategy will not be abandoned anytime soon.[95]

THE ROLE OF THE KURDS

Despite Washington's longstanding search for moderate Syrian rebels, few fighters with such an orientation are on the ground. Those who are generally lack meaningful capabilities, with one notable exception: the Kurdish units inside the Syrian Democratic Forces and other separate Kurdish militias. The Kurds are able fighters and secular at least in their outward orientation. Their commitment to democratic norms is superficially impressive, but their actual conduct both in Syria and in Iraqi Kurdistan is somewhat murkier. The Kurds' track record when it comes to democracy is better than those of other political factions in that part of the world, but it still often falls short of the Western ideal. Moreover, Kurdish politics have been trending ominously toward greater authoritarianism.[96] Additionally, disturbing evidence reveals that the Syrian Kurdish forces have committed human rights abuses.[97]

Between the two main Kurdish factions in Syria, noticeable divisions exist. One group is the rather radical-left Democratic Union Party (PYD), which controls the greatest number of militia fighters, called the Popular Protection Units (YPG). The PYD competes for influence with the somewhat more moderate Kurdish Democratic Party (KDP), a group that has ties to a similar party in Iraq. The two factions usually cooperate, but bouts of feuding have occurred on occasion.

Kurdish fighters in Syria also have displayed an impressive record of organizational competence and battlefield success.[98] In the summer and autumn of 2013, YPG forces already had scored decisive victories over both Nusra and the embryonic ISIS, proceeding to liberate most majority Kurd cities in the north.[99] Given the widespread collapse of the authority that the Assad government once exercised in that region, the Kurds had been poised to expand their power for months. As they achieved subsequent victories over Islamist forces, Kurdish leaders announced the creation of an "interim autonomous government" for that country's heavily Kurdish region,[100] and then they began to expand militarily into ethnically mixed areas. Those troops, especially components of the Kurdish-dominated Syrian Democratic Forces, played a major role in the capture of the ISIS capital, Raqqa, in October 2017.

Although able allies against ISIS, the Kurds have always pursued their own agenda—which includes securing a de facto independent state in northern Syria just as their ethnic brethren had done in Iraqi Kurdistan following the U.S.-led overthrow of Saddam Hussein. The U.S. goal of ousting Assad is not prominent on the Kurds' radar. A January 2016 incident illustrates how the Kurds' separatist agenda complicates Syria's armed conflict. In that incident, militia fighters from the Assyrian Christian community in northern Iraq clashed with Kurdish troops.[101] The episode was especially revealing because both the Assyrian Christians and the Kurds are vehement adversaries of ISIS (who at the time was a major player in that region of Syria). Logically, the Assyrian Christians and the Kurds should be tactical allies who cooperate in their military moves against the terrorist organization. However, although both hate ISIS, the former supports an intact Syria (presumably with Assad or someone else acceptable to the assortment of religious minorities in charge) while the latter does not.

By mid-2017, the accumulating victories by the Syrian Democratic Forces, the YPG militia, and other forces had expanded the amount of land under Kurdish control. It constituted a nearly continuous swath of territory along the Syrian-Turkish border from the frontier with Iraq in the east to the Turkish "thumb" jutting southward into Syria in the west near the Mediterranean Sea. That "enclave" amounted to nearly 25 percent of Syria.[102] The Kurds became steadily more politically aggressive, as well. In December 2015, they created the Syrian Democratic Council, and on March 17, 2016, they organized a conference in the city of Rmelan, along with officials from the Christian and other minority communities, to declare the establishment of the Democratic Federation of Rojava, an explicitly self-governing region. In September 2017, the authorities conducted local elections, which was the first stage in a three-stage process to establish an official, autonomous, regional government.[103]

U.S. leaders understandably welcomed military victories by a secular, somewhat democratic faction against ISIS and other militant Islamists. The Kurds seemed to be rebels worth supporting, and Washington was generous with financial aid and military hardware. But a cloud of uneasiness hangs over the project even with regard to the Kurds. Not only is the depth of their commitment to democracy and human rights somewhat uncertain, but the United States must confront the awkward reality that one of its major NATO allies, Turkey, regards the Kurdish enterprise in Syria with perhaps even greater animosity than it has viewed the existence of Iraqi Kurdistan. Ankara considers Kurdish sentiment for autonomy, or even worse, outright independence from Iraq and Syria, as a threat to its territorial integrity. President Erdoğan and other leaders have charged that the PYD is in league with the separatist, Marxist Kurdistan Workers Party (PKK) in southeastern Turkey—no minor matter, because the PKK has waged a secessionist war there for decades.[104]

Turkish fears of PYD and PKK collusion may be exaggerated, but they are not entirely unfounded, and the Erdoğan government has acted accordingly. Despite Washington's explicit wishes, Turkish planes have bombed and shelled YPG forces on several occasions.[105] When a provocative referendum in Iraqi Kurdistan produced a pro-independence vote in September 2017, Ankara's hostility toward Syrian Kurds and their counterparts in Iraq ticked up another notch.

Under growing pressure from Erdoğan, President Trump announced in November 2017 that the United States would end its military assistance to Syrian Kurds.[106] However, Washington continues to send mixed messages about its relationship with Kurdish fighters; the administration essentially deputized the Syrian Kurds, authorizing them to suppress remaining pockets of Islamic extremism in northern Syria and to guard the border with Turkey.[107] Erdoğan was enraged at that move, saying that the United States had "stabbed us in the back," and threatening to invade Kurdish-held territories in Syria.[108]

On January 21, 2018, Ankara made good on its threat: the Turkish military launched massive air strikes that it immediately followed with a full-scale invasion of Kurdish enclaves in northern Syria. Even when Washington thought it had identified an insurgent client who was both militarily effective and reasonably democratic, its support for the Syrian Kurds ended up having a very high geopolitical cost: poisoned relations with Turkey, a longtime NATO ally that U.S. leaders insist is essential to the West's security.

Yet Another Failed U.S. Policy of Backing "Democratic" Insurgents

Washington's support for the Syrian rebels belongs on a shelf alongside similarly ill-advised policy embarrassments like those in Nicaragua,

Angola, Kosovo, Iraq, and Libya. Time and again, U.S. officials have backed insurgent movements who have turned out to be as bad as, or even worse than, the regimes they sought to overthrow. In the process, Washington's regime-change efforts have destabilized already fragile states and caused massive refugee flows and other manifestations of acute human suffering. Such was the outcome in Iraq and Libya, and now it is the outcome in Syria.

With respect to the Syrian situation, Andrew Bacevich, author of *America's War for the Greater Middle East*, puts it well: "Although U.S. officials had ample justification for calling Assad 'a thug and a murderer,' his opponents were hardly paragons of virtue." Indeed, as the armed struggle wore on, a growing number of Assad's opponents included "radical Islamists more interested in promoting violent jihad than liberal values."[109] Christopher Phillips reaches a similar conclusion: U.S. and other outside support for the rebels, he contends, helped "fuel the war's development, ensure its prolongation, and facilitate the successes of militant Jihadist groups that would ultimately extend far beyond Syria."[110]

One wonders how often such an ugly experience needs to be repeated before American leaders will finally "get it" and distance U.S. policy from foreign insurgents who profess to pledge allegiance to democratic values (which some of the Syrian factions Washington supported never bothered to do even in a perfunctory manner). Unfortunately, few signs indicate that the Syrian debacle will be the last such episode for the United States.

AMERICA NEEDS A NEW
POLICY OF SKEPTICISM AND RESTRAINT

The lengthy, depressing record of U.S. support for bogus freedom fighters and democratic activists raises a question: Why are American political figures, policy experts, and journalists so susceptible to being gulled? Cynics might argue that U.S. leaders don't actually believe that most "democratic" upheavals are genuine, but instead choose to portray them as such if the insurgent faction seems amenable to Washington's economic or strategic goals. According to that theory, policymakers stress their clients' alleged democratic credentials to soothe an American public that might balk at embracing questionable (much less odious) movements or governments on the basis of realpolitik.

That thesis is a plausible one. After all, throughout the Cold War, Washington routinely portrayed friendly autocrats, no matter how corrupt and brutal, as members of the "free world."[1] Vice President George H. W. Bush hailed Philippine dictator Ferdinand Marcos for his "commitment to democratic principles," even as that country groaned under the martial law imposed by Marcos a decade earlier. Supposed human rights champion President Jimmy Carter toasted the brutally tyrannical Shah of Iran as though he were a democratic hero: "Iran, because of the great leadership of the Shah, is an island of stability in one of the more troubled regions of the world. This is a great tribute to you, Your Majesty, and to your leadership, and to the respect and admiration and love which your people give to you," Carter gushed. He added that the United States and Iran shared far more than security interests: "The cause of human rights is one that is also shared deeply by our people and by the leaders of our two nations."[2]

The notion that experienced political leaders like Bush and Carter actually believed that the tyrants they exalted were truly committed to human rights and democratic values strains credulity—far too much contrary evidence existed for them to have harbored such illusions. More likely, the praise lavished on such rulers reflected diplomatic cynicism policymakers deemed necessary to protect and advance U.S. economic and strategic interests.

Nevertheless, one cannot underestimate the capacity even of jaded politicians to engage in self-delusion. Otherwise, how does one explain the embarrassing assertion President George W. Bush made about Vladimir Putin after their first summit meeting in 2001? "I looked the man in the eye," Bush stated; "I found him to be very straightforward and trustworthy, and we had a very good dialogue. I was able to get a sense of his soul."[3]

Journalists and other opinion shapers have been even more susceptible to wishful thinking. Americans understandably are proud of the values enshrined in the Declaration of Independence and the U.S. Constitution, especially the Bill of Rights. For more than two centuries, we have wanted and expected other societies to emulate our model. The view that America is a "shining city upon a hill" that sets the political, economic, and moral example for other societies goes back to the earliest years of the Republic. However, during the 20th and 21st centuries, the United States morphed from merely encouraging foreign countries to admire and replicate her political and economic system to aggressively promoting (and sometimes even imposing) it.

From America as a Democratic Example to Democracy as a Forcible U.S. Export

Woodrow Wilson was the most prominent early proponent of that more activist approach. He famously stated that he would teach the countries of Latin America to "elect good men."[4] His military interventions in places such as Haiti, Nicaragua, and Mexico confirm that his strategy was not confined to peaceful encouragement. Wilson's Fourteen Points manifesto, which outlined his vision of a dramatically transformed world that should emerge from World War, embodied a strong push to displace the traditional royal, often multinational, autocracies in Europe and replace them with regimes that reflected both nationalist identities and democratic values.[5] That approach was merely an extension of his insistence that America had entered the war to "make the world safe for democracy."[6]

In recent decades, the Wilsonian perspective has taken strong root within certain factions in the United States, not only among liberal advocates of humanitarian intervention but also among neoconservatives who lionize the notion of U.S. "global leadership." Increasingly, those factions have come to see the democratic system not as something that must develop organically within a society but as an American product that can be exported to and then implanted in other countries (forcibly, if necessary). In 1991, Joshua Muravchik, then a scholar at the neoconservative American Enterprise Institute, espoused that very position in his book *Exporting Democracy: Fulfilling America's Destiny.*[7] Not only that, but in 2009, Muravchik doubled-down on his thesis with even greater boldness and specificity in *The Next Founders: Voices of Democracy in the Middle East.*[8] In that book, Muravchik hails an array of Middle East figures who he asserts have embraced democracy and, with America's assistance, could lead the politics of the region in a much more humane and beneficial direction.

By no means is Muravchik alone when he argues that a powerful surge of popular sentiment for Western-style democracy exists throughout the Middle East and that U.S. financial—and, if necessary, military—support is an essential catalyst for bringing such sentiment to fruition. Writing in June 2016 to U.S. presidential candidates to offer the Middle East Institute's recommendations for democracy in the region, scholar Charles Dunne argued, "Old methods of repression will not hold back the [pro-democratic] tide." The next administration, he insisted, "should increase funding for civil society in the region, among other democratization tools" to help bring in that tide.[9]

During the past few decades, democracy exportation efforts dove-tailed with the humanitarian intervention and responsibility to protect doctrines, as seen in Washington's use of military power to displace tyrannical regimes that exhibited bad human rights records. Among U.S. elites, the horrifying realities of the Holocaust and the Cambodian and Rwandan genocides strengthened both intellectual and political support for the argument that America must use military force, if neces-sary, to prevent a repetition of such atrocities. But those elites' insistence that Washington had a moral obligation to use military force in clear-cut cases of genocide soon became a justification for using military power in murkier and far less severe conflicts. Cases in point: the Balkans, Iraq, Libya, and Syria, where humanitarian arguments greatly contributed to the rationale for unwise U.S.-led interventions.

And from the belief in an obligation to prevent atrocities, human-itarian intervention proponents only had to take a small step to por-tray civilian victims of autocratic regimes as noble advocates of freedom and democracy. Embracing that view was easier and far more satisfy-ing than admitting that the United States was waging war to back fac-tions that at best were only a marginal improvement over the regimes being opposed. Therefore, advocates of humanitarian military missions and regime-change wars had powerful incentives to ignore (or at least minimize) the flaws of Washington's clients.

Exporting Democracy: A Mixed Record at Best

At times, those who have optimistically believed that a U.S. foreign policy of active democracy exportation would achieve worthy results have been vindicated. After all, the political systems implanted by the United States in Germany and Japan following World War II took hold and blossomed into pluralistic democracies. Later, and much more gradually, similar political values became dominant in South Korea and Taiwan (although in both cases, those transformations took place despite Washington's close cooperation with previous autocratic gov-ernments). After the collapse of the Soviet satellite empire in Eastern Europe, most of the political systems that emerged were reasonably democratic; in some cases, such as the Czech Republic and the three Baltic republics, they were impressively so. Moreover, those nations also tended to look to America for guidance and support, in large part because the United States had been the principal opponent of their imperial Soviet oppressor.

But in too many other cases, Americans have mentally shoehorned foreign political movements into the liberal democracy category. In some instances (most notably, Poland's Solidarity Movement), democratic activists were in fact the dominant faction, and Washington's support of the movement was at least morally justified. But most of the other allegedly democratic insurgencies around the world have fallen far short of that ideal. Ronald Reagan's likening of the Nicaraguan Contras to America's founding fathers was a considerable exaggeration. Likewise, the Maidan revolutionaries in Ukraine and participants in the Rose Revolution in Georgia were an unsettling mixture of genuine democrats and unsavory, often corrupt, ultra-nationalist elements. The balance between democratic and authoritarian players in the Kosovo Liberation Army and the government it birthed was skewed even more toward the authoritarians.

Sadly, many of the foreign political movements that the United States has supported cannot be qualified as even quasi-democratic. Portraying a murderous thug like Angola's Jonas Savimbi as a democratic freedom fighter, for example, makes a mockery of both democracy and freedom fighters. The same is true of efforts to paint the Afghan muja-hideen as anything other than a group of religious zealots determined to establish a repressive theocracy in their country. The insurgents who overthrew Libya's Muammar Qaddafi (with extensive assistance from the United States and NATO, one might add) turned out to be pri-marily undemocratic factions that were more interested in looting and establishing militarized satrapies than in creating a tolerant and effective national polity. A similar reality now has emerged among the insurgents in Syria. In Libya and Syria, legitimate secular democrats are both few and militarily weak.

Of course, it is always possible that U.S. policymakers were keenly aware that they were supporting foreign insurgents who were not committed to democracy and individual liberty in the least, but their statements at the time and later point to a different conclusion. Their impassioned arguments suggest a genuine belief in the people and causes that looked to America for active support. Ronald Reagan's entries in his private diary differ little from his often gushing public comments regarding the anti-communist rebels that Washington was backing. Additionally, given America's horrid experience in Iraq, the Obama administration likely would not have embraced a military intervention in Libya had officials truly believed that the anti-Qaddafi forces were little better than the incumbent dictator, and that the postwar outcome would be utter chaos.

Similarly, Ahmed Chalabi's American supporters likely would not have been so consistently laudatory of him had they known he was not only a corrupt operator but also a de facto political ally of Iran. Especially for neoconservatives, who regard Iran as America's most dangerous adversary in the Middle East, supporting Chalabi despite such knowledge would have been utterly irrational.

Moreover, even if a few Machiavellian officials falsely portrayed corrupt, brutal, authoritarian insurgents as freedom-loving democrats, that does not explain why so many academics, journalists, and democracy promotion activists did likewise. They had little to gain from deliberately misrepresenting the nature of such factions. Indeed, they courted embarrassment and damage to their own professional reputations, as *New York Times* correspondent Judith Miller sorely discovered when the truth about Chalabi emerged. Yet many people in similar influential positions were passionate, uncritical proponents of the self-proclaimed democratic insurgents and their causes.

Rather than being real-life examples of cynical realpolitik, then, U.S. support for unworthy foreign political movements more likely reflects an insufficient amount of skepticism on the part of American officials and opinion leaders, as well as a sincere desire to see Western values flourish in other regions of the world. Such a desire is healthy, borne of the proper conclusion that societies based on democratic principles are more humane and enable their populations to live freer, happier, and more fulfilled lives. During and after the Cold War, American proponents of liberal democracy encountered activists from countries in the greater Middle East, Africa, Latin America, and the former communist bloc in Eastern Europe who professed allegiance to the same values and goals. Too many Americans took the so-called freedom fighters at their word, even when worrisome signs of possible duplicity surfaced. In short, they believed what they desperately wanted to believe.

Foreign factions have become adept at exploiting Americans' sincere desire for the spread of enlightened liberal capitalist ideals. To win crucial diplomatic, economic, and military support from the United States, the leaders of those factions have shrewdly told American policymakers and opinion leaders what they wanted to hear. However, foreign propagandists' skillful weaving does not exonerate U.S. officials, who bear ultimate responsibility for letting themselves and U.S. foreign policy be manipulated.

American Conservative columnist Daniel Larison aptly skewers officials for their willingness to be carried away by the sweet nothings whispered to them by the Ahmed Chalabis of the world. He argues that, while it is not surprising that rebels seeking outside support "tell representatives of [the U.S.] government things they want to hear, . . . it is deeply disturbing that our officials are frequently so eager to believe that what they are being told [is] true." Indeed, U.S. leaders should be more cautious, not less, when they are hearing "all the right things" from such individuals. He adds, "Not only should our officials know from previous episodes that the people saying 'all the right things' are typically conning Washington in the hopes of receiving support, but they should assume that anyone saying 'all the right things' either doesn't represent the forces on the ground that the U.S. will be called on to support or is deliberately misrepresenting the conditions on the ground to make U.S. involvement more attractive."[10]

For our own psychological (not to mention, political and strategic) well-being, Americans would be wise to pause before automatically embracing the next gathering of dissidents in some far-flung capital as though they were noble, newborn democrats deserving our financial (and, of course, military) aid. All too often, that image does not even come close to matching reality. In pointing out the mismatch, Larison identifies a major source of the rot in U.S. policy regarding supposedly democratic insurgencies:

> The fact that interventionists "want to believe" what they're told by opposition figures in other countries reflects their general naiveté about the politics of the countries where they want to intervene and their absurd overconfidence in the efficacy of U.S. action in general. If one takes for granted that there must be sympathetic liberals-in-waiting in another country that will take over once a regime is toppled, one isn't going to worry about the negative and unintended consequences of regime change. Because interventionists have difficulty imagining how U.S. intervention can go awry or make things worse, they are also unlikely to be suspicious of the motives or goals of the "good guys" they want the U.S. to support.[11]

GREATER SKEPTICISM NEEDED ABOUT
FOREIGN INSURGENT MOVEMENTS

The bruising experiences of supporting the likes of the Afghan mujahideen, the Nicaraguan Contras, the Kosovo Liberation Army, the Iraqi National Congress, the anti–Qaddafi Libyan rebels, and the anti–Assad Syrian rebels confirm the wisdom of earlier U.S. leaders who maintained a prudent distance between America's values and interests and those of foreign insurgent movements. Reagan's willingness to equate those movements' well-being and ours was emblematic of a dangerous attitude that has become far too common. Speaking to an October 1988 World Affairs Council meeting in Los Angeles, Reagan cited the growing roster of so-called freedom fighters around the world and stated: "There is something in our spirit and history that makes us say these are our own battles and that those who resist [tyranny] are our brothers and sisters."[12]

That is precisely the ideological and emotional trap that U.S. leaders must avoid. Washington's embrace of those movements has bred consequences ranging from embarrassing to disastrous. The most charitable assessment one can make of U.S. officials and opinion leaders who touted such organizations as being committed to the advancement of freedom is that they were astonishingly gullible. Their lack of healthy skepticism is troubling. Many of them seemed in awe that foreign political activists insisted that they supported Western political and economic values. But what would American enthusiasts expect them to say? That they were really Islamic extremists, mundane autocrats, or just corrupt opportunists? Foreign activists told potential American sponsors exactly what they knew those sponsors wanted and needed to hear. Even modest due diligence would have revealed that the actions of most of the "freedom fighters" did not comport with their inspiring rhetoric.

Figuring out that Jonas Savimbi was not a Jeffersonian democrat who embraced the economic philosophy of Milton Friedman but instead was a corrupt, murderous socialist didn't take a rocket scientist—no matter how the African leader tried to cloak himself in admirable values. Likewise, considerable evidence of Ahmed Chalabi's corruption and pro-Iranian behavior had surfaced years before the Clinton and Bush administrations embraced him. And in places like Afghanistan, Libya, and Syria, no one should have been surprised that genuine secular democrats were hard to come by, while Islamists of varying extremes were everywhere. Even in more subtle cases like Nicaragua, Kosovo, Georgia, and Ukraine, copious warning signs indicated that the factions Washington was backing were, at best, highly imperfect democratic models.

Unfortunately, even now, as revealed by the continuing simplistic endorsements of supposedly pro-Western "moderate" factions in Syria and Ukraine, policymakers and opinion leaders have not learned from their predecessors' mistakes. The comments of Florida Senator and 2016 GOP presidential candidate Marco Rubio illustrate the persistence of wishful thinking about allegedly democratic movements. In an eerie echo of George Shultz's 1985 Reagan Doctrine speech (see Introduction, p. 7), Rubio argues that "oppressed peoples still turn their eyes toward our shores, wondering if we can hear their cries." We cannot ignore those cries, he contends, because we "have a responsibility to support democracy."[13] He doesn't even seem to consider the possibility that some of those democracy-professing movements are simply façades for other, sometimes even sleazy, objectives. And yet the historical record confirms that, in a distressing number of cases, sleazy objectives are the real goal, not democracy. If the United States is to avoid repeating the blunders of the past, our policymakers need to learn that basic lesson.

Moreover, whether foreign movements are genuinely democratic should have little bearing on the substance of U.S. foreign policy. Even if Jonas Savimbi, Hashim Thaçi, Ahmed Chalabi, Mikheil Saakashvili, or Petro Poroshenko were the second coming of James Madison, the United States would be unwise to meddle in turbulent regions and risk unnecessary wars. For example, when Russian forces went to war against Saakashvili's Georgia in 2008, it would have been folly for Washington to go nose-to-nose with a nuclear-armed Russia. Likewise, even if the Maidan Revolution had not produced a regime that included unsavory ultra-nationalist and neo-fascist elements, Washington was ill-advised to help unseat a duly elected, pro-Russian government and foment a new cold war with Moscow over Ukraine's geopolitical orientation.

John Quincy Adams was right about the nature of a proper and wise foreign policy for America. A crucial distinction must be made between sympathizing with causes whenever "the standard of freedom and independence has been or shall be unfurled" and having the U.S. military go abroad "in search of monsters to destroy." Adams captured that distinction and its policy requirements perfectly when he emphasized that America "is the well-wisher to the freedom and independence of all. She is the champion and vindicator only of her own."[14] U.S. leaders and the American public must revive their commitment to an Adams-like foreign policy and must refrain from quixotic crusades to impose democracy on other societies—an especially important point, because while many foreign insurgent movements unfurl the standard of freedom when it suits their purposes, they actually have little or no commitment to freedom in practice. Blindly backing foreign insurgent movements undermines America's interests and degrades her values; the United States must make a decisive course correction away from such a policy.

NOTES

INTRODUCTION

[1]"Ukraine Crisis: Transcript of Leaked Nuland-Pyatt Call," BBC News, February 7, 2014.

[2]Connor Finnegan, "A Look at the Factions Battling in Syria's Civil War," ABC News, ABC, April 11, 2017, http://abcnews.go.com/International /inside-syrias-multiple-fighting-factions/story?id=46731830.

[3]John Quincy Adams, "Speech to the U.S. House of Representatives on Foreign Policy," July 4, 1821, transcript, Miller Center, University of Virginia, Charlottesville, VA, https://millercenter.org/the-presidency/presidential-speeches /july-4-1821-speech-us-house-representatives-foreign-policy.

[4]Tim Weiner, *Legacy of Ashes: The History of the CIA* (New York: Doubleday, 2007), pp. 43–45.

[5]Peter Schweizer, *Victory: The Reagan Administration's Secret Strategy That Hastened the Collapse of the Soviet Union* (New York: Atlantic Monthly Press, 1994), p. 58.

[6]Schweizer, *Victory*, pp. 68, 228–29. By February 1986, the United States began providing substantial funds to underground groups in Czechoslovakia. See p. 228.

[7]Schweizer, *Victory*, p. 69.

[8]Schweizer, *Victory*, pp. 75, 85–90, 101. He contends further that "the CIA was in contact with Solidarity activists on a regular basis," p. 121.

[9]Robert McFarlane quoted in Schweizer, *Victory*, p. 120. For the figure regarding cash assistance, see p. 225.

[10]Schweizer, *Victory*, p. 75.

[11]George P. Shultz, "America and the Struggle for Freedom," Speech given to the Commonwealth Club of California, San Francisco, February 22, 1985, *Department of State Bulletin*, 85, no. 2097, April 1985, pp.16–21, https://archive.org/stream/departmentofstatb1985unit/departmentofstatb1985unit_djvu.txt.

[12]Shultz, "America and the Struggle for Freedom," p. 16.

[13]Shultz, "America and the Struggle for Freedom," p. 17.

[14]Shultz, "America and the Struggle for Freedom," p. 20.

[15]Shultz, "America and the Struggle for Freedom," p. 20.

[16]In his memoirs, published eight years later, Shultz still seemed to believe that supporting anti-communist insurgents automatically meant promoting democracy. See George P. Shultz, *Turmoil and Triumph: My Years as Secretary of State* (New York: Charles Scribners Sons, 1993), pp. 525–26.

[17]That tendency persisted even after they left office, despite mounting evidence about the actual nature of those fighters. See, for example, Shultz, *Turmoil and Triumph*, pp. 692, 1088.

[18]Ronald Reagan, "Remarks at the Annual Dinner of the Conservative Political Action Conference," March 1, 1985, transcript, American Presidency Project, University of California, Santa Barbara, http://www.presidency.ucsb.edu/ws/?pid=38274.

[19]Quoted in Schweizer, *Victory*, p. 246.

[20]Shultz, *Turmoil and Triumph*, p. 1113.

[21]Shultz, *Turmoil and Triumph*, p. 1116.

[22]Quoted in Richard Dowden, "Not as Nice as He Looked," *Independent* (UK), October 16, 1992.

[23]Jonathan Kwitny, *Endless Enemies: The Making of an Unfriendly World* (New York: Congdon & Weed, 1984), pp. 136, 692.

[24]Quoted in Linda Wheeler, "Marchers Strut Support for Independent Kosovo," *Washington Post*, April 28, 1999, https://www.washingtonpost.com/archive/local/1999/04/28/marchers-strut-support-for-independent-kosovo/961df9f7-4a8b-471c-9797-c4c8d92b8f9d/?utm_term=.19bdc4c762b5.

[25]See Ted Galen Carpenter, "Empowering the Body Snatchers," *National Interest Online*, December 30, 2010, http://nationalinterest.org/blog/the-skeptics/empowering-the-body-snatchers-washington%E2%80%99s-appalling-kosovo-4650. Also see Nebi Qena, "Organ Recipient Testifies at Trial in Kosovo," Associated Press, March 23, 2013, https://www.usnews.com/news/world/articles/2012/03/23/organ-recipient-testifies-at-trial-in-kosovo?offset=50; and Nebi Qena, "Kosovo: 3 Get Jail Time in Organ Trafficking Case," Associated Press, April 29, 2013, http://www.sandiegouniontribune.com/sdut-kosovo-3-get-jail-time-in-organ-trafficking-case-2013apr29-story.html.

[26]Jack Fairweather and Anton La Guardia, "Chalabi Stands by Faulty Intelligence That Toppled Saddam's Regime," *Telegraph*, February 19, 2004, http://www.telegraph.co.uk/news/worldnews/northamerica/usa/1454831/Chalabi-stands-by-faulty-intelligence-that-toppled-Saddams-regime.html.

[27]Finnegan, "A Look at the Factions Battling in Syria's Civil War."

CHAPTER ONE

[1]George Shultz, *Turmoil and Triumph: My Years in the State Department* (New York: Charles Scribner's Sons, 1993), pp. 291–292. Also see Philip W. Travis, *Reagan's War on Terrorism in Nicaragua: The Outlaw State* (New York: Lexington Books, 2016); and Alexander M. Haig Jr., *Caveat: Realism, Reagan, and Foreign Policy* (New York: Macmillan, 1984), pp. 88–89.

[2]Benjamin Schwarz, "Dirty Hands," *Atlantic*, December 1998, https://www.theatlantic.com/magazine/archive/1998/12/dirty-hands/377364/.

[3]Ronald Reagan, "Remarks at the Annual Dinner of the Conservative Political Action Conference," March 1, 1985, American Presidency Project, University of California, Santa Barbara, http://www.presidency.ucsb.edu/ws/?pid=38274.

[4]Ronald Reagan, *An American Life* (New York: Simon and Schuster, 1990), pp. 300, 484, 485.

[5]Reagan, *An American Life*, p. 480.

[6]Douglas Brinkley, ed., *The Reagan Diaries* (New York: Harper Collins, 2007), p. 308.

[7]Diary entry for February 18, 1986, in Brinkley, *The Reagan Diaries*, p. 391.

[8]James A. Baker III, with Thomas M. DeFrank, *The Politics of Diplomacy: Revolution, War & Peace, 1989–1992* (New York: G. P. Putnam's Sons, 1995), p. 54.

[9]"Psychological Operations in Guerrilla Warfare," Central Intelligence Agency, October 18, 1984, p.1, https://www.cia.gov/library/readingroom/docs/CIA-RDP86M00886R001300010029-9.pdf.

[10]United Press International, "Casey's Widow Gives $140,000 to Help Contras," *Los Angeles Times*, December 2, 1987, http://articles.latimes.com/1987-12-02/news/mn-17448_1_contra.

[11]Gregory F. Treverton, *Covert Action: The Limits of Intervention in the Postwar World* (New York: Basic Books, 1987), p. 109.

[12]Ted Galen Carpenter and Malou Innocent, *Perilous Partners: The Benefits and Pitfalls of America's Alliances with Authoritarian Regimes* (Washington: Cato Institute, 2015), pp. 28–37.

[13]Treverton, *Covert Action*, p. 110.

[14]Haig, *Caveat*, p. 90. For a discussion of Washington's cozy relationship with the Argentine junta during both the Ford and Reagan administrations, see Carpenter and Innocent, *Perilous Partners*, pp. 17–19, 87.

[15]Haig, *Caveat*, p. 129.

[16]For a detailed discussion of the role such factors played in Nicaragua, see Bernard Diederich, *Somoza and the Legacy of U.S. Involvement in Central America* (Princeton, NJ: Markus Wiener Publishers, 2007).

[17]Carpenter and Innocent, *Perilous Partners,* pp. 11–39.

[18]An example of an especially damaging action was the 1954 CIA-orchestrated coup against the leftist (but democratically elected) government of President Jacobo Arbenz Guzman in Guatemala. That step paved the way for a succession of brutal dictatorships and a simmering civil war in that country that claimed well in excess of 100,000 lives over the course of the next several decades. For an account of the coup and its aftermath, see Richard H. Immerman, *The CIA in Guatemala: The Foreign Policy of Intervention* (Austin, TX: University of Texas Press, 1982).

[19]Treverton, *Covert Action*, p. 111.

[20]James M. Scott, *Deciding to Intervene: The Reagan Doctrine and American Foreign Policy* (Durham, NC: Duke University Press, 1996), p. 155.

[21]Scott, *Deciding to Intervene*, p. 155.

[22]Treverton, *Covert Action*, p. 112.

[23]Treverton, *Covert Action*, p. 118.

[24]Treverton, *Covert Action*, pp. 118–19.

[25]Quoted in Russell Crandall, *America's Dirty Wars: Irregular Warfare from 1776 to the War on Terror* (New York: Cambridge University Press, 2014), p. 289.

[26]Crandall, *America's Dirty Wars*, pp. 289–90.

[27]Tim Weiner, *Legacy of Ashes: The History of the CIA* (New York: Doubleday, 2007), p. 383.

[28]*Final Report of the Select Committee to Study Governmental Operations with Respect to Intelligence Activities, United States Senate: Together with Additional, Supplemental, and Separate Views*, U.S. Sen. Rep. No. 94-755, 94th Cong., 2nd sess. (April 26, 1976), https://archive.org/stream/finalreportofsel01unit/finalreportof sel01unit_djvu.txt.

[29]Treverton, *Covert Action*, p. 144.

[30]Quoted in "U.S. Aid to Nicaraguan Rebels—Lawmakers Speak Out," *U.S. News & World Report*, May 2, 1983, p. 29.

[31]George F. Will, "Our Central America Myopia," *Newsweek*, August 1, 1983.

[32]Quoted in William Johnson, "U.S. House Votes to Aid Contras," *Globe and Mail*, June 13, 1985.

[33]Quoted in Steven Roberts, "House Reverses Earlier Ban on Aid to Nicaragua Rebels," *New York Times*, June 13, 1985.

[34]Quoted in Treverton, *Covert Action*, p. 113.

[35]Quoted in Treverton, *Covert Action*, p. 113.

[36]Weiner, *Legacy of Ashes*, p. 406.

[37]Shultz, *Turmoil and Triumph*, p. 411.

[38]Carpenter and Innocent, *Perilous Partners*, pp. 25–28.

[39]Quoted in Shultz, *Turmoil and Triumph*, p. 413.

[40]Reagan, *An American Life*, pp. 238–39. For similar hyperbole from a conservative scholar and activist, see John Norton Moore, *The Secret War in Central America: Sandinista Assault on World Order* (Bethesda, MD: University Publications of America, 1987).

[41]Accounts of the Iran-Contra episode include Jonathan Marshall and Peter Dale Scott, *The Iran-Contra Connection: Secret Teams and Covert Operations in the Reagan Era* (Boston: South End Press, 1987); Theodore Draper, *A Very Thin Line: The Iran-Contra Affair* (New York: Hill and Wang, 1991); and Malcolm Byrne, *Iran-Contra: Reagan's Scandal and the Unchecked Abuse of Presidential Power* (Lawrence, KS: University Press of Kansas, 2015).

[42]Carpenter and Innocent, *Perilous Partners*, pp. 28–33.

[43]Quoted in Robert Kagan, *A Twilight Struggle: American Power and Nicaragua, 1977–1990* (New York: The Free Press, 1996), p. 356.

[44]Kagan, *A Twilight Struggle*, p. 362.

[45]Quoted in Kagan, *A Twilight Struggle*, p. 362.

[46]Kagan, *A Twilight Struggle*, p. 795, n. 4. For another take on the composition of the Contra leadership, see James LeMoyne, "Nicaraguan Guerrillas Ponder Chances without U.S. Help," *New York Times*, March 18, 1985.

[47]Douglas Brinkley, *The Reagan Diaries*, pp. 396–97.

[48]Joel Brinkley, "Rights Report on Nicaragua Cites Recent Rebel Atrocities," *New York Times*, March 6, 1985.

[49]Paul J. Komyatte, "Contras Human Rights Record Attacked," *Chicago Tribune*, January 10, 1987, http://articles.chicagotribune.com/1987-01-10/news/8701030407_1_americas-watch-contra-rebels-amnesty-international.

[50]That allegation first surfaced in a series of articles by Gary Webb in the *San Jose Mercury News*. See Alex Hannaford, "The CIA, the Drug Dealers, and the Tragedy of Gary Webb," *Telegraph*, March 22, 2015, http://www.telegraph.co.uk/culture/film/11485819/kill-messenger-gary-webb-true-story.html. Also see Ryan Grim, Matt Sledge, and Matt Ferner, "Key Figures in CIA-Crack Cocaine Scandal Begin to Come Forward," *Huffington Post*, December 6, 2017.

[51]Examples of accounts favorable to the allegations include Eric Umansky, "Total Coverage: The CIA, Contras, and Drugs," *Mother Jones*, August 15, 1998, https://www.motherjones.com/politics/1998/08/total-coverage-cia-contras

-and-drugs/; Andrew Marshall, "CIA Turned a Blind Eye to Contras' Drug Smuggling," *Independent*, November 7, 1998, http://www.independent.co.uk /news/cia-turned-a-deliberate-blind-eye-to-contras-drug-smuggling-1183305 .html; and Robert Parry, "Big Media's Contra-Cocaine Cover-up," *Consortium News*, December 9, 2016, http://www.independent.co.uk/news/cia-turned -a-deliberate-blind-eye-to-contras-drug-smuggling-1183305.html. For examples of skeptical or negative accounts, see Craig Delaval, "Cocaine, Conspiracy Theories, and the CIA in Central America," PBS, *Frontline*, 2014, https://www.pbs.org/wgbh /pages/frontline/shows/drugs/special/cia.html; Roberto Suro and Walter Pincus, "The CIA and Crack: The Evidence Is Lacking," *Washington Post*, October 4, 1996, https://www.washingtonpost.com/archive/politics/1996/10/04/the-cia-and -crack-evidence-is-lacking-of-alleged-plot/5b026731-c5de-4234-b3bd-9e0f d2e21225/?utm_term=.0ed8bd15b0c9; and Jeff Leen, "Gary Webb Was No Jour- nalism Hero, Despite What 'Kill the Messenger' Says," *Washington Post*, October 10, 2014, https://www.washingtonpost.com/opinions/gary-webb-was-no-journalism -hero-despite-what-kill-the-messenger-says/2014/10/17/026b7560-53c9-11e4 -809b-8cc0a295c773_story.html?utm_term=.2948b6cea7dd.

⁵²Baker and DeFrank, *The Politics of Diplomacy*, p. 53.

⁵³Ibid.

⁵⁴Mark A. Uhlig, "Turnover in Nicaragua; Nicaraguan Opposition Routs Sandinistas; U.S. Pledges Aid, Tied to Orderly Turnover," *New York Times*, February 27, 1990, http://www.nytimes.com/1990/02/27/world/turnover -nicaragua-nicaraguan-opposition-routs-sandinistas-us-pledges-aid-tied.html ?pagewanted=all; Richard Boudreaux, "Chamorro Wins in Nicaragua: Ortega Says He Will Accept Foe's Popular Mandate," *Los Angeles Times*, February 17, 1990, http://articles.latimes.com/1990-02-27/news/mn-1312_1_national-assembly.

⁵⁵John Otis, "Former Contras and Sandinistas Join Forces in Town Takeover," United Press International, March 10, 1992, http://www.upi.com /Archives/1992/03/10/Former-Contras-and-Sandinistas-join-forces -in-town-takeover/8366700203600/.

⁵⁶Dan La Botz, "Daniel Ortega: Nicaragua's Nov. 6 Election and the Betrayal of a Revolution," *New Politics*, October 17, 2016.

⁵⁷Shultz, *Turmoil and Triumph*, p. 961.

CHAPTER TWO

¹Robert Gates, *From the Shadows: The Ultimate Insider's Story of Five Presidents and How They Won the Cold War* (New York: Simon and Schuster, 1996).

²See Brzezinski's admission during a 1998 interview. "The CIA's Intervention in Afghanistan: Interview with Dr. Zbigniew Brzezinski," *Le Nouvel Observateur*,

Paris, January 15–21, 1998, translated by Bill Blum, http://global research.ca /articles/BRZ110A.html. For an original English transcript of an interview with Brzezinski, see Jeffrey St. Clair and Alexander Cockburn, "How Jimmy Carter and I Started the Mujahideen," *Counterpunch*, January 15, 1998, http://www.counter punch.org/1998/01/15/how-jimmy-carter-and-i-started-the-mujahideen/.

[3]Quoted in "Carter Would Fight for Persian Gulf; Seeks to Resume Draft Registration," *Washington Post*, January 20, 1980.

[4]Clark Clifford, with Richard Holbrooke, *Counsel to the President: A Memoir* (New York: Random House, 1991), p. 640.

[5]William Claiborne, "Reports of More Aid to Afghan Rebels Stir Feuds," *Washington Post*, February 7, 1985.

[6]Robert Pear, "Arming Afghan Guerrillas: A Huge Effort Led by U.S.," *New York Times*, April 18, 1988, http://www.nytimes.com/1988/04/18/world/arming -afghan-guerrillas-a-huge-effort-led-by-us.html?pagewanted=all.

[7]Douglas Brinkley, ed., *The Reagan Diaries* (New York: HarperCollins, 2007), pp. 117, 128, 411, 481, 586.

[8]James M. Scott, *Deciding to Intervene: The Reagan Doctrine and American Foreign Policy* (Durham, NC: Duke University Press, 1996), p. 79.

[9]Scott, *Deciding to Intervene*, pp. 79–80.

[10]Steve Coll, *Ghost Wars: The Secret History of the CIA, Afghanistan, and Bin Laden, from the Soviet Invasion to September 10, 2001* (New York: Penguin Books, 2004), pp. 39–41.

[11]Coll, *Ghost Wars*, p. 8.

[12]Jeri Laber, "Afghanistan's Other War," *New York Review of Books*, December 18, 1986, http://www.nybooks.com/articles/1986/12/18/afghanistans -other-war/.

[13]Peter Schweizer, *Victory: The Reagan Administration's Secret Strategy That Hastened the Collapse of the Soviet Union* (New York: Atlantic Monthly Press, 1994), p. 9.

[14]Tim Weiner, *Legacy of Ashes: The History of the CIA* (New York: Doubleday, 2007), p. 384.

[15]Schweizer, *Victory*, p. 10.

[16]Quoted in Schweizer, *Victory*, p. 10.

[17]Quoted in Pear, "Arming Afghan Guerrillas."

[18]George Crile, *Charlie Wilson's War* (New York: Grove Press, 2003).

[19]Crile, *Charlie Wilson's War*, pp. 243–244.

[20]Jack Wheeler, "Fighting the Soviet Imperialists: The Mujaheddin in Afghanistan," *Reason*, September 1984, http://reason.com/archives/1984/09/01 /fighting-the-soviet-imperialis1.

[21]"The Reagan Doctrine: Should It Stay or Should It Go?" *Reason*, June 1987, http://reason.com/archives/1987/06/01/the-reagan-doctrine/.

[22]Daniel Schulman, "Dana Rohrabacher's War," *Mother Jones,* March/April 2010, http://www.motherjones.com/politics/2010/03/dana-rohrabacher-afghanistan-war.

[23]Pear, "Arming Afghan Guerrillas."

[24]For a discussion of Pakistan's objectives regarding Afghanistan, see Ted Galen Carpenter and Malou Innocent, *Perilous Partners: The Benefits and Pitfalls of America's Alliances with Authoritarian Regimes* (Washington: Cato Institute, 2015), pp. 126–32, 175–76, 429–35, 463–64.

[25]Brinkley, *The Reagan Diaries*, p. 117.

[26]Crile, *Charlie Wilson's War*, pp. 104–105.

[27]Schweizer, *Victory*, p. 63.

[28]Weiner, *Legacy of Ashes*, p. 385.

[29]Quoted in Weiner, *Legacy of Ashes*, p. 421.

[30]Weiner, *Legacy of Ashes*, p. 385.

[31]Scott, *Deciding to Intervene*, p. 81.

[32]Schweizer, *Victory*, p. 214.

[33]Schweizer, *Victory*, p. 213.

[34]Weiner, *Legacy of Ashes*, p. 420.

[35]George P. Shultz, *Turmoil and Triumph: My Years as Secretary of State* (New York: Scribner, 1993), p. 570.

[36]Schweizer, *Victory*, pp. 205–06.

[37]Schweizer, *Victory*, p. 232.

[38]Schweizer, *Victory*, pp. 271, 283.

[39]Schweizer, *Victory*, p. 181.

[40]Schweizer, *Victory*, p. 178.

[41]Schweizer, *Victory*, p. 152.

[42]Portions of this section are based on my earlier article "The Unintended Consequences of Afghanistan," *World Policy Journal* XI, no. 1 (Spring 1994): 76–87.

[43]Schweizer, *Victory*, p. 152.

[44]Wheeler, "Fighting the Soviet Imperialists."

[45]Quoted in Sheila Tefft, "Rebel Leaders Struggle for Unity," *Christian Science Monitor*, October 3, 1989.

[46]Marvin G. Weinbaum, "War and Peace in Afghanistan: The Pakistani Role," *Middle East Journal* 45 (Winter 1991): p. 78.

[47]Carpenter and Innocent, *Perilous Partners*, pp. 176–77.

[48]Weiner, *Legacy of Ashes*, p. 421.

[49]Donald Ritter, U.S. House of Representatives, *United States Policy toward Afghanistan*, Testimony before the Subcommittees on Europe and the Middle East and Asian and Pacific Affairs, House Committee on Foreign Affairs, 101st Cong., 2nd sess., March 7, 1990, p. 14.

[50]Ritter, *United States Policy Toward Afghanistan*, p. 14.

[51]Howard B. Schaffer, *Developments in Afghanistan and Their Implications for United States Policy*, Testimony before the Subcommittee on Asian and Pacific Affairs of the House Committee on Foreign Affairs, 101st Cong., 1st sess., February 21, 1989, p. 17.

[52]Robert A. Peck, *The Situation in Afghanistan*, Testimony before the Subcommittee on Asian and Pacific Affairs of the House Committee on Foreign Affairs, 99th Cong., 2nd sess., May 1, 1986, pp. 28, 73.

[53]See Ted Galen Carpenter, "U.S. Aid to Anti-Communist Rebels: The Reagan Doctrine and Its Pitfalls," Cato Institute Policy Analysis no. 74, June 24, 1986.

[54]Selig S. Harrison, *Developments in Afghanistan and Their Implications for United States Policy*, Testimonies before the Subcommittee on Asian and Pacific Affairs of the House Committee on Foreign Affairs, 101st Cong., 1st sess., February 21, 1989, and June 14, 1989, p. 98.

[55]Ritter, *United States Policy Toward Afghanistan*, p. 8.

[56]Ritter, *United States Policy Toward Afghanistan*, p. 13.

[57]Robert A. Peck, U.S. House of Representatives, *United States Policy toward Afghanistan*, Testimony before the Subcommittees on Europe and the Middle East and Asian and Pacific Affairs, House Committee on Foreign Affairs, 101st Cong., 2nd sess., March 7, 1990, p. 49.

[58]Crile noted that Humphrey "became so obsessed with the cause that he went so far as to commit over 60 percent of the efforts of his Senate staff to Afghanistan." Crile, *Charlie Wilson's War*, p. 326.

[59]Sen. Gordon Humphrey, Hearing, May 1, 1986, p. 5.

[60]Scott, *Deciding to Intervene*, p. 77.

[61]Scott, *Deciding to Intervene*, p. 78.

[62]Ted Galen Carpenter, "Bait and Switch in Afghanistan," *National Interest*, August 24, 2010, http://nationalinterest.org/blog/bait-switch-afghanistan-3958.

[63]Jimmy Carter, interview by David Letterman, *Late Night with David Letterman*, CBS, March 24, 2014, https://www.youtube.com/watch?v=qEBQe0PongA.

[64]Shultz, *Turmoil and Triumph*, p. 692.

[65]For examples, see Shultz, *Turmoil and Triumph*, pp. 692, 1086, 1087.

[66]Gregory F. Treverton, *Covert Action: The Limits of Intervention in the Postwar World* (New York: Basic Books, 1987), p. 219.

[67]Quoted in Weiner, *Legacy of Ashes*, p. 385.

[68]Quoted in Weiner, *Legacy of Ashes*, pp. 420–21.

CHAPTER THREE

[1]For accounts of Angola's civil war and Jonas Savimbi's role in it from various ideological perspectives, see Fred Bridgland, *Jonas Savimbi: A Key to Africa* (New York: Paragon House, 1987); Elaine Windrich, *The Cold War Guerrilla: Jonas Savimbi, the U.S. Media, and the Angolan War* (Westport, CT: Greenwood

Press, 1992); Karl Maier, *Angola: Promises and Lies* (London: Serif, 1996 and 2007); and Piero Gleijeses, *Visions of Freedom: Havana, Washington, Pretoria, and the Struggle for Southern Africa, 1976–1991* (Chapel Hill, NC: University of North Carolina Press, 2013).

[2]Peter Schweizer, *Victory: The Reagan Administration's Secret Strategy That Hastened the Collapse of the Soviet Union* (New York: Atlantic Monthly Press, 1994), p. 113.

[3]Gleijeses, *Visions of Freedom*, p. 14.

[4]Washington apparently had been courting Roberto since 1960, long before the Angolan civil war erupted. Gregory F. Treverton, *Covert Action: The Limits of Intervention in the Postwar World* (New York: Basic Books, 1987), p. 151.

[5]Ted Galen Carpenter and Malou Innocent, *Perilous Partners: The Benefits and Pitfalls of America's Alliances with Authoritarian Regimes* (Washington: Cato Institute, 2015), pp. 249–73.

[6]Tim Weiner, *Legacy of Ashes: The History of the CIA* (New York: Doubleday, 2007), p. 349.

[7]Treverton, *Covert Action*, p. 152.

[8]Tad Szulc, "Our Man Mobutu," *New Republic*, February 21, 1976, p. 6.

[9]James Brooke, "C.I.A. Said to Send Weapons via Zaire to Angola Rebels," *New York Times*, February 1, 1987.

[10]John Prados, *Presidents' Secret Wars: CIA and Pentagon Covert Operations since World War II* (New York: Morrow, 1986), p. 347.

[11]Maier, *Angola: Promises and Lies*, 2007 edition, p. ix.

[12]Gleijeses, *Visions of Freedom*, p. 298.

[13]William F. Buckley Jr., "Help Savimbi," *National Review*, February 28, 1986, p. 62.

[14]Quoted in Windrich, *The Cold War Guerrilla*, p. 37.

[15]Arnaud de Borchgrave and Roger Fontaine, "Savimbi Cites Guerrillas' Gains, Marxist Losses in Angola," *Washington Times*, May 21, 1984.

[16]Quoted in Phil McCombs, "The Salute to Savimbi," *Washington Post*, February 1, 1986, https://www.washingtonpost.com/archive/lifestyle/1986/02/01/the-salute-to-savimbi/b37b8411-a9fe-4cf3-8040-bb189e936d4a/?utm_term=.0ff9e414e5b7.

[17]McCombs, "The Salute to Savimbi."

[18]Douglas Brinkley, ed., *The Reagan Diaries* (New York: HarperCollins, 2007), p. 303.

[19]*Congressional Quarterly Weekly Report*, June 15, 1985, p. 1143.

[20]Gleijeses, *Visions of Freedom*, p. 291. Also see Windrich, *The Cold War Guerrilla*, pp. 52–53.

[21]Orrin Hatch, "Why We Should Aid Savimbi," *Washington Times*, February 7, 1986.

[22]Jonas Savimbi, "Don't Sacrifice Angola on the Altar of Socialism," *Wall Street Journal*, June 2, 1986.

[23]"The Week," *National Review*, July 4, 1986.

[24]George P. Shultz, *Turmoil and Triumph: My Years as Secretary of State* (New York: Scribner, 1993), p. 1111.

[25]Norman Podhoretz, "Savimbi's Promise," *Washington Post*, January 29, 1986, https://www.washingtonpost.com/archive/politics/1986/01/29/savimbis -promise/a348d313-276e-471a-b11b-2df8551714d6/?utm_term=.6ad87 c6d1bd7. Also see Windrich, *Cold War Guerrilla*, p. 52.

[26]Podhoretz, "Savimbi's Promise."

[27]Shultz, *Turmoil and Triumph*, pp. 1115–16.

[28]Shultz, *Turmoil and Triumph*, p. 1126.

[29]Shultz, *Turmoil and Triumph*, p. 1113.

[30]Shultz, *Turmoil and Triumph*, p. 1118.

[31]United Press International, "Kemp Calls on Shultz to Resign, 'Nearly Crip- pled' Reagan's Policy," February 21, 1987, http://articles.sun-sentinel.com/1987 -02-21/news/8701110582_1_kemp-reagan-doctrine-conservatives.

[32]Shultz, *Turmoil and Triumph*, p. 1118.

[33]Quoted in Chester A. Crocker, *High Noon in Southern Africa: Making Peace in a Rough Neighborhood* (New York: W.W. Norton, 1993), p. 284.

[34]Brinkley, *The Reagan Diaries*, p. 367.

[35]Brinkley, *The Reagan Diaries*, p. 367.

[36]Quoted in Gleijeses, *Visions of Freedom*, p. 299.

[37]Gleijeses, *Visions of Freedom*, p. 299.

[38]Quoted in Windrich, *The Cold War Guerrilla*, p. 10.

[39]Shultz, *Turmoil and Triumph*, p. 1119.

[40]Shultz, *Turmoil and Triumph*, p. 1128.

[41]Shultz, *Turmoil and Triumph*, p. 1128.

[42]Jonas Savimbi, "The Coming Winds of Democracy in Angola" (lecture no. 217, Heritage Foundation, Washington, DC, October 5, 1989), p. 1.

[43]Savimbi, "The Coming Winds of Democracy in Angola," p. 1.

[44]Savimbi, "The Coming Winds of Democracy in Angola," p. 1.

[45]Savimbi, "The Coming Winds of Democracy in Angola," p. 3.

[46]James M. Scott, *Deciding to Intervene: The Reagan Doctrine and American Foreign Policy* (Durham, NC: Duke University Press, 1996), p. 137.

[47]Treverton, *Covert Action*, p. 220.

[48]David B. Ottaway, "Massacre Charges Taint 'Freedom Fighters,'" *Washington Post*, July 29, 1986, https://www.washingtonpost.com/archive/politics/1986/07/29 /massacre-charges-taint-freedom-fighters/76b6478b-1ee8-4ef4-92e9-7be65b4aa1a6 /?utm_term=.73959c3c28b1.

[49]Bridgland, *Jonas Savimbi: A Key to Africa*, p. 242.

[50]Fred Bridgland, "Angola's Secret Bloodbath," *Washington Post*, March 29, 1992. https://www.washingtonpost.com/archive/opinions/1992/03/29/angolas -secret-bloodbath/c2bf6ed2-7dc2-4568-8ba5-23bc15165fc2/?utm_term =.aaaf3259ea77. Also see Richard Dowden, "Not as Nice as He Looked," *Independent* (UK), October 16, 1992.

[51]Windrich, *The Cold War Guerrilla*, p. 105.

[52]Bridgland, "Angola's Secret Bloodbath." Also see Craig Whitney and Jill Jolliffe, "Ex-Allies Say Angolan Rebels Torture and Slay Dissenters," *New York Times*, March 11, 1989; and Craig Whitney, "A Onetime Backer of Savimbi Corroborates Torture Charges," *New York Times*, March 12, 1989.

[53]Radek Sikorski, "The Mystique of Savimbi," *National Review*, August 18, 1989, pp. 36–37.

[54]For an account of Savimbi's decidedly radical left leanings during the 1970s, see Jonathan Kwitny, *Endless Enemies: The Making of an Unfriendly World* (New York: Congdon & Weed, 1984), p. 136.

[55]Maier, *Angola: Promises and Lies*, 2007 edition, p. 47.

[56]Peter Worthington, "Angola's Unknown War," *National Review*, November 1, 1985, p. 54.

[57]Windrich, *The Cold War Guerrilla*, p. 4.

[58]Quoted in Windrich, *The Cold War Guerrilla*, p. 29.

[59]James A. Baker III, *The Politics of Diplomacy: Revolution, War, and Peace, 1989–1992* (New York: G. P. Putnam's Sons, 1995), p. 598.

[60]Baker, *The Politics of Diplomacy*, p. 600.

[61]Baker, *The Politics of Diplomacy*, p. 600.

[62]Carpenter and Innocent, *Perilous Partners,* pp. 274–75.

[63]Carpenter and Innocent, *Perilous Partners,* p. 273.

CHAPTER FOUR

[1]For a discussion of the George H. W. Bush administration's initial assessment of these developments and Washington's policy responses, see James A. Baker III, *The Politics of Diplomacy: Revolution, War, and Peace, 1989–1992* (New York: G. P. Putnam's Sons, 1995), pp. 634–51.

[2]Andy Wilcoxson, "The Exoneration of Milošević: The ICTY's Surprise Ruling," *Counterpunch*, August 1, 2016.

[3]Dan Bilefsky, "Bosnian Elections Reinforce Longstanding Ethnic Divisions," *New York Times*, October 14, 2014, https://www.nytimes.com/2014/10/15 /world/europe/bosnian-elections-reinforce-longstanding-ethnic-divisions .html?_r=0; and Julian Borger, "Bosnia's Bitter, Flawed Peace Deal, 20 Years On,"

Guardian, November 10, 2015, https://www.theguardian.com/global/2015/nov/10/bosnia-bitter-flawed-peace-deal-dayton-agreement-20-years-on.

[4]David Chandler, *Bosnia: Faking Democracy after Dayton*, 2nd edition (London: Pluto Press, 2000), pp. 2–3, 50–55, 118–19, 156–58.

[5]Gary Dempsey, "Kosovo Crossfire," *Mediterranean Quarterly* 9, no. 3 (Summer 1998): 96–99.

[6]For a discussion of the various causes of the demographic shift in Kosovo's population, see David N. Gibbs, *First Do No Harm: Humanitarian Intervention and the Destruction of Yugoslavia* (Nashville, TN: Vanderbilt University Press, 2009), pp. 175–78.

[7]For a detailed discussion, see Ted Galen Carpenter, "Cynical Myths and U.S. Military Crusades in the Balkans," *Mediterranean Quarterly* 22, no. 3 (Summer 2011): 10–25.

[8]James George Jatras, "NATO's Myths and Bogus Justifications for Intervention," in *NATO's Empty Victory: A Postmortem on the Balkan War*, ed. Ted Galen Carpenter (Washington: Cato Institute, 2000), p. 21.

[9]Jatras, "NATO's Myths and Bogus Justifications for Intervention," p. 22.

[10]Madeleine Albright, *Madame Secretary* (New York: Miramax Books, 2003), pp. 379–80.

[11]Rajan Menon, *The Conceit of Humanitarian Intervention* (New York: Oxford University Press, 2016), p. 131.

[12]Albright, *Madame Secretary*, p. 381.

[13]Bill Clinton, *My Life* (New York: Alfred E. Knopf, 2004), pp. 848–51.

[14]Quoted in Philip Shenon, "U.S. Says It Might Consider Attacking Serbs," *New York Times*, March 13, 1998.

[15]Christopher Deliso, *The Coming Balkan Caliphate: The Threat of Radical Islam to Europe and the West* (Westport, CT: Praeger, 2007), pp. 41–42.

[16]That development was also reported in the *Sunday Times* of London. See Tom Walker and Aidan Laverty, "CIA Aided Kosovo Guerilla Army," *Sunday Times* (UK), March 12, 2000.

[17]Quoted in Linda Wheeler, "Marchers Strut Support for Independent Kosovo," *Washington Post*, April 28, 1999.

[18]Gibbs, *First Do No Harm*, p. 188.

[19]Christopher Layne, "Miscalculations and Blunders Lead to War," in *NATO's Empty Victory*, p. 16.

[20]Layne, "Miscalculations and Blunders Lead to War," p. 16.

[21]Layne, "Miscalculations and Blunders Lead to War," p. 16.

[22]Bradley Graham, "Report Says NATO Bombing Killed 500 Civilians in Yugoslavia," *Washington Post*, February 7, 2000, http://www.washingtonpost.com/wp-srv/WPcap/2000-02/07/000r-020700-idx.html.

[23]B92 and *Tanjug* News Service, "Serbia Marks Anniversary of Start of NATO Bombing," March 24, 2016, http://www.b92.net/eng/news/society .php?yyyy=2016&mm=03&dd=24&nav_id=97466.

[24]Albright, *Madame Secretary*, p. 386.

[25]Tom Doggett, "Cohen Fears 100,000 Kosovo Men Killed by Serbs," *Washington Post,* May 16, 1999, https://www.washingtonpost.com/wp-srv/inatl /longterm/balkans/stories/cohen051699.htm.

[26]David Chandler, *From Kosovo to Kabul: Human Rights and International Intervention* (London: Pluto Press, 2002), p. 73.

[27]UKFAC (United Kingdom Foreign Affairs Committee), *Fourth Report*, Session 1999–2000, United Kingdom, House of Commons Foreign Affairs Committee, May 23, 2000, https://publications.parliament.uk/pa/cm199900 /cmselect/cmfaff/28/2802.htm.

[28]Quoted in George Kenney, "Kosovo: On Ends and Means," *The Nation*, December 27, 1999.

[29]Quoted in Gibbs, *First Do No Harm*, p. 181.

[30]Benjamin Schwarz and Christopher Layne, "The Case against Intervention in Kosovo," *Nation*, April 19, 1999, https://www.thenation.com/article/case -against-intervention-kosovo/.

[31]Ivo Daalder and Michael O'Hanlon, *Winning Ugly: NATO's War to Save Kosovo* (Washington, DC: Brookings Institution, 2000), p. 12.

[32]Albright, *Madame Secretary*, p. 381.

[33]Quoted in Chandler, *From Kosovo to Kabul*, p. 185.

[34]Chandler, *From Kosovo to Kabul*, p. 74.

[35]Kenney, "Kosovo: On Ends and Means."

[36]Kenney, "Kosovo: On Ends and Means."

[37]Chandler, *From Kosovo to Kabul*, p. 15.

[38]See *Repression and Violence in Kosovo,* and *Kosovo: The Humanitarian Perspective*, two hearings before the Commission on Security and Cooperation in Europe, 105th Cong., 2nd sess., March 18, 1998, and June 25, 1998, https://www.csce.gov/sites/helsinkicommission.house.gov/files/Official %20Transcript%20-%20repression%20and%20violence%20in%20 kosovo%20and%20hearing%20on%20kosovo%20the%20humanitarian%20 perspective.pdf.

[39]Veteran journalist Peter Brock provides a detailed analysis of the systematic media bias and incompetence regarding coverage of the Balkan wars. Peter Brock, *Media Cleansing, Dirty Reporting: Journalism and Tragedy in Yugoslavia* (Los Angeles: GM Books, 2005).

[40]Ted Galen Carpenter, "Kosovo and Macedonia: The West Enhances the Threat," *Mediterranean Quarterly* 13, no. 1 (Winter 2002): 23–25.

[41]Morgan Meaker, "Roma in Kosovo: The Justice That Never Came," *Al Jazeera*, January 26, 2017, http://www.aljazeera.com/indepth/features/2017/01/roma-kosovo-justice-170112134149767.html.

[42]Meaker, "Roma in Kosovo."

[43]U.S. Ambassador to NATO William H. Taft IV even asserted that the violence in Kosovo largely resulted from the sense of insecurity *on the part of Albanian inhabitants*—the very people doing the ethnic cleansing. William H. Taft IV, "Speaking for Kosovo," *Washington Post*, April 14, 2000.

[44]Nicholas Wood and David Binder, "Treasured Churches in a Cycle of Revenge," *New York Times*, April 3, 2004, http://www.nytimes.com/2004/04/03/arts/treasured-churches-in-a-cycle-of-revenge.html.

[45]Deliso, *The Coming Balkan Caliphate*, p. 117.

[46]Deliso, *The Coming Balkan Caliphate*, p. 116.

[47]See Ted Galen Carpenter, "Empowering the Body Snatchers," *National Interest Online*, December 30, 2010, http://nationalinterest.org/blog/the-skeptics/empowering-the-body-snatchers-washington%E2%80%99s-appalling-kosovo-4650. Also see Nebi Qena, "Organ Recipient Testifies at Trial in Kosovo," Associated Press, March 23, 2013, https://www.usnews.com/news/world/articles/2012/03/23/organ-recipient-testifies-at-trial-in-kosovo?offset=50; and Nebi Qena, "Kosovo: 3 Get Jail Time in Organ Trafficking Case," Associated Press, April 29, 2013, http://www.sandiegouniontribune.com/sdut-kosovo-3-get-jail-time-in-organ-trafficking-case-2013apr29-story.html.

[48]Statement by the Chief Prosecutor Clint Williamson, July 29, 2014, http://sitf.eu/index.php/en/news-other/42-statement-by-the-chief-prosecutor-clint-williamson. Also see Chuck Sudetic, "The Bullies Who Run Kosovo," *Politico*, July 21, 2015, http://www.politico.eu/article/kosovo-hashim-thaci-un-special-court-tribunal-organ-trafficking-kla-serbia-milosevic-serbia-ramush/.

[49]Brock, *Media Cleansing, Dirty Reporting*, especially pp. 126–40.

[50]Indeed, the Albanian–American Civic League still boasts of its work on behalf of the KLA and Kosovo's independence, http://www.aacl.us/aaclhistory.htm.

[51]"Senator Bob Dole Led Delegation Visit to Kosova, 1990," YouTube video, February 1, 2013, https://www.youtube.com/watch?v=ZVxeewfuPVM.

[52]See, for example, "Written Testimony of Senator Bob Dole," Atrocities in Kosovo, Hearing before the Commission on Security and Cooperation in Europe, 105th Cong., 2nd sess., March 18, 1998, and May 6, 1999, pp. 34–36, https://www.csce.gov/sites/helsinkicommission.house.gov/files/Official%20Transcript%20-%20Atrocities%20in%20Kosovo%20-%20Shattuck%20and%20Dole%20Report.pdf.

[53]Council on Foreign Relations, "Campaign 2008, Morning Update," February 19, 2008, http://blogs.cfr.org/campaign2008/2008/02/19/morning-update-three-cheers-for-kosovo/.

[54]Nicholas Burns, Under Secretary of State for Political Affairs, "Teleconference Briefing on Kosovo," Washington, DC, February 18, 2008, https://2001 -2009.state.gov/p/us/rm/2008/100976.htm.

[55]Ted Galen Carpenter, "Kosovo Precedent Prevails," *National Interest Online*, August 26, 2008, http://www.cato.org/publications/commentary/kosovo-precedent -prevails.

[56]Robert M. Gates, *Duty: Memoirs of a Secretary at War* (New York: Alfred A. Knopf, 2014), p. 168.

[57]Sudetic, "The Bullies Who Run Kosovo." Also see Paul Lewis, "Report Identifies Hashim Thaçi as 'Big Fish' in Organised Crime," *Guardian*, January 24, 2011, http://www.theguardian.com/world/2011/jan/24/hashim-thaci-kosovo -organised-crime.

[58]Palash Ghosh, "Tip of the Iceberg: French Police Arrest Albanian Heroin Traffickers, but Balkan Criminal Gangs Tighten Their Grip Across Europe," *International Business Times*, October 26, 2014, http://www.ibtimes.com/tip-iceberg -french-police-arrest-albanian-heroin-traffickers-balkan-criminal-gangs-tighten -grip. Also see Maggie O'Kane, "Kosovo Mafia Supply Heroin to Europe," *Guardian*, May 12, 2000, http://www.theguardian.com/world/2000/mar/13/balkans.

[59]Sudetic, "The Bullies Who Run Kosovo."

[60]Ismet Hajdari, "Kosovo Albanians Flee Misery for EU Promised Land," Agence France Presse, February 12, 2015, http://news.yahoo.com/kosovo -albanians-flee-misery-eu-promised-land-155437138.html; and Nebi Qena, "Kosovo's Joy Now Despair on Anniversary of Independence," Associated Press, February 16, 2015, http://www.twincities.com/news/ci_27541049/kosovos-joy -now-despair-anniversary-independence.

[61]Kristen Chick, "Thousands Flee Economic Despair in Kosovo for EU Countries, Welcome or Not," *Los Angeles Times*, February 15, 2015, http:// www.latimes.com/world/europe/la-fg-kosovo-refugees-20150215-story.html #page=1.

[62]Hannah Roberts, "Hungary Building 13 Ft High, 110-Mile Fence along Its Border with Serbia to Stop the Flow of Illegal Migrants," *Daily Mail* (UK), August 10, 2015, http://www.dailymail.co.uk/news/article-3128631/Hungary -building-13ft-high-110-mile-fence-border-Serbia-stop-flow-illegal-migrants .html.

[63]"Macedonian President Warns of Albanian Threat to Sovereignty," Voice of America, March 7, 2017, https://www.voanews.com/a/macedonian-president -warns-of-albanian-threat-to-sovereignty/3754238.html.

[64]"Macedonia 'Playing with Fire,' Former Peace Envoy Warns," *Telegraph*, April 20, 2017, http://www.telegraph.co.uk/news/2017/04/29/macedonia -playing-fire-former-peace-envoy-warns/; "Macedonian President Refuses

Again to Sign Bill Boosting Albanian Language," Radio Free Europe/Radio Liberty, March 15, 2018, https://www.rferl.org/a/macedonian-president -ivanov-refuses-again-sign-bill-boosting-albanian-language/29100939.html.

[65]Ismet Hajdari, "Kosovo Postpones Controversial Border Deal Vote," Reuters, September 1, 2016, https://www.yahoo.com/news/kosovo-postpones -controversial-border-deal-vote-174933478.html.

[66]Florent Bajrami and Llazar Semini, "Germany Urges Kosovo to Pass Border Deal with Montenegro," ABC News, April 13, 2017, http://abcnews.go.com /International/wireStory/germany-urges-kosovo-pass-border-deal-montenegro -46775738.

[67]"Serbia Stops 'Promo Train' to Kosovo's North," Radio Free Europe/Radio Liberty, January 14, 2017, http://www.rferl.org/a/28233304.html.

[68]Ben Kentish, "Kosovo Stops Serbian Train Crossing Border in Move Declared 'Act of War,'" *The Independent* (UK), January 15, 2017, http://www .independent.co.uk/news/world/europe/kosovo-stops-serbia-train-crossing -border-belgrade-war-isa-mustafa-aleksandar-vucic-a7528361.html.

[69]Associated Press, "McCain Urges Kosovo Resume Dialogue with Serbia," *Fox News*, April 13, 2017, http://www.foxnews.com/world/2017/04/13 /mccain-urges-kosovo-resume-dialogue-with-serbia.html.

[70]Fatos Bytyci, "NATO Urges Kosovo, Serb Leaders to Ease Tensions," *Globe and Mail*, February 3, 2017, http://www.theglobeandmail.com/news/world/nato -urges-kosovo-serbia-leaders-to-ease-tensions/article33894528/.

[71]Reuters, "Kosovo Bows to U.S., NATO Pressure, Puts Off Plan to Create Army," Voice of America, April 7, 2017, http://www.voanews.com/a /kosovo-bows-to-us-nato-pressure-puts-off-plan-to-create-army/3801503 .html.

[72]Leonat Shehu, "Kosovo Moves to Establish Army, Defying Belgrade," Voice of America, March 8, 2017, http://www.voanews.com/a/kosovo-moves -to-establish-army-defying-belgrade/3754084.html.

[73]Washington was adamant in opposing that move—especially since Thaçi had violated the country's constitution to push the proposal forward. Associated Press, "U.S. Official Calls on Kosovo to Retract Law on Creating Army," *Daily Progress*, March 29, 2017, http://www.dailyprogress.com/us-official-calls-on-kosovo-to -retract-law-on-creating/article_00e45c92-561a-59b8-9a6e-8454cf5f0844 .html.

[74]Reuters, "Kosovo Bows to U.S., NATO Pressure."

[75]Krsto Lazarević, "Kosovo's Path from Secular Nation to Europe's Jihadist Stronghold," *Die Welt*, July 13, 2017.

[76]Garentina Kraja and William J. Kole, "3 in Dix Plot from Pro-U.S. Balkans Area," *Washington Post*, May 9, 2007.

[77]Quoted in Aidan Hehir, "How the West Built a Failed State in Kosovo," *National Interest Online,* August 31, 2016, http://nationalinterest.org/feature/how-the-west-built-failed-state-kosovo-17539.

[78]Hehir, "How the West Built a Failed State in Kosovo."

[79]See Richard Holbrooke, "America: A European Power," *Foreign Affairs* 74 (March–April 1995): pp. 38–51. That flawed thinking persists. See *New York Times* columnist Roger Cohen's essay, "Holbrooke: A European Power," in *The Unquiet American: Richard Holbrooke in the World,* ed. Derek Chollet and Samantha Power (New York: Public Affairs, 2011), pp. 164–75.

[80]Mitra Nazar, "Kosovo Fears for U.S. Ties under Trump," *Deutsche Welle,* January 19, 2017, http://www.dw.com/en/kosovo-fears-for-us-ties-under-trump/a-37186938.

[81]Nazar, "Kosovo Fears for U.S. Ties under Trump."

[82]Martin Egnash, "U.S. Soldiers Deploy to Kosovo amid Rising Tensions," *Stars and Stripes,* July 13, 2017, http://www.military.com/daily-news/2017/07/13/us-soldiers-deploy-to-kosovo-amid-enduring-tensions.html.

Chapter Five

[1]Robert Legvold, capsule review of *The Color Revolutions,* by Lincoln A. Mitchell, *Foreign Affairs* 92, no. 1 (January–February 2013): p. 198.

[2]Anders Aslund, "The Ancien Régime: Kuchma and the Oligarchs," in *Revolution in Orange: Origins of Ukraine's Democratic Breakthrough,* ed. Anders Aslund and Michael McFaul (Washington, DC: Carnegie Endowment for International Peace, 2006), pp. 9–28; Andrew Wilson, *Ukraine's Orange Revolution* (New York: Yale University Press, 2006), pp. 26–45; and Lincoln A. Mitchell, *Uncertain Democracy: U.S. Foreign Policy and Georgia's Rose Revolution* (Philadelphia, PA: University of Pennsylvania Press, 2008), pp. 20–42.

[3]Lincoln A. Mitchell, *The Color Revolutions* (Philadelphia, PA: University of Pennsylvania Press, 2012), pp. 17–39.

[4]Mitchell, *The Color Revolutions,* pp. 32–39.

[5]George W. Bush, *Decision Points* (New York: Crown Publishers, 2010), p. 430.

[6]Bush, *Decision Points,* p. 430.

[7]For a detailed account of the events and factors leading up to the Rose Revolution and Shevardnadze's resignation, see Mitchell, *Uncertain Democracy,* pp. 43–68.

[8]Wilson, *Ukraine's Orange Revolution,* pp. 45–46.

[9]Peter Baker, "Bush Promises More Help to Ukraine," *Washington Post,* April 5, 2005, http://www.washingtonpost.com/wp-dyn/articles/A24568-2005Apr4.html.

[10]Bush, *Decision Points*, p. 430.

[11]"Bush: Georgia 'Beacon of Liberty,'" *CNN.com*, May 11, 2005, http://edition.cnn.com/2005/WORLD/europe/05/10/bush.tuesday/.

[12]Office of Sen. John McCain, "McCain, Clinton Nominate Presidents of Georgia, Ukraine for Nobel Peace Prize," news release, January 25, 2005, https://www.mccain.senate.gov/public/index.cfm/press-releases?ID=877da268-ee6a-4e47-97ca-28b65df158f9.

[13]Mitchell, *Uncertain Democracy*, pp. 69–78.

[14]Human Rights Watch, "Crossing the Line: Georgia's Violent Dispersal of Protestors and Raid on Imedi Television," *Human Rights Watch*, 19, no. 8 (December 2007), https://www.hrw.org/sites/default/files/reports/georgia1207web.pdf.

[15]Human Rights Watch, "Crossing the Line," p. 11.

[16]Human Rights Watch, "Crossing the Line," p. 1.

[17]Human Rights Watch, "Crossing the Line," p. 1.

[18]Human Rights Watch, "Crossing the Line," p. 3.

[19]Human Rights Watch, "Crossing the Line," p. 3.

[20]Salome Asatiani, "Georgia: The Ally Who Turned on Saakashvili," Radio Free Europe/Radio Liberty, September 27, 2007.

[21]Jaba Devdariani, "Georgia's Okruashvili Scandal: Loud Bang with Uncertain Fallout," *Central Asia-Caucasus Analyst*, October 17, 2007, https://www.cacianalyst.org/publications/analytical-articles/item/11498-analytical-articles-caci-analyst-2007-10-17-art-11498.html.

[22]"Former Georgian Politician Seeks Asylum in France," *Deutsche Welle*, January 10, 2008, http://www.dw.com/en/former-georgian-politician-seeks-asylum-in-france/a-3049525; and Nina Akhmenteli, "Georgia: France Grants Political Asylum to Ex-Saakashvili Ally," *Eurasianet*, April 23, 2008.

[23]International Crisis Group, "Georgia: Sliding towards Authoritarianism?" Report no. 189, December 19, 2007, https://www.crisisgroup.org/europe-central-asia/caucasus/georgia/georgia-sliding-towards-authoritarianism.

[24]Human Rights Watch, "Crossing the Line," p. 6.

[25]Freedom House, *Freedom in the World, 2009: Country Report: Georgia,* https://freedomhouse.org/report/freedom-world/2009/georgia.

[26]Freedom House, *Freedom in the World, 2009: Georgia.*

[27]Human Rights Watch, "Crossing the Line," p. 6.

[28]Mitchell, *The Color Revolutions*, pp. 182–83.

[29]Freedom House, *Freedom in the World, 2009: Georgia.*

[30]"Georgia's Ruling Party Concedes Defeat in Parliamentary Elections," *CNN.com*, October 3, 2012, http://www.cnn.com/2012/10/02/world/europe/georgia-elections/index.html.

[31]"Saakashvili Rival Emerges as Winner in Georgia's Presidential Election," *Deutsche Welle*, October 27, 2013, http://www.dw.com/en/saakashvili-rival-emerges-as-winner-in-georgias-presidential-election/a-17186442.

[32]Margarita Antidze, "Georgian Prosecutors Charge Ex-President Saakashvili," Reuters, July 28, 2014, http://www.reuters.com/article/us-georgia-saakashvili-charges/georgian-prosecutors-charge-ex-president-saakashvili-idUSKBN0FX15M20140728.

[33]"Georgia Calls Interpol to Prosecute Ex-President Saakashvili," *112UA*, August 1, 2015, http://112.international/politics/Georgia-calls-Interpol-to-prosecute-ex-president-Saakashvili-361.html.

[34]Jason Horowitz, "Exile in Brooklyn, with an Eye on Georgia," *New York Times*, September 19, 2014, https://www.nytimes.com/2014/09/20/world/europe/mikheil-saakashvili-georgias-ex-president-plots-return-from-williamsburg-brooklyn.html?mcubz=0.

[35]Robert M. Gates, *Duty: Memoirs of a Secretary at War* (New York: Alfred A. Knopf, 2014), p. 167.

[36]Bush, *Decision Points*, pp. 434–35.

[37]Dick Cheney, *In My Time: A Personal and Political Memoir* (New York: Threshold, 2011), p. 513.

[38]Nathan Hodge, "Did the U.S. Prep Georgia for War with Russia?" *Wired*, August 8, 2008, https://www.wired.com/2008/08/did-us-military/.

[39]Bush, *Decision Points*, p. 435.

[40]Robert Stacy, "McCain: We're All Georgians Now," *American Spectator*, August 12, 2008, https://spectator.org/14931_mccain-we-are-all-georgians-now/.

[41]Gates, *Duty*, p. 169.

[42]For discussions of the onset of the Orange Revolution and its initial successes, see Wilson, *Ukraine's Orange Revolution*; and various essays in *Revolution in Orange*, ed. Aslund and McFaul. For a broader discussion of that episode and its eventual unraveling, see Paul J. D'Anieri, ed., *Orange Revolution and Aftermath: Mobilization, Apathy, and the State in Ukraine* (Baltimore, MD: Johns Hopkins University Press, 2010).

[43]George H. W. Bush, "Statement on Signing the Freedom Support Act," October 24, 1992, American Presidency Project, http://www.presidency.ucsb.edu/ws/?pid=21658.

[44]Wilson, *Ukraine's Orange Revolution*, pp. 183–89.

[45]Wilson, *Ukraine's Orange Revolution*, pp. 82–83, photos 11 and 12.

[46]Quoted in Wilson, *Ukraine's Orange Revolution*, p. 184.

[47]Human Rights Watch, *Ukraine: Events of 2005*, https://www.hrw.org/world-report/2006/country-chapters/ukraine.

[48]Freedom House, *Freedom in the World, 2006: Country Report: Ukraine.* https:// freedomhouse.org/report/freedom-world/2006/ukraine.

[49]Richard Sakwa, *Frontline Ukraine: Crisis in the Borderlands* (London: I. B. Tauris, 2015), p. 52.

[50]"Gas Princess Tymoshenko Elected Ukraine's PM," *Novinite.com*, December 18, 2007, http://www.novinite.com/articles/88643/Gas+Princess+Tymoshenko +Elected+Ukraine%27s+PM.

[51]Christopher Dickey, "Yulia Tymoshenko: She's No Angel," *Daily Beast*, February 23, 2014, http://www.thedailybeast.com/yulia-tymoshenko-shes-no-angel.

[52]Dickey, "Yulia Tymoshenko."

[53]Quoted in Sakwa, *Frontline Ukraine*, p. 53.

[54]"Ukraine: Yushchenko Discusses Energy, Russia, Defense Reform, Domestic Politics," *Wikileaks,* January 25, 2006, https://wikileaks.org/plusd/cables /06KIEV333-a.html.

[55]Sakwa, *Frontline Ukraine,* p. 53.

[56]U.S. Cables Extract, "Scenesetter for Codel Corker Visit to Kyiv," *Wikileaks: Ukraine,* October 30, 2008, https://wikileaksua.wordpress.com/2008/10/30 /08kyiv2174-scenesetter-for-codel-corker-visit-to-kyiv/, paragraph 5.

[57]Peter Finn, "Ukraine's President Fires Cabinet," *Washington Post*, September 9, 2005, http://www.washingtonpost.com/wp-dyn/content/article/2005/09/08 /AR2005090800243.html.

[58]Sakwa, *Frontline Ukraine*, p. 53.

[59]Sakwa, *Frontline Ukraine*, pp. 53–54.

[60]Nick Paton Walsh, "Son's Antics Vex Yushchenko," *Guardian*, July 28, 2005, https://www.theguardian.com/world/2005/jul/29/ukraine.nickpatonwalsh.

[61]"Yushchenko Angers Ukrainian Press," *BBC News,* July 26, 2005, http:// news.bbc.co.uk/2/hi/europe/4719659.stm.

[62]"Yushchenko Angers Ukrainian Press."

[63]Andrew Meier, "Ukraine's Endangered Revolution," *National Geographic*, March 2006, http://ngm.nationalgeographic.com/print/features/world/europe /ukraine/ukraine-text.

[64]Condoleezza Rice, *No Higher Honor: A Memoir of My Years in Washington* (New York: Crown Publishers, 2011), pp. 670–71.

[65]Rice, *No Higher Honor*, p. 671.

[66]Freedom House, *Freedom in the World, 2009: Country Report: Ukraine*, https:// freedomhouse.org/report/freedom-world/2009/ukraine.

[67]Gregory Feifer, "Unloved but Unbowed, Ukraine's Viktor Yushchenko Leaves Office," Radio Free Europe/Radio Liberty, February 24, 2010, https:// www.rferl.org/a/Unloved_But_Unbowed_Ukraines_Viktor_Yushchenko _Leaves_Office/1967436.html.

[68]Feifer, "Unloved But Unbowed."

[69]Sakwa, *Frontline Ukraine*, p. 62.

[70]Ellen Barry, "Former Ukraine Premier Is Jailed for 7 Years," *New York Times*, October 11, 2011, http://www.nytimes.com/2011/10/12/world/europe/yulia -tymoshenko-sentenced-to-seven-years-in-prison.html?mcubz=0.

[71]Sakwa, *Frontline Ukraine*, p. 55.

[72]David Stern, "Saakashvili, Ukraine's New Governor in Odessa, Splits Opinion," *BBC News*, June 2, 2016, http://www.bbc.com/news/world-europe -32975794.

[73]"Ukraine Strips Citizenship of Ex-Georgia Leader Saakashvili," Associated Press, June 26, 2017, https://www.apnews.com/fe895fd1d91241bd8078b54077 bd7391/Ukraine-strips-citizenship-of-ex-Georgia-leader-Saakashvili; and Sergei Karazy and Margaryta Chornokondratenko, "Ex-Georgian Leader Saakashvili Barges Across Ukraine Border," Reuters, September 10, 2017, https://www .reuters.com/article/us-ukraine-saakashvili/ex-georgian-leader-saakashvili- barges-across-ukraine-border-idUSKCN1BL0NN.

[74]Alec Luhn and Charlotte Krol, "Georgia Ex-President Mikheil Saakashvili Freed after Dramatic Rooftop Arrest in Ukraine," *Telegraph*, December 5, 2017, http://www.telegraph.co.uk/news/2017/12/05/georgian-ex-president-saakashvili -arrested-ukraine-amid-protests/; and Simon Marks, "Ex-Georgian President Saakashvili Arrested in Ukraine," *Politico*, December 9, 2017, https://www.politico .eu/article/ex-georgian-president-saakashvili-arrested-in-ukraine/.

[75]Human Rights Watch, *Crossing the Line*, p. 6.

[76]Luke Harding, "Bush Backs Ukraine and Georgia for NATO Membership," *Guardian*, April 1, 2008, https://www.theguardian.com/world/2008/apr/01/nato .georgia.

[77]"NATO Rebuffs Bush on Ukraine, Georgia," *CBS News.com*, April 2, 2008, https://www.cbsnews.com/news/nato-rebuffs-bush-on-ukraine-georgia/.

[78]Rice, *No Higher Honor*, p. 671.

CHAPTER SIX

[1]"PNAC Letters Sent to President Bill Clinton, January 26, 1998," Information Clearing House, http://www.informationclearinghouse.info/article5527.htm.

[2]See, for example, David Wurmser, *Tyranny's Ally: America's Failure to Defeat Saddam Hussein* (Washington: AEI Press, 1999).

[3]ABC News, *Nightline*, Interview with Sen. Al Gore, September 18, 1991, https://www.nexis.com/results/enhdocview.do?docLinkInd=true&ersKey =23_T26519396627&format=GNBFI&startDocNo=0&resultsUrlKey=0 _T26519396640&backKey=20_T26519396641&csi=8277&docNo=2.

[4]For the text of the letter, see Juan Cole, "Neocons to Clinton: Launch War on Iraq (1998)," *Informed Consent*, January 28, 2007, http://www.juancole.com/2007/06/neocons-to-clinton-launch-war-on-iraq.html.

[5]David Trotta, "Iraq War Cost U.S. More than $2 Trillion: Study," Reuters, March 13, 2013, https://www.reuters.com/article/us-iraq-war-anniversary-id USBRE92D0PG20130314.

[6]John Dizard, "How Ahmed Chalabi Conned the Neocons," *Salon.com*, May 4, 2004, http://www.salon.com/2004/05/04/chalabi_4/.

[7]Dizard, "How Ahmed Chalabi Conned the Neocons."

[8]James Bamford, "The Man Who Sold the War," *Rolling Stone*, November 18, 2005, http://www.commondreams.org/headlines05/1118-10.htm.

[9]Quoted in Bamford, "The Man Who Sold the War."

[10]Quoted in Jane Mayer, "The Manipulator," *New Yorker*, June 7, 2004, p. 8, https://www.newyorker.com/magazine/2004/06/07/the-manipulator.

[11]Quoted in Mayer, "The Manipulator," p. 8.

[12]Quoted in Mayer, "The Manipulator," p. 8.

[13]Cole, "Neocons to Clinton: Launch War on Iraq."

[14]Donald Rumsfeld, *Known and Unknown: A Memoir* (New York: Sentinel, 2011), p. 417.

[15]William J. Clinton, "Statement on Signing the Iraq Liberation Act of 1998," October 31, 1998, http://www.presidency.ucsb.edu/ws/?pid=55205.

[16]Dizard, "How Ahmed Chalabi Conned the Neocons."

[17]Rumsfeld, *Known and Unknown*, pp. 488–89.

[18]Rumsfeld, *Known and Unknown*, pp. 488–89.

[19]George Tenet with Bill Harlow, *At the Center of the Storm: My Years at the CIA* (New York: HarperCollins, 2007), p. 419.

[20]Rumsfeld, *Known and Unknown*, p. 489.

[21]Quoted in Rumsfeld, *Known and Unknown*, p. 489.

[22]Judith Miller, *The Story: A Reporter's Journey* (New York: Simon and Schuster, 2015), p. 153.

[23]Richard Bonin, *Arrows of the Night: Ahmad Chalabi's Long Journey to Triumph in Iraq* (New York: Doubleday, 2011), pp. 2–5.

[24]Condoleezza Rice, *No Higher Honor: A Memoir of My Years in Washington* (New York: Crown Publishers, 2011), p. 267.

[25]"Bush's War," PBS, *Frontline*, March 8, 2008, transcript, https://www.pbs.org/wgbh/pages/frontline/bushswar/etc/script.html.

[26]For more on this scheme and earlier versions, see Muhammad Idrees Ahmad, *The Road to Iraq: The Making of a Neoconservative War* (Edinburgh, Scotland: Edinburgh University Press, 2014), pp. 129–30.

[27]Rumsfeld, *Known and Unknown*, pp. 489–90.

[28]Bob Woodward, *State of Denial: Bush at War, Part III* (New York: Simon and Schuster, 2006), p. 156.

[29]Patrick E. Tyler and John Tagliabue, "Czechs Confirm Iraqi Agent Met with Terror Ringleader," *New York Times*, October 27, 2001, www.nytimes .com/2001/10/27/international/europe/27IRAQ.html.

[30]Sabah Khodada, quoted in Tyler and Tagliabue, "Czechs Confirm Iraqi Agent."

[31]Miller, *The Story*, p. 154.

[32]David Wurmser, "Ahmad Chalabi, Evangelist for Middle East Reform," *National Review*, November 5, 2015, http://www.nationalreview.com/article /426660/ahmad-chalabi-evangelist-middle-east-reform-david-wurmser.

[33]CIA briefing paper, "Terrorism Discovery That 11 September 2001 Hijacker Mohamed Atta Did Not Travel to the Czech Republic on 31 May 2000," https:// www.documentcloud.org/documents/368985-2001-12-08-terrorism-discovery -that-11-september.html.

[34]"Text: Cheney on Bin Laden Tapes," Meet the Press, December 9, 2001, *Washington Post,* December 10, 2001, http://www.washingtonpost.com/wp-srv /nation/specials/attacked/transcripts/cheneytext_120901.html.

[35]"Bush's War," PBS, *Frontline*.

[36]Ahmad, *The Road to Iraq*, p. 111.

[37]William Safire, "Mr. Atta Goes to Prague," *New York Times*, May 9, 2002, https://www.nytimes.com/2002/05/09/opinion/mr-atta-goes-to-prague.html.

[38]Ahmad, *The Road to Iraq*, p. 111.

[39]"Gunning for Saddam," PBS, *Frontline*, November 8, 2001, https://www .pbs.org/wgbh/pages/frontline/shows/gunning/etc/script.html.

[40]Ahmad, *The Road to Iraq*, pp. 111–12.

[41]Ahmad, *The Road to Iraq*, pp. 111–12.

[42]Aram Roston, *The Man Who Pushed America to War: The Extraordinary Life, Adventures, and Obsessions of Ahmad Chalabi* (New York: Nation Books, 2008), pp. 194–97.

[43]Judith Miller, "A Nation Challenged: Secret Sites; Iraqi Tells of Renovations at Sites for Chemical and Nuclear Arms," *New York Times*, December 20, 2001.

[44]Roston, *The Man Who Pushed America to War*, p. 196.

[45]Bamford, "The Man Who Sold the War."

[46]Ahmad, *The Road to Iraq*, p. 142.

[47]Bamford, "The Man Who Sold the War." Miller's close personal relationship with Chalabi went back to the early 1990s. Ahmad, *The Road to Iraq*, p. 147.

[48]Bamford, "The Man Who Sold the War."

[49]Quoted in Jack Fairweather and Anton La Guardia, "Chalabi Stands by Faulty Intelligence That Toppled Saddam's Regime," *Telegraph*, February 19, 2004

(emphasis added), http://www.telegraph.co.uk/news/worldnews/northamerica/usa/1454831/Chalabi-stands-by-faulty-intelligence-that-toppled-Saddams-regime.html.

[50]Judith Miller, "The Iraq War and Stubborn Myths: Officials Didn't Lie, and I Wasn't Fed a Line," *Wall Street Journal*, April 3, 2015, http://www.wsj.com/articles/the-iraq-war-and-stubborn-myths-1428087215.

[51]Miller, *The Story*, pp. xi–xiv, 205–38.

[52]Veteran Intelligence Professionals for Sanity (Scott Ritter et al.), "Judith Miller's Blame-Shifting Memoir," *Consortium News*, April 7, 2015, https://consortiumnews.com/2015/04/07/judith-millers-blame-shifting-memoir/.

[53]Miller, *The Story*, p. xiii.

[54]Jason M. Breslow, "Colin Powell: U.N. Speech 'Was a Great Intelligence Failure,'" PBS, *Frontline*, May 16, 2016, http://www.pbs.org/wgbh/frontline/article/colin-powell-u-n-speech-was-a-great-intelligence-failure/.

[55]See, for example, Fred Kaplan, "How Did I Get Iraq Wrong? I Trusted Colin Powell and His Circumstantial Evidence—For a Little While," *Slate*, March 17, 2008, http://www.slate.com/articles/news_and_politics/politics/2008/03/how_did_i_get_iraq_wrong_10.html.

[56]Woodward, *State of Denial*, p. 157.

[57]Andrew J. Bacevich, *America's War for the Greater Middle East* (New York: Random House, 2016), p. 256.

[58]Bacevich, *America's War for the Greater Middle East*, p. 256.

[59]Dov S. Zakheim, *A Vulcan's Tale* (Washington: Brookings Institution Press, 2011), p. 163.

[60]Bacevich, *America's War for the Greater Middle East*, pp. 256–57.

[61]Roston, *The Man Who Pushed America to War*, pp. 261–62.

[62]Woodward, *State of Denial*, p. 295.

[63]Woodward, *State of Denial*, p. 421.

[64]Rumsfeld, *Known and Unknown*, p. 499.

[65]Rich Lowry, "A Theology of Freedom," *National Review*, July 17, 2017, http://www.nationalreview.com/corner/145976/theology-freedom-rich-lowry.

[66]Rumsfeld, *Known and Unknown*, p. 499.

[67]Dick Cheney with Liz Cheney, *In My Time: A Personal and Political Memoir* (New York: Threshold Editions, 2011), p. 387.

[68]Cheney, *In My Time*, p. 387.

[69]Cheney, *In My Time*, p. 390.

[70]"Bill Kristol," Notable Names Database (NNDB), http://www.nndb.com/people/401/000048257/. See also, Eric Alterman, "Bill Kristol's Guide to Failing Upward," *Guardian*, April 24, 2009, https://www.theguardian.com/commentisfree/cifamerica/2009/apr/24/william-kristol-bradley-prize-iraq.

[71]Mayer, "The Manipulator."

[72]Tanya Nolan, "FBI Investigating Intelligence Leaks to Iran," ABC News, May 26, 2004, http://www.abc.net.au/worldtoday/content/2004/s1116275.htm.

[73]Julian Borger, "U.S. Intelligence Fears Iran Duped Hawks into Iraq War," *Guardian*, May 24, 2004, https://www.theguardian.com/world/2004/may/25/usa.iraq10.

[74]Knight Ridder Tribune News, "U.S. Cuts Off Former Iraqi Exiles," *Houston Chronicle,* May 19, 2004, https://www.chron.com/news/article/U-S-cuts-off-former-Iraqi-exiles-1991169.php.

[75]Mayer, "The Manipulator."

[76]"From the Editors: *The Times* and Iraq," *New York Times*, editorial, May 26, 2004, http://www.nytimes.com/2004/05/26/world/from-the-editors-the-times-and-iraq.html?_r=0.

[77]Quoted in Dizard, "How Ahmed Chalabi Conned the Neocons."

[78]Quoted in Dizard, "How Ahmed Chalabi Conned the Neocons."

[79]Dizard, "How Ahmed Chalabi Conned the Neocons."

[80]Dizard, "How Ahmed Chalabi Conned the Neocons."

[81]Quoted in Dizard, "How Ahmed Chalabi Conned the Neocons."

[82]Danielle Pletka, "U.S. Only Wounded Itself When It Betrayed Chalabi," *Los Angeles Times*, June 4, 2004, http://www.aei.org/publication/u-s-only-wounded-itself-when-it-betrayed-chalabi/.

[83]Pletka, "U.S. Only Wounded Itself."

[84]Michael Rubin, "On Demonizing Chalabi," *Commentary*, July 5, 2014, https://www.commentarymagazine.com/foreign-policy/middle-east/iraq/on-demonizing-chalabi/.

[85]Aram Roston, "Ahmad Chalabi, Who Conned America into War, Now Aims to Lead Iraq," *Buzzfeed*, June 21, 2014, http://www.buzzfeed.com/aramroston/ahmad-chalabi-conned-america-into-war-now-aims-; and Adam Taylor, "Déjà vu? Neocons Tout Ahmed Chalabi as Iraq's Next Leader," *Washington Post*, July 9, 2014, https://www.washingtonpost.com/news/worldviews/wp/2014/07/08/deja-vu-neocons-tout-ahmed-chalabi-as-iraqs-next-leaader/?utm_term=.830474bbe20b.

[86]Nicole Gaouette, "Wolfowitz Sees Chalabi as Viable Iraq Leader Even with Iran Ties," Bloomberg, July 4, 2014, http://www.bloomberg.com/news/print/2014-07-03/wolfowitz-sees-chalabi-as-viable-iraq-leader.

[87]Wurmser, "Ahmad Chalabi, Evangelist for Middle East Reform."

[88]Mayer, "The Manipulator."

[89]Quoted in Mayer, "The Manipulator."

[90]Quoted in Mayer, "The Manipulator."

Chapter Seven

[1]Jonathan Masters, *Mujahadeen-e-Khalq*, CFR Backgrounder, Council on Foreign Relations, July 28, 2014, p. 1, https://www.cfr.org/backgrounder/mujahadeen-e-khalq-mek. Also see Ali Gharib and Eli Clifton, "Long March of the Yellow Jackets: How a One-Time Terrorist Group Prevailed on Capitol Hill," *Intercept,* February 26, 2015, https://firstlook.org/theintercept/2015/02/26/long-march-yellow/.

[2]Masters, *Mujahadeen-e-Khalq*, p. 1.

[3]Masters, *Mujahadeen-e-Khalq*, p. 2. Also see Ariane Tabatabai, "Beware of the MEK," *National Interest Online*, August 24, 2014, http://nationalinterest.org/feature/beware-the-mek-11118.

[4]Masters, *Mujahadeen-e-Khalq*, p. 2.

[5]John Kifner, "President and Premier Die in Bomb Blast in Teheran; 5 Others Reportedly Killed," *New York Times*, August 31, 1981, http://www.nytimes.com/1981/08/31/world/president-and-premier-die-in-bomb-blast-in-teheran-5-others-reported-killed.html.

[6]Masters, *Mujahadeen-e-Khalq*, p. 2.

[7]MEK, "Biography of Maryam Rajavi," https://www.maryam-rajavi.com/en/biography.

[8]Masters, *Mujahadeen-e-Khalq*, p. 3.

[9]Quoted in Masters, *Mujahadeen-e-Khalq*, p. 2.

[10]Former MEK members have described how the Rajavis dominate the organization and have enforced, sometimes quite harshly, a cult of personality around the husband and wife team. See Adam Forrest, "A Former MEK Member Talks about the Extremist Cult," *Vice.com*, September 2, 2014, https://www.vice.com/read/masoud-banisadr-mek-cult-184.

[11]Jeremiah Goulka, Lydia Hansell, Elizabeth Wilke, and Judith Larson, "The Mujahedin-e Khalq in Iraq: A Policy Conundrum," Rand Corporation, National Defense Research Institute, 2009, http://www.rand.org/content/dam/rand/pubs/monographs/2009/RAND_MG871.pdf.

[12]Gharib and Clifton, "Long March of the Yellow Jackets."

[13]Masters, *Mujahadeen-e-Khalq*, p. 3.

[14]For example, see accounts of Rudolph Giuliani's continued lobbying efforts on behalf of the MEK. Ishaan Tharoor, "Is Regime Change in Iran Part of Trump's Agenda?" *Washington Post,* May 7, 2018, https://www.washingtonpost.com/news/worldviews/wp/2018/05/07/is-regime-change-in-iran-part-of-trumps-agenda/?utm_term=.6d18d81ed2ba; Christopher A. Preble, "Meet the Organization Pushing Regime Change in Iran—And Its Willing American Accomplices," *The Skeptics* (blog), *National Interest,* July 15, 2018, https://nationalinterest.org/blog/skeptics/meet-organization-pushing-regime-change-iran%E2%80%94and-its-willing-american-accomplices.

[15]Quoted in Guy Taylor, "McCain: U.S. Must Do More to Protect Iranian Dissident Group," *Washington Times*, October 7, 2015, http://www.washingtontimes.com/news/2015/oct/7/mccain-us-must-do-more-protect-iranian-dissident-g/.

[16]Seymour M. Hersh, "Our Men in Iran?" *New Yorker*, April 5, 2012, http://www.newyorker.com/news/news-desk/our-men-in-iran.

[17]Quoted in Eli Clifton, "AIPAC's Military 'Expert' Loves the MEK and GOP's Islamophobic Fringe," *Lobeblog.com*, August 21, 2015, https://lobelog.com/aipacs-military-expert-loves-the-mek-and-gops-islamophobic-fringe/.

[18]Clifton, "AIPAC's Military 'Expert.'"

[19]Chris McGreal, "MEK Decision: Multimillion-Dollar Campaign Led to Removal from Terror List," *Guardian*, September 12, 2012, https://www.theguardian.com/world/2012/sep/21/iran-mek-group-removed-us-terrorism-list.

[20]McGreal, "MEK Decision."

[21]Gharib and Clifton, "Long March of the Yellow Jackets."

[22]Quoted in David Francis, "Former State Official Helped Delist the MEK as a Terror Threat. That Doesn't Mean That He Wants to Testify with Them," *Foreign Policy*, April 27, 2015, http://foreignpolicy.com/2015/04/27/former-state-official-helped-delist-the-mek-as-a-terror-threat-that-doesnt-mean-he-wants-to-testify-with-them/. Also see Carnegie Council for Ethics in International Affairs, "MEK: When Terrorism Becomes Respectable," October 17, 2012, https://www.carnegiecouncil.org/publications/ethics_online/0074.

[23]Quoted in McGreal, "MEK Decision."

[24]Quoted in Scott Shane, "Iranian Dissidents Convince U.S. to Drop Terror Label," *New York Times*, September 21, 2012.

[25]U.S. Department of State, "Delisting of the Mujahedin-e-Khalq," September 28, 2012, https://www.state.gov/j/ct/rls/other/des/266607.htm.

[26]Tabatabai, "Beware of the MEK."

[27]Daniel Benjamin, "Giuliani Took Money from a Group That Killed Americans. Does Trump Care?" *Politico*, November 23, 2016, http://www.politico.com/magazine/story/2016/11/giuliani-mek-terrorist-group-money-bolton-iran-214479.

[28]Jeremiah Goulka, "The Cult of MEK," *American Prospect*, July 18, 2012, http://prospect.org/article/cult-mek. Also see Gharib and Clifton, "The Long March of the Yellow Jackets."

[29]Quoted in Goulka, "The Cult of MEK."

[30]Quoted on Twitter, Iran Freedom, Twitter post, July 1, 2017, 7:49 a.m., https://twitter.com/4FreedominIran/status/881162790374961152.

[31]Quoted in Evan McMurry, "Giuliani Tells Fox He's Meeting with Iranian Dissident Group," *Mediaite.com*, March 4, 2015, https://www.mediaite.com/tv/giuliani-tells-fox-hes-meeting-with-iranian-dissident-group/.

[32]Elizabeth Flock, "Iranian Terrorist Group M.E.K. Pays Big to Make History Go Away," *U.S. News & World Report*, July 12, 2012.

[33]Mehdi Hasan, "Here's Why Washington Hawks Love This Cultish Iranian Exile Group," *The Intercept*, July 7, 2017, https://theintercept.com/2017/07/07/mek-iran-rajavi-cult-saudi-gingrich-terrorists-trump/.

[34]Quoted in Eli Clifton, "Michael Rubin Blasts Washington's MEK Supporters," *LobeLog.com*, February 24, 2011, http://www.lobelog.com/michael-rubin-blasts-washingtons-mek-supporters/.

[35]Shane, "Iranian Dissidents Convince U.S. to Drop Terror Label"; Julian Pecquet, "MEK Uses Congressional Spotlight to Push Regime Change in Iran," *U.S. News & World Report,* April 30, 2015; and Jim Lobe, "Sen. Menendez Top Recipient of MEK-Related Campaign Funding," *LobeLog.com*, February 27, 2015, http://www.lobelog.com/menendez-top-recipient-of-mek-related-campaign-funding/.

[36]Quoted in Goulka, "The Cult of MEK."

[37]Scott Peterson, "Iranian Group's Big-Money Push to Get Off U.S. Terrorism List," *Christian Science Monitor*, August 8, 2011, https://www.csmonitor.com/World/Middle-East/2011/0808/Iranian-group-s-big-money-push-to-get-off-US-terrorist-list.

[38]Eli Clifton, "Tom Cotton Allies Himself with the MEK," *LobeLog.com*, May 6, 2015, https://lobelog.com/tom-cotton-allies-himself-with-the-mek/.

[39]Shane, "Iranian Dissidents Convince U.S. to Drop Terror Label."

[40]Quoted in Clifton, "Michael Rubin Blasts Washington's MEK Supporters."

[41]Julian Pecquet, "Congressional Invite to MEK Sparks Furious Backlash," *Al-Monitor,* April 28, 2015, http://www.habilian.ir/en/201504292239/news/congressional-invite-to-mek-sparks-furious-backlash.html.

[42]Quoted in Jessica Schulberg and Akbar Shahid Ahmed, "Why Congress Is Embracing Former Iranian Terrorists," *Huffington Post*, May 5, 2015.

[43]Quoted in Schulberg and Ahmed, "Why Congress Is Embracing Former Iranian Terrorists."

[44]Quoted in Pecquet, "Congressional Invite to MEK Sparks Furious Backlash."

[45]Quoted in Pecquet, "MEK Uses Congressional Spotlight to Push Regime Change in Iran."

[46]Tabatabai, "Beware of the MEK."

[47]John R. Bolton, "To Stop Iran's Bomb, Bomb Iran," *New York Times*, op-ed, March 26, 2015, https://www.nytimes.com/2015/03/26/opinion/to-stop-irans-bomb-bomb-iran.html.

[48]Abbas Milani, "Iran Primer: The Green Movement," PBS, *Frontline*, October 27, 2010, https://www.pbs.org/wgbh/pages/frontline/tehranbureau/2010/10/iran-primer-the-green-movement.html.

[49]Daniel Larison, "Bolton and the MEK," *American Conservative*, March 27, 2015, http://www.theamericanconservative.com/larison/bolton-and-the-mek/.

[50]Daniel Larison, "The MEK and Its American Supporters," *American Conservative*, November 23, 2016, http://www.theamericanconservative.com/larison/the-mek-and-its-american-fans/.

[51]Quoted in Shane, "Iranian Dissidents Convince U.S. to Drop Terror Label."

[52]Tabatabai, "Beware of the MEK."

[53]Goulka, "The Cult of MEK."

[54]Quoted in Gharib and Clifton, "The Long March of the Yellow Jackets."

[55]Gharib and Clifton, "The Long March of the Yellow Jackets." One interesting question is how has the MEK gotten the millions of dollars it has used to cultivate American political leaders and hire high-priced lobbying firms? As with many cults, the rank-and-file members likely provide a major portion of the resources, but that source seems insufficient for the large sums of money involved; another source might be wealthy Iranian exiles who are not officially affiliated with the organization. But one has to wonder if U.S. intelligence agencies also might be channeling funds to the group as part of a larger strategy to undermine Iran's clerical government. For a somewhat speculative discussion of the funding issues, see Daniel Tovrov, "MEK Pays U.S. Officials, But Where Do the Iranian Exiles Get Their Money?" *International Business Times*, March 3, 2012, http://www.ibtimes.com/mek-pays-us-officials-where-do-iranian-exiles-get-their-money-214388.

[56]Quoted in Adrienne Mahsa Varkiani, "Tillerson Calls for Regime Change in Iran," *ThinkProgess.org*, June 15, 2017, https://thinkprogress.org/tillerson-calls-for-regime-change-in-iran-ad2ded82f945.

[57]Varkiani, "Tillerson Calls for Regime Change in Iran."

[58]Olivia Beavers, "Cotton: U.S. Policy Should Be Regime Change in Iran," *The Hill*, June 25, 2017, http://thehill.com/homenews/senate/339392-cotton-us-policy-should-be-regime-change-in-iran.

[59]Christopher A. Preble, "Meet the Organization Pushing Regime Change in Iran."

[60]Alireza Jafarzadeh, "Iran Protests: Here Is What the U.S. Should Do Now," People's Mojahedin Organization of Iran, January 3, 2018, https://www.mojahedin.org/newsen/60439/Iran-protests-Here-is-what-the-US-should-do-now.

[61]Callum Paton, "Iran Protests: Who Are the Iranian Opposition, and Who Will Rule if the Regime Falls?" *Newsweek*, January 5, 2018, http://www.newsweek.com/iran-protests-who-are-opposition-and-who-will-rule-if-regime-falls-772045.

[62]"Iran Blames CIA for Anti-Government Protests; U.S. Denies Any Role," *CBSNews.com*, January 4, 2018, https://www.cbsnews.com/news/iran-blames-cia-for-anti-government-protests-u-s-denies-any-role/.

[63]Quoted in "UN Meeting on Iran Protests Called by U.S. Criticized at Security Council," *Reuters,* January 5, 2018, https://www.reuters.com/article /uk-iran-rallies-un/u-n-meeting-on-iran-protests-called-by-u-s-criticized-at -security-council-idUKKBN1EU27Q?il=0.

[64]Dana Rohrabacher, "A Reagan Doctrine for Iran?" *National Interest Online*, January 25, 2018, http://nationalinterest.org/feature/reagan-doctrine -iran-24220.

[65]"Bolton: 'Our Goal Should Be Regime Change in Iran,'" *Fox News Insider*, January 1, 2018, http://insider.foxnews.com/2018/01/01/john-bolton-trump-us -goal-should-be-regime-change-iran.

[66]Anne and Massoud Khodabandeh, "The Iran Protests, Regime Change, and the MEK," *LobeLog,* January 17, 2018, https://lobelog.com/the-iran-protests -regime-change-and-mek/.

[67]Daniel Larison, "The Foolish Embrace of the MEK," *American Conservative*, July 6, 2011, http://www.theamericanconservative.com/larison/the-foolish -embrace-of-the-mek/.

[68]Hasan, "Here's Why Washington Hawks Love This Cultish Iranian Exile Group."

CHAPTER EIGHT

[1]For a skeptical assessment of the responsibility to protect rationale in international affairs, see Rajan Menon, *The Conceit of Humanitarian Intervention* (New York: Oxford University Press, 2016), pp. 6–10, 43–44, 83–84, 89–97.

[2]"Bush, Blair: Libya to Dismantle WMD Programs," *CNN.com*, December 20, 2003, http://www.cnn.com/2003/WORLD/africa/12/19/bush.libya/index .html.

[3]See Alan J. Kuperman, "Lessons from Libya: How Not to Intervene," Policy Brief, *Quarterly Journal: International Security,* September 2013, http://belfercenter .ksg.harvard.edu/publication/23387/lessons_from_libya.html.

[4]Secretary of Defense Robert Gates was one of the few U.S. officials to understand Libya's fragility and the problems that the regional and ethnic divisions posed. See Robert M. Gates, *Duty: Memoirs of a Secretary at War* (New York: Alfred A. Knopf, 2014), pp. 522–23.

[5]Menon, *The Conceit of Humanitarian Intervention*, p. 111.

[6]Christopher S. Chivvis, *Toppling Qaddafi: Libya and the Limits of Liberal Intervention* (New York: Cambridge University Press, 2014), p. 182.

[7]Gail Russell Chaddock, "Five Senators Push Obama to Do More in Libya," *Christian Science Monitor*, March 22, 2011, https://www.csmonitor.com/USA /Politics/2011/0322/Five-senators-push-Obama-to-do-more-in-Libya/.

[8]Daniel Larison, "Clinton's Libyan War and the Delusions of Interventionists," *American Conservative*, February 29, 2016, http://www.theamericanconservative .com/larison/clintons-libyan-war-and-the-delusions-of-interventionists/.

[9]Chaddock, "Five Senators Push Obama to Do More in Libya."

[10]"John McCain Praises 'Heroic' Rebels on Visit to Libya," *Guardian*, April 22, 2011, https://www.theguardian.com/world/2011/apr/22/john-mccain-praises -libya-rebels.

[11]Chaddock, "Five Senators Push Obama to Do More in Libya."

[12]Ed Schultz, *The Ed Show*, MSNBC, March 30, 2011, https://www.youtube .com/watch?v=dXDZ2AogetA.

[13]See, for example, "Responsibility to Protect in Libya: Calls for Intervention Intensify," *NATO Watch*, February 24, 2011, http://natowatch.org/node/472; "Libya Revolt: Gaddafi in Crimes against Humanity Probe," *BBC News*, March 3, 2011, http://www.bbc.com/news/world-africa-12636798; and Atika Shubert, "Gadhafi Faces Investigation for Crimes against Humanity," *CNN.com*, March 3, 2011, http://www.cnn.com/2011/WORLD/meast/03/03/libya.war.crimes/.

[14]That campaign accelerated once the NATO military intervention commenced. See "UN: Qaddafi Forces Committed War Crimes," *CBS News*, June 1, 2011, http://www.cbsnews.com/news/un-qaddafi-forces-committed-war -crimes/.

[15]Ross Douthat, "100,000 Libyan Casualties?" Opinion, *New York Times*, March 24, 2011, http://douthat.blogs.nytimes.com/2011/03/24/100000-libyan -casualties/.

[16]Menon, *The Conceit of Humanitarian Intervention*, p. 111.

[17]Hillary Rodham Clinton, *Hard Choices* (New York: Simon and Schuster, 2014), p. 370.

[18]For a good, critical treatment of that narrative and its discrepancy from the actual events, see Kuperman, "Lessons from Libya: How Not to Intervene."

[19]David Bromwich, "The Roots of Hillary's Fascination with War," *National Interest* 144 (July/August 2016): 14, http://nationalinterest.org/feature/the-roots -hillarys-infatuation-war-16787.

[20]Menon, *The Conceit of Humanitarian Intervention*, pp. 111–12.

[21]Alan J. Kuperman, "5 Things the U.S. Should Consider in Libya," Opinion, *USA Today*, March 22, 2011, https://usatoday30.usatoday.com/news/opinion /forum/2011-03-22-column22_ST_N.htm.

[22]Stephen M. Walt, "Top 5 Reasons We Keep Fighting All These Wars," *Foreign Policy*, April 4, 2011, http://foreignpolicy.com/2011/04/04/top-5-reasons -we-keep-fighting-all-these-wars/.

[23]Gates, *Duty*, p. 518.

[24]Menon, *The Conceit of Humanitarian Intervention*, p. 112.

[25]Menon, *The Conceit of Humanitarian Intervention*, p. 112.

[26]"Gaddafi's Army Will Kill Half a Million, Warn Libyan Rebels," *Guardian*, March 12, 2011, https://www.theguardian.com/world/2011/mar/12/gaddafi -army-kill-half-million.

[27]For discussions of Clinton's central role, see Benjamin H. Friedman, "The Real Benghazi Scandal Everyone Is Missing," *National Interest Online*, October 28, 2015, http://nationalinterest.org/feature/the-real-benghazi-scandal-everyone-missing -14185; and Jo Becker and Scott Shane, "Hillary Clinton, 'Smart Power' and a Dictator's Fall," *New York Times*, February 27, 2016, https://www.nytimes .com/2016/02/28/us/politics/hillary-clinton-libya.html?ref=todayspaper&_r=0.

[28]For Clinton's account of the meeting, see *Hard Choices*, pp. 363–64, 369–70.

[29]Clinton, *Hard Choices*, p. 364.

[30]Becker and Shane, "Hillary Clinton, 'Smart Power' and a Dictator's Fall."

[31]Clinton, *Hard Choices*, p. 370.

[32]Ahmad Rahim, "Libya Former MP Lashes Out at International Community," *Al-Monitor*, August 29, 2016, http://archive.fo/SvmLw.

[33]Chivvis, *Toppling Qaddafi*, p. 159.

[34]Gates, *Duty*, p. 518. The defense secretary stated in his memoirs that Obama later told him the Libya intervention had been "a 51–49 call for him." Gates, *Duty*, p. 519.

[35]Menon, *The Conceit of Humanitarian Intervention*, p. 111.

[36]Clinton, *Hard Choices*, p. 367.

[37]Martin Chulov, "Saudi Arabian Troops Enter Bahrain as Regime Asks for Help to Quell Uprising," *Guardian*, March 14, 2011, https://www.theguardian .com/world/2011/mar/14/saudi-arabian-troops-enter-bahrain.

[38]UN Security Council, Resolution 1973, S/Res/2973 (March 17, 2011), http://www.un.org/ga/search/view_doc.asp?symbol=S/RES/1973%20 %282011%29.

[39]UN Security Council, Resolution 1973, sec. 4, p. 3.

[40]Nearly two weeks after passage of the resolution and commencement of the aircraft and missile attacks, President Obama still sought to portray the mission as a limited one intended to protect innocent civilians. "Remarks by the President in Address to the Nation on Libya," National Defense University, March 28, 2011, https://www.whitehouse.gov/the-press-office/2011/03/28/remarks-president -address-nation-libya. Also, see Gates's depiction of his often uncomfortable testi- mony before the armed services committees in both the House and Senate. Gates, *Duty*, p. 521.

[41]Gates, *Duty*, p. 530.

[42]Gates, *Duty*, p. 519.

[43]Friedman, "The Real Benghazi Scandal Everyone Is Missing."

[44]Gates, *Duty*, p. 521.

[45]Gates, *Duty*, p. 522.

[46]"McCain: I Hope U.S., Others Arm Libyan Rebels," *CBS News,* March 22, 2011, www.cbsnews.com/news/mccain-i-hope-us-others-arm-libyan-rebels.

[47]Mark Hosenball, "Exclusive: Obama Authorizes Secret Help for Libya Rebels," Reuters, March 30, 2011, www.reuters.com/article/2011/03/30/us-libya -usa-order-idUSTRE72T6H220110330.

[48]"U.S. Agents Were in Libya Before Obama Secret Order," Reuters, March 31, 2011, http://af.reuters.com/article/idAFN31101481201110331?sp=true.

[49]Sam Dagher, "To Ease Allies' Fear, Rebels Attempt to Rein-in Militias," *Wall Street Journal,* June 13, 2011, https://www.wsj.com/articles/SB10001424052 7023045631045763628209811611198.

[50]Amnesty International, *The Battle for Libya: Killings, Disappearances and Torture,* 2011, pp. 70–78, 82–87, https://www.amnesty.org/en/documents/MDE19 /025/2011/en/; David Smith, "Murder and Torture 'Carried Out by Both Sides' of Uprising against Libya Regime," *Guardian,* September 12, 2011, www.theguardian.com/world/2011/sep/12/murder-torture-both-sides-libyan -regime; and Seumas Milne, "If the Libyan War Was about Saving Lives, It Was a Catastrophic Failure," *Guardian,* October 26, 2011, www.theguardian.com /commentisfree/2011/oct/libya-war-saving-lives-catastrophic-failure.

[51]For an example of the latter, see Chivvis, *Toppling Qaddafi,* p. 175, where he accepts the inflated estimates of civilian casualties by government forces without mentioning a word about rebel atrocities.

[52]Menon, *The Conceit of Humanitarian Intervention,* pp. 118–19.

[53]Menon, *The Conceit of Humanitarian Intervention,* p. 113.

[54]One rebel leader epitomized the prevailing cynicism: "I can't say whether I like or dislike NATO," he said, but "without them we would have been finished." Quoted in Chivvis, *Toppling Qaddafi,* p. 189. That attitude hardly reflected international democratic solidarity, nor was it the foundation of a lasting friendship.

[55]"Clinton on Qaddafi: 'We Came, We Saw, He Died,'" *CBS News,* October 20, 2011, http://www.cbsnews.com/news/clinton-on-qaddafi-we-came-we-saw-he -died/. Her attitude was not unique. Political scientist Benjamin Barber noted that Qaddafi had refused to flee the country, stating that he would live or die in Libya; "The Libyan freedom fighters granted him his wish," Barber stated. Benjamin Barber, "Libya's Revolution Has Triumphed, But Will Democracy?" *Guardian,* October 21, 2011, https://www.theguardian.com/commentisfree/2011/oct/21 /libya-revolution-democracy-muammar-gaddafi.

[56]Don Lothlan, "Obama on Libya: 'Tripoli Is Slipping from the Grasp of a Tyrant,'" *CNN.com,* August 22, 2011, http://www.cnn.com/2011/POLITICS /08/22/obama.libya.statement/index.html.

[57]Lothlan, "Obama on Libya: 'Tripoli Is Slipping from the Grasp of a Tyrant.'"

[58]Kareem Fahim and Rick Gladstone, "U.S. Senate Delegation Offers Praise and Caution to Libya's New Leaders," *New York Times*, September 29, 2011, http://www.nytimes.com/2011/09/30/world/africa/senate-delegation-offers -praise-and-caution-to-libyas-new-leaders.html.

[59]Quoted in Andrew J. Bacevich, *America's War for the Greater Middle East* (New York: Random House, 2016), p. 329.

[60]Ivo H. Daalder and James G. Stavridis, "NATO's Success in Libya," *New York Times,* October 30, 2011, http://www.nytimes.com/2011/10/31/opinion/31iht -eddaalder31.html.

[61]Quoted in Conor Friedersdorf, "Did Libya Prove War Hawks Right or Wrong?" *Atlantic*, July 29, 2014, https://www.theatlantic.com/international/archive /2014/07/did-the-war-in-libya-prove-the-interventionists-right-or-wrong/375211/.

[62]Nicholas Kristof, "'Thank You, America!'" *New York Times*, August 31, 2011. http://www.nytimes.com/2011/09/01/opinion/kristof-from-libyans-thank -you-america.html?_r=0.

[63]Glenn Greenwald, "A Progressive Case for Obama's Foreign Policy Great-ness?" *Salon*, August 24, 2011, https://www.salon.com/2011/08/24/obama_149/.

[64]Chivvis, *Toppling Qaddafi*, p. 175.

[65]Chivvis, *Toppling Qaddafi*, p. 159.

[66]Chivvis, *Toppling Qaddafi*, p. 183.

[67]Chivvis, *Toppling Qaddafi*, pp. 170–71.

[68]Chivvis, *Toppling Qaddafi*, pp. 171–72.

[69]Menon, *The Conceit of Humanitarian Intervention*, pp. 145–46.

[70]See Chivvis, *Toppling Qaddafi*, pp. 172, 179.

[71]Chivvis, *Toppling Qaddafi*, p. 173.

[72]Bacevich, *America's War for the Greater Middle East*, p. 330.

[73]Glenn Greenwald, "State Department Attacks CNN for Doing Basic Journal-ism," *Guardian*, September 24, 2012, https://www.theguardian.com/commentisfree /2012/sep/24/cnn-journal-libya.

[74]"ISIS Video Appears to Show Beheadings of Egyptian Coptic Christians in Libya," *CNN.com*, February 16, 2015, http://www.cnn.com/2015/02/15 /middleeast/isis-video-beheadings-christians/index.html.

[75]Andrew Engel, "A Way Forward in Benghazi," Washington Institute for Near East Policy, *PolicyWatch,* no. 2088, June 12, 2013, p. 1.

[76]Engel, "A Way Forward in Benghazi," p. 2.

[77]Engel, "A Way Forward in Benghazi," p. 2.

[78]Conor Friedersdorf, "Hillary Defends Her Failed War in Libya," *Atlan-tic*, October 14, 2015, http://www.theatlantic.com/politics/archive/2015/10 /hillary-clinton-debate-libya/410437/.

[79]Friedersdorf, "Hillary Defends Her Failed War in Libya."

[80]Leon Panetta with Jim Newton, *Worthy Fights: A Memoir of Leadership in War and Peace* (New York: Penguin Books, 2014), p. 382.

[81]Chivvis, *Toppling Qaddafi*, p. 175.

[82]Esther Yu Hsi Lee, "Why So Many Refugees Are Fleeing to Europe from Libya," *ThinkProgress*, June 2, 2016. https://thinkprogress.org/why-so-many-refugees-are-fleeing-to-europe-from-libya-f95d570f4d81/.

[83]Human Rights Watch, "World Report 2017: Libya: Events of 2016," p. 1, https://www.hrw.org/world-report/2017/country-chapters/libya.

[84]Panetta, *Worthy Fights*, p. 310.

[85]Panetta, *Worthy Fights*, p. 381.

[86]Barbara Starr, Joe Sterling, and Azadeh Ansari, "U.S. Embassy in Libya Evacuates Personnel," *CNN.com*, July 26, 2014, http://www.cnn.com/2014/07/26/world/africa/libya-us-embassy-evacuation/index.html.

[87]Andrew Engel and Ayman Grada, "Libya's Other Battle," Washington Institute for Near East Policy, *PolicyWatch,* no. 2295, July 28, 2014, http://www.washingtoninstitute.org/policy-analysis/view/libyas-other-battle.

[88]William Danvers, "Next Steps in Libya," Center for American Progress, July 27, 2016, https://www.americanprogress.org/issues/security/reports/2016/07/27/141805/next-steps-in-libya/. In a considerable understatement, Danvers observes, "Libya is struggling to unify its government."

[89]Jason Ditz, "Heavy Losses Claimed as U.S. Warplanes Pound Libyan City of Sirte," *Antiwar.com*, August 1, 2016, http://news.antiwar.com/2016/08/01/heavy-losses-claimed-as-us-warplanes-pound-libyan-city-of-sirte/. For background on that rivalry, see "Libya's UN-Backed Government Sails into Tripoli," *Al Jazeera,* March 31, 2016, http://www.aljazeera.com/news/2016/03/libya-backed-unity-government-arrives-tripoli-160330125804929.html.

[90]For an early analysis of Haftar's views and apparent policy preferences, see Barak Barfi, "Khalifa Haftar: Rebuilding Libya from the Top Down," Washington Institute for Near East Policy, *Research Notes*, no. 22, August 2014, http://www.washingtoninstitute.org/policy-analysis/view/khalifa-haftar-rebuilding-libya-from-the-top-down.

[91]Jon Lee Anderson, "The Unravelling: In a Failing State, an Anti-Islamist General Mounts a Divisive Campaign," *New Yorker*, February 23 & March 2, 2015, http://www.newyorker.com/magazine/2015/02/23/unravelling.

[92]Missy Ryan, "A Former CIA Asset Has Become a U.S. Headache in Libya," *Washington Post*, August 17, 2016; https://www.washingtonpost.com/world/national-security/a-former-cia-asset-has-become-a-us-headache-in-libya/2016/08/17/a766e392-54c6-11e6-bbf5-957ad17b4385_story.html. Also see Anderson, "The Unravelling."

[93]"Libya Strongman Says Backs 2018 Elections," AFP, December 29, 2017, https://www.yahoo.com/news/libya-strongman-says-backs-2018-elections-135724296.html.

[94]"Support for Libyan Unity Government 'Crumbling': UN Envoy," Reuters, August 12, 2016, http://www.reuters.com/article/us-libya-security-un-id USKCN10N0S9.

[95]Daniel McAdams, "U.S. Airstrkes Hit Libya to Bolster UN-Created Government," *Antiwar.com*, August 1, 2016, http://original.antiwar.com/daniel-mcadams/2016/08/01/us-airstrikes-hit-libya-bolster-un-created-government/.

[96]Aidan Lewis and Ulf Laessing, "UN Condemns Civilian Deaths from Air Attack in East Libya," Reuters, October 30, 2017, http://www.reuters.com/article/us-libya-security/u-n-condemns-civilian-deaths-from-air-attack-in-east-libya-idUSKBN1CZ2NM.

[97]Egypt is just one of several Middle East powers backing one faction or another in Libya. Others include Saudi Arabia, Qatar, United Arab Emirates, and Turkey. That geostrategic meddling by regional powers was already prominent in 2014. See Gilad Wenig and Andrew Engel, "Battlefield Libya," Washington Institute for Near East Policy, *Policy Analysis,* September 17, 2014, http://www.washingtoninstitute.org/policy-analysis/view/battlefield-libya; see also Simon Henderson, "U.S. Allies Bombing Islamists: The UAE Airstrikes on Libya," Washington Institute for Near East Policy, *Policy Analysis,* August 25, 2014, http://www.washingtoninstitute.org/policy-analysis/view/u.s.-allies-bombing-islamists-the-uae-airstrikes-on-libya.

[98]Ahmed Salah Ali, "Libya's Warring Parties Play a Dangerous Game Working with Madkhali Salafists," Atlantic Council, *MENA Source*, November 3, 2017, http://www.atlanticcouncil.org/blogs/menasource/libya-s-warring-parties-play-a-dangerous-game-working-with-madkhali-salafists.

[99]"Armed Groups Clash at Key Libya Border Post," AFP, January 5, 2018, https://www.yahoo.com/news/armed-groups-clash-key-libya-border-post-175712862.html.

[100]Mohamed Eljarh, "Struggling to Advance in Post-Spring Libya," Washington Institute for Near East Policy, *Beyond Islamists & Autocrats*, January 2017, p. 5, http://www.washingtoninstitute.org/uploads/Documents/pubs/BeyondIslamists-Eljarh.pdf.

[101]Andrew Engel, "After the Islamic State in Libya: All-Out War?" Washington Institute for Near East Policy, *PolicyWatch*, no. 2749, January 11, 2017, http://www.washingtoninstitute.org/policy-analysis/view/after-the-islamic-state-in-libya-all-out-war.

[102]"Libya Rivals Agree 'Historic' Election Plan," *BBC News*, May 29, 2018, https://www.bbc.com/news/world-africa-44289516.

[103]Ghaith Shennib, Tarek El-Tablawy, and Gregory Viscusi, "Macron Brokers Libyan Consensus on December Elections," *Bloomberg.com*, May 29, 2018, https://www.bloomberg.com/news/articles/2018-05-29/libya-rivals-reach-consensus-on-december-elections-adviser-says.

[104]Patrick Wintour and Chris Stephen, "Libyan Rival Leaders Agree to Ceasefire after Macron-Hosted Talks," *Guardian*, July 25, 2017, https://www.theguardian.com/world/2017/jul/25/france-raises-hopes-of-deal-between-libyan-rival-factions.

[105]Mel Frykberg, "Agreement to Hold Libyan Elections Could Be Misleading," *IOL News*, May 31, 2018, https://www.iol.co.za/news/africa/agreement-to-hold-libyan-elections-could-be-misleading-15249382.

[106]Mat Nashed, "Holding Libyan Elections in 2018 Could Be Disastrous," *Al-Monitor*, March 15, 2018, https://www.al-monitor.com/pulse/originals/2018/03/libya-elections-conditions-un-envoy-risks-backfire-war-soon.html.

[107]Ben Fishman, "Libya's Struggle for Stability May Require Greater Western Involvement," Washington Institute for Near East Policy, *PolicyWatch*, no. 2651, July 11, 2016, http://www.washingtoninstitute.org/policy-analysis/view/libyas-struggle-for-stability-may-require-greater-western-involvement.

[108]David Mack, "Kick-Starting Governance in Libya," *Middle East Institute*, July 7, 2016, http://www.mei.edu/content/article/kick-starting-governance-libya.

[109]Friedman, "The Real Benghazi Scandal Everyone Is Missing."

[110]Kuperman, "Lessons from Libya: How Not to Intervene."

[111]Mark Landler, *Alter Egos: Hillary Clinton, Barack Obama, and the Twilight Struggle Over American Power* (New York: Random House, 2016), p. 187.

[112]Bromwich quoted in Friedersdorf, "Hillary Defends Her Failed War in Libya," p. 14.

[113]Becker and Shane, "Hillary Clinton, 'Smart Power,' and a Dictator's Fall."

[114]Larison, "Clinton's Libyan War and the Delusions of Interventionists."

[115]Bacevich, *America's War for the Greater Middle East*, p. 330.

Chapter Nine

[1]Richard Sakwa, *Frontline Ukraine: Crisis in the Borderlands* (London: I. B. Tauris, 2015), p. 57.

[2]Sakwa, *Frontline Ukraine*, pp. 72–73.

[3]Sakwa, *Frontline Ukraine*, p. 57.

[4]Sakwa, *Frontline Ukraine*, p. 56.

[5]Sakwa, *Frontline Ukraine*, p. 57.

[6]Samuel Charap and Timothy J. Colton, *Everyone Loses: The Ukraine Crisis and the Ruinous Contest for Post-Soviet Eurasia* (London: Routledge, 2017), p. 121.

[7]Charap and Colton, *Everyone Loses,* p. 121.

[8]See Susan Eisenhower, "The Perils of Victory," in Ted Galen Carpenter and Barbara Conry, eds., *NATO Enlargement: Illusions and Reality* (Washington: Cato Institute, 1998), pp. 103–19; Alton Frye, "The New NATO and Relations with Russia," in *NATO Enters the 21st Century*, ed. Ted Galen Carpenter (London: Frank Cass Publishers, 2001), pp. 92–110; and Amos Perlmutter, "The Corruption of NATO: NATO Moves East," in *NATO Enters the 21st Century*, pp. 129–53.

[9]Sakwa, *Frontline Ukraine,* pp. 54–55.

[10]John J. Mearsheimer, "Why the Ukraine Crisis Is the West's Fault," *Foreign Affairs* 93, no. 6 (September/October 2014): 77–89.

[11]"How the EU Lost Ukraine," *Der Spiegel*, November 25, 2013, http://www .spiegel.de/international/europe/how-the-eu-lost-to-russia-in-negotiations -over-ukraine-trade-deal-a-935476.html.

[12]Charap and Colton, *Everyone Loses,* p. 122.

[13]Sakwa, *Frontline Ukraine,* p. 67.

[14]Thomas C. Theiner, "Corruption You Can't Imagine," *Euromaidan Press*, July 13, 2014, http://euromaidanpress.com/2014/07/13/16899/#arvlbdata.

[15]Typical accounts include Askold Krushelnycky, "The Fight for the Maidan," *Foreign Policy*, December 13, 2013, http://foreignpolicy.com/2013/12/13/the -fight-for-the-maidan/; Olena Perepayda and Markian Ostaplaschuk, "Berkut: Ukraine's Protest-Suppression Unit," *Deutsche Welle*, December 10, 2013, http:// www.dw.com/en/berkut-ukraines-protest-suppression-unit/a-17284637; Victoria Butenko and Sergei Loiko, "Ukraine Police Storm Protest Camp, Witnesses Say," *Los Angeles Times*, December 13, 2013, http://articles.latimes.com/2013 /dec/10/world/la-fg-ukraine-protests-20131211; and "Protestors, Police Clash in Ukraine over President's Pro-Russia Policy," *FoxNews.com*, December 2, 2013, http://www.foxnews.com/world/2013/12/02/thousands-pro-eu-demonstrators -angry-with-government-march-through-ukraine.html.

[16]Tim Judah, "Fighting for the Soul of Ukraine," *New York Review of Books*, January 9, 2014, http://www.nybooks.com/articles/2014/01/09/fighting-soul -ukraine/.

[17]Timothy Snyder, "Fascism, Russia, and Ukraine," *New York Review of Books*, March 20, 2014, http://www.nybooks.com/articles/2014/03/20/fascism-russia -and-ukraine/.

[18]Charap and Colton, *Everyone Loses,* pp. 122–23.

[19]Gilbert Doctorow, "A Look at Ukraine's Dark Side," *Consortium News*, February 7, 2016, https://consortiumnews.com/2016/02/07/a-look-at-ukraines-dark-side/.

[20]Sakwa, *Frontline Ukraine,* p. 21.

[21]Sakwa, *Frontline Ukraine,* p. 21.

[22]*Yid* is an ethnic slur referring to a Yiddish-speaking Jew. Sakwa, *Frontline Ukraine,* p. 22.

[23]Sakwa, *Frontline Ukraine,* p. 84.

[24]Will Englund, "Ukraine Enacts Harsh Laws against Protests," *Washington Post*, January 17, 2014, https://www.washingtonpost.com/world/europe/ukraine-enacts-harsh-laws-against-protests/2014/01/17/365f377a-7fae-11e3-93c1-0e888170b723_story.html?utm_term=.f977ace0930f.

[25]Will Englund, "In Concession to Opposition, Ukraine Repeals Anti-Protest Laws; Prime Minister Resigns," *Washington Post*, January 28, 2014, https://www.washingtonpost.com/world/in-concession-to-opposition-ukraine-repeals-anti-protest-laws-prime-minister-resigns/2014/01/28/59f26e60-8813-11e3-a5bd-844629433ba3_story.html?utm_term=.85f3bba541bd.

[26]Charap and Colton, *Everyone Loses*, p. 124.

[27]Andrew Foxall and Oren Kessler, "Yes, There Are Bad Guys in the Ukrainian Government," *Foreign Policy*, March 18, 2014.

[28]Harriet Salem, "Who Exactly Is Governing Ukraine?" *Guardian*, March 4, 2014, https://www.theguardian.com/world/2014/mar/04/who-governing-ukraine-olexander-turchynov.

[29]Charap and Colton, *Everyone Loses*, p. 126.

[30]Charap and Colton, *Everyone Loses*, p. 126.

[31]Charap and Colton, *Everyone Loses*, p. 125.

[32]Raf Casert, "Spurned by President, EU Embraces Ukraine Protest," Associated Press, December 12, 2013, http://www.sandiegouniontribune.com/sdut-spurned-by-president-eu-embraces-ukraine-protest-2013dec12-story.html.

[33]Quoted in Bernd Riegert, "EU Parliament Backs Ukraine Protesters," *Deutsche Welle*, December 11, 2013, https://www.dw.com/en/eu-parliament-backs-ukraine-protesters/a-17286792.

[34]Robert Zubrin, "How We Can Help Ukraine," *National Review*, January 2, 2014, http://www.nationalreview.com/article/367372/how-we-can-help-ukraine-robert-zubrin.

[35]Quoted in Brian Whelan, "Far-Right Group at Heart of Ukraine Protests Meet U.S. Senator," Channel 4 News (UK), December 16, 2013, https://www.channel4.com/news/ukraine-mccain-far-right-svoboda-anti-semitic-protests.

[36]Quoted in "John McCain Tells Ukraine Protesters: We Are Here to Support Your Just Cause," *Guardian*, December 15, 2013, https://www.theguardian.com/world/2013/dec/15/john-mccain-ukraine-protests-support-just-cause.

[37]Sakwa, *Frontline Ukraine*, p. 86.

[38]"Ukraine Crisis: Transcript of Leaked Nuland-Pyatt Call," BBC News, February 7, 2014, http://www.bbc.com/news/world-europe-26079957.

[39]Ted Galen Carpenter, "U.S. Hypocrisy on Election Meddling," *Huffington Post*, January 31, 2017, https://www.cato.org/publications/commentary/us-hypocrisy-election-meddling. Also see John Mueller, "Hypocrisy on Election Interference," Cato at Liberty (blog), January 4, 2017, https://www.cato.org/blog/hypocrisy-election-interference; Ishaan Tharoor, "The Long History of the U.S.

Interfering with Elections Elsewhere," *Washington Post*, October 13, 2016, https://www.washingtonpost.com/news/worldviews/wp/2016/10/13/the-long-history-of-the-u-s-interfering-with-elections-elsewhere/; and Nina Agrawal, "The U.S. Is No Stranger to Interfering in the Elections of Other Countries," *Los Angeles Times*, December 21, 2016, http://www.latimes.com/nation/la-na-us-intervention-foreign-elections-20161213-story.html.

[40]"Ukraine Crisis: Transcript of Leaked Nuland-Pyatt Call," BBC News.

[41]"Ukraine Crisis: Transcript of Leaked Nuland-Pyatt Call," BBC News.

[42]Robert Parry, "Yats Is No Longer the Guy," *Consortium News*, April 11, 2016, https://consortiumnews.com/2016/04/11/yats-is-no-longer-the-guy/.

[43]"Ukraine's Next Chapter," *Washington Post*, editorial, February 24, 2014, https://www.washingtonpost.com/opinions/ukraines-next-chapter/2014/02/24/a26822be-9d87-11e3-a050-dc3322a94fa7_story.html.

[44]James Carden and Jacob Heilbrunn, "Post Apocalyptic," *National Interest* 135 (January–February 2015): 17.

[45]Timothy Snyder, "Ukraine: The Haze of Propaganda," *New York Review of Books*, March 1, 2014, http://www.nybooks.com/daily/2014/03/01/ukraine-haze-propaganda/.

[46]James Kirchick, "Putin's Imaginary Nazis," *Politico*, March 31, 2014, https://www.politico.com/magazine/story/2014/03/putins-imaginary-nazis-105217.

[47]See, for example, Peter Ackerman, Maciej Bartkowski, and Jack Duvall, "Ukraine: A Nonviolent Victory," *Open Democracy*, March 3, 2014, https://www.opendemocracy.net/civilresistance/peter-ackerman-maciej-bartkowski-jack-duvall/ukraine-nonviolent-victory; and Nadia Diuk, "Euromaidan: Ukraine's Self-Organizing Revolution," *World Affairs*, March–April 2014, http://www.worldaffairsjournal.org/article/euromaidan-ukraine%E2%80%99s-self-organizing-revolution.

[48]"Profile: Ukraine's Ultra-Nationalist Right Sector," *BBC News*, April 26, 2014, http://www.bbc.com/news/world-europe-27173857.

[49]Gabriel Gatehouse, "The Untold Story of the Maidan Massacre," *BBC News*, February 15, 2014, http://www.bbc.com/news/magazine-31359021.

[50]Gordon Hahn, "The Ukrainian Revolution's Neo-Fascist Problem," *Fair Observer*, September 23, 2014, https://www.fairobserver.com/region/europe/the-ukrainian-revolutions-neo-fascist-problem-14785/; and David Stern, "Ukraine Underplays Role of Far Right in Conflict," *BBC News*, December 13, 2014, http://www.bbc.com/news/world-europe-30414955.

[51]Michael McFaul, "Ukraine Imports Democracy: External Influences on the Orange Revolution," *International Security* 32, 2 (Fall 2007): 74. The principal vehicles were the ostensibly "nongovernmental organizations" affiliated with the two major U.S. political parties, the International Republican Institute and the National Democratic Institute.

[52]Sakwa, *Frontline Ukraine,* pp. 88–89.

[53]Quoted in Sakwa, *Frontline Ukraine,* p. 75.

[54]Sakwa, *Frontline Ukraine,* p. 55.

[55]Julian Coman, "On the Frontlines of Europe's Forgotten War in Ukraine," *Guardian,* November 12, 2017, https://www.theguardian.com/world/2017/nov/12/ukraine-on-the-front-line-of-europes-forgotten-war.

[56]"Ukrainian Nationalists Destroyed Tent City in Uman," *Haaretz,* September 8, 2015, http://www.haaretz.com/jewish-world/jewish-world-news/1.675138.

[57]Quoted in Sakwa, *Frontline Ukraine,* p. 65.

[58]Michael Birnbaum and Fredrick Kunkle, "In Ukraine Presidential Election, Chocolate Tycoon Poroshenko Claims Victory," *Washington Post,* May 25, 2014, https://www.washingtonpost.com/world/ukrainians-head-to-the-polls-to-elect-a-new-president-except-in-the-restive-east/2014/05/25/2680fad4-e9f7-4118-923e-852b01351b39_story.html.

[59]Yuras Karmanu, "Ukraine Prime Minister Arseniy Yatsenyuk Resigns and Opens Way for New Government," *Independent* (UK), April 10, 2016, http://www.independent.co.uk/news/world/europe/ukraine-prime-minister-arseniy-yatsenyuk-resigns-a6977421.html; and Parry, "Yats Is No Longer the Guy."

[60]Volodymyr Chemerys, "Human Rights after Euromaidan," *Counterpunch,* January 22, 2016, http://www.counterpunch.org/2016/01/22/human-rights-after-euromaidan/.

[61]John Dalhuisen, "Ukraine's Spate of Suspicious Deaths Must Be Followed by Credible Investigations," *Amnesty International News,* April 17, 2015, https://www.amnesty.org/en/latest/news/2015/04/ukraine-suspicious-deaths-need-credible-investigations/.

[62]Hayla Coynash, "Controversial Ukrainian Blogger/Journalist Freed after 18 Months in Prison," Kharkiv Human Rights Protection Group, July 15, 2016, http://khpg.org/en/index.php?id=1468506145.

[63]"Ukraine Confirms Ban of 'Fascist' Russian Books," *Deutsche Welle,* August 12, 2015, http://dw.com/en/ukraine-confirms-ban-of-fascist-russian-books/a-18646342.

[64]Agence France Presse, "Ukraine Slaps Broadcast Ban on 13 Artists—Including Depardieu," *The Straits Times,* August 8, 2015, https://www.straitstimes.com/lifestyle/entertainment/ukraine-slaps-broadcast-ban-on-13-russian-artists-including-actor-gerard.

[65]Quoted in "Ukraine Bans 38 Russian 'Hate' Books Amid Culture War," *BBC News,* August 11, 2015, http://www.bbc.com/news/world-europe-33863697.

[66]Nataliya Vasilyeva, "Ukraine Takes BBC Journalists off Its Sanctions List," *Associated Press,* September 17, 2015, http://bigstory.ap.org/article/5d16aae23b254463b9d13380e7f19c14/uk.

[67]Human Rights Watch, "Ukraine: Foreign Journalists Barred or Expelled," September 1, 2017, https://www.hrw.org/news/2017/09/01/ukraine-foreign -journalists-barred-or-expelled.

[68]Dalhuisen, "Ukraine's Spate of Suspicious Deaths Must Be Followed by Credible Investigations."

[69]"Council of Europe Blasts Ukraine Investigations into Odesa Violence," Radio Free Europe/Radio Liberty, November 4, 2015, https://www.rferl.org/a /ukraine-odesa-fire-council-europe-report/27345601.html; and Daryna Krasnolutska and Kateryna Choursina, "Ukraine Failing to Probe Pro-Russia Protestor Deaths, Panel Says," *Bloomberg,* November 4, 2015, https://www.bloomberg.com/news /articles/2015-11-04/ukraine-failing-to-probe-pro-russia-protester-deaths-panel-says.

[70]Doctorow, "A Look at Ukraine's Dark Side."

[71]Tom Parfitt, "Ukraine Crisis: The Neo-Nazi Brigade Fighting Pro-Russian Separatists," *Telegraph,* August 11, 2014, http://www.telegraph.co.uk/news /worldnews/europe/ukraine/11025137/Ukraine-crisis-the-neo-Nazi-brigade -fighting-pro-Russian-separatists.html.

[72]Tadeusz Olszański, "A Strong Vote for Reform: Ukraine after the Parliamentary Elections," *OSW,* October 29, 2014, https://www.osw.waw.pl/en/publikacje /analyses/2014-10-29/a-strong-vote-reform-ukraine-after-parliamentary -elections.

[73]"Ukraine Far Right Battles Police at Parliament in Kiev," *BBC News,* October 14, 2014, http://www.bbc.com/news/world-europe-29611588; Andrey Kurkov, "Kiev's Week of Violence Is a Crisis of Its Own Making," *Guardian,* September 2, 2015, https://www.theguardian.com/commentisfree/2015 /sep/02/kiev-violence-ukraine-crisis-russia; and Joshua Cohen, "Ukraine's Ultra-Right Militias Are Challenging the Government to a Showdown," *Washington Post,* June 15, 2017, https://www.washingtonpost.com/news/democracy -post/wp/2017/06/15/ukraines-ultra-right-militias-are-challenging-the -government-to-a-showdown/?utm_term=.c56a998da691.

[74]Masha Gessen, "The Assault on Kiev Pride," *New Yorker,* June 6, 2015, https://www.newyorker.com/news/news-desk/the-assault-on-kiev-pride.

[75]Alexander Clapp, "The Maidan Irregulars," *National Interest* 143 (May–June 2016): 26–33.

[76]Lev Golinkin, "The Ukrainian Far Right—and the Danger It Poses," *Nation,* December 5, 2016, https://www.thenation.com/article/the-ukrainian-far-right -and-the-danger-it-poses/.

[77]Cnaan Liphshiz, "'Jews Out' Marchers Celebrate Legacy of Ukraine Nationalist Stepan Bandera," *Forward,* January 3, 2017, https://forward.com/news/breaking-news -358920/jews-out-marchers-celebrate-legacy-of-ukraine-nationalist-stepan-bandera/.

[78]Tom Parfitt, "Ukraine's 'History Laws' Purge It of Communist Symbols but Divide the Populations," *Telegraph,* June 30, 2015, http://www.telegraph.co.uk

/news/worldnews/europe/ukraine/11674511/Ukraines-history-laws-purge-it
-of-communist-symbols-but-divide-the-population.html; and Josh Cohen, "Dear
Ukraine: Please Don't Shoot Yourself in the Foot," *Foreign Policy*, April 27, 2015,
http://foreignpolicy.com/2015/04/27/dear-ukraine-please-dont-shoot-your
self-in-the-foot-nationalists-russia-bandera-rada/.

[79]Graham Stack, Sergei Kuznetsov, and Ben Aris, "Poroshenko's Empire:
The Business of Being Ukraine's President," *Intellinews*, August 29, 2016, http://
www.intellinews.com/long-read-poroshenko-s-empire-the-business-of-being
-ukraine-s-president-103790/.

[80]Yuras Karmanau, "Ukraine's Anti-Corruption Agency Faces Strong Resistance," Associated Press, December 11, 2017, https://apnews.com/4ce07970f5b
743a0a79e8c57ae4bd52b/Ukraine%27s-anti-corruption-agency-faces
-strong-resistance; and Oleksandra Ustinova and Brian Dooley, "Poroshenko Is
Targeting Ukraine's Anti-Corruption Campaigners," *Newsweek*, January 8, 2018,
http://www.newsweek.com/poroshenko-targeting-ukraines-anti-corruption
-campaigners-773212.

Chapter Ten

[1]Muhammad Idrees Ahmad, *The Road to Iraq: The Making of a Neoconservative War* (Edinburgh, UK: Edinburgh University Press, 2014), p. 249.

[2]Hillary Clinton, *Hard Choices* (New York: Simon and Schuster, 2014), p. 450.

[3]UN Security Council Reports, Middle East S/2011/612, October 4, 2011,
https://www.securitycouncilreport.org/un-documents/document/syria-s2011
-612.php.

[4]Clinton, *Hard Choices*, p. 452.

[5]Clinton, *Hard Choices*, pp. 452–53.

[6]Ernesto Londono and Greg Miller, "CIA Begins Weapons Delivery to
Syrian Rebels," *Washington Post*, September 11, 2013, https://www.washington
post.com/world/national-security/cia-begins-weapons-delivery-to-syrian-rebels
/2013/09/11/9fcf2ed8-1b0c-11e3-a628-7e6dde8f889d_story.html?utm
_term=.548e58f6542a.

[7]Quoted in Clinton, *Hard Choices*, p. 454.

[8]Clinton, *Hard Choices*, p. 457.

[9]Josh Rogin, "McCain and Lieberman Meet with the Free Syria Army,"
Foreignpolicy.com, April 10, 2012, http://foreignpolicy.com/2012/04/10/mccain
-and-lieberman-meet-with-the-free-syria-army/.

[10]Ted Galen Carpenter and Malou Innocent, *Perilous Partners: The Benefits and Pitfalls of America's Alliances with Authoritarian Regimes* (Washington: Cato Institute, 2015).

[11]For a discussion of the early years of the Free Syrian Army, see Christopher Phillips, *The Battle for Syria: International Rivalry in the New Middle East* (New Haven, CT: Yale University Press, 2016), pp. 126–29.

[12]Michal Shmulovich, "Free Syrian Army Fighters Aren't Extremists or 'Al-Qaeda Types,' Group's DC Fundraiser Insists," *Times of Israel*, September 29, 2012, https://www.timesofisrael.com/free-syrian-army-fighters-arent-extremists -or-al-qaeda-types-groups-dc-fundraiser-claims/.

[13]Mark Hosenball and Phil Stewart, "Kerry Portrait of Syria Rebels at Odds with Intelligence Reports," *Reuters,* September 5, 2013, http://www.reuters .com/article/us-syria-crisis-usa-rebels/kerry-portrait-of-syria-rebels-at-odds -with-intelligence-reports-idUSBRE98405L20130905.

[14]Hosenball and Stewart, "Kerry Portrait of Syria Rebels at Odds with Intel- ligence Reports."

[15]Phillips, *The Battle for Syria*, p. 130.

[16]Phillips, *The Battle for Syria*, p. 129.

[17]David Enders, "Weeks Spent with Syrian Rebels Reveal a Force of Sunni Muslim Civilians," *McClatchy Newspapers*, June 25, 2012, http://www.mcclatchydc .com/news/nation-world/world/article24731650.html.

[18]Clinton, *Hard Choices*, p. 449. The figures that Clinton cites are both slightly different and puzzling. According to her, the population breakdown is Sunni Arabs, "more than 70 percent"; Alawites, 12 percent; Christians, 10 percent; Kurds, 9 percent; and Druze, 3 percent. One obvious problem with her calculation is that the total adds up to more than 100 percent.

[19]Clinton, *Hard Choices*, p. 450.

[20]Chas W. Freeman Jr., *America's Continuing Misadventures in the Middle East* (Charlottesville, VA: Just World Books, 2016), p. 114.

[21]Gareth Porter, "A U.S.-Fueled Syrian Sectarian Bloodbath," *Consortium News*, August 31, 2016, https://consortiumnews.com/2016/08/31/a-us-fueled -syrian-sectarian-bloodbath/.

[22]Phillips, *The Battle for Syria*, pp. 67–68, 149–54. Also see Jeffrey White, "Assad's Indispensable Foreign Legions," Washington Institute for Near East Policy, *Policywatch* 2196, January 22, 2014, http://www.washingtoninstitute.org /policy-analysis/view/assads-indispensable-foreign-legions.

[23]For a discussion of the crucial importance of the Sunni-Shia split throughout the Middle East, see Geneive Abdo, *The New Sectarianism: The Arab Uprising and the Birth of the Shi'a-Sunni Divide* (New York: Oxford University Press, 2016).

[24]Leon Panetta with Jim Newton, *Worthy Fights: A Memoir of Leadership in War and Peace* (New York: Penguin Books, 2014), p. 449.

[25]Clinton, *Hard Choices*, p. 461.

[26]Gareth Porter, "How America Armed Terrorists in Syria," *American Conservative*, June 22, 2017, http://www.theamericanconservative.com/articles/how-america-armed-terrorists-in-syria/?mc_cid=1d35590a64&mc_eid=a6aa34c728.

[27]Porter, "How America Armed Terrorists in Syria."

[28]Porter, "How America Armed Terrorists in Syria."

[29]Quoted in Porter, "How America Armed Terrorists in Syria."

[30]Michael R. Gordon and Mark Landler, "Backstage Glimpses of Clinton as Dogged Diplomat, Win or Lose," *New York Times*, February 2, 2013, http://www.nytimes.com/2013/02/03/us/politics/in-behind-scene-blows-and-triumphs-sense-of-clinton-future.html?mtrref=undefined.

[31]Ewen MacAskill, "Mitt Romney: Arm the Syrian Rebels," *Guardian*, October 8, 2012, https://www.theguardian.com/world/2012/oct/08/mitt-romney-arm-syrian-rebels.

[32]Phillips, *The Battle for Syria*, pp. 131–32.

[33]Phillips, *The Battle for Syria*, p. 132.

[34]For a detailed discussion of Jabhat al-Nusra's origins, ideological orientation, and emergence as a leading insurgent group in Syria, see Charles R. Lister, *The Syrian Jihad: Al-Qaeda, the Islamic State, and the Evolution of an Insurgency* (New York: Oxford University Press, 2015), pp. 51–116.

[35]Lister, *The Syrian Jihad*, p. 85.

[36]Phillips, *The Battle for Syria*, pp. 132–33.

[37]Clinton, *Hard Choices*, p. 460.

[38]Lister, *The Syrian Jihad*, pp. 210–11.

[39]Hamid Khatib, "Jabhat al-Nusra Al-Qaeda's Largest Formal Affiliate in History," *Al-Monitor*, July 10, 2016, https://www.al-monitor.com/pulse/originals/2016/07/syria-amnesty-nusra-alqaeda-torture-killing.html#ixzz4E882wSYh. See also, Testimony Before the Senate Foreign Relations Committee on "Global Efforts to Defeat ISIS," Witness Statement of The Honorable Brett H. McGurk, Special Presidential Envoy for the Global Coalition to Counter ISIL, June 28, 2016, https://www.foreign.senate.gov/imo/media/doc/062816_McGurk_Testimony.pdf.

[40]Susan Heavey and Andrew Quinn, "U.S. Blacklists al Qaeda-Linked Syrian Rebel Group," *Reuters*, December 11, 2012, https://www.reuters.com/article/us-syria-usa/u-s-blacklists-al-qaeda-linked-syrian-rebel-group-idUSBRE8BA0IB20121211.

[41]Phillips, *The Battle for Syria*, p. 133.

[42]Phillips, *The Battle for Syria*, p. 133. Also see Lister, *The Syrian Jihad*, pp. 7–8.

[43]Porter, "A U.S.-Fueled Sectarian Bloodbath."

[44]Lister, *The Syrian Jihad*, p. 131.

[45]Clinton, *Hard Choices*, p. 450.

[46]Steven Heydemann, "Supporting Syria's Rebels Is No Fantasy," *U.S. News and World Report*, August 14, 2014, https://www.usnews.com/debate-club

/should-obama-have-armed-syrian-rebels-sooner/supporting-syrias-rebels -is-no-fantasy.

[47]Hardin Lang et al., "Supporting the Syrian Opposition," Center for American Progress, Security Report, September 12, 2014, https://www.americanprogress .org/issues/security/reports/2014/09/12/96990/supporting-the-syrian-opposition/.

[48]Clinton, *Hard Choices*, p. 461.

[49]Karen DeYoung, "Obama Asks for Authorization to Provide Direct Military Training to Syrian Rebels," *Washington Post*, June 26, 2014, https://www .washingtonpost.com/world/national-security/obama-backs-us-military-training -for-syrian-rebels/2014/06/26/ead59104-fd62-11e3-932c-0a55b81f48ce_story .html?utm_term=.329b345760f1.

[50]Kenneth M. Pollack, "An Army to Defeat Assad," *Foreign Affairs* 93, no. 5 (September–October 2014): 114.

[51]Jonah Goldberg, "Team Obama Has Spent $500M to Train 'Four or Five' Syrian Rebels," *New York Post*, September 18, 2015, http://nypost.com/2015/09 /18/team-obama-has-spent-500m-to-train-four-or-five-syrian-rebels/.

[52]Helene Cooper, "Few U.S.-Trained Syrians Still Fight ISIS, Senators Told," *New York Times*, September 16, 2015, https://www.nytimes.com/2015/09/17 /world/middleeast/isis-isil-syrians-senate-armed-services-committee.html.

[53]Lt. Col. J. Stewart Welch and Comd. Kevin Bailey, "In Pursuit of Good Ideas: The Syria Train and Equip Program," Washington Institute for Near East Policy, Research Notes, No. 36, September 2016, http://www.washingtoninstitute.org /policy-analysis/view/in-pursuit-of-good-ideas-the-syria-train-and-equip-program.

[54]"U.S. Offers 'Military Support' to Syrian Rebels," *Al Jazeera*, June 14, 2013, http://www.aljazeera.com/news/americas/2013/06/2013613212110550.html.

[55]Eric Margolis, "U.S. vs. U.S. in Syria," *UNZ Review*, September 2, 2016, http://www.unz.com/emargolis/us-vs-us-in-syria/.

[56]Nabih Bulos, W. J. Hennigan, and Brian Bennett, "CIA-Armed Militias Are Shooting at Pentagon-Armed Ones in Syria," *Los Angeles Times*, March 26, 2016, http://www.chicagotribune.com/news/nationworld/nationalsecurity/ct-syria -militias-us-cia-islamic-state-20160326-story.html.

[57]Joby Warrick, "More than 1,400 Killed in Syrian Chemical Weapons Attack, U.S. Says," *Washington Post*, August 20, 2013, https://www.washingtonpost.com /world/national-security/nearly-1500-killed-in-syrian-chemical-weapons -attack-us-says/2013/08/30/b2864662-1196-11e3-85b6-d27422650fd5_story .html?utm_term=.6b0004e4c4c6.

[58]Brad Knickerbocker, "War-Weary Americans Wary of U.S. Attacking Syria," *Christian Science Monitor*, August 29, 2013, https://www.csmonitor.com/USA /Politics/2013/0829/War-weary-Americans-wary-of-US-attacking-Syria.

[59]Ray McGovern, "When Putin Bailed Out Obama," *Antiwar.com*, August 31, 2016, http://original.antiwar.com/mcgovern/2016/08/31/putin-bailed-obama/.

[60]C. J. Chivers, "New Study Refines View of Sarin Attack in Syria," *New York Times*, December 28, 2013, http://www.nytimes.com/2013/12/29/world/middleeast/new-study-refines-view-of-sarin-attack-in-syria.html?ref=world&_r=1.

[61]Seymour M. Hersh, "The Red Line and the Rat Line," *London Review of Books*, April 17, 2014, https://www.lrb.co.uk/v36/n08/seymour-m-hersh/the-red-line-and-the-rat-line.

[62]Theodore Postol, "MIT Scientist Disputes 'Evidence' of Syria Chemical Weapons Attack," *MintPress News*, April 14, 2017, http://www.mintpressnews.com/mit-scientist-disputes-evidence-of-syria-chemical-weapons-attack/226847/.

[63]Michael Gordon, "White House Accepts 'Political Reality' of Assad's Grip on Power in Syria," *New York Times*, March 31, 2017, https://www.nytimes.com/2017/03/31/us/politics/trump-bashar-assad-syria.html; and Michelle Nichols, "U.S. Priority on Syria No Longer Focused on 'Getting Assad Out': Haley," *U.S. News and World Report*, March 30, 2017, https://www.usnews.com/news/world/articles/2017-03-30/us-un-ambassador-says-washingtons-focus-no-longer-on-removing-assad-in-syria.

[64]Robert Parry, "A New Hole in Syria-Sarin Certainty," *Consortium News*, September 7, 2017. https://consortiumnews.com/2017/09/07/a-new-hole-in-syria-sarin-certainty/.

[65]Steve Almasy and Richard Roth, "UN: Syria Responsible for Sarin Attack That Killed Scores," *CNN.com*, October 27, 2017, http://www.cnn.com/2017/10/26/middleeast/syria-khan-sheikhoun-chemical-attack-sarin/index.html.

[66]Elliott Abrams, *Realism and Democracy: American Foreign Policy after the Arab Spring* (New York: Cambridge University Press, 2017), p. 109.

[67]Abrams, *Realism and Democracy*, pp. 109–110.

[68]Phillips, *The Battle for Syria*, p. 189.

[69]Stephen Kinzer, "The Media Are Misleading the Public on Syria," Opinion, *Boston Globe*, February 18, 2016, https://www.bostonglobe.com/opinion/2016/02/18/the-media-are-misleading-public-syria/8YB75otYirPzUCnlwaVtcK/story.html.

[70]Kinzer, "The Media Are Misleading the Public on Syria." For other accounts of rebel rule in Aleppo, see Marwan Hisham, "Scenes from Inside Aleppo: How Life Has Been Transformed by Rebel Rule," *Vanity Fair*, July 26, 2015, https://www.vanityfair.com/news/2015/07/inside-aleppo-syria; and Eva Bartlett, "Syria War Diary: What Life Is Like Under 'Moderate' Rebel Rule," *Global Research*, August 24, 2017, https://www.globalresearch.ca/syria-war-diary-what-life-is-like-under-moderate-rebel-rule/5605559.

[71]Paul R. Pillar, "Heartstrings and Aleppo," *National Interest*, December 18, 2016, http://nationalinterest.org/blog/paul-pillar/heartstrings-aleppo-18782.

[72]Patrick Cockburn, "There's More Propaganda than News Coming out of Aleppo this Week," *Independent*, December 16, 2016, http://www.independent

.co.uk/voices/aleppo-crisis-syrian-war-bashar-al-assad-isis-more-propaganda
-than-news-a7479901.html.

[73]Quoted in Robert Parry, "Debate Moderator Distorted Syrian Reality," *Consortium News*, October 11, 2016, https://consortiumnews.com/2016/10/11/debate-moderator-distorted-syrian-reality/.

[74]Leon Wieseltier, "Aleppo's Fall Is Obama's Failure," *Washington Post*, December 12, 2016, https://www.washingtonpost.com/opinions/aleppos-fall-is-obamas-failure/2016/12/15/5af72640-c30f-11e6-9a51-cd56ea1c2bb7_story.html?utm_term=.b284f35ff256.

[75]Pillar, "Heartstrings and Aleppo."

[76]Amnesty International, "Abductions, Torture and Summary Killings at the Hands of Armed Groups," July 5, 2016, https://www.amnesty.org/en/latest/news/2016/07/syria-abductions-torture-and-summary-killings-at-the-hands-of-armed-groups/.

[77]Human Rights Watch, "'You Can Still See Their Blood': Executions, Indiscriminate Shootings, and Hostage Taking by Opposition Forces in Latakia Countryside," October 10, 2013, https://www.hrw.org/report/2013/10/10/you-can-still-see-their-blood/executions-indiscriminate-shootings-and-hostage.

[78]Lister, *The Syrian Jihad*, p. 161.

[79]Nancy A. Youssef, "CIA and Pentagon Bicker While Russia Wipes Out U.S.-Backed Rebels," *Daily Beast*, June 9, 2016, https://www.thedailybeast.com/cia-and-pentagon-bicker-while-russia-wipes-out-us-backed-rebels?mc_cid=8409ce5c10&mc_eid=fac81ed64d.

[80]Christopher Hope and Peter Dominiczak, "David Cameron Admits 70,000 Moderate Syrian Army Contains 'Relatively Hardline Islamist Militants,'" *Telegraph*, January 26, 2016, http://www.telegraph.co.uk/news/worldnews/middleeast/syria/12096133/David-Cameron-admits-70000-moderate-Syrian-army-contains-relatively-hardline-Islamist-militants.html.

[81]Jake Tapper, "Exclusive: Petraeus Explains How Jihadists Could Be Peeled Away to Fight ISIS—and Assad," *CNN.com*, September 1, 2015, http://www.cnn.com/2015/09/01/politics/david-petraeus-al-qaeda-isis-nusra/index.html.

[82]Katie Zavadski, "U.S.-Backed 'Moderate' Rebels Behead a Child Near Aleppo," *Daily Beast*, July 19, 2016, https://www.thedailybeast.com/us-backed-moderate-rebels-behead-a-child-near-aleppo.

[83]"John Kerry Condemns Russia's 'Repeated Aggression' in Syria and Ukraine," *Guardian*, February 13, 2016, https://www.theguardian.com/us-news/2016/feb/13/john-kerry-condemns-russias-repeated-aggression-in-syria-and-ukraine.

[84]Gareth Porter, "Obama's 'Moderate' Syrian Deception," *Antiwar.com*, February 16, 2016, http://original.antiwar.com/porter/2016/02/16/obama's-moderate-syrian.

[85]Lister, *The Syrian Jihad*, pp. 7–8.

[86]TOW is an abbreviation for tube-launched, optically tracked, wire-guided missiles.

[87]Mohammad Ghannam, "2 Military Bases in Syria Fall to Rebels," *New York Times*, December 15, 2014, http://www.nytimes.com/2014/12/16/world /middleeast/2-military-bases-in-syria-fall-to-rebels.html?_r=0.

[88]Porter, "Obama's 'Moderate' Syrian Deception."

[89]Jeffrey White, "Rebels Worth Supporting: Syria's Harakat Hazm," Washington Institute for Near East Policy, *Policywatch* 2244, April 28, 2014, http:// www.washingtoninstitute.org/policy-analysis/view/rebels-worth-supporting -syrias-harakat-hazm.

[90]Conner Finnegan, "A Look at the Factions Battling in Syria's Civil War," *ABC News*, April 11, 2017, http://abcnews.go.com/International/inside-syrias -multiple-fighting-factions/story?id=46731830.

[91]Nicholas Heras, "From the Bottom, Up: A Strategy for U.S. Military Support to Syria's Armed Opposition," Center for a New American Security, May 10, 2016, https://www.cnas.org/publications/commentary/from-the-bottom-up-a -strategy-for-u-s-military-support-to-syrias-armed-opposition.

[92]Ehud Ya'ari, "The Southern Front in Syria: Washington Should Support Rebel Gains," *Foreign Affairs*, May 24, 2016, https://www.foreignaffairs.com /articles/syria/2016-05-24/southern-front-syria.

[93]Greg Jaffe and Adam Entous, "Trump Ends Covert CIA Program to Arm Anti-Assad Rebels in Syria, a Move Sought by Moscow," *Washington Post*, July 19, 2017, https://www.washingtonpost.com/world/national-security /trump-ends-covert-cia-program-to-arm-anti-assad-rebels-in-syria-a-move -sought-by-moscow/2017/07/19/b6821a62-6beb-11e7-96ab-5f38140b38cc _story.html?utm_term=.2fb80e9a29fd.

[94]Daniel R. DePetris, "Trump Ends the CIA Syria Pipeline: An Admission of Failure," *National Interest*, July 25, 2017, http://nationalinterest.org/blog /the-skeptics/trump-ends-the-cia-syria-pipeline-admission-failure-21663.

[95]Michael Gordon, "U.S. Is Sending 400 More Troops to Syria," *New York Times*, March 9, 2017, https://www.nytimes.com/2017/03/09/world/middleeast /us-troops-syria.html.

[96]Ted Galen Carpenter, "A Sober Look at the West's Kurdish Allies," *Aspenia Online*, November 23, 2017, https://www.cato.org/publications/commentary /sober-look-wests-kurdish-allies; and "Kurdish Parties Opposed to Barzani Report Attacks on Offices Overnight," *Reuters,* October 29, 2017, https://www.reuters .com/article/us-mideast-crisis-iraq-kurds-attacks/kurdish-parties-opposed -to-barzani-report-attacks-on-offices-overnight-idUSKBN1CZ0E6.

[97]Human Rights Watch, "Syria: Abuses in Kurdish-Run Enclaves," June 28, 2014, https://www.hrw.org/news/2014/06/18/syria-abuses-kurdish -run-enclaves; and Roy Gutman, "Have the Syrian Kurds Committed War

Crimes?" *Nation*, February 7, 2017, https://www.thenation.com/article/have-the-syrian-kurds-committed-war-crimes/.

[98]Phillips, *The Battle for Syria*, pp. 133–34.

[99]Erika Solomon, "Syrian Kurds Make Fresh Military Gains after Declaring Self-Rule," *Reuters*, November 13, 2013, http://www.reuters.com/article/us-syria-crisis-kurds/syrian-kurds-make-fresh-military-gains-after-declaring-self-rule-idUSBRE9AC0JZ20131113.

[100]Richard Hall, "Syria's Kurds Move Towards Autonomy with Announcement of Transitional Government," *Independent*, November 12, 2013, http://www.independent.co.uk/news/world/middle-east/syrias-kurds-move-towards-autonomy-with-announcement-of-transitional-government-8935441.html.

[101]Diana Al Rifai, "Assyrians and Kurds Clash for First Time in North Syria," *Al Jazeera*, January 12, 2016, http://www.aljazeera.com/news/2016/01/assyrians-kurds-qamishli-160112165041894.html.

[102]"With Control of 25 Percent of Syria, Kurds Seek to Establish Self-Rule," *Haaretz*, October 8, 2017, https://www.haaretz.com/middle-east-news/syria/1.816172.

[103]"Syrians Vote in Kurdish-Held Northern Region," *Al Jazeera*, September 22, 2017, http://www.aljazeera.com/news/2017/09/syrians-vote-kurdish-held-northern-region-170922142621848.html.

[104]"Turkey v. Syria's Kurds v. Islamic State," *BBC*, August 23, 2016, http://www.bbc.com/news/world-middle-east-33690060.

[105]Amberin Zaman, "Turkish-YPG Clashes Rage around Sites in Northern Syria," *Al-Monitor*, July 17, 2017, https://www.al-monitor.com/pulse/originals/2017/07/turkey-increases-ypg-attacks.html.

[106]Carol Morello and Erin Cunningham, "Trump Tells Turkish President U.S. Will Stop Arming Kurds in Syria," *Washington Post*, November 24, 2017, https://www.washingtonpost.com/world/national-security/trump-tells-turkish-president-us-will-stop-arming-kurds-in-syria/2017/11/24/61548936-d148-11e7-a1a3-0d1e45a6de3d_story.html?utm_term=.58f295d92fe5.

[107]Anne Barnard, "U.S.-Backed Force Could Cement a Kurdish Enclave in Syria," *New York Times*, January 5, 2018, https://www.nytimes.com/2018/01/16/world/middleeast/syria-kurds-force.html.

[108]Quoted in Nabih Bulos, "Turkey Says U.S. 'Stabbed Us in the Back' by Aligning with Kurds on Syrian Border," *Los Angeles Times*, January 16, 2018, http://www.latimes.com/world/middleeast/la-fg-kurds-border-force-20180116-story.html.

[109]Andrew J. Bacevich, *America's War for the Greater Middle East* (New York: Random House, 2016), p. 331.

[110]Phillips, *The Battle for Syria*, p. 125.

CONCLUSION

[1]Ted Galen Carpenter and Malou Innocent, *Perilous Partners: The Benefits and Pitfalls of America's Alliances with Authoritarian Regimes* (Washington: Cato Institute, 2015).

[2]*Public Papers of the Presidents of the United States, Jimmy Carter, 1977* (Washington: General Services Administration, 1977), pp. 2221–22.

[3]Caroline Wyatt, "Bush and Putin: Best of Friends," *BBC News*, June 16, 2001, http://news.bbc.co.uk/2/hi/europe/1392791.stm.

[4]Quoted in George F. Will, "Teaching Latin America to Elect Good Men," *Washington Post*, July 31, 1983. https://www.washingtonpost.com/archive /opinions/1983/07/31/teaching-latin-america-to-elect-good-men/e8bed301 -5802-49b8-be54-85d4e1dd12a3/?utm_term=.ee38edc4ef73.

[5]"President Woodrow Wilson's 14 Points (1918)," https://www.ourdocuments .gov/doc.php?flash=false&doc=62.

[6]"Woodrow Wilson, War Message to Congress, 1917," http://wps.prenhall .com/wps/media/objects/107/110495/ch22_a2_d1.pdf.

[7]Joshua Muravchik, *Exporting Democracy: Fulfilling America's Destiny* (Washington: AEI Press, 1991).

[8]Joshua Muravchik, *The Next Founders: Voices of Democracy in the Middle East* (New York: Encounter Books, 2009).

[9]Charles W. Dunne, "Middle East Democracy: Recommendations for the Next President," Middle East Institute Policy Focus Series, June 2016, http://www .mei.edu/sites/default/files/publications/PF13_Dunne_democracy_web.pdf.

[10]Daniel Larison, "Clinton's Libyan War and the Delusions of Interventionists," *American Conservative*, February 29, 2016, http://www.theamericanconservative .com/larison/clintons-libyan-war-and-the-delusions-of-interventionists/.

[11]Larison, "Clinton's Libyan War and the Delusions of Interventionists."

[12]Quoted in Elaine Windrich, *The Cold War Guerrilla: Jonas Savimbi, the U.S. Media, and the Angolan War* (Westport, CT: Greenwood Press, 1992), p. 84.

[13]Quoted in Doug Bandow, "The Bad and the Ugly of the GOP's Foreign Policy, Part II," *Cato at Liberty*, August 13, 2015, http://www.cato.org/blog/bad-ugly -gops-foreign-policy-part-ii.

[14]John Quincy Adams, "Speech to the U.S. House of Representatives on Foreign Policy," July 4, 1821, transcript, Miller Center, University of Virginia, Charlottesville, VA, https://millercenter.org/the-presidency/presidential-speeches /july-4-1821-speech-us-house-representatives-foreign-policy.

INDEX

Note: Information in footnotes is indicated by n followed by the note number.

ABOUT THE AUTHOR

Ted Galen Carpenter is a senior fellow at the Cato Institute and previously served as the Institute's vice president for defense and foreign policy studies. Dr. Carpenter is the author of eleven books and more than 700 articles and studies on international affairs. His previous books include *Perilous Partners: The Benefits and Pitfalls of America's Alliances with Authoritarian Regimes* (2015); *The Fire Next Door: Mexico's Drug Violence and the Danger to America* (2012); and *Smart Power: Toward a Prudent Foreign Policy for America* (2008). His articles have appeared in *Foreign Affairs*, the *New York Times*, the *Washington Post*, the *Wall Street Journal*, the *National Interest*, and many other publications. He is a frequent guest expert on radio and television programs in the United States and throughout the world. Dr. Carpenter received his Ph.D. in history from the University of Texas at Austin in 1980. He is a contributing editor to the *National Interest* and serves on the editorial board of the *Journal of Strategic Studies*.

Cato Institute

Founded in 1977, the Cato Institute is a public policy research foundation dedicated to broadening the parameters of policy debate to allow consideration of more options that are consistent with the principles of limited government, individual liberty, and peace. To that end, the Institute strives to achieve greater involvement of the intelligent, concerned lay public in questions of policy and the proper role of government.

The Institute is named for *Cato's Letters*, libertarian pamphlets that were widely read in the American Colonies in the early 18th century and played a major role in laying the philosophical foundation for the American Revolution.

Despite the achievement of the nation's Founders, today virtually no aspect of life is free from government encroachment. A pervasive intolerance for individual rights is shown by government's arbitrary intrusions into private economic transactions and its disregard for civil liberties. And while freedom around the globe has notably increased in the past several decades, many countries have moved in the opposite direction, and most governments still do not respect or safeguard the wide range of civil and economic liberties.

To address those issues, the Cato Institute undertakes an extensive publications program on the complete spectrum of policy issues. Books, monographs, and shorter studies are commissioned to examine the federal budget, Social Security, regulation, military spending, international trade, and myriad other issues. Major policy conferences are held throughout the year, from which papers are published thrice yearly in the *Cato Journal*. The Institute also publishes the quarterly magazine *Regulation*.

In order to maintain its independence, the Cato Institute accepts no government funding. Contributions are received from foundations, corporations, and individuals, and other revenue is generated from the sale of publications. The Institute is a nonprofit, tax-exempt, educational foundation under Section 501(c)3 of the Internal Revenue Code.

CATO INSTITUTE
1000 Massachusetts Ave., N.W.
Washington, D.C. 20001
www.cato.org